DEBTOR NATION

POLITICS AND SOCIETY IN TWENTIETH-CENTURY AMERICA

SERIES EDITORS

William Chafe, Gary Gerstle, Linda Gordon,
and Julian Zelizer

A list of titles in this series appears at the back of the book

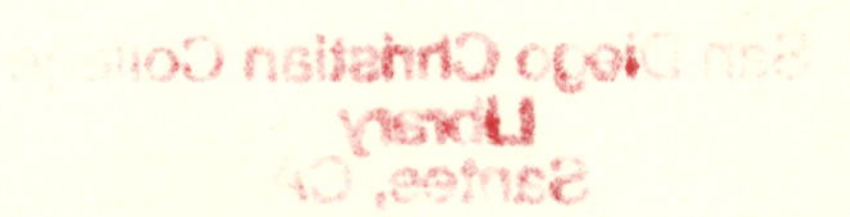

DEBTOR NATION

THE HISTORY OF AMERICA IN RED INK

Louis Hyman

PRINCETON UNIVERSITY PRESS   PRINCETON AND OXFORD

Published by Princeton University Press, 41 William Street, Princeton, New Jersey 08540

In the United Kingdom: Princeton University Press, 6 Oxford Street, Woodstock, Oxfordshire OX20 1TW

press.princeton.edu

Cover illustration by Tom Lovell, 1956. Image courtesy of The Advertising Archives.

Third printing, and first paperback printing, 2013
Paperback ISBN 978-0-691-15616-3

The Library of Congress has cataloged the cloth edition of this book as follows

Hyman, Louis, 1977–
Debtor nation : the history of America in red ink / Louis Hyman.
p. cm. — (Politics and society in twentieth-century America)
Includes bibliographical references and index.
ISBN 978-0-691-14068-1 (hbk. : alk. paper)
1. Consumer credit—United States—History—20th century. 2. Debt—United States—History—20th century. 3. Loans, Personal—United States—History—20th century. 4. United States—Economic conditions—20th century. 5. United States—Economic policy—20th century. I. Title.
HG3756.U54H96 2011
332.70973—dc22 2010031594

British Library Cataloging-in-Publication Data is available

This book has been composed in Sabon

Printed on acid-free paper. ∞

Printed in the United States of America

10 9 8 7 6 5 4 3

For Greg Kuzbida

Contents

Illustrations

DEBTOR NATION

An Introduction to the History of Debt

IT IS DIFFICULT TO consider debt as having a history, because it seems like debt might be that impossible thing in history, something that has existed forever. In 1917, one popular historian described debt as a "semi-slavery . . . [which] existed before the dawn of history, and it exists today."[1] People, in a certain sense, have always lent money to one another: over the dinner table to a wayward brother; across a saloon bar to a good customer; over a lunch pail to a hard-pressed co-worker. But even by 1917, as that popular history was written, the ancient, personal relationship of debt was changing into something that had never happened before.

While personal lending had always existed, before 1917 it had never been legal to charge interest rates high enough to turn a profit and, equally important, lenders had never been able to resell their customers' debts or borrow against them. In short, personal debt had never been able to be a normal business. Personal debt remained disconnected from the great flows of capital—confined to the margins of the economy. The big money in America was made by turning the hard work of Americans into commodities, not by lending those workers money. The wealthy could get personal loans at banks, alongside their business affairs, but for everybody else credit remained outside the conventional economy. Why would the Carnegies and Morgans of the world want to tie up their capital in loans to steelworkers, when they could make so much more money by building steel plants? When friends and family were tapped out, loan sharks—whose interest rates dwarfed even the most subprime of lender's rates today—could provide cash, but these small-timers could never compare in power or wealth to the Gilded Age titans of steel and rail. By the end of the twentieth century, however, such petty loans to workers had become one of American capitalism's most significant products, extracted and traded as if debt were just another commodity, as real as steel. Consumer finance had moved from the shadowy margins of capitalism into its brightly lit boardrooms, remaking, in its wake, the entirety of the American economy. In *Debtor Nation*, I explain how this financial revolution happened.

Personal debt assumed a new role within American capitalism once it became legal, sellable, and profitable. These developments did not occur all at once, but happened over the course of the twentieth century, beginning after World War I, and resulting as much from entrepreneurial innovation as governmental policy. These shifts in lending and borrowing practices were neither inevitable nor obvious. Policymakers, in numerous instances, often acted with the best of intentions, seeking to solve pressing economic and social problems, like unemployment, wealth inequality, and discrimination. Yet the policies, once enacted, often had far-reaching, unexpected consequences. For lenders, figuring out ways to extend credit met with both success and failure. The short-hand way in which historians describe capitalist decision-making as "profit maximizing" obscures the gut-wrenching difficulty of discovering new ways to make money. But once discovered, whether borne by profit or inscribed in law, new ways to lend spread throughout the economy. At certain junctures, which are the focus of this book, sudden changes in the larger political, economic, and social structures surrounding debt abruptly reoriented lending practices.

These moments of transformation came from all quarters, and while the most powerful institutions—commercial banks, corporations, government agencies—frequently played the most crucial roles, those with less power in America, when organized, contributed to the changes as well. Common to all these shifts, however, were new ways of regulating and reselling debt. Regulation—either its presence or its absence—made legal lending possible, but its relative strength and enforcement propelled lending in some unexpected directions. As much innovation in consumer lending resulted from evading government regulation as from obeying it. Laws and regulations, such as those on installment contracts and mortgage loans, created standards for how debt was lent, allowing investors to evaluate the worth of the loans. With known values, debts could be sold like commodities or borrowed against like assets. All modern consumer lending relied on creditors' abilities to act as middlemen, either directly by reselling the debt or indirectly by borrowing themselves. Resale allowed lenders to extend far more money than they themselves possessed by tapping into mainstream sources of capital. These networks of indebtedness enabled capital to flow from investors to lenders to borrowers. These debt markets, essential for the growth of American borrowing, relied not only on private capital but government intervention. The government made the resale of debt possible, not just through the enforcement of contracts, but in many instances by actually creating the basic institutions for buying and selling loans—making markets—like the government-made quasi-corporation Fannie Mae.[2] Government regulators sought to control economic life by regulating positively and negatively, creating incentives for businesses or punishing them for defiance. Allocating capital to invest in consumer debt was neither natural nor inevitable and the state had the power, within limits set by profit, to guide the economy. Frequently in *Debtor Nation*, it was not by the invisible hands of the market but by the visible minds of policymakers that new financial instruments and institutions were invented, causing these moments of rapid change. These two features—regulation and resale—combined in some unexpected ways to radically expand American borrowing.

Debtor Nation begins in that heady period after World War I, when installment credit and legalized personal loans first became big business. In chapters 1 through 4, consumer credit enters the mainstream of American financial life, as business and government forge new links between consumers and capital. Consumer credit, as we know it today, did not precede the mass production economy of the 1920s. Though the core profits of American capitalism were realized through manufacturing, for the first time consumers needed financing to pay for all the goods that were turned out.[3] Usury laws, at the same time, were relaxed around the country, as progressive reformers attempted to create a profitable alternative to loan sharks for industrial workers. During the 1930s, in an attempt to right the floundering economy, New Deal policymakers devised the mortgage and consumer-lending policies that convinced commercial banks that consumer credit could be profitable, despite the bankers' long-held reluctance to lend to consumers. During World War II the government attempted to regulate installment lending in order to contain inflation, but this intervention only pushed retailers to devise debt relations outside the regulations, disseminating a new hybrid form of credit—revolving credit—across the country. The postwar world underpinned by debt emerged from these practices, developed intentionally and unintentionally through government intervention.

Following World War II, new suburbanites realized the American dream through borrowing. In chapters 5 and 6, we see how consumer credit is inextricable from the postwar dream. Borrowing was at the core of both postwar affluence and its decline, demanding a reconsideration of our nostalgia for the postwar economy. Suburban Americans left government-mortgaged homes in installment-financed cars to shop on revolving credit at shopping centers. These consumers borrowed more but they could also pay back what they owed. Americans learned to borrow in the midst of prosperity when, confident of stable future incomes, debt enabled consumers to buy more and live well. While growth persisted, indebted consumers experienced few deleterious effects. Consumers borrowed because they believed that their incomes would continue to grow in the future—and they were right. Incomes rose steadily after the war from 1945 to 1970. Money borrowed today could be paid back more easily tomorrow and—as a bonus—consumers could buy that new television today! Financial institutions lent more money, and borrowers paid it back. In a time of rising incomes that were stable, consumers' expectations and borrowing were quite reasonable.[4] Unfortunately the postwar period, which defined "normalcy" to a generation of borrowers, was the aberration.

As postwar growth transitioned into stagflation, cracks began to appear in the foundation of the economy. In chapter 7, our contemporary debt system emerges through the popularization of credit cards and debt securitization. In the 1970s, unpaid debt skyrocketed not because consumers began to borrow, but because they *continued* to borrow as they and their parents had done since World War II, but without the postwar period's well-paying jobs. Consumers of the 1980s increasingly borrowed to deal with unexpected job losses and medical expenses as much as to live the good life, returning to a credit world that had more in common with the 1920s than with the 1950s.[5] A credit system premised on rising wages and stable employment was reappropriated to shore up uncertain employment and income inequality. Though credit could be used to grapple with short-term unemployment and decreased income, in the long-term loans still had to be repaid. Credit could dampen the swings of short-term fortunes, but it could not change long-term fates. Buoyed by a long-boom in housing prices, Americans used asset-growth to substitute for wage-growth, which worked fine as long as house prices continued to rise.

Consumer borrowing in the 1970s was not new, but the amount that creditors were willing to lend was. While earlier twentieth-century lending depended on the resale of debt, that resale was always between two parties that knew each other—mortgage company and insurance company or finance company and commercial bank. These networks of resale enabled the flow of capital from investors to borrowers, but these channels of resale were necessarily limited to networks of skilled buyers and sellers. While borrowers and lenders referred to "debt markets," these highly structured, highly regulated networks bore little resemblance to the chaos of a market. After the 1970s, however, new financial instruments, asset-backed securities, allowed these networks to become markets. Credit markets were deep, anonymous, and global. Capital could come from anywhere or anyone and be invested in consumer debt. This financial marvel, born of both Washington and Wall Street, midwifed the grand expansion of late-twentieth-century borrowing, enabling Americans to borrow more even while their incomes became more precarious. Capitalist structures changed more than consumers' thriftiness.[6] Because of the clever structuring of the financial instruments, the supply of lending capital was nearly limitless.

The particular forms that borrowing took—installment contract, credit card, balloon mortgage—mattered as much as how much people borrowed. Simple aggregate statistics, while meaningful and easy to understand, do not convey how debt made consumer lives possible, or how they constrained those lives. Each chapter focuses on particular debt practices and how they were created by the struggles between borrowers, lenders, and investors in a particular historical moment. The lending methods recounted in this book are but a streamlined sample of the nearly infinite ways devised to extend credit. Yet, even within that variety, a few forms took root, proliferated, and dominated. Placing debt instruments at the center of the narrative between consumers, business, and the state, shows how the formal arrangements of debt reshaped and reflected economic power. Simply telling the experiences of individuals, without the larger story of instruments and institutions, would mask the murky processes that put borrowers into debt.

If the debt relation between borrowers and lenders always took a specific form, then behind the lenders always resided the always protean capital. For borrowers, the fungibility of money meant that one form of debt could be paid off with another. The modern debt regime relied on this convertibility, not only to transform installment contracts into personal loans or credit card debts into home equity plans, but to turn the wages of labor into debt repayment as well. The transformation of labor into capital, and debt into other debt, is the crux of how the credit economy operates. To cordon off these transformations one from another, as we do when we, for instance, sanctimoniously discuss "non-mortgage debt" separately from "mortgage debt," obscures the indispensable commutability of capital. For lenders, transforming capital into debt was the essence of their business.

Capital ultimately comes from somewhere. When we need money, most of us wonder only if we can get it, and aside from the person who gives us the money, do not really care where the money comes from. Yet, once you start to think about it, how can credit card companies finance the trillions that Americans owe them? Trillions, even to bankers, is a lot of money. The source of that capital, while finite, is vast, and over the century it began to come largely from outside banks' own coffers. The story of how lenders, bankers, and non-bankers acquired the capital to lend must therefore also be told, if we are to comprehend the history of debt. Finding new sources of capital allowed for new kinds of lending. Credit cards, which in a lender's utopia, are never paid off, are extremely capital-intensive. Only when capital can be had cheaply and in vast quantities can such lending be possible. To understand how the debt economy works, we need to know not just the last instance of lending—when we get our loan—but the vast network of capital that funds that loan. Tracking the movement of capital, and how it changes over time, explains a great deal about the ultimate choice that that lender makes in giving or denying a loan. To truly discern the operations of capitalism, we must grapple with how capital gets allocated in our economy and how this allocation affects our everyday lives.

The expansion of American borrowing deals with the very foundation of capitalism: How is capital allocated? The institutional connections of capital between different forms of capitalist enterprise made the choice to borrow—to get that auto or house or surgery—possible. The flow of capital, within and between businesses, must necessarily be at the center of that history. Yet, no sinister capitalist cabal put Americans in debt.[7] The same banal investment decisions—where can this dollar get the greatest return?—that produced our nation's wealth-producing farms and factories also produced our omnipresent indebtedness. The increasing relative profitability of consumer lending is what has driven the expansion of consumer borrowing. Debt's rising profitability attracted capital that otherwise would have been invested in other enterprises. What made our indebtedness possible was that it became profitable.

The two features of modern lending—regulation and resale—made consumer lending profitable, but the profits of investing in debt relative to other investment opportunities varied over time. In the early twentieth century, installment debt helped large manufacturing companies realize the profit on their production, but could not compare in profitability. Personal loans, while a good small business, were ignored by large banks until the 1930s, when banks began lending to consumers only out of desperation and government policy. In the postwar period, consumer debt, especially revolving credit, began to become more profitable, but was still not as profitable as retail or manufacturing. In short, consumer credit, while important, was a means to end. By the 1960s, and increasingly in the 1970s and 1980s, consumer credit became an end in itself, as a rapidly expanding profit center. The profitability of personal debt—emerging after World War I, consolidating in the postwar period, and accelerating in the 1970s and 1980s—slowly reoriented American banks and corporations away from producing and distributing goods to financing them, with dire consequences for both the long-run stability of their enterprises and for the American worker.[8]

Searching for the "human" face of capitalism has led historians to focus too much on cultural ideas of debt—neglecting the history of business and politics, fundamentally misinterpreting what has happened, and missing the opportunity to tell an all-too-human story of how our choices, large and small, have brought this debt-driven economy to pass. There exist shockingly few histories of the modern credit system and those that do exist focus on culture—framed as morality—to the exclusion of business.[9] Such elisions are not unique to the history of debt, but are endemic within the history of American capitalism. Recent historiographic debates over twentieth-century capitalism, usually framed as consumer capitalism, have largely transpired on capitalism's surface, ignoring the deeper connections of finance.[10] Cultural historians have pointed to advertising, while consumer historians, entranced by the everyday world of goods surrounding them, have largely ignored the institutions that financed and created them. Such a prioritization has been understandable given that, for most consumers, this is where capitalism intersects with their lives. How people experience the world of things is important. At the same time, historians of all stripes have tended to fetishize consumer goods, overlooking the flows of capital that brought those goods into existence.

Our financial lives cannot be understood apart from the rest of our lives. Seeing the world of finance as elite and somehow outside the purview of social history, historians have largely neglected one of the key sources of power in our society. Credit operated not in opposition to categories of race and gender but through them. Part of what makes race and gender meaningful in our society is how capitalism relies on them to organize the relations of production, distribution, and consumption. At a basic level, consumer lending depended on gender, and its associated naturalized operations of power, to legitimate systems of control between male lenders and female borrowers. In related, but not equivalent ways, lending was circumscribed and transmitted along lines of race. A simple story of how African Americans and women were excluded from credit might make for impassioned historiography but would also be inaccurate. African Americans and women always had access to credit, but not always the same credit as white men, whose credit was cheaper and easier to get. In many ways, the modern credit system of the twentieth century was built by white men for white men, leaving other Americans to borrow in older, more expensive and dangerous, ways. Mortgage lending has been the most widely discussed way in which race has shaped credit relationships, but race, in more indirect ways, has also constrained the credit options for poor, urban African Americans in the postwar period that would have been inconceivable for the rest of America. While on some level, the history of credit discrimination is an important component of the narrative of this book, I also take pains to emphasis that credit is but one part of American capitalism, whose inequities cannot be simply solved by guaranteeing raceless and genderless credit access. Politicians in the 1960s, witnessing the success of credit access for postwar white people, seized on mortgages as an easy fix for income and wealth disparities, with sometimes dire consequences. The distribution of power in an economic system structured through race and gender cannot be easily freed of those categories, particularly if the economic roles that such social categories play are not fully acknowledged. Helping to return capitalism to the center of twentieth-century historiography will bring together the divergent scholarships of financial and social history, giving us a fuller picture of the twentieth-century United States.[11]

Despite capital's global mobility, every place has produced its own unique way to practice lending and repayment.[12] Installment credit was widespread in Western Europe in the first third of the twentieth century, as in the United States. Developing similar institutions, like finance companies, Europeans provided installment credit for the same purposes as Americans—to finance their manufacturing economies. European manufacturers, especially auto manufacturers, encountered the same challenges as their American counterparts. World War II provided a decisive break between the United States and other countries. While the rest of the developed world scraped together capital to rebuild the industrial infrastructure lost during the war, the United States exulted in its prosperity, as the sole remaining capitalist superpower.[13] While other countries also had uranium, wheat, and oil, no other country possessed our surplus of capital. This abundant capital allowed the United States to finance its postwar consumer prosperity. Other countries needed capital to put into financing production, but we had enough to also finance consumption. Abundant capital made possible, but not inevitable, the forms and extent of consumer financing that developed during World War II and in its aftermath. To understand the path of American financial development, we need to pay particular attention to the hard decisions made by firms and regulators during and after the war that led to that uniquely American invention—revolving consumer credit. A truly global history of debt would compare these two trajectories in the developed world until the war, and then show how they diverged after the war until the mid-1960s, when the capital imbalance between the United States and the globe began to shift back to what it had been traditionally. The breakdown of this temporary order, most visible in the collapse of the Bretton Woods system, prefigured a transition back to a more volatile world of global integration and competition, where the flows were not nearly so unilateral and once again, capital investment was more difficult to carry out profitably. While a global history of debt would, no doubt be fascinating, it was beyond the scope of this work to do so. What is lost in comparative perspective, I hope, is gained in the specificity of the American experience. In the United States, we see the first example of an economy based upon debt that can be resold at a profit, with all its associated possibilities and dangers.

This history of the infrastructure and practices of American debt will both help us to understand the financial history of the postwar period and, more generally, to come to grips with the choices that have created our contemporary indebted society. No single cause can explain the entire history of borrowing and lending: profit motive, government policy, technological progress, and even chance all played necessary but not sufficiently all-encompassing roles. Though to be sure there were hucksters who gamed the system, the choices responsible for today's economic crisis were not hidden, but done in the open, and often with the best of intentions. More terrifying than individual malfeasance or trickery is the idea that the structure of our economy itself is fundamentally out of alignment. This fear is not new. Anxieties about America's future are as old as the republic itself and fears about debt older still. But the present organization of our economy and our lives is as it has never been before. Despite the high profit of high finance, we may not be able to build as resilient an economy from debt as we did from steel. To understand today's credit system requires understanding the history of how consumer credit and twentieth-century American capitalism co-evolved to create both our prosperity and our insecurity.

Chapter One

Making Credit Modern

THE ORIGINS OF THE DEBT INFRASTRUCTURE IN THE 1920s

WHEN THE NEW INSTITUTIONS of the modern credit system took shape after World War I, its innovations frequently went unnoticed. Even to some trained financial experts, it appeared like nothing had changed at all. As one banker, Charles de B. Claiborne, later remarked in the 1930s, "We have always had installment buying, in my mind, for few ever bought for cash. The housewife bought and bought; she paid and paid, from month to month and from time to time."[1] The "charge account" or "open book account," where a retailer put a purchase on the books and a customer repaid at some uncertain future point, was the most common form of consumer credit for rich and poor, urban and rural, throughout late-nineteenth-century America.[2] Understood as a convenience, not as a profit source, charge accounts imposed no fees on the customer, unless the retailer had "credit" prices higher than "cash" prices. In some sense, Claiborne was superficially right: Americans still borrowed. Behind that borrowing, however, emerged new networks of capital that changed the meanings, the institutions, and the possibilities of lending. After World War I, personal debt in American capitalism began to become commercially profitable, institutionally resellable, and legally available on level unknown before.

Modern debt after World War I was defined through two new debt practices, installment credit and legalized personal loans, which reflected the social and economic order that emerged out of the new industrial economy. Installment credit allowed consumers to buy more, retailers to sell more, and manufacturers to make more, all at lower prices. Personal loans, meanwhile, enabled those industrial workers who made all those goods weather the uncertainties of capitalism's labor market. In tandem, the two debt practices developed for two distinct purposes inaugurated a new relationship between credit and capitalism, connecting personal lending to the larger circulation of investment capital in the American economy.

Retailers, perhaps, experienced the greatest transformation as debt became resellable. While the butcher, the baker, and the candlestick maker had always allowed their customers to charge their purchases, no retailer liked it. Consumer credit was a losing proposition that all retailers sought to avoid.[3] Lending, particularly the "open book credit" that small retailers used, was the surest way to the poorhouse. Customers didn't always pay. Record keeping was complicated. Credit bureaus did not exist yet for consumers as they did for businesses. Nonetheless, competition forced many merchants to offer credit, usually losing money in the process. Charging more for "credit prices" could drive business away, even as offering liberal credit could bring customers in. Retailers were not banks and did not have the excess capital to tie up in what amounted to unsecured loans to customers. Retailers were caught between the need to expand volume and consumers' desire for credit. This common sense thinking, that lending was unprofitable, is exactly opposite from our intuition today, when lending drives our economy. Retailers, unable to resell their debt or to finance it in other ways, had to perform the roles of bank, merchant, and collector—an untenable situation. Self-financed retailers tended to charge customers more and, through the mechanisms of repossession, had considerable incentive to cheat their customers. Only the largest self-financed merchants and manufacturers, like Singer, who financed its sewing machines or Sears, Roebuck who seemed to finance everything else, could do so without withering their own business and their customers' wealth. Even these large enterprises lost money on credit, but were able to make up for those losses on volume, something that a local merchant could not.

In the 1920s, for the first time, retailers could sell their debts to another institution—the finance company—and this simple possibility inaugurated the rise of the financial infrastructure that backed the proliferation of personal debt in the twentieth century, beginning the long process of realigning our financial common sense. This reselling of debt began through that most quintessentially American of inventions—the automobile. Financing the vast inventory of automobile dealers and the vast appetites of Americans for autos initially proved too large for auto companies, creating an entrepreneurial role for the finance company. In turn, the finance company enabled the profitable expansion of other forms of installment lending, expanding the flow of capital into nearly all areas of consumer durable spending. Through installment credit, working- and middle-class Americans could enjoy the fruits of the industrial economy, budgeting the payments to coincide with their now regular paychecks.

While consumers slaked their desire for former luxury goods like phonographs and automobiles through installment credit, Americans after World War I could also legally borrow for more pressing essentials—personal loans. If the industrial economy produced automobiles at prices Ford's workers could afford, it also produced structural unemployment, work injuries, and all the other hazards of industrial life beyond the control of individuals. Such hazards for working people were nothing new. Working-class Americans pressed for emergency cash had traditionally turned to personal networks of friends and family, themselves often financially constrained, and when those networks ran out, the local loan shark. With the legalization of personal loans—what was called "small loan" lending in the 1920s similar to what is called "payday" lending today—Americans discovered a means of financial self-reliance outside the judgmental eyes of family and community and outside the grasp of predacious loan sharks.

All Americans needed financing to benefit from and survive in the new modern world. Whereas the installment plan enabled middle-class consumers to enjoy the modern products such an economy made, personal loans enabled workers, who were always also consumers, to weather its brutal vicissitudes. While borrowing grew, the great suppliers of capital, the commercial banks, and the great organizers of capital, the manufacturing companies, initially kept the business at arm's length, leaving its risky lending for the hungriest entrepreneurs seeking the last scraps of profit. At a time when banks were distracted by the spectacular profits from manufacturing investments and the stock market, the unorthodox business models of finance companies and personal loan companies bridged the banks' capital to the consumer. Loan sharks began to move their capital from dank backrooms into the legal personal loan businesses, forming legalized national lending networks. At the same time, new independent finance companies, initially just connected to the automobile industry, eventually extended to all durable goods. Linking credit to the larger circulations of capital made credit cheaper and safer for consumers. Consumers finally had an alternative to the expensive, self-financed retailers and the illegal collection methods of the loan shark. Contrasting these new forms of credit with what came before—loans sharks vs. personal loans and self-financed retailers vs. automobile dealers—shows how the new credit system helped manufacturers, retailers, and consumers. For the middle-class, and the native-born whites of the working class, this new credit system displaced the old. For African Americans and for immigrants, access to this new credit system was more uncertain, and for those without access, lending remained as predatory as it had been before.

The rise of these new forms of debt was neither entirely beneficial nor entirely detrimental for borrowers but both at once, in complicated and often unexpected ways. Entrepreneurs, as well as reformers, created new institutions to meet these needs—creating profit for some and penury for others. Installment credit enabled people to achieve a level of consumption unattainable without the use of debt. With this improved standard of living came, at the same time, the risk of losing a family's possessions if the debtor missed a single payment. Did debt make good the promise of democratic consumption or was it only a quixotic dream of modern luxury for everyone? The Americans of the 1920s, of different classes, moral outlooks, and economic interests, had a variety of answers to these questions. For reasons of class, race, or nationality, those who did not have access to this credit paid more than those who did. Modern debt, whatever its benefits and drawbacks, refashioned the ways in which Americans bought, worked, and lived, in keeping with the harsh demands and unparalleled delights afforded by the modern industrial economy.

The Price of Risk: Loan Sharking and Small Loans

If a single place had to be pointed to as the origin of the modern debt economy, one might choose the backroom of a Minneapolis jewelry shop in the late 1870s, where a young John Mackey, a thirty-four year old man with a "substantial" inheritance, had recently set up shop to loan hopeful "settlers from both the East and from Europe" money as they made their way to the Dakota territories.[4] Mackey's small operation would eventually become, by the 1920s, the most widespread small loan company in the United States, the Household Finance Company, and then eighty years later, find itself at the center of American subprime and credit card lending. The story of his business represents, in some sense, a long thread of the history of American debt. Mackey's business could charitably be called a pawnshop, but the pawnshop was just for show. John Mackey was a loan shark, lending money at 10 percent per month, which added up to 185 percent per year.

Loan sharks, like Mackey, existed because there was no legal alternative for personal loans. In a utopian world, profit would not be necessary to get people what they need. Loans, for instance, could be lent with little or no interest and repaid when the borrower found it convenient, as many charitable societies attempted, with little success, at the turn of the century. Constrained by a lack of capital, these societies withered. Loan sharks, however, prospered. No legal alternative existed.

Profitable lending required the borrower to pay enough in interest and fees to offset the risk that debt would not be repaid. Charging interest on loans, per se, was not illegal, just usurious rates like those that Mackey charged. The definition of usury varied by state, but was always so low—typically 1 to 1.5 percent a month or 13 to 20 percent annually—that reputable businessmen could not make money lending to consumers. Though 13 percent seems high enough to us today, consider how much more difficult it would be to collect from a customer around 1900. Personal loans, by virtue of their size and the customer, made them more expensive to provide profitably under existing usury laws. Administering small personal loans was much costlier than commercial loans because the office work was at least as much for a small loan as for a large loan, if not more. Businesses had a paper trail of income and expenses, while individuals, few of whom paid income taxes, could be less transparent. Borrowers tended to have few assets to use as collateral. A unique identity, without a social security number, would be hard to ascertain. Without a phone, contacting references would have been arduous. Even if you knew someone personally, knowing who was a good credit risk was impossible without a credit rating, or at least expensive. The interest rate had to cover the risk of the loan, and without information, the risk was always high. Between paperwork and higher risk, small loan lenders needed a higher rate of interest than the 6 percent common in business loans to make a profit.

For loan sharks, the difficulty of collection was compounded by their having operated illegally. No court would enforce the loan. No bank would lend money to grow his business. Mackey had access to only a limited amount of money to lend. The scarcity of capital and the risk of borrower default made his money more valuable to him. Thirteen percent interest would not have allowed him to operate profitably. It is more than enough to offset risk today, but the relative cheapness of our credit is made possible through today's technology to enforce debts, regulation to compel us to pay, and lenders' ability to resell our debt to investors. These differences make possible profitable lending at 13 percent rather than 185 percent.

Mackey's business, despite these obstacles, grew with these high interest rates and by 1881 he opened an office separate from the shop.[5] Quasi-legal, these loan-sharking syndicates operated in the open, but with furtive methods to conceal their usurious rates. In 1885, he had the first of many usury lawsuits brought against him for charging exorbitant interest rates, which in annual terms topped 300 percent (he had evidently raised his rates). Though the lower courts found in his favor, the supreme court of Minnesota reversed the lower court's decision, finding Mackey guilty of usury. Despite the loss, however, Mackey took his fine in stride as a business expense and expanded his enterprise. In the next two decades, despite breaking the law, Mackey opened a chain of lending offices across many states.[6]

Why did people borrow from loan sharks like Mackey? Banks would not lend small amounts to ordinary people. For those who had exhausted the limits of charge account credit, there was no alternative. They had to pay their bills at the grocer or the butcher before they could get more food.[7] For those without access to other working-class credit sources, like a benevolent bartender, an ethnic credit circle, or friends and family, or were fearful of the ensuing shame of needing to borrow from someone they knew, the loan shark was often the only alternative.[8] Loan sharks, like Mackey, were an active and important part of working-class life in early twentieth-century cities.

Records from Mackey's Illinois offices in 1917 reveal that the firm served the needs of people working in diverse occupations—yet nearly always working class—as they struggled to make ends meet.[9] Working-class life was precarious. A sudden illness or job loss, especially for those with little or no savings, could mean calamity. A little money—two-thirds of loans were for less than $50—meant the difference between disaster and safety. Among Illinois offices, of 9,136 loans, the most common amounts borrowed were $25 (1,134), $50 (1,303), and $100 (1,189).[10] Loans like these, even at exorbitant rates, were often preferable to the alternatives of cold, starvation, and no medical care. A laborer required $25 to "pay up bills" because he had been sick.[11] A brush maker who could not get enough hours needed money for "living expenses."[12] A laundress wanted $10 for her family's shoes.[13] Sickness, back debts, rent, coal, and minor expenses were all too common.[14] Though the personal loan, to some extent, displaced the traditional interpersonal borrowing of working-class people, families used loans to help their families. Whether loan entries were tragic, like a "mattress maker" who borrowed $32.50 to "make good his sons [*sic*] forged check," or joyful like the fireman who borrowed $30 "to assist in bringing his two children from Europe," the small loan business helped families take care of one another, despite limited resources.[15] Necessity, not profligacy, drove this borrowing.

These loans were not charity. Though Mackey's profits varied, from 3.3 percent in one office to 16.6 percent in another, all made money.[16] In Illinois alone, the firm lent over a half million dollars in 1917.[17] Mackey's organization made money off the uncertainty and desperation attendant to risky working-class lives, not working-class profligacy or extravagance. Loan sharking "syndicates," as they were known, did everything they could to maximize their profit on this uncertainty. Mackey's storefronts, advertising "money to lend," lured in desperate working-class people. Coming in, an employee would quote a price to the borrower.[18] If that seemed too high, the customer would leave to try another lender. Unbeknownst to the customer, most of the other potential loan shark outfits, all with different names, would be operated by the Mackey organization as well, which controlled the bulk of the moneylending in Chicago. The "word" would be put out that the borrower was looking to borrow. Each store that the borrower visited would, in turn raise the quoted rates until the borrower was corralled back to the original store.[19] Without alternative credit sources, the borrower would have to pay what Mackey demanded. The shame of debt, which necessitated its secrecy, pushed the desperate to fall into the jaws of the loan shark.

Through his chain of loan shark offices, Mackey became fantastically wealthy, enjoying polo and yachting, owning property in California, Newport, and Europe, and even at one point entertaining the king of Great Britain.[20] Yet his offices, which occupied an "entire floor in the Willoughby building," according to newspaper accounts, were completely secretive.[21] Until Mackey's outing in 1910, no one outside his organization really knew what went on there.

The exposure in 1910 of the source of his wealth in Chicago newspapers as the "head of a gigantic loan shark 'trust,'" led to his expulsion from elite society.[22] Replying to critics, he justified his business: "Usurious interest? Certainly, as high as 20 per cent or more in some instances. What of it? Is it anybody's business but mine? I am not ashamed of it."[23] Though he did not challenge the claims that he charged usurious rates, he denied it was anyone's business but his and his clients,' insisting on an older, interpersonal model of lending.[24] Mackey felt that there was a "legitimate need" for his business and he felt no "stigma" for it.[25] Mackey's outlook, unfortunately for him, was not shared by the refined company that he preferred to keep. Rejected, Mackey retreated to the exclusive, one million dollar Leamington Hotel in Minneapolis, which he had built. Despite his social collapse, his company somehow persisted and grew.

While his social ambitions faltered, Mackey's business did not. The legal environment for small loan lending was about to change, and for Mackey's organization that would bring unprecedented and unexpected growth. The source of Mackey's good fortune came from a small group of devoted anti–loan shark reformers fixed on driving Mackey and his ilk out of business.

Profit and Regulation

The successful movement to foster profitable personal loans for the working class came from an unlikely nonprofit source: the newly created Russell Sage Foundation (RSF). Though named for Mr. Sage, a railroad baron who had little love for the working class, the RSF was the creation of his wife, Margaret, after his death. Very active in turn-of-the-century charity and philanthropy, Margaret Sage envisioned an organization for "the improvement of social and living conditions in the United States of America."[26] Even before the creation of the foundation, Margaret Sage's secretary, who managed her charity gifts, received thousands of letters from desperate New Yorkers. Many of these letters detailed their struggle with loan sharks, who broke the usury laws of New York and kept their borrowers in perpetual debt. Responding to these letters, the foundation decided to investigate by funding two dissertations on illegal lending in

New York, by Columbia graduate students Arthur Ham and Clarence Wassam.[27]

Their findings confirmed the letters that Mrs. Sage's secretary had received and both authors came to the same conclusion: the uncertain risk of workers' lives demanded that they have access to small loans to deal with their unexpected misfortune, and a legal form of small loan lending needed to be created. Usury laws intended to protect poor people from high interest rates and predacious lenders did not protect them from unemployment, illness, or the myriad other uncertainties facing an industrial workforce without recourse to a welfare state or a strong union. Instead, such restrictions on interest rates forced working-class people to turn to the very people they were intended to put out of business—loan sharks. These loan sharks charged borrowers between 60 and 480 percent per year.[28] Without a legal source for small loans, desperate borrowers had no other choice. Raising the legal rate of interest to a level at which lenders could make money, but would also not burden borrowers, would create a legal alternative to the loan sharks. Doubling the legal interest rate to 3 percent per month or 43 percent per year, they estimated, would create enough incentive for lenders to legally extend loans and still be substantially below the interest rates demanded by loan sharks. Calling for the reform of usury laws, the creation of legal small loan lenders, and the end of loan sharks, Arthur Ham joined the Russell Sage Foundation and emerged as the voice of the small loan reform movement in the 1910s.[29]

While supporting the quixotic efforts of the remedial loan societies, Ham worked for the rest of the 1910s on the creation of a model loan law that would not exploit borrowers, but would provide a reasonable rate of profit for the lender.[30] By 1916, Ham, in consultation with illegal lenders open to reform, finished what came to be known as the Uniform Small Loan Law. Ham defined small loans as personal loans of $300 or less.[31] Borrowers would pay a maximum of 3.5 percent a month to lenders, but without any hidden fees or charges.[32] The interest would only be charged on the unpaid balance rather that the original amount borrowed. The law also established the clear supervision of agencies in each state to enforce compliance. Small loan lenders could be profitable, but under state supervision, reformers hoped that they could not be predatory.

Through careful scientific examination, based on "intelligence instead of hysteria," experts believed they had found the best way to right this unintended wrong—the Uniform Small Loan Law. States that enacted this law would drive out the loan sharks.[33] Legislators heard that the borrowers were not "drunks" and "bums" like they had imagined, but the "exact reverse." Sickness, death, home repairs, education, unemployment, and other household emergencies were the reasons that people borrowed.

Money borrowed was not "to get drunk or for other evil purposes" but to deal with the uncertainties of an industrial economy.[34] Making the "scientific rate" of 3.5 percent legal would bring these moral borrowers out of the arms of the evil loan sharks.[35] Ham also promoted the small loans through ideals of hard work and ownership, citing in public speeches and writings how small loans could help a worker start his own business or a widow get by until she found employment.[36] All accounts of borrowing ended with working and generally owning one's own business. Reformers hoped small loans would be a bridge from owing to owning.

Such arguments to various legislatures worked. In 1917, four states introduced the small loan lending law and it was enacted in Illinois, Indiana, and Maine.[37] By 1928, adapted to local pressures, some form of the law was passed in twenty-five states covering over 60 percent of the U.S. population.[38] The businesses enabled by this reform called themselves a variety of names, all of which drew on the reformist language of the remedial associations and emphasized their legality: industrial banks, personal finance companies, or licensed lenders.[39] Industrial banking was the most frequently used in the 1920s because it was in industrial districts and for industrial workers that small loan lending found its initial niche. Because working-class borrowers tended to own little property, household goods were used as collateral in 90 percent of the loans.[40] A chattel mortgage was taken out on the borrower's furniture and other assets.[41] If the borrower failed to pay, the lender could take the borrower's collateral. Such foreclosures happened rarely—only 0.4 percent of the loans ended in this way.[42] Because of these chattel mortgage contracts, co-signers were not usually required on the loan.[43] Borrowing could be taken out in secrecy, without the social stigma of borrowing from friends or family but with the knowledge that the borrower was self-reliant and not taking charity.

In contrast to the mere tens of charity-driven remedial loan associations, by the early 1930s profit-driven industrial lenders numbered in the thousands.[44] The profits of small loan lenders were very respectable. In 1925, net profits in Virginia, New Jersey, and Massachusetts, the only public rates published, were 11.58 percent, 13 percent, and 7.7 percent respectively.[45] If Mackey's organization in Illinois in 1917 was any comparison, legal small loan lending, despite its lower interest rates, was just as profitable as illegal loan-sharking because unlike loan sharks, such businesses could use courts and police to enforce the debts, borrow from commercial banks to expand their operations, and operate in the open, all of which reduced costs and lowered default risks.

The profitability of legal personal lending was not lost on loan sharks. For many loan sharks, legalized small loan lending was a new opportunity to turn their ill-gotten gains into legal businesses. In the changing legal environment of the post–World War I period, the very business that led to Mackey's disgrace also led to his organization's greater expansion as it reorganized as a corporation in compliance with the new small loan laws. What had been a quasi-secret network of loan companies, operating under many different names, by the early 1920s could come into the light. Although unable to charge the rates they had previously set, lenders could now legally extend loans and use the powers of the state to enforce their contracts, which made earning profits much easier. In 1925 Mackey's chain of lending offices, now extending across the country, incorporated as the Household Finance Corporation.[46] By 1929, the Household Finance Corporation achieved the distinction of being the first small loan company to issue stock. The back-room loan shark had become a stock-issuing corporation. Previously illegal, lending had become big business.

The decision to go legitimate was not as easy as it might seem. Laws could always be changed. The transition to legal lending fostered its own difficulties. Some loan sharks, of course, resisted giving up their business just because of some new law, doubting whether it would last. An Atlanta loan shark, P. E. Leake, while referring to the new small loan law, "did not believe the bill [was] constitutional" and directed his underworld employees to "work hard to keep your customers in line and paying."[47] If customers asked about the new law, Leake instructed his employees to tell borrowers that the company "may be able to operate under the new law and all customers in good standing would be eligible for loans up to $300.00."[48] Uncertain of the future, many loan sharks continued their illegal operations, hedging against a possibly legal future, and trying to keep making their profit. By the 1930s, with the new inspection abilities of the state, such noncompliance was to be met sternly and swiftly. Loan-sharking had to go further underground to maintain its viability, but in doing so it lost its previously central role in working-class communities, as legal, well-capitalized small loan companies took its place.

Other loan sharks, however, like the Mackey syndicate and Henry French, tried to go straight and in the process reaped tremendous profits. In Georgia, the King brothers, Rufus and Charles, had built themselves a financial empire along similar lines to that of Mackey and French. Upon his death in 1933, the *Atlanta Constitution* described Rufus's business, Security Bankers' Finance Corporation (SBFC), as "operat[ing] subsidiary companies all over the United States, extending credit in time of need for vast numbers of people," which were known for their "sound business methods and able and conservative administration." SBFC grew, like the Household Finance Company, out of a vast interstate network of clandestine loan-sharking operations.[49] Like Mackey's syndicate, companies were registered under an assortment of names, but ownership was ultimately with the King brothers. An investigation done in the late 1920s found companies in the Rufus network in New York, Georgia, Pennsylvania, Missouri, and several other states.[50]

Like Mackey's, this illegal network used the new small loan laws to form a legal corporation in the mid-1920s.[51] Taking money previously made in loan-sharking, they used the new small loan laws to open small lending companies across the country, and to turn their previously illegal operations into legitimate ones. Incorporating in 1927, the SBFC of Atlanta, Georgia acted as a holding company for these small loan companies. SBFC's annual report credited the continued spread of the Russell Sage's Uniform Small Loan Law as the reason for its existence.[52] With "twenty-four states [having] prepared and endorsed" the law, the SBFC annual report claimed that the "subsidiary corporations" of SBFC had the support of "almost every civic and social organization in America" and the legal enforcement of the "State Banking Department," where they operated. The executives of SBFC who had "more than a quarter of century's experience in the small loan business," brought their acumen of loan-sharking along with them into the now legal small loan lending business.[53] Though the company initially had only a few subsidiaries, more were added every year. Within its first year, it loaned over $1 million to 7,310 families, earning $116, 968 in interest.[54]

Reformers seeking to destroy loan sharks may have undercut their business model, but they did not stop the businessmen themselves. Leon Henderson, soon to be at the center of the Roosevelt Administration but who then ran the remedial loan department of the RSF, approved of King's new direction, if not King himself. [55] Though the social stigma of moneylending remained, small loan law proponents did their best to encourage the transition to legal and regulated lending. The market-drive reforms of the RSF during the 1920s remade working-class borrowing. By raising the legal rate of lending, small loan reformers enabled a new profitable, legal financial industry to emerge from the shadows of the economy. Loan-sharking remained vestigial as part of the urban economy, but for most borrowers a legal alternative existed.

The industrial economy, however, was not all suffering. Modern conveniences and commodities promised workers an unprecedented standard of living, which, through installment credit, they began to enjoy.

Automobiles and the Origin of the Finance Company

Impossible to imagine today, before 1919 most cars were sold for cash.[56] Only after World War I did the automobile change from a rich man's novelty into a mass-produced commodity. As the quintessential luxury good, everything the factories turned out was sold. The creator of General Motors Acceptance Corporation (GMAC), John Raskob, said that "there has never appeared among mankind, in all its history, an object which has been more generally desired than the automobile."[57] Cars were not just a commodity; they had, according to Raskob, "given Americans new values in life . . . given us all something worth working for."[58]

By 1920, however, as the annual report of General Motors describes it, automobiles began the transition from what were "commonly known as 'pleasure cars'" to being "economical transportation."[59] Everyone who could afford to buy an auto for cash had done so.[60] To continue growth, the consumer base would have to broaden. Cars could no longer be luxury goods. As automobile production exploded in the 1920s, so too did the need for automobile financing for both consumers and dealers alike.[61]

The capital requirements of more expensive, mass-produced goods led retailers and entrepreneurs to explore new options in consumer finance and, in the process of meeting their own immediate needs, created a novel financial institution that was neither an informal lender nor a commercial bank—the finance company. Modern, pervasive installment credit found its institutional bedrock in the financial innovation of the early automobile industry. The financial infrastructure of installment credit grew out of the very requirements of heavy capital manufacturing for mass production, but once created, finance companies found other markets outside of the automobile industry. They turned to less capital-intensive retail sectors, which enabled the expansion of installment credit throughout the American economy. The automobile's historically unique combination of high expense, mass appeal, and independent dealers required an entirely new financial apparatus; it needed finance companies to enable the distribution and purchase of an expensive good on a widespread scale.

Automobile sales to customers occurred at the end of a chain of relationships. Manufacturers sold autos to dealers, which were independently owned by small businessmen. In turn, these dealerships sold the autos to customers. Upon delivery of a shipment of cars to a dealership, the dealer paid the manufacturer in cash. Before 1920, this system worked fine. Manufacturers made as many autos as they could and dealers were able to sell their inventories quickly. As the economy slowed after World War I and the cash-buying market was saturated, this system began to break down. Profitable auto factories had to be run constantly. Manufacturers invested heavily in productive capital, and letting it sit idle wasted money. The problem for automakers was that though production was year-round, consumers liked to buy cars in the late spring and summer.[62] General Motors (GM) and Ford could not produce all the autos they needed for the spring in just February. By producing year-round they lowered the average cost of production, which enabled them to lower the consumer's price to a level that made mass consumption possible.[63] The problem, for manufacturers, was how to lower inventory costs. Storing all those autos could become prohibitively expensive.

Manufacturers wanted dealers to bear those storage costs, by taking delivery from the factories year-round. At small volumes, dealers might have the capital and space for all these cars, but as volumes increased they did not. Dealers required "wholesale financing," that is, a loan to buy inventory to give the manufacturers the cash they demanded. Neither dealer nor manufacturer wanted to pay for the inventory costs, but manufacturers had the upper hand.

Manufacturers created wholesale finance companies for dealers to resolve these production pressures. Such manufacturer-organized finance companies, like GMAC, concerned themselves with wholesale financing and not, as GMAC would later claim, retail financing. Manufacturers, seeking to hold down storage costs that resulted from year-round production, forced dealers to take on stock out of season, often pushing them to the limits of their credit.[64] And the credit always had interest. The more autos the dealer took, the more money was made by the manufacturer, but the dealers now had to pay the inventory costs. Dealers who refused autos were in danger of losing their contract with the manufacturer.[65] Manufacturers denied this. GM insisted that "no dealer is required or permitted to carry stocks beyond that point" of necessary accumulation "during seasons of relatively low retail deliveries" so as to "facilitate prompt deliveries" and "to maintain manufacturing and distributing economies afforded by a reasonably level rate of production."[66] Despite such claims, dealers reluctant to take inventory knew other dealers could always be found. Turnover in dealerships was rapid. One independent finance company executive remarked that in northern Illinois he could not "find two automobile dealers in our town that were there five years ago."[67] What the manufacturer and the dealer thought were reasonable inventories could be quite different, as neither wanted to pay the associated costs of unsold inventories. As a result, their interests were in conflict. GM's goal of being "free from the evils resulting from excess accumulation of stocks" was as much theirs as the dealers, since for both, inventory costs cut into profits.[68]

For manufacturers, the expense of expanding production demanded all their available capital. With wholesale financing to handle the production problems, diverting scarce capital into the less profitable consumer debt, or "retail financing," made little sense. As economist Milan Ayres noted in 1928, "Why should not many of these manufacturers or merchants be glad to turn over that part of their business to finance companies, and thus conserve their capital, or credit resources, for the expansion of their primary business?"[69] An auto finance company that made a net profit of a few percent on its investment was considered to be making a good profit, but this was still far less profitable than the capital invested in auto manufacturing.[70] In the face of capital scarcity, manufacturers logically chose to place their money where it would be most profitable. Equally important was the sense from manufacturers that they sold cars to dealers, not consumers. Surprisingly it was not until 1924 that GM used "sales to consumers" as their "fundamental index" for measuring success instead of just sales to dealers.

Manufacturer finance companies' initial focus on financing dealers and not consumers provided an opening in the early 1920s for the emergence of small automobile finance companies. This gap in financing allowed independent finance companies with no automobile factories in which to invest, to invest instead in consumer retail financing. The much larger profits inherent to retail finance than to wholesale finance came quickly.

The lure of these profits pulled in entrepreneurs all over America. In 1922, for instance, Thomas E. Courtney of De Kalb, Illinois took out a $3,000 mortgage on his home to start a small finance company. Profits for Courtney, like for so many local finance companies in the early 1920s, were tremendous. By the end of the first year, the assets of his company, Northern Illinois Finance Company, totaled $30,000.[71] Like Courtney, most of these "newcomers" were locally oriented with limited financial resources. As one banker later remarked, a "line of business [which] has a rapid growth . . . attracts some who are entitled neither by ability, character, nor experience to manage a business, and installment financing [was] no exception to this rule."[72] Many saw the opportunity, but few made money as easily as Courtney, who went on to be a leader among small finance companies.[73] Yet for those who could tame the exploding industry, profits could be had. Within five years of Courtney's mortgage, the industry went, according to a vice-president of Commercial Investment Trust, from being virtually unknown to "employing an invested capital of nearly a half a billion dollars."[74] "In little more than a decade," a Chicago banker observed, finance companies "have acquired a capital that our largest banks have taken half a century to attain."[75]

Courtney's financing niche existed because commercial banks, like manufacturers, had little interest in filling it. Banks, with rare exceptions, stayed out of the automobile financing business in the 1920s. Of course, in the 1920s banks had many other, more traditional opportunities to make profits. Manufacturing was booming. The stock market, by the late 1920s at least, offered a fantastic site of investment for stock speculators borrowing on the margin, and stocks could be easily liquidated to repay such debts. The consumer finance market, though growing, was not a necessity. Most banks could not risk the investment in collections and consumer investigations. As the president of a large auto finance company noted in 1929, "[w]hen consumer credit first appeared in volume, about ten years ago, many bankers, particularly those of the ultra conservative type, were opposed to it. Theretofore the banker had concerned himself practically altogether with producer credit, and no attention had been paid by financial institutions to consumer credit."[76] Consumer credit was lending money for something that produced no value. Stocks and business loans produced return. Cars did not. A conservative banker would not lend money on an asset that produced no additional value, since it was through that additional value that the loan was to be repaid. The logic of business lending and the logic of consumer lending were totally at odds. And practical matters were as important as those logical differences. Banks had never provided installment credit for automobiles and did not know how to go about it. Even the most well thought-out idea could miss an important angle.

As finance companies expanded, however, they turned to commercial bankers for additional capital. Though bankers had neither the inclination nor infrastructure to directly lend to consumers, they could look at the balance sheets—and profits—of finance companies that needed capital to expand. Commercial bankers had plenty of experience examining balance sheets to determine how much money to lend to entrepreneurial businessmen, even if they did not know—or want to know—how to profitably lend to consumers. Finance company executives took pains to draw analogies between their businesses and banks to emphasize the soundness of consumer lending. One executive compared the finance company's receivables and notes to the bank's loans and deposits. Emphasizing the objectivity of balance sheets over cultural preconceptions, Alexander Duncan, an executive with Commercial Credit Company, remarked that "[c]ommercial Bankers feel, and experience has proven, that they are doing a safe and conservative business." If bankers agreed with that statement, then Duncan hoped bankers would see "that a well managed Finance Company is also doing a safe and conservative business, as shown by its actual experience, and that when its experience begins to prove otherwise it will quickly change its policy."[77] Balance sheets might convince bankers to lend to businesses, but not directly to consumers. The habits of a lifetime were more credible than a few years of profits.

The "success of a few stimulated the organization of many," observed another finance company executive in 1928.[78] The company and its services appeared seemingly overnight and changed the entire auto sector. The rapid expansion of installment credit in auto sales was fantastic. In contrast to before World War I, when there were virtually no auto installment sales, within ten years installment sales grew to 60 percent of the total number of auto purchases.[79]

Within a couple of years of the initial rush of hopeful entrepreneurs into the finance industry, competition began to take its toll. Executive Alexander Duncan remarked in 1925 that for the previous "two years there [had] been, and for the next several years there [would] continue to be, a gradual process of elimination which will ultimately benefit the strong and well managed Companies." Believing in the efficient operation of the market, Duncan saw the competition between finance companies as benefitting both the finance companies and consumers. With competition, nevertheless, profits dropped. Profitable finance companies who lent loosely in 1922, quickly saw their profits shrink by the mid-1920s.[80] By the end of the decade, bankers favorably remarked on the "gradual elimination from [finance companies'] ranks of the incompetently or dishonestly managed finance company."[81] GM's annual report for 1926 noted that in the finance industry "there [had] been a marked tendency toward more conservative policies" in retail auto finance.[82]

Though initially created just to finance the wholesale credit of dealers, after a couple of years manufacturer finance companies began to catch on to the profitability of retail finance as well. By 1924 GMAC provided about 5 percent of the annual profit for GM and its subsidiaries.[83] Whereas the GM annual report for 1919 describes the primary purpose of GMAC as, "to assist dealers in financing their purchase of General Motors' products," by 1927 the GMAC annual report describes "provid[ing] credit to the consumer of goods as its most important function."[84]

Only by the mid-1920s did GM begin to realize it had a relationship with the consumer as well as the dealer, in terms of product appeal and its profit growth. In the 1923 annual report, retail finance was, for the first time, on an equal footing with wholesale finance, with the stated purpose of GMAC to "assist dealers in financing their wholesale commitments and uses in the purchase of autos on the deferred payment plan."[85] By 1925 GM recognized the importance of time sales to its essential business plan, noting in its annual report that "at the present time its importance can hardly be overestimated."[86]

Clearly by the late 1920s, as GMAC became its own institution with its own set of problems and solutions separate from its parent company, it turned increasingly toward the retail business as a source of profit, putting a squeeze on local finance companies. While the GM annual report recognizes the importance of GMAC to its product distribution in the mid-1920s, the GMAC annual report had a different perspective on its role in the organization. GMAC provided wholesale and export financing, "but the most important, from the standpoint of operations, volume, business policy and administration is, of course, the retail business."[87] Unlike their parent institutions, who booked profits on manufacturing, these finance companies made profits only by lending money. Institutionally, they were set up to lend. Though the manufacturers had a definite idea about the purpose of these subsidiaries, institutional autonomy engendered more autonomous goals, leading to a revision of both their original purpose and their history. Inaccurately revising GMAC's history, its creator, John Raskob, recounted in 1927 the purpose of GMAC's creation as to fight the neighborhood "fly-by-night" financing of cars, which was "not sound or safe" for the consumer and who charged "outrageous" rates.[88] By the mid-1920s, these manufacturer finance companies began to compete with the independent finance companies for the consumer auto debt.

For independent finance companies, competition from manufacturer-organized finance companies could not have occurred at a worse time. The decrease in domestic new auto sales added to finance company woes by the late 1920s. Though more autos were manufactured in 1928 than in any previous year, the number sold in America was fewer than in 1923, 1925, and 1926.[89] Unlike the early 1920s, when a finance company could count on rising auto sales and little competition, sales by the mid-1920s had fallen and competition had increased. Manufacturer-organized finance companies, like GMAC, also increasingly looked at retail finance as a key component of their business. In 1926 GM produced one-third of all cars made in America.[90] From 1926 to 1927, it increased the number of autos still being financed at the end of the year from 646,000 to 824,190.[91] GMAC financed slightly over one million GM cars in 1927. Even as auto production sales fell, manufacturers nonetheless increased their share of the retail financing.

Independent finance companies decried the infringement of manufacturer finance companies on their territory. They saw the expansion of companies like GMAC the result of unfair "pressure" on dealers. The national association of the independent finance companies passed resolutions to demand "that the automobile manufacturer should desist from any attempt to compel its dealers to sell their time paper [consumer auto debt] to any particular company."[92]

Manufacturers denied this. A representative of the Motor Dealers Credit Corporation (MDCC), who financed Studebaker, "steadfastly refused" to recognize that his company had brought "pressure to bear" on the dealers, despite the fact that, as he acknowledged, MDCC would have liked to.[93] A GMAC representative claimed that his company "never used coercive measures in acquiring business, nor has the General Motors Corporation any such policy."[94] Ford's financing company, Universal Credit Corporation, expressed similar policies "opposed to factory compulsion and/or coercion which would compel dealers to do anything against their free will."[95]

Manufacturers did not need to pressure dealers. The structural realities of automobile distribution did the work for them. In the popular press, manufacturing executives like GMAC head Raskob, called the process of financing dealers, manufacturing goods, and lending to consumers part of one continuous process. For General Motors, retail finance was as central to their business as making the cars. The early separation of production, distribution, and financing began to be erased rhetorically. Though the "motor-car dealer" was "responsible for his debt," GMAC took "over the debt from him, at a reasonable cost for the service and his books [were] clear."[96] Raskob contrasted GMAC, a "real banking concern," with those "fly-by-night" finance companies that would fleece customers. GMAC claimed to protect customers from excess debt, by not selling autos "to persons who have no right to try to buy them." By presenting the benevolent face of the professional credit man, Raskob contrasted GMAC with the conventional "loan shark" image of the finance company owner. With their greater resources and institutional connections to dealers, manufacturer-organized finance companies steadily displaced independent finance companies in the automobile market.

Financing Everything

In the face of increased auto financing competition, some finance companies looked to diversify their accounts. In the early 1920s, independent finance companies could rely on auto financing for steady profits. As domestic sales fell and manufacturer finance company competition increased, finance companies approached those that had traditionally financed their own sales. Though finance companies were not initially necessary for the financing of other commodities, their services were still useful. The model of the finance company developed for automobiles was adapted for other goods.[97] Some financing companies specialized, like the American Finance Co. of Cincinnati (radios) or Refrigeration Discount Co. of Detroit (electric refrigerators).[98] Most of these firms, however, had matured through the automobile industry's easy profits at the beginning of the 1920s and turned to these new products as their older revenue dried-up. By purchasing their customers' debt, finance companies allowed these other manufacturers and retailers, to provide installment credit to their dealers and customers as if radios and refrigerators were the same as automobiles.

Unlike in the early automobile finance industry, easy profits did not exist at first to attract many independent finance entrepreneurs into household appliance financing. Manufacturers still needed, however, to finance dealers' inventories. Starting with General Electric (GE), manufacturers set up subsidiary financing companies for wholesale financing, and then, later, retail financing. GE made finished consumer goods as well as parts, like motors, for other manufacturers. In conjunction with some of its manufacturing partners, GE started six finance companies across the country, in New York, Pennsylvania, Ohio, Illinois, California, and Texas.[99] Initially, these companies had minority stockholders from other durable goods manufacturers who used GE motors in their machines, but as GE expanded into more lines, like washing machines and vacuum cleaners that allowed them to compete with their previous partners, those relationships fell apart. In 1921, GE formed its first totally subsidiary finance company that was the forerunner to the General Electric Contracts Corporation (GECC), leading the way for financing companies to become part of non-automotive manufacturers' business.[100]

Manufacturer competition determined the boundaries of lending in which the subsidiary finance companies engaged. Like in auto manufacturing, the primary aim of these finance companies was to promote the manufacturer's product lines. GECC, for instance, financed only GE-manufactured products, even though it could have easily, and profitably, financed other manufacturers' goods as well. Companies that used GE motors complained to government investigators in the early 1920s that if they used any non-GE motors in their machines, "General Electric Co. would refuse to sell us any motors and would refuse to allow the Purchase Corporation [GECC] to finance our dealers."[101] Though the head of the GECC, E. W. Miner, claimed they would sell motors to anyone, he confirmed that without the exclusive use of GE motors it was the "general practice" not to finance any of their products.[102] GE's goal was profits from manufacturing, not financing, particularly if those financing profits encouraged the sales of competitors' products.

Some large manufacturers, like Westinghouse, turned to existing commercial wholesale finance companies for their credit needs rather than forming an internal finance company. In 1922 Westinghouse contracted with the well-known Commercial Credit Company (CCC) of Baltimore, Maryland.[103] Unlike GECC, CCC had interests other than Westinghouse, but in exchange for Westinghouse's business its contract stipulated that CCC had to "recommend exclusively the use of the Westinghouse commercial credit plan" to distributors, dealers, and other manufacturers.[104] Despite no explicit arrangement to prevent CCC from financing Westinghouse competitors, it was understood that it could only promote Westinghouse. CCC, while financing Westinghouse, refused financing to its competitors, including the large motor manufacturer Robbins & Myers.[105] Though not explicitly a manufacturer-organized financing company, it operated largely the same.[106]

By the mid-1920s, installment financing for both retailers and consumers became necessary to remain competitive. Robbins & Myers, for instance, found that "it was losing customers on account of the credit facilities of the other large motor manufacturers."[107] A large manufacturer Robbins & Myers could create its own financing company, which it did, but for smaller manufacturers the choice was not so easy. Small manufacturers, shut off from the big wholesale finance companies, turned to the small, independent finance companies that emerged out of the auto industry, and these companies had a great deal of experience in lending to consumers.

These independent finance companies enabled small manufacturers to focus on their core business and leave the trouble of financing to someone else. A pamphlet from the Apex Electrical Distributing Company, who made home appliances, explained to its dealers that it had a financing arrangement with the Republic Finance & Investment Company because Apex's "business is to manufacture; your business is to sell; the Republic's business is to finance."[108] These independent finance companies tended to mask their role in credit relationships. By design, consumers often had no idea who the finance company was, and were often led to believe that the dealer financed the contract, like in the older, familiar forms of charge account credit that lacked the opprobrium of installment credit. Apex's pamphlet to dealers explained that "under this plan you never lose your identity with the customer. He does not know that the financing company is financing this paper for you. He deals with you alone, and knows nothing whatever about your financing arrangements." By maintaining the fiction of retailers providing the credit, it was hoped that customers would feel gratitude towards them. At the very least, when paying their bill at the store, customers might buy some additional merchandise.[109] Having the store as the collection agent for the account also provided incentives for the retailer not to lend money on accounts that were uncollectible.

Down payments and retailer collections made sure every party involved had an incentive to insure that the customer paid. For example, if a customer bought an appliance from a dealer using the GE finance company, the money would be exchanged in the following way. If the cash price of the appliance was $100, then the credit price would be set at $110.[110] The customer would give the retailer $10 as down payment and agree to pay the additional $100 over the following 10 months at $10 per month. The finance company would buy the installment contract of $100 for $83. The retailer then had, immediately, $93. The finance company, in turn, had $100 receivable over 10 months for $83. In addition, the finance company would pay the retailer a 10 percent collection fee, so upon the completion of the contract, if all payments were made, the retailer would receive an additional $10. The down payments and collection fees made sure that the retailer had a stake in the actual collection of the total debt. In total, the retailer would make $103 from the installment sale compared to $100 from the cash sale. In ten months, the finance company would earn $7 in total for an investment of $90, which was the equivalent of an annual interest rate of 21.7 percent.[111] For the finance company, profits were made on large numbers of accounts. A finance company with $100,000 worth of such accounts could earn over $20,000 in ten months. With many such accounts, the finance company could turn to the commercial bank and borrow whatever funds were needed. For the retailer, installment collections could, beyond the additional $3 in profit, produce more sales.

For customers, these installment plans, despite their apparently high interest charges, could seem like a good deal. A vacuum cleaner financed by the Republic Finance Company for $52.50 could have an interest rate of 62.4 percent per year.[112] From the customer's perspective, however, the credit charge was only $5.25, payable in five months.[113] Customers saw $5 as a worthwhile expense if they could extend their repayment whatever the interest rates. Multiplied over many borrowers, however, that $5 was an investment that returned 62 percent per year for Republic Finance.

Ironically, the arguments the finance companies made to justify lending them money—that there was little difference between a bank's and a finance company's lending—did convince some banks to enter their business, but in general banks were reluctant to invest in consumer debt during the 1920s. By the late 1920s though, some banks had begun to experiment in new fields. Though many bankers asserted that banks had no interest in consumer financing, there were notable exceptions, like National City Bank, as well as local banks, which had begun to engage in the indirect financing of installment debt. Banks that took on the functions of the newly profitable finance company were usually local banks desperate for investment opportunities.

The original reasoning behind banks not entering the consumer finance business continued to be as pertinent at the end of the decade as at the beginning. The finance business, as one small finance company owner noted, "call[ed] for a specialized credit and collection and sales department, which usually the bank [did] not have."[114] Bankers agreed. One banker reassured finance companies that banks were not in the finance business and he could "see no reason to believe that they [would]."[115] In his view "no bank [could] afford to have more than a certain proportion of its resources tied up in installment finance, and it is simpler, safer, and in the long run, probably as profitable for the banks to carry the lines of finance companies as it would be to do the business direct[ly]."[116] Lending money to finance companies did not require costly institutional adjustments of uncertain profitability. For mainstream banks, the more reliable sources of business investment continued to be primary, at least until the onset of the Great Depression.

By the end of the decade, manufacturers like GE and GM had absorbed retail finance as a key component of their business. Manufacturing profits were far greater than finance profits, but for auto finance profits could still be made. Reflecting this change, in 1929 the corporate account of GM for the first time consolidated the profits of GMAC in its annual income accounting.[117] Auto finance, if not on par with manufacturing, had come a long way from being a convenient way to deal with inventory problems. Independent finance companies, which had been born amidst the lush profits of the growing automobile industry, adapted to the increasing competition and diversified into new fields, spreading the possibility of installment credit throughout the retail world. By the end of the decade, stores and manufacturers no longer had to rely on their own capital to finance their inventories since outside companies could finance their customers. For manufacturers and retailers, the big money was still in making and selling, but finance companies filled a necessary niche in the American manufacturing economy. For consumers, the easier access to capital, through the resale of their debt, meant that they could borrow on an unprecedented scale.

Cut Off from Capital: Installment Credit without Resale

The new financial system provided merchants and borrowers a way out of the structural problems of installment credit. And finance companies offered honest merchants a way to avoid the onerous capital costs of installment selling. Reselling the debt to finance companies allowed durable goods retailers to provide the credit their customers wanted and enabled them to focus on the merchandise at the core of their business. Profits, with resellable debt, could be made just on sales alone.

While financial companies began to take over the credit services of some manufacturers and retailers, there remained significant numbers of urban retailers who did not resell their debt. As in personal loans, where loan sharks preyed on consumers, these retailers were equally exploitative. These retailers continued to finance their own sales, as they had done since before the advent of the finance company. These retailers, most importantly furniture stores, frequently used installment credit to maximize their profits by overlending to customers and then repossessing the goods when the customers could not meet their payments. The differences between retailers who held their customers' debts and those who resold them reveal the deep changes underway in the 1920s. While the finance company existed, older installment patterns continued that remained disconnected from the larger flow of capital.

This form of predatory retail would persist in the face of many other changes in retail over the century, to become the bane of poor, urban consumers everywhere. For those without alternatives, these installment sellers offered credit, but with greater risk. In the 1920s, such sellers preyed on the urban working class composed of European immigrants and African Americans. The advertising pages of African American newspapers like the Chicago *Defender* and the New York *Amsterdam News* beckoned readers with promises of the "easiest credit terms" on attractive bedroom and dining room sets.[118] Internally financed, such stores often charged more for their credit than other stores that resold their debt. For many urban customers these stores were the only option, and they ended up paying more for less on the installment system.

The laws that protected borrowers from loan sharks did not apply to predatory installment lenders. Usury laws, of course, had been weakened only recently by the small loan laws and, in many states the restrictive usury laws were still on the books. Excessive rates, usually above 3 percent, were still illegal everywhere. How then could installment contracts that typically cost several times that number be legal? In numerous state-level court cases like *GMAC v. Weinrich*, judges held that the usury laws restricting interest rates on lending were intended to protect working-class people against loan sharks, and not the perceived affluent against discretionary purchases. Unlike the numerous court cases that ruled against loan sharks, installment borrowers found no protection in the courts from high-cost installment sellers. Judge P. J. Trimble noted that the installment "purchaser is not like the needy borrower, a victim of a rapacious lender, since he can refrain from the purchase if he does not choose to pay the price asked by the seller."[119] If goods were bought on time, they were beyond the budget of the buyer, and therefore, it was thought, could not be seen as necessary. Such luxury goods could not be protected by usury laws. Seen as unnecessary, consumers who used the courts found themselves unprotected, in many ways, by usury laws. While beds and tables, particular those sold on easy credit by predatory retailers, are hard to see as luxury goods, legally they were deemed so, and as such, were outside the purview of usury laws.

The furniture industry highlights the possibilities and dangers of the installment credit system. Furniture was much more expensive in relative terms than it is today. In 1920, a four-piece bedroom suite of just middling quality cost $235, or $2,540 in 2009 dollars.[120] Furniture's expense and resale value, after all, made possible its use as collateral for small loans. For families with little savings, installment credit made such an outlay easier.

At the same time, the legal structure of installment credit created tremendous incentives for retailer duplicity. Furniture dealers selling on the installment plan retained title to the furniture until the very last payment. If the borrower defaulted, the retailer could repossess the furniture and keep all the previous payments. Unscrupulous lenders took advantage of this possibility, and tried to make that "equity" theirs. Since repossessed furniture was easy to resell, merchants could profit by their customers' defaults. Buying new inventory was a furniture retailer's greatest expense; repossession allowed retailers to sell the same merchandise twice or even more. Furniture repeatedly resold by a retailer made more money than selling new furniture. For every dollar spent by a consumer at a furniture store, about half went to the manufacturer and half to the retailer.[121] If retailers repossessed the furniture and resold it, then they would claim the whole dollar. The very structure of the installment sales contract enabled that retailer fantasy to occur in real life.

The ploy of shady furniture dealers was simple and all too common. In New York, for instance, lawyers with the Legal Aid Society, a nonprofit organization that helped the urban poor navigate the complicated legal system, spent a great deal of their time in the 1920s wrestling with the installment lending for working-class and poor borrowers. According to a Legal Aid Society report, when a young couple, "improvident persons . . . in a moment of optimism," came into the furniture store, they would be shown a new "parlor suite."[122] The salesman would showcase furniture more expensive than the couple had planned to buy, but the installment plan would bring the monthly payment to an amount the couple believed they could afford.[123] The salesman verbally reassured the couple that if there were any problems meeting the payments, the report continued, "leniency" would be shown, and the couple then would sign the contract unread.[124]

If the couple could pay off the furniture, the retailer would make money, but more profit actually would be had if they made a few payments and then defaulted. Getting a few payments out of the buyers for "a hundred or two hundred dollars" and then reselling the goods would yield a tremendous profit for the furniture houses.[125] Borrowers rarely found the leniency promised at the moment of sale when a payment was late, since such compassion was never in the contract. According to the Legal Aid Society, furniture retailers would show new furniture in the store and then deliver used furniture that had been repossessed, but "polished up to look like new."[126] The furniture the young couple had bought for "new" was probably already used. Furniture retailers who sold heavily on the installment plan had the highest profitability and the lowest inventory costs of all furniture stores. Unscrupulous furniture merchants, pushing the customers to the limits of their ability to pay, increased the likelihood that the furniture store would to be able to repossess the goods.[127] These installment sellers constituted the bulk of all furniture sales, accounting for slightly over two-thirds.[128]

Ruthless furniture sellers went to great lengths to reap the extra profit made possible by the installment credit contract. Referred to as "typical of the class of cases" involving the "unfair advantage taken of ignorant people by scheming and really dishonest firms," the Legal Aid Society annual report recounted the true story of a working-class man named "Mr. Z" (whose name was changed to protect his identity) that illustrated the lengths furniture retailers went in trying to repossess goods.[129] A middle-aged building mechanic, with "little money saved, but being assured of steady work for a considerable period of time," married and "establish[ed] a home."[130] He "furnished the girl," as the common, unfunny joke of the time put it, and the retailer furnished the furniture. Having a steady job, Mr. Z made all his weekly payments. After a period of time, he completed the full payments and went to the furniture store with his wife to finish up the paperwork and "obtain a free bill of sale."[131] While there, his wife "pressed upon him to purchase" another $350 worth of furniture.[132] The store, instead of creating a new contract, "entered up the new goods on his old account book," making both sets of purchases liable for any failure to pay.[133]

While Mr. Z worked, everything was fine, but the debt made him much more vulnerable to changing circumstances. A few months went by before tragedy struck. Mr. Z was "severely injured by being run over by a taxi" and he could no longer work.[134] Mr. Z believed the store could only repossess the last few articles he bought, but "imagine his consternation when . . . two wagons backed to his door and a City Marshal presented an order, directing that all of Mr. Z's goods be turned over."[135] Rather than an isolated incident, a 1923 Federal Trade Commission report on the furniture industry remarked that in the "several instances where inquiry was made" it found that "unless the entire account is paid the old balance is never regarded as having been paid in full."[136] Such schemes were common.

For buyers duped by such schemes, the situation could become a nightmare. Legal recourse was meaningless for buyers because the contract signed away all their rights, despite their "misfortune."[137] Buyers lost all the equity they had paid into the furniture. As a Legal Aid Society report pointed out, though such repossession was legal, the effects on the family were insidious. It led to family strife with "domestic recriminations." The money lost, also, was not insignificant. The loss of "$100 or $200 is one from which the man of small means [did] not soon recover."[138]

Overlending, of course, only made sense if the furniture dealer held title to the furniture. With the advent of the finance company, retailers found they could sell their customers' contracts. If the retailer resold the installment contracts to a finance company, as became more common over the course of the 1920s, then there was no longer an incentive to overlend. The finance company held the title to the goods and wanted its money—not some used furniture. Finance companies would not do business with retailers whose customers always defaulted, and retailers received their final payment from the finance company—which made the deal profitable for the retailer—only when their customers paid off the debt. The relationship between retailer and finance company gave retailers a strong incentive only to lend to customers who could actually pay their bills. In this way, reselling debt curbed overlending. Though reselling the debt meant retailers could no longer profit from repossession, they could lower their prices and sell a higher volume of goods. Finance companies would even give them a cut of the interest. For consumers, such retailers could offer $10 of interest on a $100 of sales, compared to the $16 of interest on $100 of sales charged by retailers who did not resell debt.[139] Retailers who sold on this system had the same profit rate and a higher volume, which meant more money. Reselling debt, then, shaped the lending and selling practices of retailers. Stores that resold debt could sell more honestly and cheaply, on average, than those that did not.[140] Only retailers who sold to the poorest customers—those actually unable to make the steady repayments—could not resell their customers' debts.

Even in the absence of overlending, job loss or illness could lead to catastrophe if borrowers were unable to meet their payments. The installment credit system created a tremendous amount of risk for the borrower. With the help of nonprofit organizations like the Legal Aid Society, dishonesty and deceit could be dealt with legally. But it was less clear how to deal with the problems of equity that grew directly out of the structure—and not the abuse—of the installment credit system. For consumers, the legalization of personal loan lending, which occurred at the same time as the expansion of installment credit, allowed borrowers an unexpected way out of the problem of equity loss. The risk of installment buying could be mitigated by consolidation loans through the newly legal small loan companies. While borrowers would rarely take out a personal loan to buy merchandise, despite the encouragement of lenders, they would use personal loans to consolidate existing debts.[141] Though the borrowers would have to confront the inspection of their finances, borrowing money from a small loan lender to repay their installment contracts rid them of the risk of losing their possessions, even if in the process they paid higher rates of interest. Though not the reason that small loan laws were passed, borrowers could use the new licensed lenders to their advantage and, in doing so, confirmed all the hesitations legislators had in passing these laws. By the late 1920s, one economist estimated the percentage of loans used to consolidate other loans, mostly installment loans, at between 50 and 75 percent.[142] Rather than just mitigating the risk of working-class life or enabling the transition to small business ownership, as the reformers had intended, by the end of the decade small loans were used to eliminate the riskiness of borrowing for the good life. While legally and institutionally separate, finance companies and small loan companies reinforced installment lending, aiding in the expansion of American indebtedness.

At the same time, separating the function of retail and finance, as many durable goods sellers could do by the end of the 1920s, reduced the incentive for fraud and deception. Reselling debt invariably reduced the cost of borrowing for consumers. For consumers who had access to these larger flows of capital and credit, installment credit offered opportunities for better living. For the urban poor whose lives were too tumultuous for their debts to be resold, borrowing remained expensive and risky, the process full of fraud and deception. For everyone else, however, the resale of installment debt brought lower prices and reputable goods, improving consumers' lives.

Installment Credit and Class Identity

Archie Chadbourne, a truck driver in Colorado, required some "luxuries." Life, for him, did "not mean merely to draw breath" but to enjoy existence. Installment credit made luxury possible for working-class consumers like Chadbourne. These borrowed-for luxuries, decried by the wealthy moralists who could easily afford them, led Chadbourne to "owe something like $681.39," which he believed he had of "as much chance to pay [off] as John D. Rockefeller [had] of dying poor," but still he did not regret his purchases.[143] He bought a car, which he justified because it would have cost the same as using the streetcar. A second-hand phonograph bought on "payments" allowed the daughters to fox-trot.[144] Enjoying life and being debt-free, a prerequisite for middle-class respectability and self-worth, was not possible for many working-class people. With installment credit, the material differences between those who did and those who did not have money lessened. Middle-class and working-class consumption converged more than every before, even if workers' incomes remained precarious. While work remained different for those employed in the factories or in offices, everyone fox-trotted and drove autos. Through installments, proponents extolled, "the laboring man with his small car can ride over the same boulevards . . . as the millionaire in his Rolls-Royce." What was class difference if everyone's consumption looked the same?

If workers had less power on the factory shop floor as union membership withered through the 1920s, they could at least have more power in the retail shop floor. Despite stagnating incomes for most Americans, credit enabled per capita consumption to rise over the 1920s.[145] Installment credit, progressive for some and dangerous for others, blurred class distinctions in the consumption arena. Did critics of debt and luxury really mean living beyond one's station when they criticized "living beyond one's means"? If, by 1925, 9 percent of American's annual retail spending was on installment goods, for both debt critics and defenders this number meant vastly different things.[146] Nine percent could be a growing threat to civilization itself, or a reasonable way for people to enjoy industrial prosperity. For working-class consumers like Chadbourne, installment credit could very well be seen as the flowering of industrial democracy, giving him the same access to consumption as wealthier citizens. Radio broadcasts sounded the same on cheap sets as on expensive sets. Similarly, "with his radio receiving set the workman can now listen to grand opera singers whose voices formerly were heard only by the socially elect." This leveling of difference in consumption even led, some argued, to "discouraging socialistic tendencies."[147] Some proponents saw the installment plan as a mark of confidence that Americans had for their future, while critics saw it as the beginning of the end of that same America.[148] Erasing class differences threatened America, but installment credit disturbed other kinds of relationships as well, most importantly gender and family.

Love, marriage and gender relations, as much as class, framed how people understood and used credit. Borrowing affected not just individuals but households, and it was through the ordering of the household, primarily through gender, that credit relationships were commonly understood. Young couples borrowed when they had little money and later, as their earnings increased, they paid off their debts. In trying to understand how credit worked, later economists of the 1950s, labeled this experience the "permanent life cycle hypothesis." Credit was not a moral failure, in this view, but a rational allocation from the future to the present, maximizing the total pleasure of a lifetime. Interest was simply the cost of this allocation. In the 1920s, as young couples found greater access to debt, installment credit allowed the life cycle hypothesis to become reality for the first time. While many young couples took advantage of the borrowing enthusiastically, the costs were frequently greater than merely the interest paid, and the choices were just as frequently made by credit managers, spouses, and bosses as by individual consumers.

Even before the ring went on the finger, the etiological narratives of debt and gender began. Single women, because of their gender's perceived intrinsic penchant for luxury, were frequently described by the media as unable to control their shopping or their credit use.[149] Women writing about credit themselves pointed to the difficulties women had in resisting buying new dresses or other "frills of life," which "women, from their earliest beginnings, have . . . found so very necessary to successful living."[150] "No young woman," one former female office worker wrote, could "be blamed for wanting to look well." The "well-dressed working girl [paid] through the nose" for clothes from "installment houses" to "compete with the wife or daughter of the richest man in town." Buying a "fur coat with a mortgage" was accompanied by "chiffon blouses, silk dresses and flimsy underwear" bought with a "dollar down the promise of a dollar a week would secure."[151] Borrowing to the limits, a woman who became "sick" or had another kind of "emergency" would miss a payment and then the collector would descend. In one writer's work experience, "not a week passed without some concern attempting to attach the salary of one or more of the girls with whom [she] was employed."[152] Siding with the "delinquent" rather than the collector, the writer believed her "moral sense . . . [had] atrophied." Yet if the moral sense atrophied, it was only from the economic reality of being a working girl. Dressing well, argued female debtors writing about their lives, enabled them to catch a better-paid man. In the quest to be attractive and worth marrying, which would end the need to *be* a working girl, these women, it was commonly thought, overextended themselves, endangering both their finances and their morality, but such choices reflected not moral improvidence but strategic choices made given the inequality of income between men and women.[153]

Anecdotes about young office girls buying too many clothes were common in anti-credit narratives of the 1920s, yet the lessons learned by such narratives were not limited to prescriptive gender roles but, more subtly, offered instruction in the tacit trust between borrower and lender. Though sellers had incentives to push unnecessary purchases on the buyers, rarely did the popular press blame retailers for the rise in installment credit. More frequently, the media encouraged buyers to trust the guidance of store credit managers. The common intuition was that no "credit man" would ever encourage the excessive use of credit because then they would not get paid. Such reasoning demanded that persistent indebtedness was caused by something or someone other than credit managers.

A story presented in *American Mercury*, the prominent literary magazine edited by H. L. Mencken, was typical of narratives surrounding female customers and credit managers. Recounted by a Cleveland credit manager, it was one of many stories involving female debtors who didn't pay. A "young woman" approaches the retail credit manager of a department store. She works in the office of a "large manufacturing concern" and her credit had been "shut off." The benevolently rational credit manager explains to her that her "trouble . . . was that she had never taken the trouble to face the facts." The woman "admitted that she knew she was in debt, but did not know exactly how much." After a long talk, with the woman "finally admit[ing] that [he] was right," she forswore the "new dress" and acknowledged that her present dress was "practically new," and then "agreed to pay her bills." The woman "stuck to it until she had paid every cent and had fully restored her credit." Her income was, naturally, sufficient to repay all of her debts but just had to be correctly budgeted.[154]

Note the assumptions in this *American Mercury* story: that debt is only for luxury; that creditors benevolently watch over the budgets of debtors; and that rational budgeting can tame even the most oversized debt. Though young office women were certainly under pressure to dress well for reasons both economic and personal, the purpose of the story goes beyond a woman's fondness for clothes or even simple assumptions about gender stereotypes. The cause of excessive indebtedness is the desire for "new things" when "old clothes" would still do. Desire is at the root of debt. As important is the role of the credit manager. He "shuts off" the woman's credit when she is too far in debt and chastises her behavior. Though initially resistant, she acknowledges the rational truth of his argument. This reasoned accounting was the only way to contain desire, and the credit manager helps the customer exert control. The credit manager would never extend credit that the borrower could not repay. For the credit manager, the answer to the question, "What should a man do to keep his credit good when he simply hasn't got the money or has had sickness or bad luck?" went unanswered. This event, as the credit manager tells it, is not the norm. Merchants and creditors would understand. He advises the sick or unemployed debtor to "tell the truth," since "honesty of purpose will carry you through and over the troublesome places."[155] These assumptions about the creditor/debtor relationship were both contested by debtors and challenged by the changing purposes and institutions of debt.

Blaming women for borrowing money did not end once the single girl got married. Installment credit enabled young consumers to meet their material expectations for luxury and love, but with serious consequences if payments were missed. The common slogan, "You Furnish The Girl," used in sales promotions to young men looking to marry, expressed all the logic of this system. The young man provides the woman and retailers provide the goods that are, in this formulation, equally necessary for a happy marriage. Happiness could be had at once, but at a price.

In a 1926 *Collier's* article entitled *You Furnish the Girl*, a prospective fiancée was ring shopping in a "sleek, smart jewelry shop just off Fifth Avenue." The young man, with only $400 to spend, inquires about a "frost of platinum set with a square ice of diamond," which turns out to be five times as expensive—$2,000. The salesman, "with no change of expression," informs him that he can use the $400 as down payment and pay the balance over eighteen months at $90 a month, or $1,620 in total. The interest of $20 for $2,000 over 18 months was not discussed in the article, but the young man's reaction was when he exclaimed, "but I could not do that *here*, could I? That's the installment plan." The salesman informed him that it was called the "deferred payment" plan and they "do it as an accommodation when people do not wish to tie up so much money at once."[156] The point of the story was to show how the installment plan, while maintaining its working-class stigma, had in practice if not name penetrated all strata of society, even Fifth Avenue jewelry stores.

Marriage and settling down into middle-class life was seen as requiring a certain set of possessions to go along with it. Many writers on debt seemed to agree with one married woman, pseudonymously calling herself "Alice," who wrote "the vicious chain of being in debt . . . was forged when I married and set up a home."[157] The "bridal outfit" had been charged, the husband had spent "several hundred dollars" on his cutaway and "a few weeks later the bills began to come in."[158] She had "naturally" given up her job, and they both resolved "to start [their new life] on a cash basis." Before the advent of installment credit, a respectable husband-to-be was expected to save until he could afford to outfit a home, or the couple lived in penury. Installment credit enabled an entirely new possibility.

The installment plan, then, enabled true romantic love. Marriage ought not have to be delayed merely for lack of savings. Couples could marry and borrow money for the all the furniture, house wares, and other signifying accoutrement of respectable married life, but in most places, unlike the ring shop, the interest would not be 1 percent for eighteen months. Borrowing for furniture by the 1920s was, as one article on marriage and credit put it, "down to a science."[159] As Alice noticed, "in [their] new little home there were constantly things needed, and [their] credit was good in many places." Beyond household goods, there were also the babies, "two of them in fairly quick succession," which created large doctor's bill that took five years to pay off.[160] From buying the ring, to financing the white dress, to paying for baby's crib, the goods of marriage could be had on credit. Yet for married people, installment credit created new sets of problems and opportunities to negotiate, often in ways tied to ideas of gender and self-respect.

Once married, borrowers trusted the credit department not to lend them too much money. The "credit man," who decided how much credit to extend, was conservative and could be expected not to give the borrower more than they could easily repay. Lending was seen not only as an economic relation but a beneficent social relation, from the generous to the grateful. Buyers habituated to charge accounts, where the seller had to be coaxed into giving more credit. They saw credit as something carefully rationed by stores—reluctantly given and never in excess. Retailers played up this image. The president of the department store Lord & Taylor, for example, affirmed this guardian image of the credit manager of a store as someone who "watches the purchase accounts of charge customers and promptly discourages their buying beyond the danger point."[161] The overextended lender would quickly fail, it was thought, and default endangered both the firm and the borrower.

Excessive debt, as credit managers explained, was the fault of weak husbands, not retailers who overlent; irresponsible husbands refused to control their wives, displacing the burden of control to retailers. Prudent husbands, credit managers insisted, would manage their wives, who, due to the weakness of their sex, could not be blamed for their natural excesses. A credit man explained that "many men give their wives free rein in buying on credit . . . but do not permit the women to handle the money directly."[162] These husbands pay the bills as they come due, but the credit man suggested that it would be better to "put their wives on a regular allowance, and let them manage their own finances."[163] The president of the Chicago Association of Credit Men, John McConnell, claimed to know "of instances in which men [had] intentionally permitted their wives' accounts to lapse into delinquency in order that the stores would refuse further credit."[164] Though letting the accounts go "injures seriously the credit of both the wife and the husband," the implicit truth was that it would be the only way that the weak husband could control his wife's spending, and that the wife would, on her own, never do so. The answers on how to deal with temptations and limitations of installment credit were often cast in terms of proper household management, which usually meant gender relations between husbands and wives, and trusting stores' credit managers, which usually meant class deference. In all these narratives of consumption, strong men with middle-class values, whether credit managers or husbands, were seen as necessary to control women's spending.

The use of credit, however, was thought to sap that male strength. While credit could allow the purchase of goods that signified respectable marriage, it also threatened the very foundations of that middle-class life. For men, indebtedness could shake the moral foundations of success, turning, as one autobiographical account of debt in the *Saturday Evening Post* warned, a successful man into a "coward." Debt transformed a healthy, thirty-two year old man of "success" into a "deadbeat" with "gray hairs and lines in [his] face from worry." Not only his body changed but his demeanor. He "los[t] a fairly decent disposition and [became] nervous, irritable, and disagreeable."[165] Once in debt, the moral erosion it caused from his feelings of being a "failure and a cheat," made him unable to conduct his business. He lost his "nerve and his wit."[166]

The debt that tortured this anonymous debtor accreted gradually. Though he earned "four to six thousand dollars a year," he and his family managed to spend more than that, adding only "six or seven hundred dollars" each year.[167] He cited doctor's bills as the principal source of debt. His first baby "swelled the total in red" and subsequent "exorbitant" bills only added to that.[168] He felt the worst about these bills since he considered the doctor his "personal friend," yet he was still unable to pay. Aside from the doctor bills, the greatest danger to his budget was the consumer credit, "which sets a trap for many ambitious and hopeful young people when it offers to make marrying . . . easy and simple by pay-by-the-month system."

Young couples, the autobiographical debtor opined, should go without rather than go into debt. The eager "young man who needs a dress suit to be married in would be far better off staying unmarried than to start into life with a monthly payment," the debtor felt.[169] Typically, he felt, "young people saddle themselves with more than they can carry, fall behind in payments, get entangled, lose heart and the goods thus contracted for, and eventually become victims of debtor cowardice."[170] Without charge accounts and installment credit, buyers would spend their money at "cash stores" and "find satisfactory substitutes much cheaper" and without the danger of "contracting debtor's cowardice." The easy satisfaction of desires made possible by the charge account, which in the writer's case included an odd fondness for leather-bound board games, preyed upon a weakness of character that debt only exacerbated.[171]

For those who could control their desires and keep their jobs, the installment system allowed American consumers to lead a better life, but for those who relied on the discipline of the lender or the good luck of the labor market, the loose supply of credit could be calamitous. Gender and class expectations guided this control—both for borrowers and lenders—reinforcing expectations and structuring the consequences of borrowing in this new credit-abundant world.

At the End of the New Era

Despite its newfound ubiquity, the future of installment credit seemed uncertain at the end of the 1920s. Was it to be the salvation of American industry or the source of its economic and moral ruin? To most people, installment credit was simply a way to buy a car and some furniture.

Those who helped create it, however, like John Raskob of GMAC, believed that "this form of banking . . . will one day grow to gigantic proportions[,] selling durable goods to deserving people on proper terms."[172] Raskob even imagined consumer credit as an alternative to socialism, since credit might make possible "the dream haven of plenty for everybody and fair shake for all, which the socialists have pointed out to mankind. But our route will be by the capitalist road of upbuilding rather than by the socialistic road of tearing down."[173]

Consumer use, retailer sales, and financier profits—rather than eschatological or utopian theories—won the debates on installment credit in the middle of the decade. Businesses prospered using it. Consumers had more of the modern goods that defined the good life. Anxious inquiries from frenzied and fearful businessmen during 1924 and 1925 to the U.S. Chamber of Commerce, disappeared suddenly in 1926. A representative there remarked "that all that worry and puzzlement seems to have dropped off" as installment credit became a common part of American life.[174] The editorial page of *Collier's* opined that "the installment business, now a five-billion-dollar affair, [made] for prosperity so long as installment buyers [kept] their head."[175] Keeping one's head meant obeying a budget for the "required payments" with "regular income," buying only high quality goods at a reasonable (regardless of installments) price, and buying only necessary goods.[176] Though all these tests seemed objective, what was "necessary," "affordable," and "reasonably priced" was highly uncertain.

The consequences of not keeping one's head, however, were not. Ill-considered use of credit was, as an author in *Collier's* admonished, "bad for you and bad for the country."[177] As good as judicious use of credit was for the country, its misuse could be equally as bad. America's downfall fueled the fears of installment critics. Even to GM, the arrival of a depression borne of profligate credit would seem to be a justified "day of reckoning."[178] The seeming profits of consumer finance drove much of the criticism. Vocal debt critic Senator James Couzens attacked the way in which finance pulled profits out of communities. Every dollar spent on installments was, Couzens believed, a "dollar sent . . . to some finance corporation lessen[ing] the purchasing power of that community." Finance companies in his view were distant parasites drawing money out of small-town America. An avid admirer of Henry Ford, the well-known manufacturer and critic of finance companies, Couzens quoted Ford at length: "when financiers flourish on credit, you may depend on it that plenty of other people are withering."[179] Large finance companies, Couzens warned, made "substantial profits" from installment buyers. If installment plans enabled consumers to take part in the pleasures of industry, it was just another way in which the worker was separated from his hard-earned dollar. Rather than connecting consumers with capital, consumer credit, in this view, disconnected Americans from their communities.

As industrial lenders and finance companies proliferated and profited, they grew fearful of commercial bankers interfering with their business. Commercial bankers, outside of a few experimental personal loan departments, however, wanted nothing to do with either one. Small loan lending was too different and too risky. Installment credit undermined the values of thrift and production that banks promoted. Most importantly, profits from business investments and margin loans on stocks were too profitable and these new types of finance too different. By the end of the 1920s, consumer credit had taken radically new forms and meanings. Even as it had grown out of that society's very demands and possibilities, debt extended into all strata of industrial, urban society—presenting a personal face but backed by increasingly powerful, increasingly impersonal institutions.

The new supply of credit offered better lives for wage-earning and salaried Americans. In the 1920s, black and white, native and immigrant, the working-class world of urban credit was the same. That similarity was soon to end as lines of race would definitively cross lines of class. For white Americans, a more stable world of growth would soon be founded amidst the recovery from the economic collapse of the Great Depression. A new credit system fostered by the federal government, drawing on and extending the developments of the 1920s, would provide white Americans new opportunities to finance abundant postwar lives.[180] While white Americans of all classes would enjoy a new credit system to provide a better life that was sustained by the flow of capital, urban black Americans would find themselves shut out. The urban retail economy would remain predatory and stagnant, as this new credit system developed in the suburbs In the next chapter, we will see how federal mortgage policies, intentionally and unintentionally, brought these changes to the center of American debt practices, extending the nascent installment system in vertiginous new directions.

Chapter Two

Debt and Recovery

NEW DEAL HOUSING POLICY AND THE MAKING OF NATIONAL MORTGAGE MARKETS

In Franklin Roosevelt's 1933 inaugural address, he told Americans that the economic crisis they faced was both unprecedented and, at the same time, within the government's ability to remedy. The problems besieging the economy were no "plague of locusts" sent by an angry god, but instead the result of the "stubbornness" and "incompetence" of the "rulers of the exchange of mankind's goods." Faith in bankers and business was slim. It was in this moment of doubt about the future of capitalism—borne of the frenzied speculation of the late 1920s and the subsequent Great Depression—that even greater government intervention experiments in the economy could be proffered. As Roosevelt said later, America was "faced by a condition and not a theory."[1] Theories of capitalism were abandoned for possible solutions. The "grim" reality demanded confrontation and not talk. Radical changes in all areas of the economy were proposed and tried, but always, as Roosevelt said, "the primary task [was] to put people [back] to work" and restore faith in the stability of the economy.[2]

The different New Deal programs embodied competing visions between the relationship of the state and the market in American capitalism. Some within the administration saw this as an opportunity to sidestep the constraints of the market economy while others saw it as a chance to create new directions for private investment. The Depression was, as economist and consumer credit activist Leon Henderson wrote, "a testing block for financial and management policies, for operating theories, [and] for enabling legislation."[3] The seeming failure of business created a protean opportunity for new directions, to which the president was open. Roosevelt wanted America, above all else, to overcome the "conditions which came very close to destroying what we call modern civilization."[4] The reduction in unemployment and rejuvenation of economic growth contained the metrics by which Roosevelt determined which policies to encourage and which to dismiss.[5] Practical solutions in a time of desperation, more than ideology, guided his policies. Those who formulated and carried out those policies, however, did not find it so easy to shed their assumptions about the economy and the state. Indeed, the competition of economic ideologies marked the early years of the New Deal.

Housing, one of the largest industries in the American economy, proved to be one of the most controversial sites of policy experimentation, as well as one of the most enduring. The first forays of the Roosevelt administration into housing policy supplanted private industry as either the builder or the lender. The Public Works Administration (PWA), among its other projects, sought to build affordable housing for low-income Americans, creating both houses and jobs for workers. The Home Owners Loan Corporation (HOLC) lent government funds through banks as a source for mortgages. However, as the limits of government lending were realized, alternative programs that more closely involved private sector funds and institutions pushed aside the PWA and HOLC. Though Roosevelt was sympathetic to housing the poor, his policies aimed, primarily, to grow the economy and reduce unemployment.[6] If this could be accomplished through housing the poor, all the better, but that was a secondary goal to restoring economic growth. Unlike the other housing programs of the New Deal, the Federal Housing Administration (FHA) promised and achieved this growth. By 1939, thanks in great part to the FHA, investment in residential housing was nearly back to its 1929 levels.[7] Channeling private capital for the public good proved to be the most effective way to achieve policy goals. The flood of funds, guaranteed profits, and standardized policies initiated through the FHA changed the way banks operated forever, turning mortgages into nationally traded commodities—and in the process changing the way Americans related to banks and debt.

The issues at stake in New Deal housing policy went beyond housing to the core relationships between markets, the state, and the modern economy. The HOLC stopped mortgage markets from collapsing in the face of mounting foreclosures, but did not have the mandate or capital to put them on a sounder footing. The PWA nobly created, and underfunded, work relief programs through its housing projects, attracting criticism from both the left and the right for doing either too little or too much. Most importantly, the PWA, by opting to plan and fund its operations directly, limited the extent of its operations through a lack of capital and by inciting the ire of the business community. Only the FHA charted a course in concert with capital, thus taking advantage of tremendous productive abilities, but in doing so limited the scope of its programs to what business believed was important. The failure of the PWA and other directly funded government agencies established a limit for direct federal intervention in housing construction. Most importantly, in the course of enacting these programs, particularly the FHA, the federal state remade not only the institutional structure of urban housing mortgages, but also other, less obvious fields of consumer finance, directly connecting, for the first time, home mortgages and anonymous institutional investors.

The real innovation of New Deal policy was neither direct state investment nor planning—as the left has celebrated and the right has denounced—but more the practical harnessing of private capital for social ends. Using markets to provide housing and stimulate the economy, and not government spending, was a controversial policy decision. People and ideas clashed within the Roosevelt administration, resulting from vastly different interpretations of how capitalism operated.[8] While some of the agencies discussed have been widely written about by historians, the controversial role played by private capital has been generally overlooked or under-examined. Harnessing private capital enabled more intercession than direct federal spending, but the range of possible interventions in the economy was circumscribed by the compliance of the business community. The different assumptions about the economy built into those programs, as well, simultaneously enabled and constrained the effectiveness of these policies. Attempting to solve the crisis of the Great Depression, federal policymakers effectively made new markets through which home mortgages could be bought and sold, enabling an unprecedented level of home ownership, and indebtedness, in the United States.

Mortgage and Crisis

During the freewheeling years of the 1920s, capital may have seemed to flow too freely, but the easy credit was not limited to consumer goods. During this period, mutual savings banks and building and loan societies lent huge sums to the growing urban population as well. But these home mortgages were not what we today consider traditional mortgages. Balloon mortgages dominated urban lending. In these "balloon notes," the principal was paid back in whole or in part at the end of the loan term and whatever difference remained had to be refinanced.[9] The average length of a mortgage was three to five years, and was not amortized.[10] Amortized loans—that is, loans where the borrower pays down both the principal of the loan as well as the interest on the loan every month so that the payments are roughly equal—existed, but during the boom years, interest-only loans meant home buyers could borrow more money. Borrowers hoped to pay it off quickly, or to sell and reap a profit. Most borrowers, however, rolled over the mortgage every few years.[11] The bank, if it chose to, could renew the mortgage and keep the borrower in a state of what the later chairman of the Federal Home Loan Bank Board, John Fahey, called "more or less permanent indebtedness."[12]

Before the late 1920s, mortgages were seen as just a short-term debt with a certain claim on property, like any other form of consumer lending. Home mortgages, without their later ethical auras, were seen as short-term debts, not long-term investments.[13] Later postwar economists agreed with housing economist Leo Grebler's assessment that "the reluctance of home owners to incur mortgage debt, a characteristic of earlier decades [than the 1950s], was undoubtedly reduced in keeping with the change in general attitudes toward all forms of consumer debt."[14] And like other forms of peripheral lending, like personal loans and installment credit, the big commercial banks were not involved. In 1924, the McFadden Act allowed commercial banks to write mortgages for only five years—up from one year in 1916.[15] State banks had only 16 percent of their assets in mortgages and this accounted for 95 percent of all commercial bank ownership of mortgage loans.[16] Home mortgages were dominated by small lending institutions.

When the short-term mortgages came due after the stock market crash, investors, recognizing an increasing risk, refused to renew borrowers' loans. Nervous investors and prudent banks everywhere increasingly withdrew their capital from the mortgage market, making it more expensive and difficult for borrowers to renew their mortgages. Many smaller banks funded their mortgages by issuing bonds, called participation certificates, to local investors. As investors refused to reinvest in these bonds, banks had no choice but to refuse to refinance balloon mortgage holders. Available mortgage funds dropped precipitously in 1929.[17] For borrowers, when a single lender chooses not want to renew, it is inconvenient; when all lenders choose not to renew for structural reasons, it is a calamity. Borrowers unable to pay off the principal on their balloon mortgages faced foreclosures. Foreclosures during the Depression resulted as much from the drop in home owner's income as from the withdrawal of short-term mortgage funds from the market, making refinance impossible. By 1933 the mortgage market was effectively dead, and with it the housing industry.

Without mortgages, the housing industry collapsed. Housing investment fell from $68 billion in 1929 to $17.6 billion in 1932. By 1934, the construction industry, as a whole, was one-tenth the size it had been in the late 1920s.[18] Wage earners from a third of the families on relief were employed in construction.[19] Indirectly, the collapse of the housing industry hit other sectors of the economy as well. Construction also had tremendous linkages to other sectors of the economy to a much greater extent than most industries. Ten percent of American factories manufactured building materials for construction.[20] Twenty percent of freight cars carried those materials across the country.[21] Unskilled labor carried material. Skilled labor put it together. Metal and wood of all shapes and types were needed for almost any project. Muscle and machine were needed alike. Clearly, restoring the economy turned on restoring the construction industry. What was less certain was how to bring about new construction. New Deal policymakers focused on the housing industry in their efforts to restart the economy because it had fallen so hard and so fast.

Stopping the Collapse: The Home Owner's Loan Corporation (HOLC)

The creation of the HOLC was not intended to expand the housing market, but to arrest its free fall. In 1932 and 1933, lenders foreclosed over a half million urban homes.[22] By the middle of 1933, the foreclosure rate hit over a thousand mortgages a day.[23] Beginning with the crash in 1929, mortgages had been increasingly difficult to refinance as anxious investors withdrew their money from participation certificates. The tremendous flood of foreclosed properties onto the market threatened to erase the value not only of the foreclosed houses, but all the others as well. The instability of the market demanded action. The HOLC stepped in to put an end to what amounted to a major crisis for the U.S. housing market.

The HOLC resurrected the American mortgage markets by providing much needed liquidity. Begun in the summer of 1933, the HOLC created ways for both creditors and debtors to maintain the value of their investment, despite the feeble demand for such properties. So many properties being sold on the market at one time was rapidly eroding the value of the nation's housing stock. Selling foreclosed property often brought much less money than the creditor wanted or would have received even a few years earlier. The HOLC intervened, allowing creditors to opt for long-term bonds in exchange for mortgages in danger of foreclosure. Then the HOLC refinanced the mortgages on longer terms, up to fifteen years.[24] The hope was that by lowering the monthly payments owners could meet their obligations.

The HOLC worked. Distressed home owners quickly filed more than 400,000 applications by September and they continued strongly through the next spring.[25] On average, they asked for $3,272, but amounts varied widely by state. In New York, the average was $5,129, while in Texas it was only $2,313.[26] In total, 54 percent of applications were approved for $3.1 billion in loans.[27] Almost 10 percent of all homes in America were mortgaged to the HOLC.[28]

Never seen as a long-term program, the HOLC shut down the bulk of its operations within the year. By November of 1934, 92.5 percent of the agency's total applications had been received.[29] In total, about 1.9 million home owners applied for $6.2 billion in refinancing, of which half was approved. The HOLC refinanced about 40 percent of all qualifying property and about one-fifth of the total U.S. owner-occupied, non-farm homes.[30] In taking over these mortgages, the HOLC also took over lenders' unsound loan choices. Nearly 20 percent of HOLC loans ended in foreclosure, leaving the agency with properties that weren't completely liquidated until after WWII.[31] But its primary aim of restoring liquidity to markets was successful.

The HOLC's policies, with a 20 percent foreclosure rate, were not sustainable, and its reach was necessarily limited by a lack of funds. The HOLC rejected half of the applicants in distress, like the fictional Mr. Hoe. HOLC administrators did the best they could do with their limited resources. Without a self-sustaining stream of income, the HOLC's proponents repeatedly returned to Congress, hat in hand, asking for more money. Every time its needs exceeded its expectations it had to return to Congress to ask for more money. By 1934, the publicity made the HOLC seem like a government-run money pit.

Despite its popularity among distressed home owners, the HOLC garnered its share of criticism from business. As a business, the HOLC could never work. By 1934, 30 percent of borrowers were late with their payments; 12 percent were more than sixty days overdue.[32] Many business leaders were suspicious of the HOLC's methods, believing the government was incapable of identifying a good credit risk, only confirming that the business of government was not in lending. Though the immediate crisis was averted, business was incredulous of the HOLC's methods.

Restricted to refinancing mortgages in default, the HOLC was successful in stopping the hemorrhaging of the value of housing stock, but had no mechanism to revive new construction. Despite calming the markets for the moment, the larger structural problem of private investors withdrawing their funds from the market continued. Without a way to mobilize those funds, the markets would again grind to a halt. The temporary stabilization of the market, however, allowed other New Deal policies to step in to get construction started again.

Building for the Poor: The Public Works Administration (PWA)

The PWA was founded in 1933 as Title II of the National Industrial Recovery Act. Initially allotted $3,300,000,000, the PWA faced the staggering challenge of properly allocating those funds. Overseen by Secretary of the Interior Harold Ickes, one of Roosevelt's most trust advisors, PWA projects ran the gamut from playgrounds to bridges. Yet it was the PWA's housing division—which sought to rehabilitate the urban slums—that inspired the most debate among its supporters and critics.

At the heart of this debate was the question of whether the nation's economic and social problems could be better addressed by public programs or private enterprise. For Harold Ickes, the origins of the depression were clear: "We have left it so far to private enterprise, and the conditions we have are the result." PWA policymakers and, most importantly Ickes himself, believed that the public could "not depend upon private enterprise or limited dividend corporations to initiate comprehensive low-cost housing and slum clearance projects."[33] Ickes had lost faith in the private sector's ability to restart the economy, much less to rebuild urban slums. According to the PWA bulletin, "the answer was simple and inevitable."[34]

For Ickes, resolving the slum problem was necessary for the larger project of renewing the economy, which he believed depended, in turn, on a revival of the cities. In his words: "the future financial stability of many of our urban centers depends upon the prompt reclamation of their slum areas."[35] In Ickes's view, slums were a sort of cancer. Without checking their growth, slums and blight would spread into the industrial and commercial areas, choking off any possibility of economic recovery. Moreover, slums consumed more taxes every year than they paid, inhibiting other uses of local tax dollars.[36] In the absence of private profit motive, Ickes believed the federal government had a need and a right to intercede in the housing sector. By November of 1933, 14.7 percent, or $485,100,000 of the total PWA project budget had been designated for "low-cost housing and slum clearance."[37] Creating a subsidiary, "Public Works Emergency Housing Corporation," Ickes planned "to build low-cost apartment houses as slum clearance projects throughout the country."[38]

PWA's creators viewed the housing division as a way to solve both the problem of slums and the larger economic problem at the same time. Substandard housing threatened the economic integrity of the cities and the moral integrity of the citizenry. In their view, which clearly favored government intervention, "blighted areas [would] continue to spread in extent and grow progressively worse" without drastic action. Critics of such government involvement were quick to blast PWA's housing division because it so forcefully charged the federal government with the task of improving the urban poor's "bad housing conditions and bad health, delinquency, and lower standards of family life." PWA housing programs seemed to represent the fulfillment of the government's potential to provide solutions to social problems, providing large-scale, affordable housing to the poor.[39] It employed the unemployed and it included more racially progressive policies than most other New Deal programs.

Whether or not the PWA was radical, it certainly seemed that way to many members of the business community at the time. The clamor against directly funded federal housing began almost at once. The private sector's animosity was a combination of a perceived threat to private enterprise and what they saw as a profligate waste of public funds. Ickes's critics saw little to commend the PWA housing projects, and they considered Ickes himself to be demagogic at worst and ineffective at best. When the press splashed "Ickes Urges Billions For Larger PWA Plan" across the headlines, criticism whipped to a new peak.[40]

The business community's hostility did not reflect a desire to undertake the types of projects sponsored by the PWA. Private firms had little incentive to invest in so-called slum clearance. Even if the PWA had had such lofty (and politically suicidal) aspirations, it didn't have the capital to compete with the private sector. The PWA $400 million dollar budget paled before the vast monies that changed hands in private mortgage markets.

While irritating the Right, PWA also irked those on the Left. The PWA housing projects never fulfilled the ambitions of the social reformers and went too far for those who opposed its actions on principle.[41] Most projects originally planned by the PWA never occurred. Criticism of PWA housing programs, for instance, even came from local government officials, for whom the federal government had provided either too little or too much. New York Tenement House Commissioner Langdon Post attacked the PWA programs because, he believed, the grants and loans actually provided very little money to the city for carrying out the housing programs. He estimated that after the state of New York had paid interest on the federal loans (which were 4 percent annually) the federal government ended up only contributing between 15 to 22 percent of the costs of the projects.[42] The PWA decided what to do and how to do it, but passed most of the cost to the local government. Many projects never came to fruition because local authorities couldn't find the supplementary funds.[43] Though the projects were ambitious, the funds were insufficient.

By the next summer of 1934, only $171,801,000 was designated for housing, about one-third of the original estimates for housing expenditures.[44] Ickes complained "that most of the projects that came before [the PWA] were conceived more for the speculative benefit of their promoters than for the advantage of the people who need modern housing at a low price."[45] Construction businesses contracted to build these projects never responded in the altruistic fashion Ickes had hoped for and, despite the national crisis, continued to search for more profit. Lacking funding, Ickes's vision for restoring the economy by restoring the cities came to little.

The PWA and HOLC programs, though well-meaning, operated under the assumption that capitalism had largely failed and could not recover. Alternatives to the market, in this view, had to be found in state-run projects. Reacting to the criticism from business, and the financial limitations of a government building program, other New Deal policymakers conceived of a new direction that took advantage of what capitalism was good at—making money—and creatively induced business toward new housing initiatives to restart the economy. It was this program, the Federal Housing Administration (FHA), that ultimately reshaped the way in which Americans borrowed mortgage funds and in the process remade where and how people lived, and how a new American economy was ultimately financed.

Rethinking Assumptions: The Federal Housing Administration

The innovative solution to the crisis of housing finance came unexpectedly from a veteran Federal Reserve economist named Winfield Riefler.[46] The best way to get the economy moving again, in Riefler's view, was to focus on the construction industry.[47] Unlike the housing boom of the 1920s, which was financed with balloon mortgages and speculative building, Riefler imagined a new kind of "mortgage instrument which will be the soundest thing in the market, the most approved standards, which will be amortizing and paying off."[48] Borrowers would not renew, but would pay off the loan slowly with a long-term, amortized mortgage. Homes would be owner-occupied and not speculative instruments. This new kind of mortgage would be primarily for "model homes" and "not distress instruments," to resolve the bad choices of the New Era home buyer. The time for the stopgap measures of the HOLC was over. It was time to rebuild on a more stable footing. He envisioned a new kind of mortgage through which the power of private financing, guided through federal policy, would expand home ownership in America and restart the economy. The FHA that resulted from Riefler's unusual economic theory took the country in a very different direction than that of the PWA. Unlike the HOLC or PWA, this new plan relied on private planning, private funds, and private incentives to carry out federal policy.

As the future commissioner of the FHA, Julian Zimmerman, wrote in the 1950s, "twenty-five years later, the basic scheme seems simple and logical. At the time it was proposed, it was such an innovation that many people considered it radical and unworkable."[49] But to Zimmerman twenty-five years later, and some of the New Dealers at the time, "it was the last hope of private enterprise. The alternative was socialization of the housing industry."[50]

The National Housing Act was passed on June 27, 1934, implementing Riefler's policy to create the FHA. Financing the pent-up demand for housing to create jobs, the goal of the act was to free the "'key log' in the credit jam which [had] been holding back the building industry."[51] The National Housing Act created two loan programs and one new organization to buy and sell those loans: Title I home improvement loans, Title II home mortgage loans, and the Federal National Mortgage Association (FNMA). Title I loans were for modernization. Home owners could borrow money to repair roofs, install electricity, or buy non-movable durables, like oil burners or air-conditioning systems. These loans were expected to be relatively small—only a few hundred dollars. Without a down payment, hard-pressed home owners could more easily borrow, and pay the loan back on an amortized schedule. Title II home mortgages were similarly amortized and low-interest, but for an entire house and for at least ten years—much longer than the short balloon mortgages of the 1920s. Prospective buyers, who still existed even during the Depression, could buy well-made houses at reasonable prices. FHA guidelines would deem what kinds of properties a loan could be procured for—to avoid the shoddy, speculative construction that had been the norm in the 1920s. Every mortgage would be amortized and every buyer would be able to pay back what he borrowed. Since the quality of these homes was assured by FHA inspectors and the mortgages standardized, investors from all over the country would know exactly what a particular mortgage was worth. A standardized mortgage could be resold like a commodity, which made possible the third provision of the National Housing Act. National Mortgage Associations, authorized as the third component of the National Housing Act, were intended to trade these mortgages from around the country, creating a secondary market for home mortgages.[52] Like any other standardized commodity, mortgages then could be resold nationally, which would enable the money of the capital-rich east to flow south and west. Between these three programs, the financial infrastructure of America was remade, sometimes in unexpected ways.

The plan was simple, if novel. The government would lend no money. Instead the government would create an insurance program for lenders so that they could safely loan funds. If borrowers defaulted, the insurance program would repay the principal to the lenders.[53] The FHA mandated interest rates would be low—below 5 percent—but the profits would be guaranteed by the insurance and the risk would be nonexistent.[54] The insurance program would be paid for by a small half-percent slice of the interest from every FHA loan, and if there were no defaults the lenders even got all their insurance payments back.[55] Borrowers could go to any lender subject to government inspection—which encompassed a variety of financial institutions from specialized mortgage companies to general-purpose commercial banks—and get the mortgages that they wanted. The federal government organized the FHA, but private capital paid for it and profited from it.

Unlike other New Deal programs, the FHA was not aimed at those hit hardest by the Depression. It did not provide food relief like the Federal Emergency Relief Administration (FERA). It did not directly provide jobs like the PWA. FHA policies helped those who were getting by and doing fine—home owners or those wanted to be home owners—with stable incomes. By focusing on those who were already doing well, the FHA drew fire from critics who believed the government should be helping the millions out of work and struggling, not burdening the solvent with more debts. Did the New Dealers want to bring down the stable portion of society still left? To a country that had recently elected Roosevelt on a platform of balanced budgets that they believed would right the economy, the idea of expanding American debt, even if privately lent, seemed suspect at best. If senators questioned Riefler's plan for adding "another billion and a half to the debts of the Nation," Riefler's response echoed the new economic thinking of the day: Any measure that increased employment, would add wealth and thereby repay that debt.[56]

The conventional justification for government intrusion, framed as large-scale charity, was completely reversed for the National Housing Act programs. The PWA elevated charity to a new level, which opened itself to the criticism that it was nothing but a "rent dole" instead of a wage dole, diverting taxes to pay for the "chiselers" who lacked the character to support themselves.[57] While the PWA was justified by doing work that the private sector could not or would not do—a conventional argument for government action—the FHA created the opportunity for the private sector to act. The FHA's purpose was confusing. As the program's proponents took pains to explain, this money was not "emergency, distress, or relief money."[58] It was not dole. It was not taxpayer money. The government was "simply attempting to induce lending," not to lend money itself.[59] Why did it need to exist if business lent its own money?

Risk, Regulation, Insurance

The senators who presided over the passage of the National Housing Act questioned why the government needed to intervene if the banks were doing it all themselves. If this money surplus was available, "why don't they [banks] supply this need?"[60] Why did the government need to intervene if the government was not providing any money? The answer was that commercial banks, who had most of the country's capital, did not think of mortgages or any form of consumer lending as a good opportunity for profit. Banks did not extend the money themselves for the same reason that several Congressmen questioned the soundness of putting money into housing. While the opportunity for profit existed, government intervention was necessary to reduce the risk of investment.

The big housing lesson of those years was the danger of foreclosure. Housing was too risky to lend money on. Riefler's ingenuity was in combating exactly that problem of expected risk. The insurance program got rid of the risk entirely. The only way to unleash private capital in a manner that would significantly reduce unemployment was to reduce that risk. Future Fed chairman, then under-secretary of the treasury, Marriner Eccles, explained that "without this insurance program" bank's potential mortgage funds would not be lent.[61] In other words, FHA proponents believed the opportunity for profit existed, but institutional assumptions about risk prevented that profit from being realized.

The insurance program gave lenders broad assurance that they could not lose money as long as they lent prudently. The FHA offered to insure, on complying loans, up to 20 percent of total losses.[62] As a *New York Times* article noted at the time, the insurance "furnish[ed] a margin of security more important in its psychological effect on investors than the government's actual financial commitment."[63] Since bankers still remained liable for 80 percent of the loans, FHA supporters had little fear of overextension of mortgage credit. Bankers still did not want to lose their money. There were limits on the amount of insurance, but barring outrageously unsound lending, those limits could never—and in practice were never—reached. If the mortgage foreclosed, lenders would get their money back from the insurance program, but not in a particularly liquid form, so as to create a disincentive for unsound lending. The insurance payments would be bonds for the cost of the mortgage payable in three years. For three years the bank's capital would be tied up in a bond earning no interest.[64] Bad investments would not be disastrous but there would still be a cost for reckless lending. Though it emboldened bankers psychologically, it could not make them impetuous.[65]

The insurance was not only a way to bring back private funds to the market, it was also a means to structurally reduce the risk to home buyers of overborrowing. Compliance with FHA guidelines was mandatory for the insurance. If the loan did not conform to the rules, in either the kind of property it was used to buy or in the way in which the loan was extended, then the insurance was void. Banks did not have the option of amortized or unamortized loans. Loans could not be interest-only and then become amortized. The financial chicanery of the 1920s was at an end. Title II regulations were clear: "the mortgage must contain complete amortization provisions . . . [such] that the total principal and interest payments in each month shall be substantially equal." The loans not only had to amortize the interest, but real estate taxes, special assessments, and fire insurance.[66] FHA punctiliousness gave the banks a tremendous incentive to follow the letter of the law.

Home buyers could also borrow more under the FHA loan program. Compared to the loans of the 1920s, FHA loans were generous. Though they were restricted to new homes, they could be up to 80 percent of the home's worth and up to $16,000.[67] This fraction of the purchase price was unprecedented. Only through the FHA insurance plan could bankers be persuaded this was a good—or even halfway sane—proposition. Before the FHA program, lenders were loathe to cover more than half of a home's cost in a mortgage, so potential borrowers often needed a second, more expensive mortgage, with up to a 20 percent interest rate, to make up the difference.[68] Few first mortgages covered more than 50 percent of the cost. These second mortgages charged higher rates, both because they were being lent to people who, by definition, had fewer resources and because the second mortgage had a subordinated claim to the real estate.[69] For those who had mortgages in the 1920s, these junior mortgages were commonplace, but under the FHA program they were forbidden.[70] FHA loans covered a much greater fraction of the home's cost, so such second mortgages were deemed unnecessary.[71] Their high costs would have defeated the entire point of lending money cheaply to the buyer. Mortgage lenders, meanwhile, financed these larger loans because their risk would be substantially reduced with the FHA insurance and guidelines.

Through the lever of insurance, the FHA loans changed the way that periodic recessions interacted with mortgage renewal. As discussed earlier, most mortgages before the FHA loans were short-term (three to five year) loans on which the borrowers paid only interest until the end of the term, when either the loan was renewed or the principal paid back.[72] The FHA financing plan, with its twenty-year mortgages, offered escape from this pernicious cycle. Extending the mortgage over many business cycles would stabilize the supply of mortgage money. Investors, already committed to the lengthy terms, could no longer be scared away from investing. By amortizing payments, the massive need to refinance the principal at the end of twenty years would be gone. Borrowers would be capable of meeting their monthly obligations without the fear that when the mortgage came due, they would lose their house if they were unable to find additional financing. The loan would have the means of its repayment built into it.

Aside from protecting against another mortgage crisis, amortization provided another effect that was more important in the long run: it greatly increased the number of Americans who could afford to buy homes. Extending terms allowed aspiring home owners—particularly middle-class families—to borrow much more per month. Most borrowers, the FHA believed, did not care about the sum of the principal and the interest, just the monthly payment.[73] What mattered was that amortization and longer terms reduced monthly payments. At certain times, federal programs allowed borrowers to mortgage up to 100 percent of the cost of the house. Consumers eagerly took on such loans, despite the long repayment period and vast amount of interest that it involved. Though this created more interest and lengthy repayment, it was eagerly used because of the desire to own a home.[74] Most potential home owners looked only at the monthly payment, so these mortgages really expanded those who were able to borrow money.[75]

This new insight, that amortized payment plans were far more predictable and less risky, proved the installment credit in the 1920s to be a successful lesson. FHA administrator James Moffett hoped this new system would substantially diminish "the residential building booms and consequent collapses of past experience."[76] The goal, he announced, was nothing less than "to give our home financing system a thorough overhauling, with the long-term amortized mortgage at a low interest to become the standard practice."[77] For the FHA to succeed, banks and business would have to follow its regulations, and they did. With such large penalties for non-compliance and such large incentives for compliance, the stick and carrot of the FHA remade American mortgage lending.

For President Roosevelt, the FHA mandated low interest rates to counter "exorbitant and usurious rates charged in many cities," which justified the whole program.[78] He considered 8 or 12 percent rates far too high. Both to encourage borrowing and because the loans were less risky, the government mandated a relatively low interest rate. Banks were to charge borrowers 5 percent interest per year. Four percent of that interest would go to the bank, or the investors who later bought the mortgage, and 1 percent would go to a special insurance fund.[79] Mortgages would be classed according to risk and maturity date. For each class of mortgage there would be a separate fund.[80] This insurance fund would cover the losses on loans that did default and whose owners would need compensation. Despite the moniker, "federally insured," the government did not insure the loans, but merely set up a system that would function by itself and at the same time provide low-cost loans to consumers. Government regulations enabled private capital to realize its maximum profits.

Appealing to Business: The Title I Modernization Loan Program

Unlike the HOLC or PWA programs, business enthusiastically endorsed the FHA. Since the banks lent the money, bankers had no fear of being "crowded out" by the FHA, as they might have been by a direct government lending program. Operating through banks, the government retained bankers' support and accomplished its policy goals.[81] The head of the FHA, James Moffett, attempted to differentiate its activities from "just another government campaign." By working through private channels, the FHA did not seem like another one of Roosevelt's unnecessary, possibly socialist, or fascist, boondoggles, but a valid capitalist enterprise.

In promoting the FHA, Moffett was working against a great tide of resentment against the recent programs coming out of Washington. Roosevelt hoped that appointing an administrator with strong business credentials would help stave off criticism. Moffett was not only the former director of Standard Oil of New Jersey, but his father had been as well. To Harold Ickes's disgust, Moffett "[was] against a [government-funded] housing program of any sort. He [did] not want to interfere with private capital." To Ickes's consternation, "He belong[ed] to the capitalist class."[82] Progressives like Ickes resented Moffett's wealth but Roosevelt appreciated that his social status and class outlook would help legitimate the FHA program. Moffett employed exactly the people who could not fit in at Ickes's PWA, often hiring the very people he had fired. In appointing Moffett, Roosevelt sought to shore up the capitalist credentials of the FHA and, by extension, the entire New Deal agenda.

Moffett drew on experienced businessmen to organize the FHA, which preempted antigovernment critiques of the new program. Upon receiving a housing contract returned from a Midwestern banker, who declared it "badly drawn up—'just like everything else that comes out of Washington these days,'" Moffett replied that it had been "drawn up by a former vice president of the National City Bank who has been doing such jobs all his life."[83] Employing businessmen, and not New Deal eggheads, Moffett could fend off the criticism that had brought down the National Recovery Administration (NRA) and other New Deal programs. Drawing on those experienced in business, rather than social planners or visionaries, Moffett implemented Riefler's innovative banking ideas that would become the backbone of the new housing finance system.

The first part of the National Housing Act to be implemented was the Title I loan program, which enabled home owners to borrow for home improvement. For home owners in need of repair and modernization, these loans presented an affordable way to improve home owner's standards of living. The intended users of Title I loans were not new buyers, but those who already owned.[84] For those who did own their own home, Title I loans were a doorway to the modern era, enabling electrification as well as the products that used electricity. Many homes, as late as 1934, lacked electricity, much less oil burners or new plumbing. Without electricity, home owners could not purchase the new appliances like radios and refrigerators, the demand for which would stimulate the economy and create jobs. While Title I could not directly finance the purchase of a radio, it could finance the electrification necessary for the radio's operation. Through a Title I loan, many modern household improvements like oil burners, air-conditioning, electric ranges, and automatic garage door openers could be easily financed. [85]

The FHA set Title I loans, like their Title II counterparts, as affordable as possible to stimulate the most demand. Unlike home mortgages insured through the FHA, modernization loans required no down payment but, like the home mortgages, were amortized. Repayment plans were flexible, from one month to five years.[86] Compared with business loans, the interest on Title I loans was expensive, but compared to installment contracts for consumer durables they were a downright bargain.[87]

The Title I program was enacted briskly. By mid-August 1934, initial rules and regulations for the modernization loans were mailed to 15,000 institutions.[88] By October, 8,000 banks had joined the program. In just a few months, banks loaned a total of $4,600,000 among 10,480 borrowers. The loans averaged $443 with a maturity of 26 months. Administrator Moffett claimed there had been a 40 percent rise every week since the program began, "equal[ing] our most optimistic expectations."[89] Such fast growth was made possible not only by the policies of federal officials, but by the hard work of local business leaders.

Cultivating the consent of business was the foundation of the FHA's successful operation. The FHA promoted its Title I loans for home modernization under the Better Housing Program, which through local volunteers committees and business associations enabled housing improvements. Business, both in finance and the building industry, lauded the plan, praising the government for "oil[ing] the credit machinery." A *Wall Street Journal* editorial observed that, "one New Deal project stands out in bold contrast with the common nature of many others. It may not be so widely understood as it should be that the National Housing Act . . . appropriates no federal funds to be distributed as gifts."[90] Businesses were being helped, possibly guided, but the entire process was voluntary.[91] Even conservative bankers could not disagree with the logic. Rudolph Hecht, president of the American Bankers Association, believed the FHA programs were "deserving of hearty support."[92] In an effort to help their members take advantage of the plan, the American Bankers Association appointed an educational liaison officer in every state to explain to uninformed lenders how the program worked. Such education was necessary because, as Moffett explained, "banks, generally, are unfamiliar with the personal credit installment payment plain." But bankers provided with the potential for profit learn quickly.

By the end of 1934, there were nearly 4,000 local Better Housing Program committees promoting Title I loans across America.[93] Relying on local volunteers and business elites, the Better Housing campaign turned a top-down Washington policy into a bottom-up local project. With the Better Housing campaign, the FHA united a national program and town pride.[94] In the "Modernize Morristown" campaign, for instance, the New Jersey town used billboards to extol owners to "repair and improve your property now" to "put Morristown to work!"[95] That Stewart F. Seibold, owner of Morristown Lumber & Supply Co., was the committee chairman (as he was in surrounding Morris Plains and Morris Township) struck no one as unethical.[96] Local business leaders were intended to lead the drive to home improvement. Patriotism and profit went hand-in-hand. Volunteers canvassed house-to-house urging home owners to modernize, and provided the names of local banks that could make that happen. Many cities and towns made the Title I improvements tax-exempt in the belief that the programs would "supply work for thousands now on relief rolls and being supported by the community." By November, 2,606 cities and towns had modernization campaigns underway like those in Morristown.[97]

At the same time, the FHA took pains to explain how "the Better Housing Program, sponsored by the Federal Housing Administration, should mean profits for you, regardless of the type of goods or services you have to sell."[98] But the important point was that the profits, first made by the "architect, supply dealer, contractor, realtor, painter, plumber, [and] electrician" would then be "felt immediately through the entire community." The "new money in circulation" would lead to "reemployment and a pick-up in business generally." The Better Housing Program's profits would not be just for builders but for everyone.[99] The promotional literature emphasized the good wages that skilled workers earned—and spent. The FHA told businessmen that of every building dollar spent, 75 cents went to labor directly or indirectly associated with the building project.[100]

Mass media got behind the program. National radio chains donated time to promoting FHA programs. On CBS a listener could hear "Your Home and Mine" on Wednesday nights, and "Master Builder" on Saturdays on ABC and NBC. Over a thousand daily newspapers, 55 percent of all dailies, had a special "better housing" section to promote the loans. Movie theaters showed "pictures and slides" to patrons and then gave out materials on where to secure those loans.[101]

In an indirect rejoinder to its pro-urban critics, the FHA newsletter of the "Better Housing" campaign even pointed to indications that some poor areas were recovering because of the modernization loans. The director of the Maryland campaign reported that the "exodus from the old section of the city" had been stopped by Title I modernization loans. Motion-picture theater owners in Baltimore, who also owned the surrounding dwellings, claimed that following the modernization of their properties they found tenants willing to pay $20 a month. The movie house business had also picked up, presumably from the money circulating again in the community.[102] Reports like this were reprinted from all over the country, from Long Beach, California where building permits had increased six-fold since June, to Fort Worth, Texas where formerly idle workers were "now seen hurrying to and from their work," to Buffalo, New York where there was a "40 to 1" ratio of modernization to business loans. Through modernization loans and the anticipation of the Title II guidelines, construction companies were hiring again. Men were working again.[103]

The FHA success put the PWA in an uncertain position. In late November 1934, Ickes proposed an even larger $2 billion low-cost housing program. The announcement reignited controversy. The president of the National Retail Lumber Dealers Association, Spencer Baldwin, speaking on behalf of the coalition of bankers, laborers, and manufacturers that supported the National Housing Act, telegrammed Moffett to declare that Ickes's "program . . . will destroy all the good work you have done, and private capital will become indisposed to come forward and uncertainty and demoralization will result."[104] Baldwin believed that "the National Housing Act has afforded us a sound policy to work on and this should be followed through in a sane and orderly way." Though Baldwin claimed, "private industry cannot compete with the government," in reality it was the government that could not compete with the resources of private capital. By the end of the first year, almost a half billion dollars of Title I improvements had been pledged for 1935 by private industry, nearly three times the expenditures for PWA for the next few years.[105]

By December, the FHA reported the results its nascent policies, which already had taken some effect. By the end of the year, 72,658 modernization loans had been insured for a little over $30 million. In the northern states, building permits continued to grow despite the onset of winter.[106] Correspondingly, large manufacturers of household building material reported substantial gains over the previous year sales. Radiators, for instance, were up 500 percent over the previous year. Plumbing supplies were up 175 percent.[107] The largest shipment of roofing supplies—ever—arrived on the West Coast in Los Angeles.[108] The construction business began to recover. The FHA annual report estimated that its programs put 750,000 men back to work in only the few months of its operation.[109] Roosevelt wrote to Moffett in March of 1935 to congratulate him on the success of the program—which was declared unconstitutional shortly before the NRA—enjoyed the support of thousands of communities, hundreds of thousands of "civic-minded" volunteers, and most crucially the continued support of business.[110]

Title II Mortgages and Suburbanization

The purpose of the FHA was to create demand for building materials and for labor. To get money moving again in the economy, the FHA guidelines helped buyers and lenders alike differentiate between a good house and a bad house. Too many home buyers had been burned by shoddy construction in the 1920s. Enacting national standards allowed investors to loan money at a distance, and allowed mortgages to be resold. Housing quality was the foundation upon which the entire FHA system resided.

In determining "good" housing, however, FHA guidelines went well beyond the proper ratio of nails to wood in addressing what had long been contentious politically and racially. The risk ratings in the primary FHA guidebook, the *Underwriting Manual*, reflected the bureaucrats who wrote them. These guidelines had implicit and explicit hierarchies of what home buyer's *ought* to want. The casual racism, antiurbanism, and pro-development assumptions of the bureaucrats drove the planning of the manual, and when developers adhered to it, as they had to if the mortgages on the homes were to be eligible for FHA insurance, the newly constructed world reflected this vision.

The FHA *Underwriting Manual* instructed lenders on which properties could be insured.[111] Through a rating scheme measuring the construction quality of the house, its layout, its neighborhood, and its access to amenities, FHA underwriters could determine whether a house was a good investment—to avoid the speculative overvaluing of houses that occurred in the 1920s and maintain the equity of both buyer and lender. Through its many pages of charts, tables, and descriptions, the manual instructed banks on where to lend and on whom to lend money to. While the manual promised objectivity, the social assumptions of the FHA planners shaped the planning criteria as much as macroeconomic considerations.

These new homes had to meet standards for construction. FHA officials feared "jerry-building," which had run rampant in the housing upswing of the 1920s.[112] Inspected regularly by FHA architects and appraisers, builders of homes that did not meet the FHA standards would lose their eligibility for FHA insurance.[113] Competition from other builders, whose buyers could get FHA loans, would ensure that the builder conformed to the building codes. Construction standards not only constituted an abstract notion of quality, but also ensured that rapid depreciation did not erode the home's value—for either the bank or the home owner.[114] Like installment contracts for furniture and other repossessable goods, the lender, or in this case the insurer of the lender, wanted to make sure that the property being lent upon would continue to have value for the duration of the loan.[115] New homes, it was believed, would last longer than previously existing ones.

The *Manual* preferred new homes both because they fit the economic purpose of the program as well as being perceived as healthier. FHA loans for existing homes were possible, but the existing homes had to meet FHA standards.[116] These standards were not only for how they were physically constructed, but also where they were located, which few extant homes could meet. Helping Americans buy older homes created no demand for either labor or materials. FHA guidelines, therefore, tended to steer potential home buyers away from existing homes toward new ones.[117] New homes created new jobs. Older homes, particularly in cities, with their cramped spaces and aging interiors, could not meet these conditions.

Following the same impulses as Ickes's PWA, FHA planners imagined the ideal home as the opposite of the crowded tenements of the urban slums. Modern space, above all else, determined the quality of the house. Layouts had to be "economical, practical, and efficient." This meant the maximum "usable floor area," as well as space for privacy, well-lit rooms, and modern bathrooms.[118] Long hallways and steep staircases, which prevented the easy moving of furniture, lowered the value, as did "broken or short wall areas [which did] not permit flexibility in furniture arrangement."[119] Space for ample and replaceable furniture was important, since allowed for greater consumption.

The area surrounding the house mattered as much as the house itself. The ideal house lot possessed "sunshine, ventilation, scenic outlook, privacy, and safety." "Effective landscaping and gardening" also added to its worth. Needless to say, downtown districts, especially in the East, rarely possessed all these qualities and "depart[ure] from the conditions [caused] ratings [to] become progressively lower."[120] Homogeneity of surrounding housing stock—houses that all looked alike—was believed to indicate stable housing prices. To get the maximum score on the mortgage evaluation, the manual mandated that a house be a part of a "sparsely developed new neighborhood . . . completed over the span of a very few years."[121] Without this homogeneity, "an undesirable age mixture of structures will result."[122] Between the types of lots and the need for similar building age, the suburban subdivision easily received a designation as a "better mortgage-lending area."[123] Urban neighborhoods found it nearly impossible to receive such a designation.

Transportation access also played into the valuation of the potential mortgage. For urban properties the FHA planners advocated public transit, as well as for low-income districts. The manual, however, acknowledged the contradiction at the core of its mortgage reasoning: the "areas with the finest transportation facilities are those situated close in to the center of the city [but] these are frequently the most [from the FHA perspective] undesirable areas."[124] For middle-income areas outside the city, automobiles were necessary.[125] Public transit systems would be preferable, especially for "getting their servants to and from their homes," but underwriters were instructed to regard automobile transport as sufficient. The automobile, the manual reminded, had "accelerated the decentralization of the cities," since "inhabitants of all income levels usually desire to live away from the crowded, older sections of the town." While FHA planners were rhetorically ambivalent toward transportation type in their rating scheme, they preferred the kinds of places automobiles could get to. For those who moved to these FHA-insured neighborhoods, purchasing an auto was essential to their transportation needs. In this regard, housing policies created a demand for autos—and automobile financing—as well as for building materials.

Investigating neighborhoods, underwriters were told to seek out the defects that could erode value from the house. Multiuse districts with "commercial, industrial, or manufacturing enterprise," threatened residential value. A declining population threatened a surplus of sales, which would decrease value. Most alarming was the mixture of classes or races in a neighborhood or the potential therefore. The "adverse influences" category of the mortgage application, which was 20 percent of its total rating, was mostly concerned with the danger of class and racial mixing. Ideal neighborhood schools ought not to have "a goodly number of the pupils represent a far lower level of society or an incompatible racial element."[126] A good neighborhood also included "prevention of the infiltration of business and industrial uses, lower-class occupancy, and inharmonious racial groups." Protection took a variety of forms—from the man-made "high-speed traffic artery" to natural "hills and ravines" to the social "college campus." Enforcement of this separation by either "established barriers" or the law was essential to a good mortgage rating. The "lack of appropriate and adequate deed restrictions" to keep out Jews, Asians, and most importantly, African Americans, jeopardized the collateral for the mortgage.[127] The most important point of these racial and class guidelines went unsaid: the potential borrower ought to be white. The sought-after borrowers were those who did not threaten housing values: middle- and upper-class whites.

Considered from the point of view of a mortgage lender, the FHA believed the city was not a good investment, making suburban lending risk-free and thus, urban lending, bad business. Very explicitly, the "central downtown core" was "considered ineligible." Such downtown areas included "business and commercial sections of the cities as well as the slum and blighted areas which almost invariably surround downtown sections of major cities."[128] Outside of the downtown core, the rest of the city was also suspect. The manual told underwriters an "examination of residential areas in any American city reveals that, with practically no exception, such districts decline in desirability with the passage of substantial periods of time."[129] Housing values would "inevitably decline" because "the older district [would remain] desirable . . . only to families whose social status or standards of living are lower."[130] Without insurance for the loans, mortgages were unlikely to flow into these areas. The worst fears of pro-urban housing advocates were realized. With the city such a bad investment, in this view the suburb was not a choice, it was *the* choice.

Suburbs fulfilled the promises of the FHA's policies. FHA technical bulletins, like the widely circulated *Planning Neighborhoods For Small Houses*, explained to potential developers everything from the proper layout of streets to the arrangements of shrubbery.[131] FHA officials believed that planning had, for too long, been the province of "'exclusive' neighborhoods or subdivisions of high priced homes," and they considered suburban planning essential to the success of the new small, but modern, home[132] "Produced devoid of plan," suburbs had seen only modest growth, with the consequence that the investment in such properties "stagnate" and "owners find little or nothing to encourage the maintenance of their properties."[133] The end result of subdivisions where "no effort was made for planning" was the decrease in property values and occupation "by owners or tenants of a markedly lower social and financial class."[134] Without increasing, or at least stable, values, the entire scheme of the long-term mortgage would become untenable. Unsurprisingly, the first Title II loan in the New York area was not in the city, but in the suburbs in Massapequa, Long Island.[135]

That FHA policy privileged new suburban housing over existing urban housing marked a major difference between the FHA and the PWA.[136] PWA policy focused on the rejuvenation of the city, where "bad housing" hindered economic growth and tax revenues. In contrast, the FHA had no special concern for the city.[137] In Roosevelt's view, while improving the city slums was a worthy goal, rejuvenating the economy was the top priority. Harry Hopkins, Roosevelt's brain trust and head of FERA, echoed Roosevelt's concerns: "my own interest in this program . . . is as a recovery measure, and as a measure which gets private funds into the picture."[138] Housing was instrumental to the larger goals. Critics, like Columbia professor Carol Aronovici, who claimed that "there remain[ed] little hope from the New Deal government in the way of low-cost housing construction and slum clearance," missed the point of what Roosevelt was trying to do. Urban or suburban, the house being built was still part of the American economy and the creation of jobs knew no location. The nation's economy, not the nation's cities, mattered most. Despite the outcry from social reformers, who declared the new Roosevelt housing programs were failing to help the very poorest, Roosevelt's programs pushed ahead.[139]

The social reformers, moreover, misunderstood what was possible for Roosevelt to do. PWA had tried to rehabilitate the urban slums—and failed from lack of funds. The FHA did not fix the slums, but it did create, at least for whites, a new place to live. As Bank of America set up its Title II loan program radio advertising for its "Timeplan Home Loans," it consciously sought "not to sell home loans, *but to sell home life.*" Amadeo Giannini, the Bank of America president, claimed that the "broadcasts [were] calculated to appeal to those home lovers whose existence in [urban] rented quarters amount[ed] to a frustration, and there [was] an abundance of them."[140] The point of the FHA program was to escape the cities, not save them. The possibility of divorcing jobs, housing, and investment from a specific location is part of what gave FHA policies their power, but also constrained their ability to redress economic inequality. Indeed, in helping to recover the economy through suburbanization, the FHA re-entrenched wealth inequality along racial lines for several generations.

FNMA: Making a National Mortgage Network

To make federal housing programs self-sustaining, the government needed to lure private capital into housing. Investing in far-away housing was risky because investors could not easily buy and sell from afar, much less be sure about what they were investing in. Making mortgages standardized enough to sell as commodities and then to make them easily tradable would decide whether the FHA mortgage program could work without the continued support of the Reconstruction Finance Corporation, which bought the mortgages in the first few years. What had been a local debt practice could become national only through federal policy. While financial institutions had been willing to lent Title I and II mortgages, ultimately the private sector proved unable to coordinate the resale of these loans. The government had to create the mortgage market.

Prior to the New Deal, mortgages were extremely local. The ability to borrow was determined by the local banker's perception of the borrower as a credit risk. Bankers calculated the risk not from a credit rating but from the personal knowledge of one's "character," which mattered as much as one's assets. Houses, too, varied tremendously across the country, requiring those knowledgeable of local building and real estate practices to determine their value. Because home mortgages were so local, it was difficult for national or out-of-state banks to lend the money from afar. Unable to lend money from a distance, capital could accumulate in slow-growth areas and be scarce in fast-growing areas. Such imbalances created disparities in the mortgage interest rates where the lack of savings made it more expensive to finance housing in regions outside of the northeast.[141] Mortgage capital was limited to the depositors in local savings-and-loans or from local investors who bought bonds issued by commercial banks to fund mortgages. With the passage of the Glass-Steagall Act in 1933, banks could no longer issue these securities, called participation certificates, which further limited the pool of capital for mortgages.[142]

With the FHA, the government's insurance of the loan guaranteed a standard of quality and a known level of risk. As the federal government began to guarantee loans for housing through the FHA and the HOLC, the organizations created a system of standards to evaluate applicants and loans.[143] In new institutions of debt, the government could insure only based on the borrower's personal worth, set down on preprinted forms within categories fully defining a given property's value. Standardization was such a prerequisite to commodity trading that FHA Administrator Moffett believed, "the conditions favorable to a nation-wide mortgage market may be expected to follow automatically from the fact that all insured mortgages will conform to standard specifications."[144] Moffett was correct that standardization was necessary for the creation of a mortgage market, but such a market did not happen automatically.[145]

A market for mortgages had to be created by a middleman, or more accurately a middle-institution, to buy and sell mortgages. Though the National Housing Act of 1934 authorized the creation of national mortgage associations to facilitate such mortgage trading, no private firm applied for a charter to do so. Authorized under Title III of that Act, national mortgage associations were to be directly regulated by the FHA administrator. These associations were able to conduct business anywhere in the country, but their operations were restricted to the purchase and sale of first mortgages.[146] The associations were authorized to borrow money, issues bonds, and acquire capital by the standard means, but their borrowing was subject to the approval of the FHA administrator. Such associations were also forbidden to invest their money in anything other than first mortgages. With so many restrictions, it is not hard to imagine why no entrepreneur applied for a charter.

Without a single company willing to undertake the business, the trade in federally insured mortgages was less liquid than intended, and by extension limited the private investment funds available for the program. The Reconstruction Finance Corporation had, since 1935, been, on a limited basis, buying FHA-insured mortgages to help some building developers, but this crucial link in the mortgage system had to be made permanent.[147] By 1938, Roosevelt was forced to setup a quasi-governmental corporation to fulfill this role, founding the Federal National

Mortgage Association (FNMA). By May 1938, FNMA bought its first federally insured mortgages, fulfilling the intended function of the Federal Housing Act's national mortgage associations. While FNMA was not private, it did enable a national private network for federally insured loans. Local mortgage companies could lend to home owners and then resell—or "assign"—those mortgages to FNMA. Mortgages, now standardized, could be bought and sold by FNMA.[148] Large institutions, such as commercial banks and insurance companies, began to buy and sell mortgages both directly from mortgage companies and through FNMA. Yet this flow of capital was more a network than a true market. Mortgages flowed, generally, unidirectionally from mortgage company to FNMA to investor rather than constantly traded. The FHA knew exactly who owned which mortgage at every moment, or that mortgage was no longer insured. Mortgages were bought and sold through long-established relationships, not the happenstance of market.[149] Still, the network removed the blockages to the national flow of mortgage capital—at least for federally insured loans—which was its purpose.

Without local financial borders to stop capital flow, but with federal impositions of maximum interest rates, mortgage rates converged. The FHA set a maximum limit on the interest rate for mortgages. This rate was set nationally. Where before there had been variation between regions and locales, the FHA committed to a standard rate for the country as a whole. In the days before the Title II guidelines were issued, Administrator Moffett met with Federal Home Loan Bank Board (FHLBB) officials as well as mortgage bankers, who all informed him that to have adequate funds available for investment, the interest rate would have to vary according to local practice. When Moffett suggested this to Roosevelt, the president very quickly made his position clear: "One of the major purposes of the National Housing Act," Roosevelt told him, "was to encourage a greater uniformity in mortgage interest rate[s] through the country and especially to eliminate as far as possible exorbitant and usurious rates charged in many places." FDR's moral notion of appropriate rates superseded established business customs. He trusted that the "excellence and security of this type of investment," fostered by the FHA insurance, would draw investor capital into the mortgage market. He had no qualms about remaking business custom to fit his vision of a moral, and functioning, economic order.[150]

As federally insured mortgages fixed a national interest rate, they also helped end mortgage capital scarcity, especially outside the northeast. If in 1890 regional mortgage rates varied by as much as 3.8 percent, by 1940 the variation was 0.6 percent and by 1950 it was practically zero.[151] Moffett correctly predicted, as he issued the first FHA guidelines, that "an investor in New York City or Chicago will be able to advance money on a home in Texas or California . . . with a sense of security quite as great as would be the case if the property were in the next block. With the Federal National Mortgage Association in operation, prepared to buy insured mortgages for cash at any time, a nation-wide market was created."[152]

Insurance companies, commercial banks, and other large institutions took advantage of national standards to invest in mortgages across the country. FHA and Veteran Administration (VA) loans, though distant, were much safer investments than local conventional mortgages. Amortized, long-term mortgages matched the long-term investment needs of institutional investors. Amortization is only possible if the lender does not need quick repayment of the principal, which is only possible if the lender has large quantities of capital, which such institutional investors did. The FHA not only acknowledged the shift to insurance companies as sources of capital, but actually took pains to emphasize that life insurance companies could be approved mortgage lenders when it issued its first mortgage guidelines in November, 1934.[153] Large institutional ownership of residential mortgage debt rose from 50 percent in 1920 to nearly 80 percent in 1953. According to the FHA, such institutional investors financed "86 per cent of the net increase in the mortgage market from 1939 to 1954."[154] From 1946 to 1948 commercial banks doubled their investment in mortgages, raising their market share to 20 percent.[155] Institutional and commercial banks quickly rose in importance in mortgage lending.

Smaller financial institutions and individual investors lost their share of the mortgage market. Local mutual savings banks fell from 25.9 percent of mortgages in 1912 to 14.2 percent by 1952. This change did not occur because savings banks changed their investment strategies. Savings banks had actually increased their mortgage investments from 31.5 percent of their assets in 1912 to 39.2 percent in 1952.[156] Savings banks simply did not have the capital to compete with the large institutions. Individual investors, almost inconceivable today, went from 60 percent of the mortgage market at the turn of the century to about 10 percent in 1962.[157] Mortgages loaned by individuals continued to exist, but only for those excluded from federally insured loans by the *Underwriters' Manual*, like urban African Americans. Large institutions took advantage of the new market opportunities to dominate the mortgage market. Local and personal mortgages quickly lost ground to national and institutional lenders backed by the federal government. These institutions could supply the massive amounts of capital needed to build the suburbs that the FHA planners dreamt of. By making a national mortgage network, FNMA remade American home ownership.

Conclusion: The Meaning of Mortgages

The FHA continued its programs long after the Great Depression ended, but in the few years following its creation the effect of federally insured lending was considerable. By 1937, the construction industry had recovered and it was easier than ever for most Americans—over half of borrowers earned less than $2,500 a year—to borrow money for a house.[158] Nearly a half billion dollars in mortgage money was lent in 1936 alone under FHA insurance.[159] By 1939, about $4 billion in insured mortgages and home improvement loans were extended, all without the federal government lending a dime.[160] In contrast to the nearly 20 percent foreclosure rate of the HOLC, only 1,200 out of 465,000 insured FHA mortgages borrowers could not meet their mortgage by 1939.[161] In the secondary market, $300 million worth of mortgages changed hands, moving capital from where it was plentiful to where it was scarce.[162]

Although there was talk of conflict between Ickes and Moffett in the press, and indeed there may have been behind the scenes, the differences that mattered were only in the proper way to resuscitate the economy.[163] Ickes believed the government could boost the economy while helping its most disadvantaged, and in the process modernize the city. In contrast, Moffett believed the best way to jumpstart the economy and set it on a sustainable footing was through the "loosening" of private capital. Only those projects that private industry was not willing to undertake should be handled by the PWA, he felt. Since low-cost housing, through the FHA system, was underway, Moffett did not see what role the PWA should have it in. In the press, Ickes and Moffett were repeatedly represented as enemies—Ickes stylized as opposed to private industry and Moffett as a free marketeer bent on the destruction of the PWA.[164] Neither was completely the case. Both undertook their activities in the best way they understood to achieve Roosevelt's goal of a functioning economy. They took pains not to step on each other's toes, despite their differences in outlook. But in the end, only one method had the power—economic and political—to truly remake the economy fundamentally. As Ickes wrote in the *New Republic*, "Social need [was] the justification for [the PWA's] low-cost housing," not economic need. The PWA's housing program in its four years of existence created 25,000 units of housing. In the same time, FHA generated almost ten times as many.[165] Roosevelt and the New Deal staff allied themselves with Moffett's belief: private industry should lead the way in housing and to a way out of the Depression.[166] The PWA's public building program remains today one of the great achievements of the New Deal, but it was the FHA that changed the way the rest of America was built and financed. The slum problem, which Ickes felt was pivotal to restoring the U.S. economy, was not solved. Though many people left the crowded cities through the FHA, others, denied access to federal mortgages, were left behind.

Through the attempts to stabilize a faltering economy, New Deal housing programs radically changed existing consumer and business practices of debt. Borrowers enthusiastically took longer mortgages as large institutional lenders enjoyed insured investments. These radical interventions in mortgage markets fundamentally altered the ways in which Americans borrowed. The short-term loan that was barely tolerated socially became, by government policy, an encouraged long-term debt, partially because the government language reframed mortgages not as a heavy debt, but as responsible long-term investments for the borrower. Americans were encouraged to become comfortable with long-term debt in a way they never had before. Between 1935 and 1951, 45 percent of mortgage funds for new construction were federally insured.[167] The ratio of residential to nonresidential mortgages rose from 14.8 percent in 1916 to 45.5 percent by 1952.[168] Only when houses began to be seen primarily as investments, and not debts, could they acquire long-term financing. After the war, ever more of residential finance filtered from distant investors through federally made markets.[169] Moreover, this debt was not of the personal kind to which they had been accustomed, but to large, impersonal corporations. Debtors gradually became accustomed to owing money in large amounts to someone they had never met.[170]

The FHA program enabled home ownership for millions of Americans, yet this home "ownership" took the form of a long-term debt. The real owners were the banks and insurance companies, who found a safe source of income in the midst of the Depression. This technicality was not enough to overcome the appeal of "owning" one's own house. Legitimated by government promotions, the stigma of mortgage indebtedness receded over the course of the 1930s. What had been a marker of financial uncertainty became a marker of financial responsibility.

Long-term FHA loans fundamentally altered the way in which Americans borrowed mortgage money. Even non-FHA mortgage loans, so-called conventional loans, began to follow the manual's lending guidelines, despite not being eligible for insurance through the FHA or for resale through FNMA. The FHA had remade what was considered a sound, and more importantly, a *normal* mortgage. Mortgages lenders generally followed the FHA guidelines even for conventional mortgages, except, of course, lenders could charge higher interest rates. The FHA had redefined what middle-class, predominately white Americans believed was possible for owning their own home—and this "ownership" was predicated on twenty years of indebtedness. Government policy had created mortgage markets and in doing so remade the American mortgage.

Chapter Three

How Commercial Bankers Discovered Consumer Credit

THE FEDERAL HOUSING ADMINISTRATION AND PERSONAL LOAN DEPARTMENTS, 1934–1938

ON FRIDAY, MAY 4TH, 1928, on New York's East 42nd Street, in a little basement room containing only three desks, four employees, a dozen chairs, and a teller's counter, National City Bank opened the nation's first personal loan department.[1] Announced to the public with only one line in a newspaper, hundreds of applicants nonetheless overwhelmed the bank on its very first day.[2] The next day, in a vain attempt to contain the crowds, "shock troops from around the bank" along with a dozen desks, according to one bank employee, were moved into adjacent corridors.[3] Carpenters and painters worked through the night to convert an adjacent second story into more office space for what would become an incredibly popular department of the bank. In its first year alone, the personal loan department extended $8 million over 28,000 loans.[4] The *Herald Tribune* remarked that as New York had been so successful in its campaign against "unscrupulous loan sharks . . . there has been developing a dearth of borrowing facilities for small-salaried individuals and 'the National City Bank [had] step[ped] into the breach.'"[5] *Newark News*, *Evening World*, *New York Times*, *Herald Tribune*, and other New York-area newspapers all praised the new personal loan department of National City Bank.[6]

Curiously, despite the popularity of the department and despite the prominence of National City Bank, one of the country's largest commercial banks, few other banks opened their own personal loan departments in the late 1920s. Nonetheless, by the end of the 1930s personal loans were a standard part of commercial banks' offerings. Why would banks begin to loan to consumers in the middle of the 1930s when jobs were so precarious, rather than in the 1920s when prosperity reigned? In answering this question, we can better understand how small loan lending to consumers became essential to the viability of the core financial institution in American capitalism—the commercial bank. At the same time, we will also see how powerful federal policy can be in transforming the most basic practices of capitalism, since it was through a previously overlooked federal program—the FHA's Title I loan program—that bankers learned consumer lending could be a good idea.

To Think Like a Banker

Though National City Bank publicly claimed profitability and that its borrowers repaid their debts, in the midst of the prosperous 1920s other commercial bankers remained doubtful about the viability of lending to consumers. Why take a risk on lending to them when business investments were doing so well? To today's reader, this hesitance seems like madness—especially since National City Bank, the forerunner of today's Citigroup, remains one of the country's largest banks—but to bankers at the end of the 1920s such reluctance was well-founded prudence. Why would bankers not want to lend money to consumers? The simple answer is that banks in the 1920s earned easy profits from lending to business in an expanding economy and had no need to explore new opportunities when their capital was already so profitably employed.[7] A more complex answer, however, is not only to be found in well-calculated profit margins but in the bankers' own experiences with prudent lending and the constraints of their institutions, which were not equipped to handle consumer lending.

Experience, more than numbers, guided bankers' conservative investment practices. Only a wholesale refashioning of that experience would alter their worldview. For smaller banks, capital was not to be gambled on new-fangled schemes and benevolent outreach programs when certain profits abounded. Even National City Bank, initially, saw the personal loan department more as public outreach than a source of profits. The department's popularity, more than profitability, had been the impetus for its creation. Roger Steffan, an ambitious vice-president at National City, who both came up with the idea for the department and oversaw it, was supervised by the head of public relations, not the head of commercial loans.[8] National City Bank, with its amassed millions in capital, could perhaps indulge in some public relations and progressive reform, but most of the nation's banks were more comfortable sticking with what they knew in the world of business finance, which in 1928 was working out pretty well for them.

Commercial bankers had long been uncomfortable with personal loans. Commercial banks had always made small loans, on the side, for good customers who borrowed large sums for their businesses. These "accommodation" loans, however, never made any money. If a businessman did a lot of business at a bank and happened to need a comparatively small amount lent on the side for personal use, the bankers, grumpily, would accede, in the name of the other accounts. These accommodation loans were a nuisance to bankers since they caused a lot of paperwork for no profit. Capital would be locked up as the loan was repeatedly borrowed, preventing the money's investment in more lucrative and sound schemes. Rather than a business loan, accommodation loans should be thought of in the same way that a bartender might lend money to a regular patron.[9] This form of consumer credit, emerging out of class-based social relationships, had more in common with mutual aid societies and ethnic lending than with commercial banking.

For those customers that the banker did not know, in whose social and economic life he was not privy to, personal loans were judged by the conservative standards of commercial banking practices—and found lacking.[10] The habits of commercial lending—the methodical review of each borrower to make sure he had the collateral to cover the loan—made personal lending seem foolhardy and unsound. People who wanted to borrow would be *exactly* the sort of people to whom the bank would not want to lend.

It was to those people, as other bankers feared, that National City Bank lent its capital. James Perkins, chairman of National City Bank, who by all accounts was as genuine as he was hard-working, believed that "behind almost every loan is a story of good citizenship." Without practical experience in personal lending to guide them, early experiments were guided by the moral outlook of bankers. To Perkins, loans for moral purposes that improved the lives of families in need were, by definition, worthy. Childbirth expenses, "lives . . . saved by timely surgical attention," and children's education were all worthy goals for personal loans.[11] Moral ideals of lending dominated, or at least equaled, those of profit. Loans, as one bank's guidelines for lending stressed, for "some luxury or whim that he ought not gratify," even if they fit the borrower's income, were not to be made.[12]

The very unexpectedness of need, in contrast to installment credit, morally justified these personal loans. A common moral criticism of indebtedness was that it resulted from irresponsibly managed budgets, from consumers who refused to save for what they wanted. Consumers who used installment credit wanted things more than they wanted the satisfaction of living within their means. Installment debt, from the bankers' moral vantage point, was an irresponsible choice—a failure of character. In contrast, a personal loan was taking responsibility for life's uncertainties. Childbirth, illness, funeral expenses, and other hazards of life could not be in the same profligate moral category as fast cars and modern furniture, and while these early lenders would happily lend for misery, they would not lend for luxury. This moral view of debt sharpened the contrast between personal loans and installment debt, giving personal loan bankers a justification for their lending, but it also firmly circumscribed the kinds of permissible loans.

Bankers who managed personal loan departments saw the existence of these unexpected expenses as the only justifiable reason for personal borrowing. Charles Mitchell, president of National City Bank, remarked in 1928 that "while it is not our purpose to encourage anyone to borrow except under the stress of circumstances, we have faith that loans so made can and will be paid where incident thereto the spirit of thrift can be kept alive."[13] The Hudson County National Bank, one of the few banks to follow National City's early lead, used this notion of worthiness to guide its lending. One of the earliest banks with a personal loan department, it would "not entertain a personal loan under any circumstances to help buy a luxury or for speculative purposes."[14] Lending such credit was as much a social service as an opportunity for profit. In contrast, everyday lending only encouraged the debtor to improperly budget, which led to both moral and economic peril. While we today might doubt the sincerity of their moralistic language, the strange repayment plans for these loans demonstrated that bankers put rehabilitating debtors' habits before profitability. The practices of lending reflected the economic as well as moral assumptions behind the loan.

Banks, with these moral purposes in mind, conducted loan repayment differently than we would expect today. As important to the bankers as repayment of the loan was inculcating habits of deposit in debtors so that they learned to save. Before they were allowed to borrow, debtors had to learn deposit. National City Bank and other banks that followed its example, like First Wisconsin National Bank, required borrowers to deposit at least $1 into a savings account at the time that the loan was made.[15] According to the bank's instructional pamphlets, borrowers would deposit into this savings account at fixed "monthly, semi-monthly or weekly intervals" the appropriate fraction of the loan so that at the end of twelve months the loan would be "paid out of the funds which [had] accumulated in the savings account." These accounts, though dedicated to repay the loan, still earned interest on the savings. At the end of the twelve months, borrowers would pay off the loan in total from the money available in this account, mimicking the practice of business loans, which were paid off in one lump sum. In this moralizing hybrid, borrowers both received and paid interest on the loan. At the end of the repayment term, borrowers would also still have a savings account, which the bankers hoped they would continue to use to avoid any future need to borrow.

Beyond the loan, bankers intended this savings account to inculcate the habit of thrift. Perkins emphasized that the monthly deposit "maintains the thrift spirit of the borrower and does not develop a debtor attitude."[16] Bankers saw personal loans not only as a way to help borrowers in a moment of crisis, but also to encourage thrift to prevent borrowers from needing to turn to the bank again. As one banking association economist described it, personal loans were only "a step to saving."[17] The "concrete experience" of depositing funds every month, even if that money was earmarked for the bank, instilled in depositors virtuous habits of thrift, which, from the bankers' point of view, was an important as the interest banks earned on the loan.

After National City Bank began its personal loan department, for each positive endorsement in the banking trade journals or popular press there were as many, or more, that negative assessments. Personal loan departments did not spread. Even by the time of the Depression, when banks became increasingly desperate for investments, other commercial banks continued to resist entering consumer lending and the conventional wisdom continued to assume that such lending could not be profitable. Writing in a banking trade magazine in late 1932, a Midwestern banker, A. Cornelius Clark, made the case that despite experimentation with personal loan departments, such schemes could not be—by inspection—widely profitable.[18]

Clark's arguments resonated with the conventional habits, experiences, and reasoning of the commercial banker. To be sure, the appeal of personal loans was seductive. A banker could imagine that borrowers who took out small loans might start to borrow business loans at the bank or at least deposit their savings there. Clark estimated that some bankers thought "20% or more of borrowers may be educated into savers and their friends [might] be induced to become customers of the bank."[19] A typical charge of $8 for a $100 loan over the course of 12 months represented a 16 percent interest rate (with an average balance of $50, the $8 was a 16 percent rate). This return would certainly have been appealing to bankers at first glance, since 16 percent was considerably more than a business loan even in the best of times.[20]

Clark, echoing the honed experience of commercial banking, dismissed these flights of fancy with hard-nosed facts. After examining the figures he had available from "six larger banks whose analysis departments have kept close check of expenses over a period of three years or more," he reckoned that for each $100 lent, a bank would earn a net profit of only 11 cents—nowhere near the gross profit of $8 because of the added expenses for staff, investigation, advertising, and collection.[21] The staff for personal loan departments had to be at least double that of a similar-sized commercial lender, he reckoned. Keeping track of the monthly payments created a lot of paperwork, in contrast to the usual business loan that was terminated with a single deposit.[22] Investigating borrowers would be a Herculean task, at least if it was done as thoroughly and traditionally as commercial bankers expected for such a loan.

Part of the difficulty Clark and other bankers had in apprehending that a personal loan department could be profitable was their failure of imagination. When the commercial banker pictured a personal loan department, he envisioned exactly the methods used for commercial loans only for much smaller amounts. He called or wrote to every reference of every borrower. He went over the applicant's financial statements in detail, ascertaining the complete inventory of his assets and liabilities. He attempted to understand every aspect of what the borrower intended to use the money for. He imagined having to hire a vast staff to process each of these individual applications. For such small amounts—$8 for all that work!—the only way to make sense of the claims of profitability was to attribute them to something as other-worldly as Hercules himself. The profits of some experimental banks could not be due to a sound system of credit analysis, according to Clark, but to the preternatural senses of bankers "so adept at reading character and approving loans that their losses are reduced to almost nothing."[23]

Without the requisite mystical ability of this exceptional loan manager, whose capacities could not be reproduced through study or training, and whose very existence seemed suspect, it would be unsafe to enter the personal loan business. To the reader of the journal, looking at Clark's argument, buttressed as it was by tables of expenses, careful calculations, and metaphysical injunctions, the easy profits of the personal loan department seemed only to be an easy way to lose money. Commercial bankers' habits and professional literature strongly resisted personal loans; it would take a widespread—and profitable—experience with consumer lending to change their minds.

To Act Like a State

The transformative experience took the unlikely form of Federal Housing Administration's Title I loan program. Created by the National Housing Act of 1934, its proponents intended the Title I modernization loan program, like the rest of the Housing Act, to stimulate the Depression-era economy.[24] Home owners could borrow money to repair their roofs, install electricity, or buy nonmovable durables like oil burners and air-conditioning systems.[25] These loans were expected to be relatively small—only a few hundred dollars. Title I loans, like their Title II counterparts, were meant to be affordable so as to stimulate as much demand as possible in the hard-hit economy of the Depression.[26] For home owners needing repairs and modernizations, these loans presented an affordable and easy way to improve their standard of living.

For bankers, the loans guaranteed profits. As discussed in chapter 2, the FHA did not lend any money directly to consumers, but relied on the profit motive of private capital to supply the financing. The government created an insurance program for lenders, so that in case of default bankers would always get back the principal of the loan, allowing them to take on more risk than they ordinarily would. The interest rates would be low, but through the government insurance program the profits would be risk free. Crucially, the Title I loan program connected a demand by consumers with a supply of capital that, in its absence, the market could not. The effects of this intervention went far beyond home repair however, as the program remade the institutional structure and intellectual assumptions of commercial banking.

By the time that the FHA announced its Title I program in 1934, formerly skeptical bankers had become desperate for sites of profitable lending. Investment opportunities in such uncertain times remained relatively hard to find as businesses avoided borrowing to expand their operations.[27] Perkins, the National City Bank chairman, remarked in a 1934 letter to Giannini, the Bank of America chairman, that National City's "excess reserves are very big. It is almost impossible to find any use for money in credits that we are willing to take, and the rates are terribly low."[28] Businesses trying to survive the Depression had no incentive for expansion and relied, to an unusual extent, on their internal funds.[29] While consumer spending fell by a fifth between 1929 and 1932, nonresidential business investment had plummeted by more than two-thirds.[30] Business had stopped borrowing.

Every year through the 1930s the percentage of commercial loans in bank portfolios dropped.[31] A 1938 Conference Board survey of 1755 firms, mostly in the manufacturing sector, showed that 91 percent had "no bank credit experience."[32] No sensible businessman borrowed. Firms did not need the money bankers were willing to lend. For most banks, like one small Missouri bank, their "income [had] been greatly reduced due to the fact that the demand for good loans [had] fallen off."[33] Good loans, in this common view, were business loans. Without profits from lending, banks could not offer interest to depositor's funds for long and would soon be out of business.

When the FHA introduced Title I, however, all of that changed. The guarantee of profits through federal insurance mitigated bankers' suspicions about consumer lending, and bankers opened FHA Title I loan departments. Though bankers remained skeptical, with a federal mandate and guaranteed profits, and no business investments to be found, bankers were willing to try something new. Though commercial banks had little to do with consumer loans before Title I, commercial banks became the main source for Title I funds, providing over 70 percent of all FHA-insured funds. Over 90 percent of all FHA lending institutions were commercial banks. The combined lending of building and loan associations, finance companies, industrial banks, credit unions, and savings banks comprised slightly less than 10 percent of all Title I lending institutions. Though personal finance companies did loan more money per firm, it was commercial banks that opened the most new loan departments and with their greater capital pools loaned more money. Title I institutionally remade American commercial banking, connecting it, for the first time, with consumer lending.[34]

That the Title I loan program formed a bridge to personal loan departments for commercial banks was no doubt helped by those that administered the program. As Congress debated the best course to recovery and framed the Federal Housing Act, some of the witnesses to the hearings came from National City Bank. Steffan, who had created National City Bank's personal loan department, his assistant vice president, Elliot Beams, and an assistant manager, J. Andrew Painter, all prepared testimony for the committee. The testimony apparently got Congress and FHA Administrator James Moffett's attention and, according to Painter, he and Steffan were "loaned" to the FHA to "help set up the Property Improvement Plan under Title I."[35]

Steffan, who had fashioned the first personal loan department, was appointed director of modernization credits to oversee the administration of Title I.[36] Though he only served for a few months and then returned to National City Bank, Steffan set the course of the program, touring the country to promote it.[37] Speaking before the American Banker's Association, ten weeks after the program began, Steffan declared that the Title I program was "based on old-fashioned and orthodox principles—to bring together *private* capital, industry, and labor to do the long overdue job of brightening up American homes—at a fair profit."[38] Steffan believed in the Title I program because of his experiences at National City Bank. Over the previous six years, he explained, the personal loan department had loaned $172,000,000 to 545,000 people with a repayment rate of 99 percent.[39] The experience of success convinced him that the Title I program would work.

From Painter's perspective, for America's commercial banks the Title I program "was a great adventure."[40] Their willingness to enter the new field of lending, he thought, was "a tribute to the readiness of the Commercial banks."[41] From Painter's view, "that experience [with Title I loans] was undoubtedly the kick-off for the commercial banks in achieving a remarkable record in providing consumer instalment [*sic*] credit."[42] But bankers' willingness to try personal loans, contrary to Painter's account, sprang more from desperation than a lust for adventure. Adventure could have been had at any time, but banks only began to open consumer lending departments after the Title I program began.

The Title I program, Steffan conceded, could not have occurred in any earlier moment. The interest rate of the loans—about 5 percent—was less than commercial bankers ordinarily would have accepted. It was as obvious to Steffan as to the bankers that "a small loan of this kind averaging $432, with monthly payments or deposits, costs relatively more to handle than a loan of several hundred or several million dollars, paid off by the writing of a single check."[43] Steffan reminded his audience of bankers that these were not normal times, and "if bank funds and bank staffs were being utilized to the limit, as they were in 1929, circumstances would not be so favorable[,] but now in most instances a comfortable volume of these loans can be handled by existing staffs." Excess capital and excess staff that otherwise would go uninvested or be fired could be employed.

When FHA administrator James Moffett seemingly exaggerated Title I as "a novel conception of credit of far-reaching and historic significance," he might have actually *underestimated* its consequences.[44] Through its modernization loan program, the FHA loan system introduced consumer lending to commercial banks. The most plentiful source of capital in the American economy had begun to see consumer lending as a source of profit. In doing so, Title I overcame the habits of practice that held commercial banks out of the personal loan field. Bankers across the country duplicated Steffan's experiment at National City Bank. Government policies had inadvertently created a market for consumer credit that went beyond the confines of the Title I program.

In the process of discovering the personal loan's profits, the personal loan became anything but personal. No longer could the businessman go to his long-time banker for an accommodation loan on the side. Loosening social bonds, the applicant for a personal loan confronted not an individual banker but an impersonal system of evaluation and profit. Commercial banks were no longer only for the wealthy businessmen, but for the new middleclass as well.[45] Personal loans, once the province of the loan shark, industrial bank, or remedial loan society, were brought into the mainstream of capitalist lending—commercial banks. In the process, commercial banks that used to cater only to wealthy businessmen opened their doors to the salaried middle class.[46]

The composition of borrowers at National City Bank and Manufacturers Trust Company, as shown in figure 3.1, reflected these concerns. Personal loan customers were not penurious workers, but as an investment magazine for bankers put it, "dependable people of relatively modest income."[47] From the available information, it is clear that the majority of borrowers were the new middle-class of white-collar employees (salesmen,

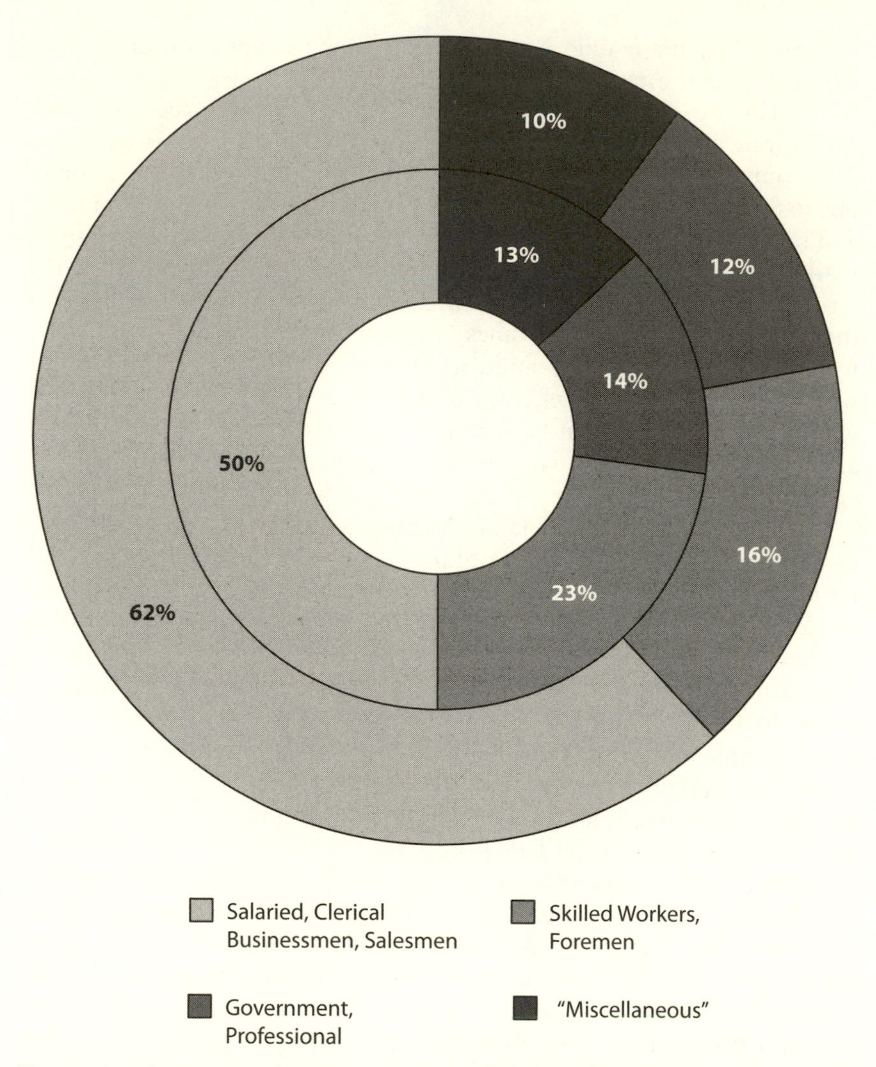

Figure 3.1. Occupational Percentage of Borrowers at Two Commercial Banks. Outer ring: National City Bank. Inner ring: Manufacturers Trust Company. Source: Irvin Bussing, *Report on Some Important Aspects of the Personal Loan Business From the Savings Bank Point of View* (1937), "Savings Banks," Box 99, Russell Sage Foundation Papers, Manuscript Division, Library of Congress, Washington, D.C.

government employees, clerical workers, and professionals) and businessmen. Personal loan departments, although they did not exclude workers, were, unlike small loan companies or remedial lenders, primarily aimed at middle-income Americans, many of whom would already have a savings account at a local bank.[48] Skilled workers and "miscellaneous" applicants together made up only between a quarter and a third of the borrowers, unlike the borrowers at more working-class-oriented small loan companies.

While applicants' incomes varied widely, their occupations were overwhelmingly middle class. One executive of the Manufacturer's Trust Company wrote that, "applicants comprise a cross section . . . with incomes ranging from $1,000 to $50,000."[49] The qualities that the banks looked for in borrowers matched those of the new middle class—stable income and long-term employment, whatever that income might be.[50] Seasonal or independent workers were not looked upon favorably. Because they generally dealt with higher income people, who were considered less risky, they could offer lower cost loans than the companies, like industrial banks, that, as one economist wrote, catered to another "economic stratum."[51] Manufacturer's Trust Company required a $3,000 a year income but also offered lending at the low rate of 4 percent per annum.[52]

What applicants borrowed for reflected the needs of this salaried, urban class. Bankers' self-described "conservative" loan policy covered a variety of purposes, from clothes to medical care. Rather than just what consumers wanted, the numbers in table 3.1 reflect the purposes for which the banks were willing to lend just as much. Medical expenses and loan consolidation drove the personal loan business. Without health insurance, the risk of illness was not only lost wages but medical expenses as well. Where the ethnic and family lending networks broke down under the strain of the Depression, personal loan departments stepped in, offering support for unplanned expenses. It is telling that older patterns of filial loans didn't disappear as lending became more formal. Five percent of Manufacturers Trust Company loans, around $2,000,000 in 1937, went to help relatives. Borrowers' unexpected emergencies continued even as banker's moral motivations were supplanted by profit.

What constituted an emergency for a borrower was not always as simple and noble as needing money for a child's doctor. Always topping the list of bank loan purposes was debt consolidation. Debt consolidation could mean paying off medical and educational loans, but more frequently it meant the consolidation of installment debts owed on consumer durables in danger of repossession.[53] The loans that were consolidated ran the gamut from furniture dealers to family to loan sharks.[54] The key differences between those loans made on the installment plan or to a loan shark and the loans at the bank, were collateral and cost. In addition to charging a much higher interest rate, missing a payment on furniture meant losing the furniture. Missing a payment to loan shark meant the possibility of what the *New York Times* referred to as "gangster methods."[55] But

TABLE 3.1

Manufacturers Trust Company		National City Bank	
Purpose	Percentage	Purpose	Percentage
Consolidation and payment of debt	30	Medical and dental	30
Medical and dental	20	Pay debts and loans	15
Business	20	Purchase home equipment	14
Home furnishings	10	Business emergency	11
Clothing	5	Payments on own home	8
Education	5	Necessary clothing	7
Mortgage payment and taxes	5	Education	5
Help relatives	5	Taxes	3

Source: Irvin Bussing, *Report on Some Important Aspects of the Personal Loan Business From the Savings Bank Point of View to the Investment Committee of the Savings Bank Association of the State of New York* (1937), "Savings Banks," Box 99, Russell Sage Foundation Papers, Manuscript Division, Library of Congress, Washington, D.C.

the personal loan at the bank required no collateral. The enforcement of its loans never meant losing a valued possession—or a limb. Personal loan departments helped people get disruptions in their income without risking the loss of their possessions or bodily harm.

Personal loans, for those able to get them, protected the wealth of borrowers as well by the relatively low interest rates for the loans and the borrower's ability to pay off other forms of debt. Personal loans could protect the equity of installment purchases.[56] Personal loans, used for debt consolidation, enabled middle-class borrowers to save their equity in installment purchases—something lost to working-class borrowers on repossession. Personal loans were also much cheaper than other conventional forms of credit. For example, by law, personal loans in New York could not exceed 12 percent per year on unpaid balances. Rates were less than the legal maximum due to competition. National City Bank charged 3 percent annually for a loan (5.7 percent on unpaid balances). The Manufacturers Trust Company offered 5 percent loans (9.7 percent on unpaid balances) with a co-signer and 4 percent loan (7.7 percent on unpaid balances) for low-risk loans without a co-signer. Though it varied by state, this percentage was always much lower than that for small loan lending companies. In New York, the personal loan rates were one-third those of small loan companies and about half of industrial banks.[57] Loan sharks' rates were much higher. Leon Henderson, Russell Sage Foundation economist, estimated loan shark earnings at three times their capital every year in interest or $300,000,000 a year, which, if accurate, is a fantastic rate of return.[58] In all cases, personal loans from banks, for those borrowers who could obtain them, were the cheapest source of funds.

Despite being cheap for borrowers, these personal loans were also profitable for the banks. While interest rates were low, losses were also extremely low. In their new FHA loan departments, against all their assumptions about sound lending, commercial bankers experienced for the first time how profitable personal loans could be. As banks offered the insured FHA modernization loans, their discomfort in lending to consumers lessened. This discomfort disappeared because these loans, contrary to the bankers' fears, were in fact quite dependable. Borrowers repaid them reliably. The federal insurance for the Title I loans was rarely used. Bankers also began to notice, through trade journals and their own personal experience, that in spite of their expectations, consumers had rarely defaulted on their installment purchases or small loans throughout the Depression.

Earlier reported numbers on personal lending became believable as bankers' own experiences in lending reinforced earlier claims of profitability. The New York State Savings Bank Association economist, Irvin Bussing, noted in 1937 that the "experience of commercial and industrial banks with personal loans appears to have been highly satisfactory."[59] Repayments of personal loans, which had always seemed so unsound to the banker's commonsense, were virtually 100 percent. By the late 1930s, the National City Bank reported losses of only one-tenth of 1 percent.[60] Painter, the assistant manager in the bank's personal loan department, in remembering the period many years later recounted with some pride that, "some have said, and I would be the last to deny it, that the bank's dividend record was maintained during the low interest rate and [the] small commercial loan volume days of the depression years by the profitable use of some of the bank's funds by the Personal Loan Dept."[61] For the Manufacturers Trust Company, also a savings bank, losses on loans made in the previous twelve months were only one-fifth of 1 percent. Less than 1 percent of their accounts were more than thirty days overdue. National City Bank, in 1933, reported losses of only 5/1000 of 1 percent. This meager loss, mind you, was in the midst of the Great Depression. Lending to salaried employees was very, very safe.

The existing infrastructure for the FHA programs made the transition into personal loans easier for commercial banks, bootstrapping the new lending field. Since consumer loan departments were set up for the FHA program, adding an additional line in personal loans was relatively simple. Personal loans were simply Title I loans for everything else and without the government guarantee. If the National City Bank was atypical in opening a personal loan department in 1928, it was more typical by 1936, in that its FHA modernization loans were handled by the same department.[62] For most banks, however, the FHA modernization loans preceded the personal loans.[63] The Manufacturers Trust Company, also of New York, was more common in the order of its operations. As it considered opening a personal loan department in 1935, it already had a small department to service the "Modernization Credit Plan" under Title I of the National Housing Act.

Like most banks before Title I, Manufacturers Trust Company had not previously had a department to lend to consumers. But with the organization of a department for Title I, a personal loan program became easy since the staff and the office space were already allocated. Employees were trained in small loans and customers knew to come to the bank to borrow these small loans. Bankers saw personal loans as the logical extension of the FHA modernization program, often reporting to the public information about their modernization loans alongside other, non-FHA types of loans to the consumer.[64] By bringing Title I and personal loans together, it became "feasible to consolidate the work and coordinate new business, credit, and collection effort[s] on monthly payment loans."[65] Indeed, acting in concert with the promotion of federal housing policies, which had, as Manufacturers Trust bank executive John Paddi put it, "[made] the public more loan-conscious," seemed patriotic as well.[66]

Bankers' culturally embedded ideas of risk and proper practice were not insurmountable. As a testament to the flexibility of bankers' minds in search of profit, what they experienced was more important than what they had read or had been taught. The practice of lending directly to consumers under Title I, and not just to business, gave banks the confidence to expand into the personal loan business, which like Title I loans also had amortized, monthly payments.[67]Again and again, bankers' positive experience with Title I loans led them to set up personal loan departments. Desperate for outlets for their surplus capital and flush with a newfound exuberance for consumer banking, increasing numbers banks began to open "personal loan" departments.

The timing of new personal loan departments in commercial banks in the 1920s and 1930s shows the centrality of the Title I lending experience. First emerging in the late 1920s with National City Bank, the number of new departments had slowed in the early 1930s as many, but not all, of the new experimental departments showed losses.[68] In the early 1930s, approximately only thirty departments were being organized per year. Then, in 1934, at the same time as FHA Title I loans began, there was a sudden surge to 84 departments per year. In 1935, 182 were organized, followed by 214 in 1936.[69] By 1936 there were three and a half times as many departments as in 1929.[70] Loan balances rocketed from $33 million in 1933 to $129 million by 1936. Before Title I, less than 1 percent of commercial banks had a personal loan department. By the end of 1934, 71 percent of the "total banking resources" did.[71] Through "the example and the introduction of FHA modernization financing," one banking journal noted, banks "established such departments through which almost every type of personal or installment financing [could then] be arranged."[72] Though, initially, banks like the Des Moines National Trust Company thought Title I would only be a "minor side line." For them and other banks it quickly became an important "revenue-producing business," a banking journal observed."[73] Personal lending helped many banks survive the depression.

Fordism at the Bank

So many banks had opened personal loan departments by 1936 that an American Bankers Association (ABA) bulletin of 1936 bemoaned that personal loans could not be, as apparently some bankers had begun to think, "a panacea for low earnings or provide a plan for investing all, or even a portion of the banks' excess reserves."[74] Yet even as ABA publications advised caution, evidence continued to mount that, contrary to traditional beliefs, profits could be had in personal lending. Two years later at the ABA conference, a Louisville banker named Elbert S. Woosley declared that "the average small borrower is the best credit risk in this nation." At his bank, the First National Bank of Louisville, the personal loan department caused him "less worry" than their "other earning assets." Woosley's worries centered not on the future of personal loans, but on what he called "this time of uncertainty."[75] Business investments, not personal loans, by the late 1930s had him nervous. By the time the second recession of the decade hit in 1937, even banks that had been waiting for business to return to normal were forced to take notice of the new opportunities in personal lending. Recovery in industrial production of the previous few years faded as production in late 1937 dropped almost as low as the nadir of the Depression in 1932.[76] National City Bank chairman Perkins anxiously wrote to a fellow banker that "commercial loans were practically non-existent."[77] The lack of commercial investments forced commercial banks to look elsewhere for profits.

Most commercial banks entering the personal loan field through Title I loans, unlike the initial pioneers, did not start their departments strictly out of a concern for consumer thriftiness but to make profits in an era of uncertain business investment. As discussed earlier, the Depression had precipitated a sharp drop-off in commercial borrowing. If personal loans could be collected and the riskiness of borrowers correctly—and cheaply—reckoned, then personal loans represented a perfect outlet for surplus funds. This combination of experience with Title I lending and the need for profits is what led to the massive increase in the number of personal loan departments organized in the mid-1930s. As homage to their origin, the personal loans echoed the structure of the Title I loans—short-term, amortized, and without down payment. Like the FHA loans, the new personal loans were all structured like installment credit. The advertising promise of Bank of America in 1936, when it like so many other commercial banks launched its new personal loan department to make "bank credit available to all qualified installment buyers," showed how far personal loans had come from the accommodation loans and moral judgment of an earlier era. Banks decreasingly sought to differentiate personal loans from installment credit.[78]

As the personal loan department became a standard part of the banking business, the early moral vision of personal lending, like that held by James Perkins, lost its influence. In 1938 the ABA conducted a survey of its membership to find out just how the personal loan department practiced their trade.[79] How could traditionalists like A. Cornelius Clark have been so wrong? The survey found that personal loans were both practical and profitable. Following the publication of this survey by America's foremost banking association, no one could argue, on the grounds of risk, that personal loans were bad business.[80]As banks entered the field with more of an eye to profit than to encouraging thrift, the number of banks offering personal loans grew as did the ways in which bankers lent.

To make profits commercial banks had to reinvent how they did business, making their offices more like Ford's assembly line than an artisan's shop. The key to profits on small loans was lowering the cost of processing each loan. The average loan of the majority of banks was between $150 and $250.[81] Whereas profits could be—and it was essential that they were—made on commercial loans through a careful investigation of each borrower, profits from small loans required investigations to be accurate—but more importantly—quick. The margin of profit could easily be lost through overly in-depth investigation.

The only way to drop the investigation costs was, like a factory, to expand the volume and take advantage of economies of scale. Rather than a few airtight loans, as commercial bankers were used to, personal loans required many loans be certain only on *average*. High loan volume, which necessitated rapid growth, was the only way in which a personal loan department could be profitable. The rapid expansion of personal loan departments was due to both their success and the way in which they became successful. Their success centered on volume lending. Either a bank's personal loan department grew very quickly or it did not make money. There was no in-between.

And volume there was. By the mid-1930s, for the 254,000 yearly borrowers from National City Bank, there were only 580 employees. Each day the bank processed 1,200 loan applications, or about two for every employee.[82] Since the dollar amounts were relatively small and defaults extremely infrequent, banks erred on the side of volume rather than certainty, hoping (correctly) that the profit on the volume would make up for the defaults. The cost for certainty outweighed the cost of default. The techniques, then, used in personal loans were very different from the detailed, plodding way business loans were determined. A federal consumer expenditure survey conducted from 1935 to 1936 showed that about a tenth of the population of New York, Atlanta, and Chicago, of the income ranges and occupations to whom banks lent, had used some form of personal loan in the past year.[83] Moreover the very profitability, dependent on volume of lending, of personal loan departments showed that many people were beginning to use this service, not only at the National City Bank, but across the country.

Not all people, however, could use the personal loan department of a commercial bank and the high rates of loan approval reflected, as much as the investigation process, the class filter of feeling comfortable walking into a commercial bank. The system created to speedily evaluate applicants reflected both the problems and possibilities inherent to a steady, monthly wage income.[84] Borrowers needed loans because of their risky position in the wage labor system, but the perceived steadiness of wage labor enabled them to borrow from expected future income—the salary.

Salaries, not assets or collateral, underpinned the personal loan system. National City Bank, when it opened its department, only lent to salaried employees. Business loans, unlike personal loans, were determined not on the expected ability to repay but on the value of liquidation of the firm's assets. Firms borrowed against their current value. Bankers asked, "if they default, can we get our money back when the firm's assets are sold off?" Anticipated future income was considered part, but certainly not the most important part, of a firm's assets in determining their eligibility for a loan.

In contrast, for personal loans salary was everything and assets nothing. In examining a personal loan application, the question was not a person's net worth but their "week to week" or "month to month" income.[85] Personal loans were not based on collateral but "character." Though the moral language of the 1920s character loan continued, by the mid-1930s one's character was, apparently, entirely determined by monthly income. The bank did not ask, "Is the applicant good for $300" but instead, "Can he repay $25 a month?"[86] The most important determinants for a loan were stability of employment and address. The greatest potential cost of a loan was the cost of collection, and that could be reduced if the borrower was easily located at either home or work. But more importantly, if he had worked at one job for a long time he probably would continue to work there in the future. For a bank in Albany that shortened its application form to less than one page, the only three questions that mattered were, "How long has the applicant lived in Albany"; "How long has he been employed by his present employer?"; and, "How much is his pay per week or month?" The extensive investigation imagined by A. Cornelius Clark never happened and was, more importantly, not necessary. In the view of that bank's manager, if the applicant had lived in Albany and had held the same job for long time, then the "chances [were] strong that he [would be] entitled to the loan."[87]

Restricting the clientele to the salaried, middle class allowed for sound loans, bankers believed, at such a large volume. The large volume, in turn, allowed for simplification and standardization of application information, which enabled new divisions of labor at the bank. To rapidly accomplish loan approval or denial, the investigation and paperwork, which in the case of business loans had been done from beginning to end by one clerk, was split up on standardized forms and distributed to many different employees. The personal loan department was the first twenty-four hour banking system. At the Manufacturers Trust Company a loan received in the afternoon would be filed and processed by clerical staff in the evening so that it might be investigated, by phone, the following morning. One clerk would check all the names under investigation that day for each reference, instead of many clerks re-contacting the same reference throughout the day.[88] One clerk confirmed employment. Another clerk confirmed addresses. For larger loans, another clerk confirmed litigation reports. In 95 percent of cases a decision on the loan would have been made by the following afternoon and a check sent off by that evening. Because such loans were often in response to emergencies, the banks gave as prompt service as possible or they risked losing the loan to another bank. Speed and division of labor made lending possible and competitive.

Beyond the simple class filter of salary, the personal loan departments also relied on the new consumer credit bureaus to decide who made a good risk. New organizations, credit bureaus were devoted to the integration of city-wide credit backgrounds on consumers. Though mercantile credit bureaus had existed since the nineteenth century, these new bureaus focused only on consumers.[89] Professional organizations like National Association of Credit Men, as well as local entrepreneurs, created information exchange systems to enable the tracking of debtors' information.[90] Two-thirds of banks claimed they gained enough information about the applicant at the first interview to decide on the case.[91] Eighty percent of banks reported that they made use of either "local merchants or credit associations" in developing credit information. These two figures can only be reconciled if the new credit bureaus of the 1930s provided all the information two-thirds of banks needed. When the Manufacturers Trust Company was considering opening their personal loan department, they felt safe doing so, in part, because of the services of New York's "central bureau" operated by the New York Credit Men's Association.[92]

Applicant interviewers, at the Manufacturers Trust Company and other banks that relied on credit bureaus, got all the information they needed at the first interview because they were given the name, address, and job information they needed to obtain the credit history of the borrower from a credit bureau. The night staff of the personal loan department "prepare[d] the cards for the interchange bureau" every evening, so that they and other lenders would be able to have information on borrowers employment, address, and most importantly, other loans.[93] These cards arrived by 8:30 a.m. the next day.[94] A few hours later the bureau contacted the "Interchange clerk" at the bank to report on all inquiries, telling him if the applicant had outstanding debt, poor payment records, or anything else that would, literally, "red card" the account.[95] Multiple applications from the same address, applications from women under maiden names, and similar acts of "fraud" to either hide a "poor credit record" or obtain "additional funds" could be found out only through the comprehensive records of the bureau.[96] The Manufacturers Trust Company reported that it had "detected and declined a total of $60,000 in Personal Loan applications filed with intent to defraud" by the methodical use of the interchange bureau.[97] Sixty thousand dollars was a small fraction of the amount loaned by Manufacturers Trust, but its loss would have made a sizable dent in its profits.

By 1937, seventeen industrial and commercial banks with personal loan departments in New York relied on the "local interchange bureau."[98] Unlike the experiences of National City Bank in late 1920s and early 1930s, no additional information needed to be investigated by the staff. The "habit of the borrower" could be more easily found through the local credit bureau.[99] According to the 1938 ABA survey, only 13 percent of banks reported not using these sources of information. Without this new system of consumer credit exchange, the volume of processing that made personal loans profitable would not have been possible. Between restricting lending to salaried employees and the ample use of credit bureaus, seemingly loose lending was made safe.

Banks were generous in their lending, reassured by their quick investigation methods both in-house and through the credit bureau, as well as by the class status of their clientele, allowing for high volume lending. Eighty-one percent of banks claimed to approve a seemingly outrageous 70 to 100 percent of loans. Only 4 percent of banks approved fewer than half of the applications. The borrowers, in turn, repaid such confidence. Ninety-eight percent of banks claimed that repayments on individual loans had been satisfactory, and 93 percent reported that even the already low delinquency rate was dropping. Such astounding figures did not go unnoticed by the ABA survey authors, who remarked that these "exceptionally high approval percentage[s] when considered in connection with the almost infinitesimal losses experienced by these banks on personal loans, seems to indicate the inherent soundness of personal loans."[100]

Low losses did not always guarantee high profits to banks. Though virtually all loans extended were repaid, the actual profits yielded on these loans were apparently highly variable. Compared to other questions on the survey, relatively few banks (62 of 258) reported their net rates of profit. Forty-nine banks reported that their profits were not "segregated" by department, 29 did not have the figures "available," and 18 banks had "new" departments. The newness of the personal loan business led 96 banks in total not to know how much money they were making with their operations. Still the median reported profit rate was between 5 and 6 percent.[101] Despite such uncertain numbers, the *Wall Street Journal* felt comfortable reporting, without qualification, that profits were between 4 and 7 percent, reporting that banks charged, on average, between 5 and 8 percent interest on the loans.[102] The salient fact was that only 2 banks of the 180 answering the question made no money on the personal loan departments, even as business loans everywhere grew more uncertain in the midst of the Great Depression.

Credit Access and Institutional Change

Even as the number of banks offering personal loans grew, so too did their profits. By 1938, commercial banks with personal loan departments were earning higher profits than those without.[103] National City's net profit increased from $9,584,953 in 1937 to $10,547,750 in 1938, despite the bleak environment for commercial lending.[104] Noticing the continued low personal loan default rate and comparing it with business loan defaults, how could bankers come to any other conclusion? A *Wall Street Journal* writer found that "the banks are beginning to consider personal loans as a definite and integral part of their business, rather than as a 'necessary evil.'"[105] By the late 1930s, personal loan departments of commercial banks rapidly pushed other small loan lenders to the margins. By 1936, the loan balances of personal loan departments exceeded those of credit unions, equaled those of industrial banks, and nearly matched those of small loan companies.[106] Small loan companies continued to cater to the working class, while commercial banks lent to the middle class.[107]

As the attention of mainstream banks turned to consumer lending, their lending volumes quickly dwarfed other personal finance institutions because better-paid, middle-class employees could borrow more money. Already by 1939, only a few years after most banks seriously entered the field, economist M. R. Neifield, one of the foremost contemporary authorities on the personal loan business, estimated that the amount of money loaned by personal loan departments was twice that of either pawn brokers or cooperative credit unions, 50 percent greater than other industrial bank companies, and nearly equal to personal finance companies.[108] The organizational ability, access to capital, and resources of commercial banks could not be matched by small loan lenders. Small loan lenders were left with only the riskiest of customers, who increased their costs.

Profits were at the center of the expansion and as the drive for profits grew more important, the moral justification for the personal loans continued to fade in importance. As more banks opened new departments, their practices took the forms shaped by principles of profit and practicality, not the moral notions of thriftiness from earlier times. Though most departments were relatively young, repeat business, after a short time, formed a large fraction of their business. The early paternalist slogan of one bank, "Out of Debt, Money in your Pocket," gave way to the needs of profit and the preferences of borrowers.[109] Despite the genuine effort of early personal loan departments to get borrowers out of debt, these departments saw a tremendous increase in repeat business in the late 1930s. Twenty-eight percent of banks reported repeat lending of between 11 and 30 percent of their business Twenty-two percent of banks reported 31 to 50 percent, and even 15 percent reported 51 to 80 percent repeat business. These loans were issued from programs that were less than four years old. The feisty scheming of small loan operators to encourage repeat borrowers seems to have been unnecessary for personal loan departments. Though early promoters of personal loan departments hoped the loans would be a stepping-stone to saving and financial independence, for some borrowers they were only a cheaper form of debt persistence.

The use of savings accounts to encourage thrift also fell to the wayside. By 1938, only slightly more than half of installment payments were repaid into savings accounts. For those banks that continued to use savings accounts in this way, encouraging thrift was no longer the main purpose. Half of them did so, the ABA survey reported, because of the "simplicity, efficiency, [and] economy" of using previously established systems for deposit. If banks already had bookkeepers, machines, and ways of dealing with deposits, why create an entirely new system? One-fifth of banks had savings deposits because of state law.[110] Six percent did so because other banks did. Only 4 percent claimed to use savings deposits to encourage thrift. Most revealing, perhaps, that "savings" accounts were used for the ease of management and not for thrift, is that less than a third of banks using savings accounts, or 13 percent of all banks, paid interest on the deposits.[111] In contrast to only a few years earlier, when banks anxiously wrote to National City Bank for blank forms and anecdotal training, only one bank by 1938 reported using savings accounts because the National City Bank did it.[112] Indeed, by 1938, not even National City Bank used savings accounts anymore. In October 1936, National City converted its personal loans to the system based on the Title I program.[113]

New personal loan departments were modeled on the Title I Loan program, not the moralistic program of National City Bank. Experiments in lending were widespread, but banks quickly learned what worked and what did not. Long lists of new and discontinued practices, rarely with frequencies higher than one bank, show the variation in practices and uncertainty with which banks stepped into this new world of personal loans. From innovations that would eventually become standard, like machine bookkeeping, to practices that would disappear, like interest on deposits, banks tried all kinds of ways to lend personal loans.[114] Within a few years, however, as information, like that from the ABA survey—about what worked and what did not work—personal loan department practices converged.

Even as methods of lending to consumers converged, the kinds of loans that were offered rapidly diverged. Commercial banks expanded outside of small loans into other branches of consumer credit. As the finance companies of the 1920s feared, commercial banks, especially as they witnessed the reliability of consumer lending in the mid-1930s, expanded into installment financing of both consumer durables and automobiles. As Bank of America president and founder Giannini commented in 1936, the "trend is toward inclusion of the individual in bank financing, through personal loans, modernization loans, and automobile finance. . . . This is the trend that will be most apparent in banking during the ensuing years."[115] Like most other banks, Bank of America had started its installment loan department under the FHA insurance program. In 1935, it loaned $18 million to borrowers under this program. Giannini vowed to expand the bank's consumer lending even if "the government cease[d] to insure modernization and equipment loans."[116]

In 1936, Bank of America (BOA) expanded the installment program to include other forms of consumer credit. The Bank of America "Time Plan" financing system allowed consumers to borrow for autos, furniture, consumer durables, or personal loans at low cost.[117] Advertisements reminded potential borrowers that each loan established better credit with the bank, ensuing easy future borrowing.[118] Without the fees associated with regular finance companies or dealers, bank auto financing loans could be much cheaper than those from finance companies.[119] BOA guaranteed that the cost of their loans would be the lowest in California.[120] Finance companies had to borrow their money from banks and then lend it. BOA and other banks could lend the money directly. With 432 branches across California, BOA could offer more convenient service than any local finance company. The costs for banks to lend installment credit, once the personal loan department was organized, was much lower than any finance company's costs.

For BOA, the Time Plan reaped tremendous profits. In 1936, the year in which it was instituted, BOA increased earnings nearly 40 percent over 1935 to $22.5 million.[121] The increased profits came, according to Giannini, from the expansion on loans of $81 million primarily in consumer credit.[122] By May 1937, Giannini told the *Los Angeles Times* that "the handling of these installment loans has trebled and quadrupled activity in our branches."[123] Giannini stated that BOA had lent, in the prior eighteen months, $140 million in loans, expanded to 479 branches, and had added 5,400 employees.[124] Consumer lending had attained maturity as a form of lending and independence from the incubating FHA Title I program.

Conclusion: Commercial Banks Discover the Consumer

Even though Congress briefly suspended the Title I loan program in April 1937, the expansion of commercial banks into consumer credit continued. Title I was later reinstituted, but consumer lending continued to expand without federal assistance. Unlike mortgage lending, consumer lending quickly became autonomous from the state, leading to our current amnesia about its origins. Writing in a bankers' magazine, Donaldson Thorburn, assistant vice-president of Bank of America, wrote that the weak environment for business loans made "retail lending the logical road to improved earnings."[125] What was incredulous a decade earlier had now become logical. As the 1930s closed, many other commercial banks began to follow BOA's aggressive lead and increase their consumer financing. The soundness and profitability of consumer lending had been proven by experience. Federal loan guarantees were no longer needed. Commercial banks had discovered the profits of consumer credit, and that discovery would, in the years to come, remake both the foundations of American capitalism and society.

Commercial banking's shift into personal lending signaled more than a new source of profit. For capital it also marked the long-run legitimacy of consumer credit. As an editorial in the New York Credit Men's Association journal noted, "whatever doubts may have existed as to the permanency of consumer credit during the last half of the Depression were definitely laid at rest with the entrance of America's largest commercial banks into the personal loan field."[126] Yet, the desireability of an economy reliant on consumer credit remained. The "two-headed monster" of credit boosted sales, but as the editorial reminded the reader, the possibility of massive default always loomed.

Most importantly, the experiences of the 1930s led bankers to think of consumers as profitable sites of investment. If commercial bankers began lending to consumers for worthy purposes, once they recognized the potential profits of such lending, their definition of a "worthy purpose" expanded. Experience with Title I and personal loan lending rapidly extended into other areas of direct and indirect consumer lending for automobiles and retail credit. The great lesson of the Depression for banks was that there were alternatives to investing in business—investing in personal debt could be profitable as well.

This discovery was the sea change that the president of BOA referred to in his 1936 letter to all of his managers announced that "the character of banking service is changing."[127] On the tenth anniversary of National City Bank's personal loan department, by then called the personal credit department for its more extensive operations, an editorial in the National City Bank employee magazine stated that the creation of the department was "viewed with raised eyebrows in an era that had never devoted much serious thought to the plight of the prospective small borrower. Today, acceptance of the idea by banks everywhere in America is the best answer to the practicability of the character loan and to National City's leadership."[128] The experiences of FHA lending, under the guidance of National City Bank's Roger Steffan, led banks to think of consumers as a profitable alternative to investing in production. Even if Steffan "gauge[d] correctly," as he believed he had, that "the original sponsors of the National Housing Act, of those administering it, and of those bankers active in the extension of personal credit on the mass plan" had no initial intention of "tak[ing] over the great bulk of time-financing that exists in this country," such intentions mattered little when compared with profitable opportunity.[129] Installment loans, deemed risky and unsound in the 1920s, were by the end of the 1930s considered a foundation of modern lending. The experience of profitably lending money with monthly repayments—with or without collateral and with or without co-signer—signaled an upheaval in how banks saw consumers that would structurally alter the postwar world, as slowly, contingently, those monthly loans became ever more divorced from the things on which they were lent.

For the middle-class borrower, the short-term personal loan and the long-run mortgage, both legacies of the New Deal's FHA program, solidified the changes in borrowing that had begun with installment loans in the 1920s. Personal debt was everywhere in America and institutional lenders, not family or social networks, provided the funds. And these funds were now provided by the largest financial institutions in the country—commercial banks. Even if you knew a commercial banker socially, a vast impersonal staff would review your application and check with the credit bureau before you received a loan. And with the purchase of your FHA house in the suburbs, your automobile loan at the bank, and your consolidation of installment payments in a personal loan, indebtedness began to spread throughout your economic life. As the BOA radio advertisements reminded its Time Plan borrowers, the bank did not extend home loans, it financed a "home life."[130] For those left out of this salaried, middle-class world of debt—poor and working-class whites, most African Americans, and all unmarried women—life continued with its risks and uncertainties; their credit sources continued to be more expensive, dangerous, and unreliable.[131] Yet for those with access, debt presented new opportunities for home ownership and a lifestyle of greater choice. The salaried, middle class could begin to count on low-cost credit to finance their "home life." What would become of this life remained to be seen after the troubles of the Great Depression ended and World War II began, where the perceived dangers of too much credit, and the subsequent attempts to regulate it, transformed consumer credit in an entirely new direction.

Chapter Four

War and Credit

GOVERNMENT REGULATION AND CHANGING CREDIT PRACTICES

Reportedly in 1950, Frank McNamara, a businessman who had left his wallet in his other suit, in a flash of inspiration, conceived of the credit card while anxiously waiting for a bill. Diner's Club International, purveyor of what has been called the first credit card, has claimed that McNamara thought to himself, "Why should people be limited to spending what they are carrying in cash, instead of being able to spend what they can afford?"[1] Historians, when they have remarked on the origin of contemporary credit, have largely gone along with this "great man" anecdote, attributing its conception to the savvy of a brilliant entrepreneur.[2]

In reality, however, the idea of the credit card did not appear ex nihilo in the mind of Frank McNamara, but emerged from a complicated network of institutions, policies, practices, and technologies that had only recently come into being. Without this existing infrastructure of debt, McNamara could never have had that insight in 1950, much less put it into practice. Though McNamara's scheme, the travel and entertainment (T&E) card Diner's Club, did succeed in providing credit for businessmen, it was more an extension of existing practices of department store customers than a true innovation. The majority of American consumers who were not traveling businessmen already had learned how to "charge it" at department stores, where revolving credit had become common during the 1940s as the inadvertent result of a federal policy called Regulation W.

As the federal government attempted to restrain inflation during World War II scarcity, it instituted both the well-known rationing program for many consumer goods, and launched the now forgotten first federal attempt to directly regulate consumer credit.[3] With Regulation W, Roosevelt authorized the Federal Reserve, under a contorted reading of the Trading With the Enemy Act, to directly regulate how much consumers could borrow and the terms under which this borrowing could occur.[4] Federal Reserve regulators, who feared another NRA-esque debacle, carefully attempted to cultivate the consent of the businessmen. Rather than acting decisively, regulators formulated rules piecemeal so as to avoid aggravating American business. Moreover, the Federal Reserve lacked the staff or experience to directly enforce the regulations on hundreds of thousands of businesses. Weak enforcement and uneven regulation remade the incentives and practices of lenders.[5]

As the war wore on, businessmen who initially agreed to Regulation W in the name of patriotism saw opportunities to obey the regulation in name but to break it in practice, so as to gain an edge against their competition. Some forms of credit, like installment credit, were heavily regulated, while others, like open accounts, went ignored. Nimbly dodging Regulation W's grasp, many American retailers reorganized their businesses to create the first revolving credit plans, which could not be effectively regulated. While Regulation W reduced the overall amount of consumer debt during the war, it also destabilized established lending practices and encouraged a hybridization of installment credit and charge accounts—revolving credit—that combined interest charges and flexibility in a form outside Regulation W. In effect, from the beginning of World War II until the Korean War, Regulation W deeply shaped the course of credit practices in the American economy, pushing retailers and consumers towards revolving credit—the nucleus of today's modern credit card.

The origin of today's credit cards can be found in the larger structures of capitalism and public policy rather than in Frank McNamara's dinner mishap. The more important question, then, is how did existing forms of consumer credit—installment credit and open account credit—converge to produce the new practice of revolving credit that became the foundation of today's credit card. Revolving credit, where consumers pay back a loan over time with interest, like an installment account, but without a specific end date—like an open book charge account—was unlike any type of credit consumers had access to before. Revolving credit shifted the onus of deciding how much to borrow from the credit manager to the borrower, giving the consumer far more agency over borrowing. Revolving credit provided consumers with ready-access to flexible amounts of credit that was unsecured by the goods themselves. That is, no repossession was possible with revolving credit. For retailers, revolving credit offered a way to bind consumers to their stores and to get them to buy more. Despite these benefits, revolving credit was an extremely different practice of credit more suited to a time of prosperity than to wartime, which, in turn, begs the question: Why did retailers and consumers abandon their conventional credit techniques for revolving credit during World War II? Regulation W successfully curtailed the growth of consumer credit while it was in effect, but produced unexpected consequences for how businesses and consumers practiced debt, ultimately fueling the postwar credit boom.

Reform and Regulation

Even before the war, Rolf Nugent and Leon Henderson, who had worked together in the Department of Remedial Loans of the Russell Sage Foundation and who later designed Regulation W, were publishing articles like "Installment Selling and the Consumer: A Brief for Regulation," that argued for an interventionist role for the government in consumer credit.[6] Consumer credit, in their view, had grown too large and too exploitative. Installment credit was rife with consumer fraud, nonstandard contracts, and excessive finance charges. The lack of regulation, they believed, "exposed large groups of consumers to abusive practices."[7] Following the Russell Sage Foundation's success in regulating the small loan field, Nugent and Henderson imagined that regulation of installment credit would help the consumer. In 1939 when Nugent had become head of the Department of Remedial Loans at the Russell Sage Foundation, he published his landmark, *Consumer Credit and Economic Stability*, which similarly argued that installment credit exacerbated the swings of the business cycle and could be best controlled with regulation of contract lengths and down payments. Nugent believed that the Federal Reserve, with its "extensive facilities for collection and interpretation of statistical data concerning business conditions and consumer credit movements," would be the best choice to regulate installment credit.[8] Under their guidance, in 1940 the Russell Sage Foundation published, *The English Hire-Purchase Act:,1938: A Measure to Regulate Installment Selling*, whose introduction called for the creation of a government agency given "direct control over instalment [*sic*] merchants" to redress the abuses of the installment credit system modeled on the British intervention of 1938.[9]

As Americans anticipated the return to war, economists and government officials contemplated the consequences of such a decision for the economy. Presented with the opportunity to join the group creating Regulation W, Henderson and Nugent brought their earlier perspectives to bear. Nugent's idea for the Fed to directly regulate installment credit became the cornerstone of the regulation. Inflation, such as had happened during World War I, was deemed one of the greatest threats to the mobilization effort. When factories converted to war production, consumer goods would surge in price as their supply dropped. One seemingly easy option to lessen demand, and thus prices, was to reduce the available credit to consumers. By restricting credit access, Henderson and Nugent believed they could reduce the number of people who could afford to buy, thus lessening demand and replacing inflationary borrowing with disinflationary saving.

Such a control on installment credit could be effective because one quarter of all American families used the installment plan on the eve of

World War II.[10] Three-fifths of this installment borrowing was for automobiles and most of the rest was for other consumer durables, all of which grew scarce as American factories retooled for war, lessening the demand for those goods.[11] Installment credit could not be allowed to enable an "unjustifiable bidding up of prices," as Federal Reserve Chairman Marriner Eccles commented.[12]Though the Supply Priorities and Allocation Board, and more generally the massive government contracts, determined what would be produced, market prices would still react to the shortage. With "two or three buyers for each automobile," Eccles believed prices would rise quickly.[13] Credit controls would mitigate the inflationary effects of demand under such scarcity.

The perceived need to regulate consumer credit pointed to both its importance and marginality. Consumer credit represented a large enough portion of the economy so that restricting it could significantly reduce consumption. Nugent had just argued in *Consumer Credit and Economic Stability* that in wartime the need to regulate consumer credit would be enormous. While there had been, according to him, a "moderate" inflationary expansion of credit during World War I, with the "more widespread use and more general availability of consumer credit" there would be a "far more substantial" increase by 1939.[14] At the same time, consumer credit was marginal enough that cutting it back would not produce economic collapse. The economy could continue independently of consumer credit, particularly if government demand replaced consumer demand.

Restricting consumer credit nonetheless required a sudden reversal of federal policy, which had focused throughout the 1930s on expanding consumer credit access. As chapters 2 and 3 have shown, federal policy in the 1930s promoted consumer borrowing to stimulate the faltering economy. Before the United States entry into World War II, these policies remained in effect. As the economy suddenly expanded through government demand for wartime goods, an about-face in economic policy became necessary. Gone were the days of coercing demand from uncertain Depression-era consumers. Instead of fears of deflation, the dangers of inflation resurged. Altering the juggernaut of federal programs could not happen as quickly as declaring war.

From the beginning of the regulation, the Federal Reserve, guided by the Utah banker Eccles, had been anxious to regain lost power. The failure of the Fed's monetary policies to stop the Depression had led to widespread doubt in its capacity to really guide the economy. New Deal agencies of the 1930s, like the Federal Housing Administration, now commanded vast control over the flow of capital in the United States. As Eccles noted to a meeting of Federal Reserve bankers, there had been "a good deal of encroachment" on the Fed's control of the "credit mechanism" of the economy, since "Acts . . . were passed in 1933 and 1934" in which the Fed "lost a considerable amount of the power . . . over the money and credit system."[15] Regulation W would restore some of that lost institutional power, but not all. Though Eccles had come to a private understanding with Roosevelt that if any additional credit control powers were created, over housing for instance, they would go to the Fed, but existing institutional powers could not be taken away.[16]As Regulation W went into effect, the Fed had to coordinate with other branches of government whose policies also affected the credit supply. The FHA, for instance, continued to use its powers to expand the supply of housing for defense workers. At the time of Regulation W's enactment, its Title I program recommended no down payments and thirty-six month repayment plans—that diametrically opposed the Fed's anti-inflation program.[17] For the Federal Reserve, Regulation W was a way to regain lost bureaucratic power and institutional respect.

Bureaucratic fiefdoms, business practices, and consumer expectations did not change as easily as the issuance of an executive order. An adroitly managed transition called for more than well-crafted policies. It required federal regulators' careful cultivation of the consent of the governed, both business and consumer alike. The Fed, accustomed to ready obedience from banks in need of loans, never anticipated how difficult it would be to police the entire U.S. economy.

Cultivating Consent for Regulation W

Economists of the Office of Price Administration (OPA) and Federal Reserve staffs met during the summer of 1941 to iron out their vision of what a politically viable control on consumer credit could look like.[18] The OPA collaborated with the Fed, through Regulation W, to ensure that rationing would not result in inflation. Their previous experiences guided them in what was feasible and what was necessary. As chairman Eccles remarked, they were "fortunate in having a staff with real experience." These experts like Henderson and Nugent, Eccles noted, had "been giving . . . thought to the fundamental questions involved in trying to operate selective credit controls for a long time," and the regulation reflected the assumptions and conclusions borne of that experience as well as the necessities of wartime.[19] Enormous difficulties confronted these framers of the regulation, but through their cunning and expertise they devised a system that they believed would accomplish their shared goal of restraining inflation.

Nugent and Henderson hoped that the regulation would lead to other long-term changes beyond the immediate concerns of inflation in a wartime economy. At the first meeting of the Federal Reserve to work out its tentative draft, Eccles announced that it was a "momentous meeting" to discuss Regulation W since it was not only an entirely new "field of action and responsibility" for the Fed, but also because "it may turn out to be a permanent instrument of control in the [Federal Reserve] System."[20] The immediate consequences to the defense effort were paramount, but as Nugent and Henderson and the rest of the staff framed the new control they imagined it to be a permanent one, along with the Fed's other powers in the economy, following Nugent's plans in *Consumer Credit and Economic Stability*. For reformers like Nugent and Henderson, the regulation presented the opportunity for success at the federal level that the Russell Sage Foundation had had at the state level in the 1920s and 30s with its small loan law campaign. Regulation W could be the way to control unscrupulous installment credit as effectively as loan sharks did under the small loan laws.

For those opposed to Nugent's substantial reforms, like the vice-chairman of the Federal Reserve, the Atlanta banker Ronald Ransom, the chief task of the regulation was helping the Fed in its primary responsibility to restrain macroeconomic inflation. Regulating the microeconomy was best left to other institutions—or just the free market.[21] Ransom believed consumer credit was "very difficult" to regulate because it was not one industry but an interconnected system that extended across many sectors. The consumer credit industry encompassed a wide variety of businesses—auto dealer and furniture retailers' installment plans, department stores' charge accounts, industrial lenders' companies, and commercial banks' personal loans. Balancing those sometimes contradictory interests would take extraordinary political and policy adroitness. While credit appeared equivalent macroeconomically, at the level of the firm restricting consumer credit could have wildly different effects. Restricting cash loans and installment credit, for instance, had a more dire effect on those businesses—like small loan lenders, auto dealers, finance companies, and retailers who sold predominately on the installment plan—than on firms for whom consumer lending formed only a portion of their business, such as department stores, or firms for whom the wartime economy presented alternative sources of profit, like commercial banks and auto manufacturers. Small loan lenders and finance companies had nothing to sell but their money, but commercial banks, for example, could invest in wartime production. Regulators would have to mediate between all the different interest groups and still come up with a workable regulation that contained inflation but did not bankrupt businesses.

Business consent, so lacking during the NRA, was carefully cultivated during the creation of Regulation W and the NRA's shortcomings came up frequently as industry representatives and regulators discussed the limits of Regulation W.[22] Leon Henderson, for instance, had worked at the NRA during its failed attempt to regulate finance companies in the 1930s.[23] During the first Fed meeting, Ransom prayed, only half in jest, "If the Lord is kind to us, this will not be a repetition of N.R.A."[24] It was, as Ransom remarked, "in the light of many of the experiences all of us had with the N.R.A. that we have approached the writing of this regulation."[25] Wanting to regulate consumer credit, but also not overstep the constitution, the regulators hemmed to the less extreme modes of enforcement: inspection, regulation, and fines.[26] Imprisonment was not discussed, but neither was exactly who would handle these inspections or who would prosecute infractions. Written with business interests in mind, the regulators hoped compliance during wartime would be voluntary. The regulators, more than counting on the negative enforcement, hoped that most sellers would "desire to comply in good faith" during the time of war and that "trade associations and the leaders in the different lines" would convince their colleagues to conform to the regulation.[27]

The Fed requested suggestions from bankers, economists, businessmen and others whose support would be necessary to maintain public legitimacy. Because of the need for business support, as the Board planned out its regulation, it also sought the feedback, as Chairman Eccles noted, of the institutions most "vitally interested" in the proposal.[28] For the regulation to be successful, the Fed needed the support of the manufacturers, distributors, and retailers who sold on the installment plan.[29] As Ransom told the first conference held of those involved in the installment trade, "without your full cooperation, without your good will, without your understanding that we are trying to do a job in a national emergency and in the public interest, we shall not make headway."[30] Whatever their feelings about government regulation, the Fed hoped that appeals to patriotism would sway the support of business.

The public support of businesses and consumers depended on how necessary the regulations appeared, and while the legal justification came from stopping inflation, public support required that the regulators rhetorically frame the regulation as a way to save scarce war materiel, like the OPA rationing program.[31] War aims could be easily defended, but not more abstract economic ideas. Citizens, even those with considerable profits at stake, understood the need to conserve strategic war materials. The abstract danger of inflation did not emotionally sway retailers and consumers like steel needed for a gun. The further a good was from defense materials, Ransom suspected—all too accurately it turned out—"administrative problems might become increasingly difficult," since sellers and buyers alike would begin to resist the regulation's imposition.[32]

By giving business input in its creation, the writers of Regulation W believed that they could win the consent of the governed. The Fed regulators hoped that the regulation could be initially enacted weakly, achieve business buy-in, and then, if necessary, be made stricter. The regulation's initial scope was, as Nugent planned, "sweeping but mild," encompassing all installment sales less than $1,000.[33] Ransom remarked that they would "much prefer to tighten [the regulations] slowly rather than put them on tight and then loosen them."[34] The kinks in the system could be worked out and then, when ready, the controls on credit and inflation truly enforced. The regulation was, above all else, malleable. The Fed wanted to act quickly but it also wanted to leave opportunity for revision and reflection. Ransom emphasized equally that the regulation was to be "flexible" and "open to amendment in the light of experience and . . . changing conditions."[35] While weakness produced consent and flexibility allowed technocratic precision, over time they also allowed Regulation W to alter its function in subtle and unexpected ways. As political and economic pressures were brought to bear, unintended effects on credit practices were created.

Inside and Outside Regulation W

Proceeding with trepidation and fearful of irritating business leaders, the Federal Reserve implemented a loose version of Regulation W on September 1, 1941. Yet for its supposed mildness, the regulation even in its weak form reshaped the entire installment credit industry. It changed the way millions of consumers and hundreds of thousands of retailers conducted their everyday business, disrupting large corporations and sometimes entirely destroying small companies. At the same time, the regulation neglected widely used kinds of credit—charge accounts and personal loans—that could be easily used to evade the restrictions on installment credit. In reshaping American borrowing, the types of credit inside the regulation mattered as much as those outside.

Following Nugent's framework in *Consumer Credit and Economic Stability*, Regulation W specified the minimum down payment and maximum contract length of a wide range of goods, but these terms were often at odds with the conventions of installment practice. Eighteen months seemed to be the maximum reasonable contract length to the regulators, with all goods requiring between 15 and 33 percent down payment, but these numbers had little to do with how installment credit worked in the real world.[36] Autos commonly had twenty-four month contracts and refrigerators thirty-six, but most installment sales were considerably less than eighteen months.[37] Such a regulation, Nugent believed nonetheless, would "have no more than a mildly restrictive effect on all but a few important commodities."[38] Though the Fed tried to be clear that these were only minimums and that retailers could at their discretion always demand higher down payments and shorter contracts, misunderstandings arose for both retailers and consumers. At the same time, however, the regulation covered nearly all consumer durables, prescribing maximum contracts lengths and minimum down payments for a wide variety of goods. Though Nugent had initially suggested that the regulation be no tighter than the most conservative lending practices, as enacted, the regulation was more uneven.[39]

Conventional contract lengths were often longer than those of Regulation W, yet at the same time the down payments were more onerous than were typical in the installment business. Even as the contract lengths were not particularly restrictive, the larger down payments roused the ire of installment-selling retailers.[40] David Craig, president of the American Retail Federation, felt that requiring "20 per cent down payment is more of a departure from current practice than [was] needed."[41] Even though such payments had clear precedent in past credit practices, the regulation compelled merchants to ask for a greater down payment than their customers were accustomed to by 1940. This frustration led even patriotic retailers to look for alternatives.

One alternative was personal loans, which, though regulated offered a different structure than installment credit. Money could never be for just one purpose. If the regulations were to work, personal loans, whose cash could be used for any purpose including buying consumer durables, had to be restricted.[42] Without the requirement for a down payment, a cash loan would be easier to acquire than an installment contract. Though thought of separately, cash loans could just as easily pay for medical bills as for a new washing machine. Borrowed money could also substitute for other expenditures. A loan could be used for rent, which would free up cash to buy a restricted article.[43] Personal loans for "medical expenses, funeral, grocery or other similar legitimate and necessitous bills [which had] no direct impact on supply," as Edward Brown, the chairman of the federal advisory council and president of First National Bank of Chicago, wrote, could seriously undermine popular support of the regulation.[44] Yet, once borrowers had the money in their hands, what seemed important might change. B. E. Henderson, president of the Household Finance Corporation, a national small loan company, said that for many borrowers the "purposes change over night."[45] Henderson did not think that his clients would always intentionally deceive, but he also did not assume that every dollar borrowed for a hospital bill necessarily went to the hospital. Borrowers might receive a $100 for a bill and have some left over to use for other purposes.[46] The regulation, however, expected each dollar to go for the purpose intended, which not only contradicted established practice, but the limits of human self-control.

When the representatives of many commercial banks' personal loan departments, as well as those of industrial banks and credit unions, met to discuss the proposed regulation, they found Regulation W's requirements unsettling for both their profits and the social purpose of personal lending.[47] Personal loan departments, National City Bank's Roger Steffan wrote, would find the regulation "so disruptive to established fundamentals" as to be "dangerous."[48] Facing this bureaucratic intrusion, Steffan thought, borrowers instead of taking out a reputable loan with the bank's personal loan department, would "apply for a second loan at another bank, loan company, or even a loan shark" rather than "going through the red tape."[49] Edgar Fowler, secretary of the American Association of Personal Finance companies, thought that deprived of one source of credit, borrowers would find another; "the whole history of loan shark legislation since 1890 proves their behavior."[50] Applied to small loans, Steffan feared the regulation's "economic dynamite" would "explode" the anti–loan shark reforms of the past twenty years, pushing borrowers to loan sharks who would ask fewer questions.[51]

As much as Regulation W's proscriptions did cover personal loans and installment credit, there were important gaps, most importantly on open book credit.[52] Open book credit's absence from the regulation mattered the most of all because it represented such a huge fraction of consumer borrowing. In 1938, $7.9 billion was transacted on such charge accounts, or nearly one quarter of all retail sales.[53] Open book credit, Ransom explained to businessmen and other Fed officials, was simply too difficult to regulate. With no contracts and no scheduled payments, their potential for regulation was nightmarish. For reform-minded regulators, open book credit was not harmful because borrowers paid no interest and never faced repossession.

Yet for retailers, the absence of regulation offered an obvious way to evade Regulation W. The "thousands, possibly millions of instances" of open book credit, as one hardware trade representative put it, ought to be regulated as well as installment credit, since they had the same economic effect.[54] If customers could borrow on unregulated open book accounts, the trade representative persisted, then would this not lead to a "situation where everyone would sell on open account"?[55] The shifting of installment credit to open book credit would fundamentally undermine the regulation.

Fed officials dismissed the regulation of open book credit because of how it was financially practiced and culturally understood. Open book credit lacked installment credit's contract, interest, and repayment schedule. Without these three features, finance companies would not buy the debt from the retailers. Without the ability to resell consumer paper, charge account sellers could not afford to extend nearly as much credit as installment sellers.[56] Evaders of the regulation who sought to substitute open book credit for installment credit, as one Fed banker conjectured, would quickly exhaust their "general line of borrowing power."[57] Unless retailers wanted to get themselves into debt, they had to limit open account credit. Installment credit, backed in the last instance by commercial banks, was a potentially massive source for inflationary funds, which gave it a much higher priority for regulation. The cultural assumption that charge accounts were repaid monthly obfuscated the reality that these accounts often went unpaid for many months. Even though Ransom and the other Fed framers realized that "a good many open book accounts [ran] for long periods without payment," the difficulty associated with their regulation and the cultural assumptions underpinning their extension made such regulation impossible.[58] This decision to regulate installment but not open book accounts, led to, what some thought, were unexpected consequences for Fed policy and business practice.

The Effects of Regulation W

Consumers, when the Fed first enacted the regulation, were unsure what to make of the new regulation. The uncertainty of the regulation paired with the government's authority made interpretation of the regulation both necessary and powerful. While retailers and regulators spent large amounts of money on advertising in trying to correct these misunderstandings, consumers caught up in the uncertain remaking of the installment credit relation, began to assert their own interpretations of what the government wanted.[59] Though the regulation did not require merchants to extend credit as liberally as permitted by the regulation, consumers often did not feel the same way, misinterpreting Regulation W's maximum contract lengths as government-mandated minimums.[60] For many consumers, the government decreed the proper lengths of contracts and amounts of down payments. In its desire, as Ransom explained, "not to put the brakes on quickly or to cause too much trouble," the Fed had inadvertently created a new credit norm for the American shopper.[61] Where the Fed regulators saw a maximum of eighteen months, consumers saw only eighteen months. For merchants to refuse to extend eighteen months of credit now seemed somehow unfair to their customers. The regulation had begun to remake socially acceptable contract lengths.

From the first announcement that regulation was coming, people rushed out to buy on the installment plan, fearing credit would soon be outlawed.[62] This reaction drove the Fed to quickly disseminate the regulation and choose a fast deadline, before the frightened shoppers drove up prices. Despite their efforts, Roscoe Rau, of the National Retail Furniture Association, reported to the Fed that all the publicity surrounding Regulation W gave consumers the "wrong impression."[63] An informal survey of auto buyers, when asked their opinion of Regulation W, found that they chose "confused" about 40 percent of the time when given the choice of "favorable," "unfavorable," or "confused."[64] Confusion extended beyond autos, however. Some consumers thought the regulation was a "tax" or that the down payment on furniture (one-fifth) was the same as the more widely discussed down payment on automobiles (one-third).[65] Retailers were confused as well. By June of 1942 about 170,000 firms had registered as installment sellers under Regulation W.[66] Of three thousand registration forms sent by retailers in the Richmond Federal Reserve district, about half contained errors.[67]

Retailers felt the effects of Regulation W almost immediately. Sales fell, not only because of fewer goods but because of reduced credit. October auto sales on the installment plan fell to two-fifths the level of a year earlier. The Dallas Federal Reserve Bank claimed that total auto sales in its area were only one-fourth of the previous year. In meetings with Dallas area auto dealers, bankers, and finance company owners, every single one reported that sales had "dropped materially."[68] From August to September, furniture sales on the installment plan dropped by nearly a third, and refrigerator sales fell by 85 percent.[69] As the months wore on, it became clear that even as durable goods sales continued to drop, installment sales fell even faster.[70] In October 1942, installment sales of furniture were down 35 percent from the previous year.[71] From August, 1941 to October, 1942, outstanding auto debt dropped from $2,313 million to $600 million, or nearly 75 percent.[72] By 1943, more money was being lent on furniture than on autos.[73] Department stores reported a 40 percent drop in installment accounts receivable from January to October of 1942.[74] Even the venerable mail order company Spiegel's reported installment sales and outstanding accounts had fallen to one-quarter of their prewar levels, which the secretary-treasurer of the company attributed entirely to Regulation W.[75]

Borrowers also cut back on personal loans. Personal finance companies and industrial banks also lost loan volume, but at only half the rate of commercial banks.[76] The outstanding loans of personal loan departments of commercial banks' loan outstanding dropped from $732 million to $460 million—37 percent—from September 1941 to September 1942.[77] Despite their more rapid decline, the regulation hit other personal loan lenders harder than commercial banks since commercial banks could fall back on business loans for firms expanding wartime production. Demand for business loans, the weakness of which had drawn commercial banks into the consumer credit business, returned with gusto as the government's need for production expanded. As Chrysler, for example, stopped making autos and started making tanks, they required a $100 million loan to switch their factories over.[78] So much demand existed for wartime business loans that the American Bankers Association feared a scarcity of investment capital and called for voluntary curtailing of money for non-defense purposes.[79] Only $153 billion of the $380 billion spent by the federal government in the war years came from taxes. The remainder was borrowed from the private sector, including $95 billion from commercial banks.[80] Other financial institutions and consumer retailers, however, sharply felt the effects of Regulation W and began to speak out.

Regulation W's success brought complaint from business owners, who as the reality of falling profit set in, began to fear for their enterprises. A Dallas department store manager told the head of the Dallas Fed that despite the reduced number of refrigerators produced, his store was still unable "to sell anywhere near the number it was able to obtain" because of Regulation W.[81] Furniture stores selling heavily on the installment plan experienced painful contractions. As feared, when contract terms constricted, profits on the loans fell. The National Retail Furniture Association reported that revenue from credit fell by as much as half for some stores. The fears of some businessmen were exacerbated by inaccurate information from their own organizations. In October, for instance, the National Automobile Dealers Association sent out a bulletin to its membership that the Fed intended to raise the minimum down payment to 50 percent and drop the maximum contract length to twelve months on automobiles. Finance companies dealing in automobile loans also read this bulletin. Such a regulation would have more than halved their business. On the basis of just this one rumor, more than a hundred letters were sent to the Federal Reserve.[82]

Consumers' consent, as much as that of business, had to be delicately managed. Evidence from confidential internal Federal Reserve meetings suggests that regulators often based decisions as much on preserving Regulation W's legitimacy as inflation or wartime need. The restriction on pianos, for instance, was not in the initial regulation but put in only after the vice-president of the Philadelphia Federal Reserve, C. A. Sienkiewicz, remarked that too many of the restrictions smacked of "class legislation."[83] By restricting goods with upper-class cachet, like pianos, the regulation hoped to avoid what Sienkiewicz called the "appearance of discrimination." Regulations on pianos were not needed to fight the axis, but to win public opinion. Sewing machines were, for the same reason, *not* restricted. Since sewing machines were, as Ransom explained, "limited so largely to a class, that by including them and involving the women of the country specifically in this regulation we bring down upon our heads a pretty solid front of opposition."[84] Ransom explained that organs, for fear of "country churches" organizing against the regulation, were also unregulated.[85] Though conceived to fight a straightforward economic agenda, the regulation framers constantly thought about the regulation in terms of practical politics. Some Fed officials objected to such a politically minded plan, calling for a straight economic approach regardless of "political expediency."[86] The reality of the situation, however, required such guile. It was not wise to have a class of people disciplined by the regulation to organize politically around a strong symbol of home such as the sewing machine or a symbol of religion such as the church organ.

As initially written, Regulation W disproportionately affected the urban poor, who did not have access to the open credit of higher-end retailers. Low-end clothing stores that sold on credit witnessed a fantastic collapse in profits. The Association of Credit Apparel Stores, a group of 451 stores that catered to lower-income patrons and sold 97 percent of their goods on installment credit, told the Fed that their businesses "[could] not survive under the regulation as now written."[87] Like furniture stores, nearly half of their sales were "add-on's," which were restricted by the regulation and whereas their down payments averaged only 7 percent, for repeat customers there was no down payment.[88] Prices at installment stores were generally higher, with a 55 percent markup compared to 40 percent markup at cash or charge account stores, but lending standards were low.[89] With the regulation extended to clothing, however, shoppers, who frequented them because of the easy credit, stopped buying.

As their 97 percent installment business constituted only 4 percent of all American installment sales, the Association of Credit Apparel Stores felt that the regulation disproportionately targeted them and, because of their small importance, had little effect on inflation, while at the same time hurting lower-income Americans.[90] Charge accounts simply accounted for more buying. In 1939, charge accounts had nearly ten times the sales volume of installment sales of clothing.[91] In contrast to the installment clothing stores, during the first few months of 1942 sales rose at department stores, where cash customers and middle-income charge customers, fearing wartime scarcity, bought absurd amounts of clothing. While low-income people had their buying curtailed, the Association argued, those able to buy with "cash or on charge accounts" had gone on a "buying spree" on woolen goods all out of proportion to their needs.[92] Installment clothing stores were marginal to the economy, but not marginal to their customers, who had no other way of buying them. Buying for a $1 down and a $1 a week at stores like New York's Dejay Clothing and Washington D.C.'s Liberal Credit Clothing, seemed unsavory to the Fed officials, but it gave low-income Americans clothing that they wanted when they wanted it.[93]

Very clearly, Fed officials aimed Regulation W at a class of people, if not the working class, then at least those who either chose to or had to use installment plans to finance their purchases. Listed articles could always be paid for in cash, regardless of the regulation, but only if the buyer had the cash to buy. At the same time, however, installment plans were not eliminated. Credit was still available. A refrigerator that normally sold on a thirty-six month contract could still be sold on an eighteen-month contract. As Nugent pointed out, for a good quality refrigerator, which sold for $150 in 1941, the difference between a thirty-six month contract and an eighteen-month contract was $5.00 per month versus $7.50 per month.[94] Ransom believed that part of Roosevelt's support for the control was that he did not want workers' "increasing income to run away because of a run-away in prices."[95] Regardless of class, if something was really desired, $2.50 could probably be found to purchase it.

As the wartime economy kicked off the long postwar boom, however, many working Americans began to find that they could come by $2.50 more easily than during the Depression.[96] As Carl Parry, one of the economists who designed Regulation W remarked, it was not the high-income group that was getting the defense economy's "new money," but the lower income.[97] The high-income group always had money, but working-class consumers had been deprived since the 1920s. This regulation restricted the group most likely to spend the money they received, not out of profligacy, but a decade of deprivation. Of course, if working-class Americans—who had been hit so hard in the 1930s—found themselves with unprecedented amounts of money in defense jobs, saved that money instead of spending it, then the regulation would not be a bad thing, so the thinking went. If it was paternalist class legislation, Regulation W had the best of intentions for both workers and the economy.

The difficulty was not, then, finding that $2.50 for many working-class Americans in the wartime economy if they really wanted that refrigerator, but in adjusting salesmen and consumers' expectations and habits. Conventionally, refrigerators had long-term repayment plans because sellers sold them at the per month price that ice delivery would cost. If consumers were used to paying X dollars per month for ice, they could pay the same X dollars and get the use of a modern electric refrigerator, which after three years they would own outright. Such pricing schemes made installments fit the conventions of prices and budgets that people had for their daily expenses. More than simply denying the lower-income consumer commodities like refrigerators, which were "really doing something for the health of his family," as one Fed official criticized, the threat of Regulation W was in the unraveling of credit conventions that made buying and selling easier for both consumer and seller.[98]

Regulation W disrupted these conventions of price and practice for both retailers and consumers. Some companies collapsed, others turned to alternative sources of profit, while still others adapted, attempting innovative new forms of credit. New market constraints created new market challenges and opportunities. The Fed might call these experiments evasions within a loose regulation, but to firms trying to get their share of the wartime profit, novel credit practices were strictly business.

Tightening the Regulation and the Spread of Hybrid Credit

The Federal Reserve regulators believed in categories. To them, the names of different kinds of credit were not just words, but scientific descriptions of the real world. Regulation W's effectiveness turned on the reality of these distinctions. Without a way to describe commercial activities, those activities could not be controlled. Regulators asserted that, "it [was] recognized by credit men that instalment [*sic*] credit is suited to one type of customer and charge credit to another," but even as they insisted among themselves that these distinctions between credit were real, retailers and consumers found ways to make new kinds of credit so as to evade the Fed's control.[99]

Part of the difficulty with regulating consumer credit was the artifice of the distinction between charge accounts and installment credit. Regulators complained that the two forms of credit had a "considerable variation in detail" and also "overlapped a great deal."[100] Fed definitions of credit meant less than retailers' practices of credit. Merchants, especially the smaller ones, answering to no one on how they ran their credit business, created whatever jury-rigged system worked. Charge accounts were for convenience and installment plans were for using future income.[101] Regulation W, not the demands of commerce, required merchants to adhere perfectly to definitions of credit in order to obey the regulations. Compliant retailers aligned their credit systems with the Fed's regulations, creating a more homogenous credit environment for borrowers and lenders alike. These retailers offered credit, Brown explained, "on the basis of the regulation's definitions rather than on the basis of the terms used by the merchants."[102] Ironically, as Regulation W defined how to practice certain kinds of credit, all a retailer needed to do was to invent a new kind of credit, outside the regulations, to give customers what they wanted—more borrowing power.

The Fed anticipated trouble with "hybrid" types of credit that were somewhere between installment credit and charge accounts. Charge account borrowers often used their accounts to spread payments out over several months. Brown believed that this practice had its roots in the "custom" created during the depression when merchants pressured customers to keep buying and to pay when they could. The practice was still called a charge account, he believed, because of the "opprobrium attached in some people's minds to the word 'installment.'" Merchants who extended charge credit to customers unable to pay off their debts in one payment not only violated the regulation but violated the customer's "good faith."[103] Giving charge accounts to those who could only pay over time would violate the regulation on installment credit, even if such partial payments were not formally required.[104]

Despite the existence of this system before Regulation W, regulators attributed the increase in the use of the serially liquidated charge account to the regulation's tightening grip. While some sellers used charge accounts in "good faith," Fed officials like E. A. Heath also believed that other merchants "obviously acted in bad faith in establishing so-called charge accounts for the express purpose of avoiding down payment requirements."[105] Fed investigators found that most stores using charge accounts with partial payments had, until the regulation, been strictly installment stores. The stores continued to provide installment payment books, verbally told customers that they ought to pay bi-weekly or monthly, and advertised "open a charge account and pay $___a week. No down payment."[106] Customers familiar with paying in installments, even if not told explicitly, would continue to pay in installments out of habit, the regulators believed. Charge account or not, lower-income "customers have been educated to instalment and almost inevitably will pay for goods purchased on credit on an instalment basis."[107] Of course, customers learned how to repay their debts not only through installment credit or charge accounts at department stores, but through charge accounts kept with grocers and butchers as well. They learned to repay debts when they could for this convenience credit. To institute a new definition of charge accounts to mean single repayment, as one regulator suggested, the Fed would not only violate customs surrounding charge accounts but begin to make the accounts more like business loans, which had interest.[108]

There were clear provisions for the regulation of charge accounts and installment credit, but how were these partial-payment charge accounts that seemed to intentionally blur the categories of control handled? How could they control lending outside of these categories? How could they decide what was one kind of credit and not the other? The regulators, though exhaustive lists of the qualities of the different forms of credit existed, seemed to even deny the possibility of hybrid forms of credit.[109] The Fed regulators debated endlessly around this problem, which they called the "Twilight Zone" question, both for its liminal, otherworldly quality and for the difficulty in seeing a solution.[110]

In the spring of 1942, the gaps in Regulation W became too big to ignore, particularly on charge accounts. Open book charge accounts, despite the Fed's early hopes to the contrary, had become a serious impediment to the regulation by 1942. Installment sellers and financiers complained that a lot of their business had moved to "department stores which [sold] on charge accounts."[111] Merchants and consumers used charge accounts to "avoid the instalment credit requirements" through "serial liquidation" of the charge account.[112] Stores intentionally allowed customers to use charge accounts to pay for goods over time, rather than just at the end of the month. Rumors had begun to flow to the Fed of department stores that would place the goods on the charge account to evade the regulation if a customer had a frozen installment account.[113] What began as an obscure maneuver to avoid Regulation W was becoming a "widespread and growing abuse of the charge account privilege," dangerously disturbing the perfect categories necessary for effective regulation.[114]

Ronald Ransom tightened the control of Regulation W, as he had imagined doing from the very beginning. The Federal Reserve extended the regulation to encompass charge accounts in the hope that such restrictions would help stop evasions. The charge account regulations were expected to make Regulation W have an even greater effect on consumer credit. The Fed tried to force retailers to only use charge accounts for convenience credit—not for long-term financing. Charge purchases would now have to be paid off within three months—on the tenth day of the second month to be exact—or the account would be frozen.[115] Charge accounts that went too long without repayment would be converted into formal installment plans, limited in size and duration by Regulation W. To help borrowers repay their charge debts, Fed officials promoted a program that would allow retailers to convert overdue charge account debt into installment debt, placing such serially-liquidating charge accounts back in the regulatory categories of Regulation W.

At the same time, installment credit also became more restrictive. Regulating charge accounts was only one part of Ransom's broad plan, by the spring of 1942, to reduce the outstanding consumer debt by nearly half over the course of the next year, from $9.5 billion to $5.5 billion.[116] Debt reduction soaked up demand and, equally importantly, allowed the consumer to borrow more during the postwar peace when many economists feared a return to depression. One Fed official declared that it was the Fed's responsibility that the debtor was "sold on the fact that this is the time to get out of debt so that he will not be overburdened when the defense program is over."[117] To this end, the Fed expanded Regulation W to cover more goods, shorten contract lengths, and raise down payments.[118] Regulating well beyond the goods needed for the war, Regulation W now covered luggage, athletic equipment, film projectors, and even opera glasses.[119] By this point, the Fed's restrictions were all more conservative than prewar lending practices, virtually guaranteeing the resistance of business. Though Ransom wanted retailers to adhere more strictly to the rules of Regulation W by further restricting installment credit, the Fed increased retailers' incentive to find ways to evade.

As the new regulation on charge accounts went into effect in the spring of the 1942, retailers froze accounts across America. In New York, retail executives estimated that stores froze a quarter of all accounts.[120] In the months preceding the enforcement's deadline, customers had made unprecedented "heavy payments" on their debts, retailers claimed. Whether it was for fear of losing the convenience of the accounts, or as James Malloy, the president of the Credit Bureau of Greater New York and the credit manager of Abraham & Strauss, believed, "the patriotic response of customers in cleaning up their credit indebtedness in line with the anti-inflation program of President Roosevelt," charge account payments came in at an unheard of rate.[121] Retailers believed that there would be an overall shift from credit to cash. They were right. Over the next few years, cash sales rose much faster than either charge account or installment sales. Even as cash sales rose, credit practices changed as stores embraced the serially liquidated charge account.

The Fed hoped the conversion would force businesses not to use charge accounts to avoid the controls on installment credit, but retailers resisted being pushed back into the Fed's categories. Department stores, even when pushed, seemed at first to rarely use it, preferring to prevent their customers from buying anything else rather than turning their charge accounts into installment accounts. In 1943, a survey of Ransom's own sixth federal reserve district, encompassing most of the South, found most stores prohibited the conversion and those few that had not used it had only a few per month.[122] For instance, Burdine's, a department store in Miami, preferred to close 7 percent of consumer's charge accounts per month rather than convert them to installment credit, claiming that Burdine's did not want to see the customer "getting himself deeper in debt by charging merchandise on open account."[123] Such noble sentiments might have been true, but it might equally have been the case that the retailers did not want to alienate good customers by forcing them onto an installment plan.

Retailers that adopted the serially liquidated charge accounts that evaded regulation were hostile to the Fed's increased attention to the problem. In Iowa, for instance, the retailers felt, "credit paying habits [had] apparently stabilized in accord with the Regulation" and this increased objection to serially paid charge accounts was unfair and would disrupt consumer confidence in the regulation and the government at large.[124] Fed official Heath met with many of Des Moines's merchants, small loan bankers, and credit men, whom he described as "definitely antagonistic."[125] Local businessmen could not understand how further regulation was meant to help the war effort and, citing the sacrifices made by Iowa's citizens already, demanded an explanation—such as the president of the largest women's clothing store in Des Moines, for "a requirement so ridiculous" as that on serially liquidated accounts.[126] People in Iowa had always paid a little bit at a time on charge accounts; restricting payment to one lump sum was "completely foreign to common practices."[127] Despite the similarity to installment credit's serial payments, the distinction to the merchants was clear, since they made "no specific agreement to make periodic payments."[128] The president of the Retail Credit Association of Des Moines objected that their credit could be classified with the installment credit of "lower priced stores and lines of merchandise."[129] Disrupting consumer practices of serial payment, moreover, was dangerous to collecting since money "easily slip[s] away for other purposes."[130] For these retailers, and others like them across the country, Regulation W provided incentives to develop new forms of hybrid credit.

Most retailers did comply with the new regulation, using new technologies like the Charga-Plate and the Addressograph to efficiently track their customers' accounts. These new technologies made the freezing of accounts easier and as they fit neatly into the regulation, and their use spread quickly throughout the country during the war. The use of Addressographs and Charga-Plates mechanized payment. The Charga-Plate was a metal card imprinted with the name and account number of the customer. The Addressograph allowed for the mechanical addressing of charge accounts. In combination, these two technologies, both of which existed before the war but were promoted by the account tracking needs of Regulation W, allowed for easier surveillance of customer accounts. In Germantown, Pennsylvania, Allen's department store, for instance, transferred the Addressograph plates of charge accounts in default to a separate drawer. Without the Addressograph plate, additional charges could not be made, and at the same time, notifications could be easily mailed in bulk, allowing Allen's to comply with Regulation W.[131] Because of their convenience for tracking accounts under Regulation W, these new devices flourished.

Charga-Plates served a similar function, equating a number with each customer and their address that would mark a sales slip as the charge was made. Initially stores kept Charga-Plates at the checkout, instead of letting customers carry them around. Some stores like Cleveland's upscale Halle Bros. Co., gave customers small paper "credit cards" to show the cashier.[132] The credit card had the Charga-plate number and the customer's name on it. If the customer had the card, the cashier did not have to look their name up in the long, repetitive list of numbers. Frozen accounts would not be on the list.[133] Though cumbersome, plates and lists of numbers were easier to keep track of than numbers written in log books. Typical of the credit cards was one from Buffalo's J. N. Adam store that told its customers that "charge accounts are now regulated by the Government. However, those customers who pay their bills . . . need have no concern regarding the Government regulations."[134] J. N. Adam sent each customer a new credit card every month if their account had been paid. The card implored the customer to "always carry it with you!" and reminded them that, "your credit card is evidence of a promptly paid account."[135] Signing one's name to the card meant you were the upstanding kind of person who paid your bills. Department store credit cards, from their very inception, were invested with the morality of credit as well as the mechanisms of surveillance.

Despite regulators' efforts, the charge account continued to hybridize to avoid the pressure of the regulation. Retailers evading the regulation promoted a new kind of charge account that customers paid back flexibly over time. Retailers that obeyed the regulation expanded the use of new technologies to track individual charge accounts, reducing the cost of offering them to customers. Though installment credit continued to have the highest outstanding levels, other practices of debt began to emerge that supplemented and sometimes substituted for installment credit. The serially liquidated charge account and the Charga-Plate were the first steps toward a new consumer credit practice—revolving credit—that would be the basis of the modern credit card.[136]

The Transition to the Postwar

Following Ransom's tightening in 1942, Regulation W's scope continued largely unchanged through the remainder of the war. Small adjustments were made, but the larger features of the program remained. Consumer debt fell tremendously, as Ransom had planned, from $2.4 billion at the end of 1941 to $455 million at the end of 1945.[137] At the end of the war, the regulation even began to loosen as the Fed decided to end controls on the ever-contentious charge accounts.[138]

Yet as the end of the war appeared in sight, Fed regulators met with business representatives in January of 1944 to decide whether or not Regulation W should continue into the peacetime. A Fed regulator reported that at a 1944 meeting of New York commercial bankers, economists, small loan lenders, and department store executives, there was a general fear that removing or relaxing the regulation after the war might "be damaging to the nation's entire credit picture and would be undesirable from a social point of view."[139] Too much credit would encourage

Americans to over-borrow. Returning to the installment credit of the 1930s might also, they feared, bring back the Depression as well. Fears of postwar inflation resulting from pent-up wartime demand and a lack of goods could be a good reason for the regulation, claimed John Paddi of the commercial bank Manufacturers Trust Company.[140]

As the war ended and peacetime appeared imminent, however, many different kinds of firms began to express their dissatisfaction with the regulation. Stores that relied on more liberal credit policies, rather than merchandizing, were increasingly more likely to oppose the regulation. Expressing a common position, clothing-store executive J. A. Kaufman, president of the Warwick's clothing chain based in New York, felt that the regulation had accomplished its wartime aims by reducing indebtedness, but as the war was coming to an end its purpose had been "completely served."[141] The Retail Credit Institute (RCI), a trade association of credit-heavy retail merchants, wrote a letter to Truman calling for the end to controls.[142] Nathan Sachs, the president of the RCI, remarked that such regulation would "be the beginning of the end of private enterprise and distribution in this country." Ample credit was needed for returning veterans to "re-equip their homes . . . after migration to a new environment" occasioned by wartime shifts in the location of industry.[143] Credit restrictions, as well, Sachs argued, would encourage workers to cash their savings to enjoy a "progressive standard of living" when that standard could, instead, be borrowed for.

Many retailers at the end of World War II remained uncertain about the strange new revolving credit emerging organically from the interstices of Regulation W. Toward the end of the war, revolving credit came up during a discussion between Fed officials and prominent department store managers. Kenneth Richmond, vice-president of New York's Abraham & Strauss, had "never gone in for revolving credit but [thought he] may have made a mistake."[144] Other prominent businessmen, at war's end, persisted in their skepticism of revolving credit. Representatives of Macy's, while discussing revolving credit with a Fed representative, were leery of a credit system that "ke[pt] the customer continuously in debt."[145] Revolving credit, with less structure than installment credit, supposedly "stimulate[d] credit" and sales, while still having more "firmly fixed" limits than a charge account.[146] Revolving credit was supposed to give the customer more flexibility and the store additional sales. Much as it might want more sales, Macy's did not want to keep its customers in perpetual debt. What would that say about the kind people who shopped at Macy's?

While opinions varied on whether credit regulation would help retailers, there was little disagreement over whether credit itself would help sales. A national survey reported in the *New York Times* found that

66 percent of retailers favored easing regulations[147] What retailers completely agreed upon was the desire to expand the use of credit in their businesses. Ninety-eight percent of retailers "plan[ned] to go after more charge account business after the war," citing the need to expand volume, increase customer loyalty, and help workers maintain their savings.[148] Ninety-six percent of retailers believed that credit would increase sales and that "credit [was] a more powerful selling force than cash." Credit was seen as the gateway to increased sales. The clock could not be turned back to 1940. Charga-Plates, Addressographs, serially-liquidating charge accounts in the twilight zone, strict charge account due dates, and the equivalence between installment and charge account credit had all become well-known practices.

Regulation W's continued existence after World War II, however, was uncertain, as the emergency that had legally justified it under the Trading with the Enemy Act ended. The Fed regulators, however uncertain about the future of the regulation, were certain in their desire to continue it and to show they could be responsible in relaxing as well as tightening the regulation. In the Fed's annual report to Congress in 1946, they reaffirmed the importance of regulating consumer credit to prevent both inflation and depression, since there was, the Fed officials believed, no way to prevent "excessive expansion and contraction except governmental regulation" of installment credit.[149] Amendments continued to be issued if only, as acting Governor Evans wrote, for "'symbolic significance' . . . to remind people that Regulation W is still in existence . . . and to show that the Board is still of no mind to relax the regulation."[150] Given the power over consumer credit, the Federal Reserve did not casually relinquish it but merely loosened it until it had no effect, creating no need to explicitly take the power away.

Charga-Plate in the Postwar Era

The new revolving credit practices developed during World War II persisted into the postwar period, even when no longer regulated. While half of stores loosened their installment terms, only about a tenth of them loosened charge accounts.[151] Eighty-eight percent of stores maintained the end of the second month policy created under Regulation W.[152] Following the war, revolving credit and the Charga-Plate were "revolutionizing credit sales and sweeping the country," as one credit professional put it.[153] The practices that were inadvertently promoted by Regulation W were all found in the new revolving credit programs, which made them easier to accept despite being different from the traditional credit practices of open book charge accounts and installment credit.

Retailers, following the war, pushed "to add new and revive dormant charge accounts."[154] Though charge accounts had grown slightly during the war from $12.4 to $12.8 billion of annual sales, retailers hoped to push those numbers even higher.[155] Prior to V-J day, 66 percent of department store sales were paid in cash, in contrast to the prewar period when cash was only 40 percent of sales.[156] There was a lot of opportunity to expand consumer borrowing. By January of 1947, consumer credit made a triumphant return without the strict wartime regulations. A National Retail Dry Goods Association (NRDGA) survey of 106 cities found that new credit applications were up 42 percent, and charge account sales up 25 percent.[157] Seventy-six percent of NRDGA retailers reported "campaigns to get customers to say 'charge it.'"[158] When one store offers "generous credit," as a one Boston department store official said, "competitors have to follow suit."[159] Behind the credit managers of these firms, however, were commercial banks, whose loans to business had risen to over $2 billion outstanding, more than a third higher than in May of 1945.[160] By August 1946, consumer credit outstanding passed $8 billion.[161] Consumer credit continued to rise in 1946, charge accounts by two-thirds and installment credit by 60 percent.[162] By 1947, the prewar, all-time high peak of $10 billion was exceeded.[163]

Revolving credit had existed before the war, albeit briefly, but was confined to only a few stores and was primarily experimental. Shortly before the war began, Bloomingdale's, the well-known New York department store, instituted a plan for "a new type of extended payments" named "permanent budget accounts" (PBAs), that in 1940 increased their installment payments outstanding by a half million dollars, or about 15 percent.[164] Regulation W ended its use.[165] Unlike the stores that used revolving credit to evade installment credit regulations, Bloomingdale's followed the spirit of the regulation, putting its permanent budget accounts on the same footing as its installment credit. Bloomingdale's only wartime advertisement that mentioned the permanent budget account, incidentally, included the PBA along with other ways to finance purchases at Bloomingdale's under Regulation W. The advertisement stated that PBAs, like installment credit, also required a down payment.[166] It is unclear whether Bloomingdale's or the Fed decided to treat the PBA like installment credit, but the effect was the same. There was little incentive for customers to use the revolving credit accounts when the charge accounts, there and elsewhere, allowed them to buy without down payments—at least at the beginning of the war. But as the war ended, Bloomingdale's, like rest of American retailers, embraced revolving credit.

While only 12 percent of stores in 1947 had PBAs like those of Bloomingdale's, 42 percent of the stores offered "easy credit" with 86 percent of those stores having 0.5 percent service charges on their charge accounts.[167]

These charge accounts looked more like revolving credit, incorporating serial liquidation and charging interest. While half the stores maintained the same terms as under Regulation W, the other half loosened their terms. Half of those stores refunded the service charge if the payment was complete in ninety days.[168] In practice, if not in name, more than half of NRDGA stores offered revolving credit.

A 1949 survey of retailers found that 75 percent of major stores had instituted revolving credit plans since the war's end.[169] The conversion to revolving credit was made substantially easier by the social and accounting similarities with open account credit. During the war, Charga-Plate systems, which were not hampered by Regulation W in any way, had become more common. All larger stores and many smaller ones used it for tracking purchases and bills.[170] All the revolving credit systems relied on the Charga-Plate to keep track of accounts. Advertisements promoting revolving credit commonly had a picture of the Charga-Plate as well. In a 1949 survey of the NRDGA stores, nearly all of the stores with revolving credit used the Charga-Plate system and 70 percent *required* the Charga-Plate to authorize the account.[171] The old days of giving a clerk one's name and address to post the bill to a charge account were gone.[172] Revolving credit and the Charga-Plate grew together.

Retailers using the Charga-Plate system for billing could easily add revolving credit. A Bloomingdale's credit manager extolled the ease of adding revolving credit, since "actual billing is the same as that of a regular charge account with the exception of the carrying charge feature."[173] R. H. Bulte, a St. Louis credit manager, told a crowd of credit managers that he did not "believe you [would] have too much of a problem in setting it up. The bookkeeping procedure is no different than on your regular account."[174] Retailers could use the "same bill and print 'permanent budget account' or 'revolving credit' on it." The service charge could just be an additional line item. With the Charga-Plate, Bulte continued, "it is an easy matter to put an identification signal on it. There isn't too much difficult with what you already have in the regular accounts."

Farrington Manufacturing, the company that sold the Charga-Plate system, encouraged the connection between Charga-Plate and revolving credit by issuing special Charga-Plate cards to be used. These cards were different in color than those of the regular charge accounts, but could be used with the same machines and allowed the customers to say the same magic words to operate them—"charge it"![175] The manager of the Charga-Plate division of Farrington Manufacturing, William Brian, reinforced the social advantages of using Charga-Plate for revolving accounts to other credit managers, since through the "special colored plate . . . *distinction* and *individuality* [were] obtained from this type of credit selling, grading up the budget buyer without conflicting with regular account buying or paying habits."[176] Because of the shoppers' experience and the ease of using the already existing Charga-Plate system, Brian reported that "retailers [were] enthusiastically accepting this new Charga-Plate service in ever increasing numbers."[177] Farrington not only offered the physical system, but instruction in "a workable plan that has been well proved" on the new revolving credit system.[178]

The many stores that converted to Charga-Plate systems, and began using revolving credit plans, also invested heavily in new machinery. For stores like Woodward & Lothrop in Washington, D.C., the conversion included not only staff training in the new systems, but installing Charga-Plate–based billing and Addressograph machines in a special credit building to take advantage of the efficiency gained from a centralized credit department for its many stores.[179] These investments allowed for greater sales, but these expenses were all sunk costs. Once the conversion was made, it was not easily undone.

The Charga-Plate's equivalence of charge and revolving credit enabled a new kind of social democracy at the checkout counter. The failure of installment coupon books, promoted unsuccessfully before the war, highlights the social appeal of revolving credit. Many retailers had created installment coupon books.[180] Half of the NRDGA membership used coupon books in their stores.[181] These coupons, though widespread, were little used. Initially, they seemed like a good idea. Installment credit could be used for smaller purchases. It was not practical for customers who wanted to buy $16.58 worth of goods to fill out a contract—work out terms and down payment, for each purchase at the cash register—while other customers waited behind them. Instead, customers would first go to the credit manager, arrange a line of credit, and receive a coupon book, usually in increments of $25. These coupon books cut down on the clerical work required for managing each individual sale. The amounts were fixed and the contracts standardized. The customer could buy exactly $25 worth of goods in one sale or buy $2.50 worth in ten sales; either way the credit department would only have to keep track of one purchase of the coupon book, which made billing much easier to handle.

Coupon books never really caught on both because they were a hassle and because they forced poorer customers to mark themselves socially when using them. Compared with the ease of revolving credit accounts, coupon books were a total hassle. Though their interchangeability with cash at the register made them easier to use for the credit department and the sales clerk, they nonetheless imposed limits on the customer that limited their appeal. The customer could not buy just an additional $5 of goods, only $25. Richmond believed that the customer had "to make up his mind . . . and then arrange for [a] book," rather than pick out the things that he or she wanted in the store and go to the checkout. Coupon books required filling out contracts and paperwork each time the book ran out.[182] Consumers and retailers frequently complained about all the "red tape" coupons entailed.

In addition to the bureaucratic hassle, shoppers who had to present coupons instead of cash or a Charga-Plate might feel stigmatized as "lower income" than those who "qualify[ied]" for a charge account and could use their Charga-Plates.[183] Reflecting a commonly reiterated statement among credit professionals, a St. Louis credit manager remarked that "the revolving credit is a little more dignified, and a more dignified way, for our customers . . . to shop, rather than the coupon method. Sometimes it might be embarrassing for a woman to pull out a coupon in the store."[184] The coupon books, because they marked a customer as someone who did not have the cash and did not qualify for a charge account, were never very popular in more affluent stores.[185] Revolving credit eliminated the need for installment coupon books. For stores that conveyed a middle- or upper-class image, unlike the discount installment clothing stores, the revolving credit account provided a means for customers to enjoy the pleasure of shopping—based partially on a certain performance of affluence, while enabling them to borrow for their purchases. For lower-income customers, the revolving credit plan allowed them to behave in stores just like the more affluent. For middle-class patrons, they could use installment credit without the threat of lost class prestige. Revolving credit allowed the performance of wealth for everyone. As a Detroit credit manager, S. C. Patterson, explained, the revolving credit customer "gets her "Charga-Plate" or other customer identification media the same as a 30-day account."[186] At the checkout line, "she can say 'Charge it'" like a rich woman, even though she paid by the month. This experience of shopping was, Patterson insisted to other credit managers, "important to your charge customer, and if you do not believe so, I think you are deluding yourself."

But while the experience of shopping became more uniform, the customers were all quite different, especially in terms of income. Bloomingdale's credit manager, Robert O'Hagan, said "the PBA taps a practically untouched field of continuous revolving business from customers who may not be eligible for a regular charge account, or who are so used to buying everything on a budget that this is the only type of account that appeals to them."[187] While credit managers emphasized that half of customers using revolving credit would be eligible for charge accounts, the flip side of that was that half would not. A credit sales manager of a large Brooklyn department store remarked that half of his competitor's new PBA accounts were new accounts.[188] Revolving credit plans brought in new customers and new sales to stores.[189] But with these new customers and sales came new expenses, as one Columbus credit manager noted.

Early revolving account managers described the system as promoting a great deal of sales and just breaking even, but that quickly changed. Increased sales brought additional profits, as did the interest on the unpaid balances. Revolving accounts, when popularized after the war, typically charged customers 1 percent per month in interest. A 1949 survey found that 65 percent of stores with revolving credit charged 1 percent, and 35 percent charged ½ percent.[190] Installment coupons had typically earned ½ percent per month; the revolving credit plan charged double that.[191] The annual interest on ½ percent per month was about 6 percent, while that 1 percent per month was about 13 percent. Bloomingdale's O'Hagan described, in 1949, their "great success in increasing store volume by opening up among the lower income groups, a practically untouched field."[192] If anything, the biggest problem stores using revolving credit reported were customers developing a "tendency to overbuy."[193] One credit manager said in 1951 that the revolving charge account was "a big source of revenue to the credit office."[194] More than breaking even, revolving credit balanced out the losses of all complete debt losses and went "a long way to pay your credit office expenses."[195] Revolving credit provided profits to those willing to make the investment in the new system.

Sales grew because shoppers, unrestrained by coupon books or quick repayments, could buy anything. Following the war, the permanent budget account became a centerpiece of Bloomingdale's advertising, with large-scale ads focusing on promoting the PBA's utility for the postwar consumer. A December 1946 advertisement, for instance, explained how the fictitious "Ann Smith" told "Bloomingdale's, I Love You . . . When [The] Credit Manager Explained How A Permanent Budget Account Work[ed]."[196] Smith's "love" resulted from the credit manager's explanation of "how she could have three evening dresses at one time" for the "New York winter season" and "some mighty attractive and attentive gentlemen," and would have eight months to pay it off.[197] Men, too, could purchase sets of matching shirts, ties, and handkerchiefs, along with quality suits, on the "Permanent Budget Account—the charge account with the many months to pay and the small service charge."[198] Clothes, cookware, lawnmowers, *anything* could be had on the new PBA. Was this the promise of consumer democracy?[199]

Revolving credit made explicit the suspicion that an account might never be completely repaid. Unlike open accounts or charge accounts, which maintained the fiction of convenience credit, revolving credit made explicit that the customer was borrowing beyond their ability to repay, if only for that month. Retailers fretted over the implications of this, but could not deny that the credit plan had boosted sales. While the revolving charge accounts were sometimes called permanent budget accounts, credit managers still seemed uncomfortable with the idea of permanent indebtedness.

Yet even as customers appeared similar at check out—all saying "charge it!"—stores also began to strictly differentiate them when the bills came due. Customers found that stores began to force them to make a choice between the open book charge account and the revolving credit account. Unlike installment credit, one customer could not have both a regular charge account and a revolving charge account. Abraham & Strauss (A&S), for example, forbade customers from having both; they offered their own PBA, "for budget-minded people."[200] Advertisements featured parents with "royally furnished" nurseries, college seniors who were "the best dressed girls on campus," and fathers who kept "the family budget on an even keel." Promoted as economical and judicious like the old A&S charge accounts of the 1920s, the PBA was nonetheless a mutually exclusive alternative to the traditional charge account.

A&S had different practices for the PBA as well. With a 1 percent interest rate, customers paid a little over a 12 percent interest rate per year on a balance that need never be fully paid off.[201] Customers were reminded that they could "continually charge the difference between what you owe and the amount of credit you have established." Customers, naturally, had to have their "identification card" containing their PBA account number to shop so that the store could make use of all the modern billing machines. The importance of the emergence of revolving credit was marked in the new dichotomous definition of "charge account"—a "regular charge account" was like the old open book credit but with firm repayment dates, and a "revolving charge account" was the new revolving credit.

While the popularity of revolving credit relied on the conflation of Charga-Plate practice with charge accounts, retailers also used the plan to clearly differentiate customers who paid in thirty days from those who paid over many months. Three-fourths of stores forbade customers from having both a regular charge account and a revolving credit account. Customers who were "slow pays," that is, tended not to pay when the bill was due, could now be switched over to the revolving account.[202] One Minneapolis department store had a small card printed with a check box that simply said, "Please transfer my regular charge account to the revolving charge plan," for customers believed to be slow in paying.[203] Most switched without complaint. Because the revolving account looked and felt like a charge account, even if the finances differed customers rarely resisted since there was no social stigma attached. Retailers could then worry less about slow paying customers, since they would be charged interest on the balance.

During the 1940s, department stores embraced revolving credit to boost sales and Charga-Plates to control costs. Most shoppers preferred revolving credit to traditional forms of credit because it gave them more control over their spending and more social status when they shopped. By the late 1940s, revolving credit and American retail had firmly entwined.

The Korean War and the Last Gasp of Regulation W

As Truman entered the war, Congress passed the Defense Production Act of 1950, which gave him broad powers over the control of the economy.[204] Truman favored the style of Regulation W rather than a return to the rationing of World War II.[205] Direct restrictions on production would, after all, hamper the "economic strength" that Truman felt made the West "superior to their enemies."[206] Fighting communism, rather than fascism, required the juxtaposition of free enterprise to communist command economies. Unlike Roosevelt, who had justified the first Regulation W in a convoluted fashion under the Wartime Powers Act, the Defense Production Act gave Truman clear authority to regulate for inflation control.[207] Even so, the effectiveness of Regulation W during World War II derived from business's consent, not from clear legal authority. As America entered the Korean War, the Federal Reserve, which Truman asked to once again enforce Regulation W, was to encounter a business community far less amenable to its regulatory goals.

The American economy had changed quickly since the end of the war, and retailers had grown very dependent on consumer credit. The stupendous growth in sales volume depended on charge accounts. By 1950, Charga-Plate systems for both charge and revolving credit accounts had become integral to American retail.[208] A NDGRA survey found that by 1951, 76 percent of credit sales were through charge accounts—with 19 percent revolving and 57 percent regular—for stores selling more than $20 million a year on credit. The Philadelphia credit bureau, in a letter intended to show the Fed that charge accounts were still being used in America, provided them with a table of Charga-Plate accounts used in large cities.[209] In some cities, the system had been in place for only a few years, but in that time charge accounts and Charga-plates had become synonymous. Charga-Plates systems could not be regulated.

Unlike installment credit, which was still carried out with pen and paper contracts, charge accounts, now mechanized, proved an enormous obstacle. Charga-Plate billing machines were not like computers today. They could not be reprogrammed. Farrington Manufacturing had hardwired assumptions about lending into the levers, relays, and gears of the accounting machines. The introduction of Regulation W with the freezing of charge accounts would make all that investment worthless. A Fed study found "it would be extremely difficult for a large number of stores to comply with a freezing mechanism on charge accounts . . . [and] some stores might be unable to comply fully even at considerable expense to themselves."[210] Employees, trained to use the machines, were unfamiliar with any other system and could not go back to an earlier model. Retailers needed mechanical billing to remain competitive, since it cut accounting costs so much. Typical of the stern letters the Fed received was one from Aaron Frank, the president of the large Northwest department store chain Meier & Frank, which explained that they doubted they could comply with a regulation that froze charge accounts.[211] Inquires made to Charga-Plate's Farrington Manufacturing, by Frank, only confirmed his fears that there was no way to reconcile the Charga-Plate system with a World War II–style regulation on charge accounts. Frank Neely, chairman of the board of Rich's department store in Atlanta, wrote one official to "call [his] attention to the fact that merchants have developed a new type of open credit in amounts that are very sizable."[212] Neely explained that revolving credit was the "big bugaboo" for the reinstitution of Regulation W, since customers could transfers balances from their open account to a revolving account to "dodge the restrictions."[213] Lamenting revolving credit's expansion, Rich also emphasized its intractable reality.

The Fed, under pressure from large retailers, recognized the constraints of the situation. If charge accounts could not be regulated, then neither could revolving credit be, since they both depended on the same technologies. The similarities that made the switch to revolving credit easy, also made them indivisible. Faced with such technical and political difficulties, the Fed did not impose charge account regulations.[214] Installment credit would be regulated, but charge credit, both regular and revolving, would not.

Regulation W was reenacted on September 18, 1950, but only for installment credit, and business opposition was immediate.[215] With widespread access to revolving credit, however, consumers could easily substitute for the regulated installment credit. Opposition to the regulation during the Korean War was anything but marginal, especially since the regulation fell unevenly on installment credit businesses that did not offer revolving credit. Most business groups actively tried to have the regulation repealed.[216] Installment sellers and their trade organizations, likewise, claimed the regulation's effects on inflation were "fallacious."[217] President of the National Foundation of Consumer Credit, John Otter, claimed that there was "no shortage of . . . radios, televisions, refrigerators, washing machines, and vacuum cleaners."[218] While during World War II government demand had cut heavily into consumer production, the expansion of the economy since the war and the comparatively smaller war in Korea, made for less of an effect on retailers' inventories.

The government's demand on the economy was much less than during World War II.[219] While nearly half of the national output was devoted to defense during World War II, less than a quarter was similarly allocated during the Korean War. Without a shortage of inventory, demand could not outstrip supply, which was the justification for the controls. Business achieved a widespread consensus against the regulation.[220] Even Federal Reserve Board members, shockingly, spoke out publicly against the use of selective controls.[221] Credit professionals, like Arthur Morris, moreover, denounced the regulations on ideological grounds, as an "abhorrent interference with individual liberty." The defense of liberty against communism, which justified the war, was turned against the regulation.

The explicit lack of restrictions on revolving credit further propelled its use. Before the Korean War, despite the preponderance of Charga-Plate, revolving credit was still restricted geographically and by the type of store that used it. Investigating revolving credit, Fed official Philip Webster found it only in large department stores of major cities, particularly on the East Coast.[222] The Atlanta Federal Reserve reported that in the South there was "extensive use of 'revolving' charge accounts" that they thought had been instituted to create "a loophole to any future Regulation W."[223] In Boston plans could be found with no down payment and twelve months to pay, to 10 percent down and six months to pay. In New York, terms were no longer than ten months and with never more than a $120 credit limit. Revolving credit seemed, at the outset of the war, to be replacing older charge accounts, not installment credit plans. Durable goods retailers still offered installment plans, for the most part. Some stores explicitly restricted the revolving credit to "soft goods."[224]

Despite wartime regulations on traditional installment credit, the reported statistics on it continued to improve because revolving credit, unregulated, was lumped with installment credit.[225] The *New York Times* reported that despite a drop in durable good sales, the decline in installment credit was "made up by the growing trend in stores toward budget plans or revolving credit."[226] By 1952, even the old installment seller standby, furniture, was being sold on revolving credit. For goods other than automobiles, revolving credit became an alternative to the installment plan. Advertisements in the *New York Times* from furniture house like Sachs and Gimbels, as well as department stores like Bloomingdale's, encouraged "young moderns" to buy their furniture on "budget accounts."[227]

By May of 1952, the opponents of the regulation had won. The "months of pressure exerted unrelentingly by manufacturers, distributors, and retailers," as the *New York Times* reported, as well as internal disagreement over the regulation's efficacy, led the Fed to end controls.[228] Installment sellers across the country immediately relaxed terms, advertising "no down payments."[229] In Dallas, installment sales grew by 50 percent in one month.[230] Televisions, air conditioners, laundry machines, and refrigerators sold especially well. Most of the country, however, saw no buying spree, showing the regulation's limited effect if consumers could use revolving credit instead.[231]

By the end of the Korean War, revolving credit became ubiquitous across the country. In 1953, Bullock's department store advertised the PBA for the first time in Los Angeles.[232] By 1955, some department stores began to do away with their installment plans altogether, consolidating all sales into either revolving credit plans or regular charge accounts.[233] A. L. Trotta, an official with the NRDGA, believed that this system would "eventually be the sole type of account maintained by stores." Though other retailers and credit managers felt this single vision of credit to be "utopian," the *New York Times* reported, Trotta believed in a future where, in terms of credit, all customers were treated equally with "no stigma . . . attached to the customer who spaces out payments." Revolving credit held out the possibility of a future where consumers of all classes could borrow in exactly the same way.

Conclusion: Regulation, Evasion, and Revolving Credit

Regulation of consumer credit of such a novel scope as Regulation W had never been seen before or since. It was the last attempt to fully restrain consumer credit. Large enough to be meaningful if reduced, consumer credit was still small enough that the economy would not topple. Consumer credit during World War II was not foundational to the U.S. economy. By the Korean War, however, retail businesses relied on consumer credit, not only for profit, but for the central operations of their businesses. Regulations so stark in scope as those during World War II could no longer be enacted. Following the Korean War, regulators of consumer credit focused not on restraining it, but in making its access more democratic. As will be shown in the next two chapters, credit had become so central to upward mobility that the government, instead of focusing on its dangers, demanded its access for all.

Department stores that took advantage of this new revolving credit system witnessed fantastic sales growth and increased profits. It is no coincidence that the stores that most fully exploited the new charge systems, Filene's, Abraham & Strauss, Bloomingdale's, Foley's, Burdine's, and others, grew to become America's largest retail conglomerate in the postwar era—Federated Department Stores. Even its nearest rival department store conglomerate, the May Department Stores Company, was composed of avid revolving credit retailers like Marshall Field's,

Kaufmann's, Meier & Frank, Famous Barr, and Lord & Taylor. Growing out of the cities and into the suburbs in the postwar period, they brought the new revolving credit to a debt-driven suburban periphery. In these department stores Americans learned the pleasures, benefits, and dangers of putting it on the card.

Chapter Five

Postwar Consumer Credit

BORROWING FOR PROSPERITY

MANY IN THE POSTWAR United States achieved a material prosperity that, in debt's absence, they could not have attained. Middle-class consumers with rising incomes shopped on credit for items that their wealthier neighbors could buy with cash.[1] Working-class Americans earned less than the professional class, yet lived very similar material lives. Even middle-class African Americans, though lacking the wealth of their white neighbors and facing racial barriers to some kinds of financing, could borrow the same amounts as white debtors and enjoy material abundance. Only the very rich and the very poor borrowed nothing. For the vast middle, borrowing and buying were thoroughly entangled. The social practice of buying had little to do with economists' abstractions of interest rates, and a lot to do with shopping habits. Consumer debt moved to the center of American life, even as the center of American life began to move to the suburbs. Debt made the good life possible.[2]

The postwar prosperity enabled suburbanites with good incomes to live as well as their perhaps wealthier neighborhoods, even if they had little savings. This equality of consumption, however, reinforced inequalities of wealth. Despite the money seeping away in higher interest rates and financing charges, the inequality of wealth mattered little as incomes continued to rise and retailers extended credit. Consumers could enjoy the houses, autos, appliances, and clothes made possible through consumer credit. The rate of savings continued to rise even as Americans borrowed. Seventy percent of households with debt continued to save. The budgeted borrowing was paid back. These new suburbanites rarely defaulted.[3] As figure 5.1 shows, though Americans continued to borrow more every year after World War II, they also paid more back. While the amount loaned grew tremendously in the postwar period, the growth rate for outstanding debt remained relatively flat. Borrowing remained a viable strategy, not only because of rising incomes, but also because all consumer credit remained tax deductible. In such a favorable climate for borrowing, Americans borrowed their way to prosperity. Consumers could provide the savings and financial institutions could relend that money back to them, boosting American manufacturing and retail. Credit

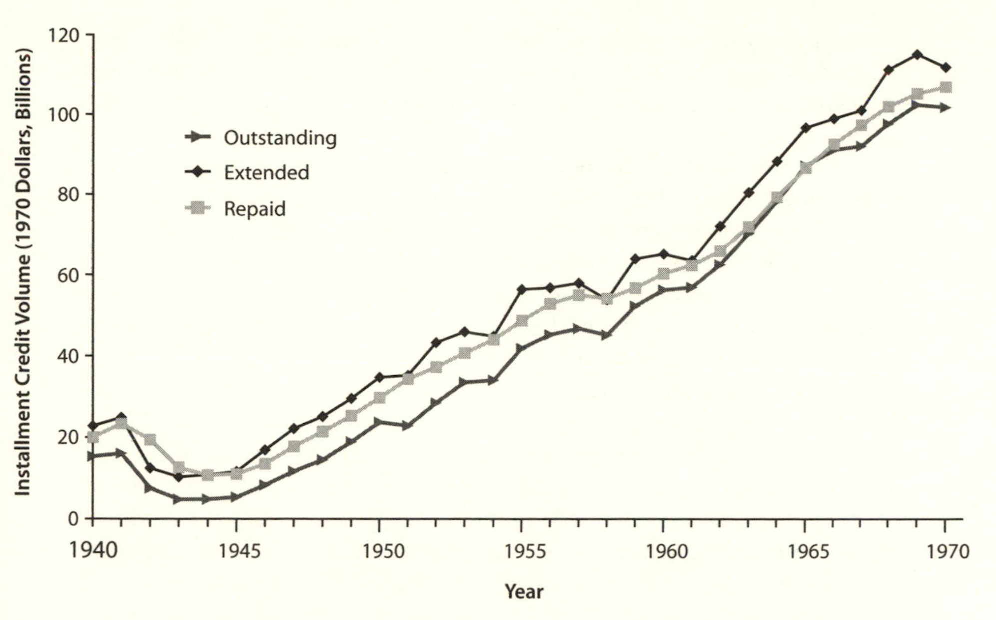

Figure 5.1. Installment Debt Extended. Source: Board of Governors of the Federal Reserve System, *Supplement to Banking and Monetary Statistics* (Washington: GPO, 1963), 57. Adjusted to 1970 dollars by author.

in the postwar period was a virtuous circle, turning future income into present-day prosperity.

Not only the good life but the good profits of the postwar period depended on debt, as retailers pushed new forms of revolving credit to spur sales growth. Retailers like Federated Department Stores followed their customers' migrations into the suburbs, tactically using revolving credit to promote their new branch stores. John Lebor, vice-president of Federated Department Stores, the prominent national chain of department stores, pronounced department stores as the "leaders" in credit innovation when he spoke to a gathering of credit managers at their annual convention in 1958.[4] It was in department stores, after all, that consumers first learned to carry the metal Charga-Plates popularized after World II. Consumers first used those charge cards with revolving budget plans to buy a multitude of small purchases, as they had previously with 30-day accounts, but to pay for them over many months, as with installment plans. Though durable goods dealers had initially promoted installment credit, and small loan companies and personal loan departments had provided microfinance across the country, it was department stores that wove consumer credit into the everyday lives of buyers. The revolving credit offered by department stores allowed for even the most mundane purchase of socks to be paid back over time, rather than the infrequent and expensive house or auto purchase for which installment credit had spread.

Though historians, sociologists, and economists have imagined an unbroken line from the first universal credit cards of the early 1950s to today's plastic, department store charge plans formed an important intermediate moment where consumers and creditors learned how and why they could make money on consumer purchasing. Save for a few examples, all the early experimental programs in universal credit cards that were promoted by banks for consumer use at local stores failed. Only specialized programs focused on traveling businessmen for nonlocal, non-ubiquitious purchases succeeded. Beyond the narrow world of business travel, the far more important arena of household consumption took place at department stores, where consumers learned to charge against the department store's own, self-financed credit plans that possessed no relation to banks and their proprietary bank card plans. The overwhelming majority of department stores would not even allow these bank-issued cards to be used. Everyday consumer credit was department store credit.

The beginning of the transition from the installment credit economy of the manufacturing era to the revolving credit economy of the service era was witnessed in the early 1960s. Before the 1960s, finance companies made marginal profits but enabled large manufacturing concerns to realize their profits on production. After the 1960s, profits on the financing became ends in themselves. General Electric, for instance, began its long arc from a company that profited mostly from manufacturing into a company that profited mostly from finance. This transition was not predestined. No wizard pulled a lever and revealed the deep mysteries of capital to retailers. The underlying shift in relative profitability propelled the transformation of America's largest corporations, and the insights that made this shift possible accumulated slowly, sometimes accidentally, in the late 1950s in America's largest retail operations—the department stores.

Competitive sales pressures between stores in the booming days of the late 1950s drove the expansion of consumer credit. Consumers had begun to spend less of their disposable income on retail goods and more on services.[5] Looking for any means to outfox their competitors in this relatively shrinking pie, stores looked to credit to drive their profitable expansions, both figuratively in terms of bottom lines, but also literally as the large retail chains moved into the suburbs and the Sunbelt. As retail firms expanded their credit offerings, they also expanded the accounts receivables that their customers owed to them. Caught in a financial catch-22, retailers had to expand their sales through credit, but in doing so confronted the limits of their own capital. By the mid-1960s, these retailers who spurned bank-issued cards in the 1950s once again had to turn to bank-issued capital to expand sales.

Rather than forced down on consumers and retailers by banks from above, credit practices trickled *up* to financial institutions as retailers responded to the limits of their capital. This chapter illustrates how the thinking and practices of credit managers who created these policies—as well as the flows of capital that made these innovations possible—slowly changed. Different retailers resolved their crisis of capital shortage differently, but in solving it they all fundamentally altered their businesses and the way in which Americans practiced debt. Despite their different aims and incentives, the necessities of capital stitched together the disjointed elements of postwar manufacturing, retail, and finance.

Tellingly, in no case did a successful business opt to restrict credit. The increased importance of consumer credit led many retailers to form separate credit divisions or even subsidiary corporations to handle their firms' needs. Some succeeded, but many looked outside their own companies for the capital needed to continue to expand their credit sales. Into this gap came finance companies and banks that had remained outside of the postwar retail credit boom. Economic changes had, by the early 1960s, rendered the installment contract a mute legal instrument and finance companies looked for alternative sites of investment. In department store revolving credit, finance companies found a new way to finance consumer debt. Consumers did not hesitate to spend more, and embraced the most recent innovation in credit in the prosperous times of the late 1950s and early 1960s—the option account—which allowed them to both buy more and owe more.

Credit in the Postwar Suburbs

The suburbs created an apparent equality of consumption, even if there remained inequalities of wealth. Consumers who could borrow from the future could live better today. In the suburbs, the broad middle class of better-paid office and factory workers could borrow more frequently and in greater amounts that ever before.[6] Only the poorest and richest households, by exclusion or by choice, abstained from borrowing.

Suburban borrowing began with the house. With twice the rate of mortgage borrowing as in the cities, mortgages made suburban home ownership possible. Conventional mortgage lenders provided two-thirds of suburban mortgages, but federally insured loans continued to be important, not only for the actual money they provided but for underwriting guidelines that shaped all suburban development. Suburban home owners borrowed more frequently than their urban counterparts, and they also borrowed more money. In the suburbs, conventional mortgages were 20 percent larger and federally insured mortgages were 50 percent larger than the average urban mortgages.[7]

The greater borrowing did not stop with the house. After controlling for other factors, simply having a mortgage raised the other indebtedness of a suburban household $571, or 42 percent of the average household nonmortgage debt.[8] Simply having a mortgage made a suburban household 3.4 times as likely as suburban households without mortgages to have other forms of consumer debt.[9] Mortgage borrowing was only the first step into of a suburban world of indebtedness.

The FHA *Underwriting Manual,* whose dictates shaped nearly all suburban construction, planned as much for autos as for houses, encouraging the constructions of streets amenable to driving automobiles. Living in the suburbs made a household twice as likely to own an auto as those living in the city.[10] That better-earning suburbanites tended to own more autos is no great stretch of the imagination, but what is important is that they tended to *even after* their higher incomes are taken into consideration. The suburbs were not just wealthier; the built environment of the suburbs promoted auto ownership, and auto ownership, despite those higher incomes, meant more debt. Just owning an auto made a household 2.3 times as likely to have other debt as an autoless one.[11] Auto owners, after adjusting for other factors, were 2.6 times as likely as non-auto owners to be in debt.[12] Mortgages and auto payments made households more likely to be in debt in other areas of their lives, but what influenced that first decision to borrow, and how much did households borrow?

While wealth determined if a household borrowed, income determined how much was borrowed.[13] Households without savings could borrow cheap mortgage funds to live among wealthier neighbors. While the average incomes of debtors and nondebtors were indistinguishable—$6,322 and $6,328 respectively—nondebtors were wealthier, with an average of $3,994 of liquid assets compared to $1,018 for debtors. Indebted households, regardless of income or occupation, had lower levels of liquid assets than nonindebted households.[14] Debt enabled those who had not saved or inherited to live as well as those who had.

Newly middle-class consumers without savings used their newfound prosperity to live better. Future income could be made into present-day prosperity. Among indebted suburban households, each additional $100 of income meant an additional $5 of consumer debt.[15] With a similar income and ability to borrow, households with very different levels of education, occupational attainment, and wealth could maintain the same lifestyle. While incomes differed, the mass production economy of the postwar era offered few choices. When suburbanites borrowed, they tended to borrow the same amount—outfitting their homes with the latest consumer durables, but no more and no less. For instance, half of factory workers and half of clerical workers lived in the suburbs, following the broad pattern of American postwar life. Clerical or factory workers, however, were 1.5 times more likely to borrow as the managers, owners, and professionals who ranked above them occupationally.[16] Better-off households did not need to borrow as frequently, but they purchased similarly to workers if they did have to borrow. The washing machines that they bought cost the same. Workers and managers, though they borrowed at different rates, borrowed the same amounts.[17] The debt economy of the postwar suburb erased many class differences in consumption.

The Suburban African American Wealth Gap

Suburbanization and credit use worked differently for African Americans than for whites, both because of differences in wealth levels, and also because of the differences in the kinds of financing available. While suburban whites of different classes did not have significant differences of wealth, suburban whites and suburban African Americans, even those with similar incomes, did. Black borrowing took on a different pattern from white borrowing, and that borrowing opened up material opportunities, that in debt's absence could not have been realized.

For moderate African American reform groups like the Urban League, consumers' use of debt was a problem. By 1959, the Urban League began an outreach to black consumers in Chicago. Edwin Berry, the executive director of the Urban League, believed them to be disproportionately affected by bankruptcies, wage assignments, and garnishments.[18] Rather than seeing credit as empowering the choices available to consumers, Berry saw African American borrowing as a rip-off that resulted from the "failure of many individuals to understand sound budgeting practices," an "inability to read and comprehend a contract," "economic cutbacks," "unethical business practices of some credit merchants," "credit houses that take a chance on poor credit risks," and "debt consolidation gimmicks." In short, retailers "exploit[ed]" African American consumers. For those "families . . . caught in the web of too much credit," Berry proposed an educational program to reeducate consumers not to borrow as much.[19] Groups like the Urban League saw credit as sapping the wealth formation of the African American community.

While the *Defender* took up the Urban League's critique of borrowing, the newspaper also promoted suburban living for its readers. The "fast-growing Negro suburbia" was, the *Defender* reported, not the norm for many African Americans, but offered an alternative made available through credit.[20] In Atlanta's Crestwood Forest, Memphis's Lakeview Gardens, New Orleans's Pontchartrain Park, Long Island's Dunbar Estates, and Philadelphia's Concord Park, to name a few, African Americans could "settle where the air is clean and . . . curse the crab grass" as well as "buy second cars and second TV sets." Mortgage costs were usually higher for black borrowers than for whites, but for the black middle class borrowing still meant "good living," as the *Defender* reiterated. While credit for African Americans in the cities only reinforced a stereotype of ignorant consumers, it represented progress for the suburban households.

This progress, however, came at a significant cost. While African Americans moved into suburbs to enjoy their version of the postwar American dream—both together with and separate from whites—this dream was far more expensive than it was for whites. Choices over the use of savings and borrowing for mortgages and other forms of suburban debt differed from whites. African American borrowing patterns reflected both the higher interest rates from systematic racial discrimination and the constraints imposed by lower average levels of wealth. While African American leaders espoused the importance of migration to the suburbs as a means of middle-class empowerment, the result in terms of long-term wealth accumulation may have been more mixed as a financed lifestyle drained off savings.[21]

While suburban black incomes remained roughly equal to those of urban households, white suburban households earned significantly more. In the suburbs, whites ($6,458) earned $2,861 more than black households ($3,597) compared to a difference of only $1,800 between urban whites ($5,610) and urban African Americans ($3,767). If white households earned nearly double that of black households, the average wealth differences were even more striking, with the average suburban white household possessing nearly twenty times ($2,428) the liquid assets of the average black household ($122). This difference was far greater in the suburbs than in the city, where the difference was only six-and-a-half times.

Changes in wealth affected black and white households differently. For white households, greater levels of liquid assets decreased the likelihood of borrowing and, if borrowing did happen, kept the amount borrowed low.[22] For black households, however, greater levels of liquid assets increased the likelihood of borrowing and then also increased the amounts. For every $100 in liquid assets, white households borrowed two *fewer* dollars than black households.

Presumably, white households with higher average asset levels than black households could choose whether or not to use their savings, while black households, living on the edge of their income, were forced to borrow. With rising assets, black households did not have much more choice in their consumption, but to lenders they did have more financial stability,

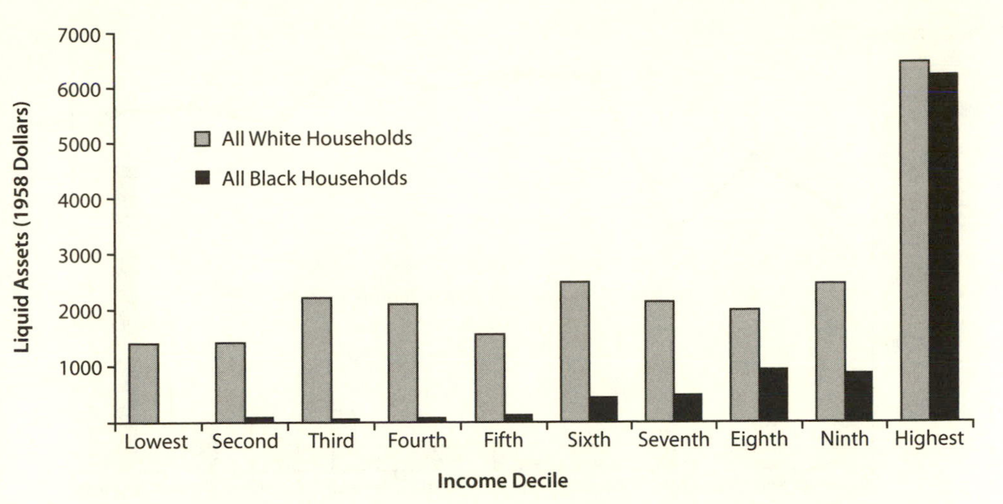

Figure 5.2. White and Black Assets. White households, at every income level, had greater wealth. Overall, the mean liquid assets for white households were 10 times greater than for black households ($2,494 vs. $247). Source: Survey of Consumer Finances, 1958.

which enabled them to borrow more. As figure 5.2 shows, even the lowest-income whites had average higher wealth levels than all but the highest-earning African Americans. Even if black consumers preferred to just purchase goods out of their savings, they often would not have had the money. While only 24 percent of white households who borrowed had no savings, 69 percent of black households with debt had no savings at all.

Considering race alone, whites were half as likely as African Americans to have an installment debt. Even after controlling for socioeconomic differences, African Americans tended to borrow more frequently than whites. Even among the lowest income groups, African Americans incurred debt at twice the frequency of whites. As figure 5.3 shows, across income deciles, blacks used debt to a higher percentage than whites. Among suburban borrowers, African Americans were even more likely to make use of installment credit than whites; they were 5.4 times more likely than whites to have an installment debt.[23] African Americans used debt with a frequency unseen among white Americans, but its use made possible the material aspirations that those suburbs held out to the readers of the *Defender* and the black middle class everywhere.

While black households borrowed more frequently than whites, both indebted households borrowed the same amount, despite their differences in income. A suburban dishwasher cost the same to all consumers. Among those with debt, white suburbanites had an average installment debt level of $814, while black suburbanites had $810. Race had no relationship with how much a household borrowed, just whether they borrowed.[24]

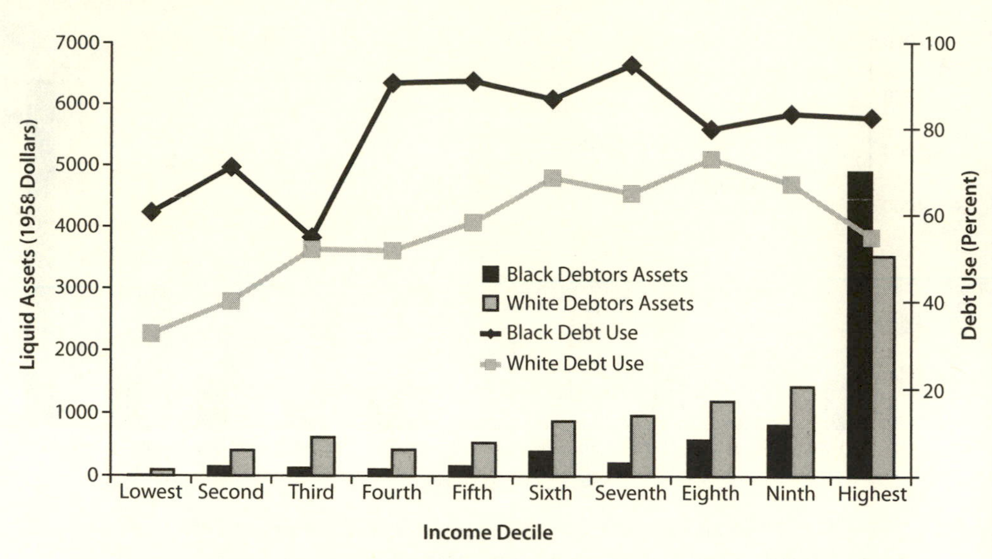

Figure 5.3. Debt Use and Assets. At every income decile, black households borrowed more than white households. Source: Survey of Consumer Finances, 1958.

Yet while black households borrowed the same amounts as whites, their incomes and assets were nowhere near as bountiful. As figure 5.3 shows, at nearly every income level whites had higher levels of liquid assets and lower rates of borrowing than African Americans. Black suburbanites did not borrow more extravagantly in absolute numbers, but relative to their incomes, they carried nearly double the debt burden of white households. While living in suburbia tended to add $106 to the debt burden of the average white household, it added nearly three times that amount, $282, to black households, even after adjusting for income.[25] Suburban black consumers were five times as likely as white consumers to borrow, even after controlling for income, wealth, and mortgage status.[26] Unlike white suburbanites, no black suburban households reported only using cash to buy durables. Among black households that bought, 81 percent bought using just credit, compared to 40 percent of whites. Black prosperity, even more than for white debtors, was a borrowed prosperity, inhibiting long-term wealth formation. African Americans paid more in interest, not only by borrowing more frequently, but in paying more for their suburban housing.

Black mortgagees paid more than whites for their housing, since whites disproportionately had greater access to lower-cost federal loan programs. Historians have correctly explained the racial composition of the suburbs through the discriminatory lending practices of federal loan programs, such as those offered by the VA and the FHA.[27] Yet, the *Under-*

writing Manual lending guidelines also preferred suburban housing to urban housing. Given the massive push toward suburbia exhibited in the FHA and VA planning documents, one might think that suburban locations in and of themselves would predict whether a mortgage was federally insured. The data do not bear out this conclusion. Though there was a higher frequency of federally insured loans in the suburbs, location was not statistically significant.[28] The difference in suburban lending was a result of racial discrimination, not a lender preference for suburban housing. While there was no statistically significant relationship between residential location and federally insured loans, being white made a household 3.69 times as likely to have a federally insured mortgage.[29]

By the 1950s, the sources of such mortgage discrimination were more complex than in the 1930s when the FHA *Underwriting Manual* simply redlined African American neighborhoods. While the early years of FHA explicitly redlined mortgages to racial and ethnic minorities, by the late 1940s, under political pressure from groups like the NAACP and the Urban League, the FHA began to rethink its policies.[30] In 1947, the FHA hired racial relations officers to oversee its lending policies to make sure they were race-neutral and to oversee a public relations campaign to convince black Americans that FHA lending was fair. In the late 1940s, FHA officials seemed to believe their policies were merely race neutral and simply reflected a naturally occurring market. Following this belief, the FHA, for instance, took a strong stance against racial covenants. Despite the *Shelley v. Kraemer* decision in 1948, which forbade court enforcement of racial covenants, such covenants persisted across the country and were enforced informally by the real estate industry, limiting the ability of Jews, Asians, and African Americans to buy property.[31] The FHA stopped recognizing the legitimacy of racial covenants in providing mortgages, and then in 1950 explicitly forbade insuring mortgages to properties with such covenants.[32] Preserving a race-neutral market was for these officials tantamount to fairness.

Even after such actions to make FHA insurance race neutral, black access to FHA-insured housing remained meager. Larger connections of race and finance choked off capital to potential black home owners. Dehart Hubbard, a FHA racial relations officer, attempting to explicate the inaccuracy of this race-neutral position, explained in a 1949 internal memo that the FHA "original Underwriting Manual and the ambiguous language of the 1947 revision" that struck out explicit racial provisions "did little to inspire confidence among minority groups."[33] Positive action was needed by the FHA if minority groups were to own homes at the same rate as whites.

The market failure puzzled FHA administrators. Builders and developers, while hesitant to build integrated housing, happily would build black-only housing, if the buyers could get financing.[34] Emanuel Spiegel, president of the National Association of Home Builders, told the Urban League at their national convention that "the greatest obstacle to better housing for Negroes is the lack of adequate financing"—that resulted from "deep-rooted racial prejudice."[35] The National Association of Home Builders attempted in the mid-1950s to push its members to develop subdivisions specifically for African Americans. Household incomes for African Americans since World War II had risen several fold, and builders wanted to take advantage of those rising incomes.[36] Financing, however, proved a stumbling block. Working to ban racial discrimination from its operations was far easier than cultivating investors willing to invest in racially mixed or minority neighborhoods.

The FHA found that while it could insure mortgages, finding buyers for those mortgages proved difficult.[37] The national resale of mortgages that supported the growth of the white suburbs did not work for African Americans. Investors, like large white-controlled insurance companies, were more likely to invest in FHA-insured apartment complexes for African Americans than individual houses.[38] Some resales of black mortgages occurred, but not with the certainty that white mortgages were resold, making housing subdivisions more risky for builders. FNMA could buy the mortgages, but unable to resell them, had to suspend purchases. While some local banks in predominantly African American areas would buy mortgages, these banks, with limited capital, could assist only local building.[39] Black insurance companies proved unable to support black suburbia in the way that white insurance companies helped build white suburbia. In 1947, for example, the fifty-five members of the National Negro Insurance Association (NNIA) had only twelve approved FHA investors, whose investments totaled only $1.5 million. One company, North Carolina Mutual Life Insurance Company, of Durham, accounted for 55 percent of this total investment.[40] Despite the pressure from the FHA to buy more mortgages, there were limits to what black insurance companies could do.[41] The top twelve white-controlled insurance company holders of owner-occupied FHA mortgages, in contrast, held $633 million in mortgages.[42] The 424 mortgages owned by the entire NNIA could not, in any realistic sense, support the housing needs of black America, and white insurance companies would not buy the mortgages. Even the black insurance companies, with $80 million to invest and over $10 million in outstanding mortgage loans, devoted less than 2 percent of their investments to FHA mortgages.[43] Limited capital rendered FHA loans for African Americans both harder to get and more expensive, limiting the kind of broad explosion of suburban housing for African Americans that whites enjoyed.

FHA administrators lamented the widespread perception that minority neighborhoods invariably lost value, believing that this was the cause for the lack of white investment. Pointing to the research of economists, FHA administrators tried to convince potential investors that conventional wisdom, created in part by FHA policies in the 1930s, had pegged African American neighborhoods all wrong.[44] Academics found housing values actually went up. Black incomes had increased three-fold since the 1930s, yet, as the FHA commissioner lamented to the annual meeting of the Urban League in 1952, many bankers and investors were unaware of the quickly rising economic resources.[45] Yet insurance companies continued to buy few African American owner-occupied mortgages. Letters to the FHA reasserted, even in the midst of these rising incomes, that African American default rates were disproportionately high. One letter from the American National Bank and Trust Company of Chicago to the FHA commissioner, claimed that though "non-white borrowers" accounted for "18% to 20%" of their borrowers, non-white borrowers accounted for "35% to 40%" of delinquent accounts.[46] Even occasional anecdotes or experiences that reinforced commonly held beliefs were hard to undo through academic studies and rhetoric. By the end of the 1950s, two-thirds of white households owned homes, compared to only one-third of black households.[47] The FHA could not force insurance companies and banks to invest and without a source of capital, black home owners could not get as many FHA or even conventional mortgages.

If a black family could get a mortgage, the amount actually borrowed was the same for both white and black households. Without taking any other factors into consideration, the mean gap between the mortgages of black and white households was substantial. After controlling for suburban status, however, there was no meaningful difference between mortgage levels.[48] Suburban living, rather than race, drove how much a household borrowed, as one might expect, since prices would differ based on location rather than the race of the borrower.[49]

African Americans paid more in interest to live in the suburbs than whites. While interest rates did not vary overall between the city and the suburb, they did vary by race.[50] Black mortgagees paid more than whites. The interest rates on federally insured loans were lower than those on conventional loans. The interest rates for black households, as shown in figure 5.4, skewed higher than for white households. Cheap FHA and VA mortgages allowed borrowers to afford the more expensive suburban housing.[51] Compared with African Americans without an FHA mortgage, households with federally insured mortgages had mortgages $3,518 higher, after adjusting for income, than the average black mortgage.[52] The FHA and VA programs, when African Americans were able to use them, allowed for much better housing choices. Having access to the federally insured loan programs, however, made African Americans no more likely than those without access to move to the suburbs.[53] African American

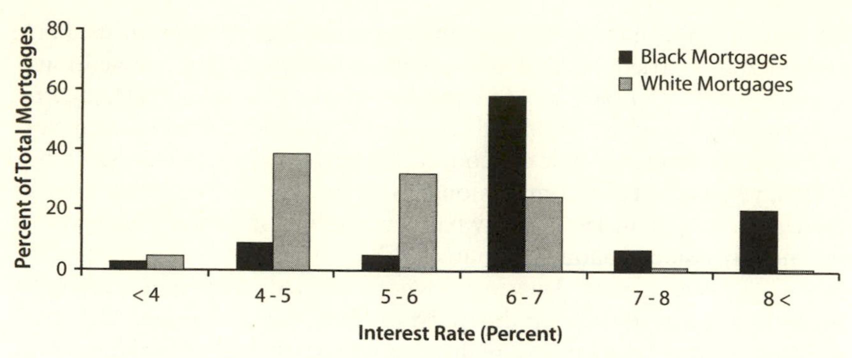

Figure 5.4. Interest Rates by Race. Black households, disproportionately denied federally-insured loans, paid higher interest rates. Source: Survey of Consumer Finances, 1958.

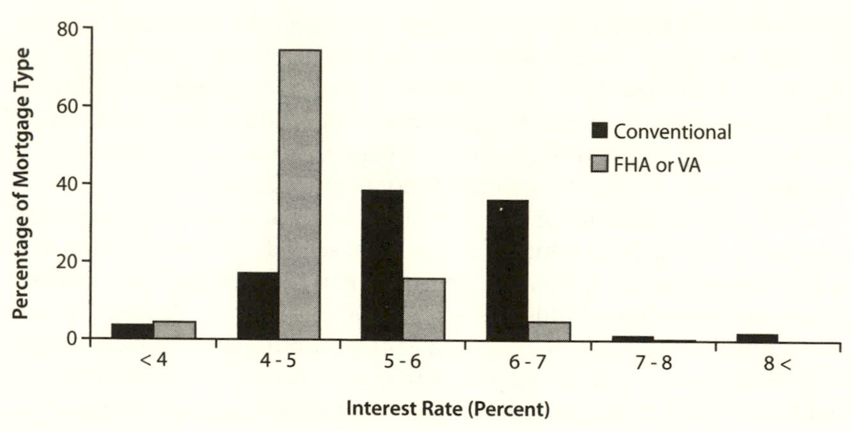

Figure 5.5. Interest Rates by Type. Federally insured mortgages had lower interest rates. Source: Survey of Consumer Finances, 1958.

mortgagees who wanted to move to the suburbs, and could find housing, did so with or without the federal loans.

Suburban African Americans had to borrow to get the life that they wanted. Yet to have this life, the black middle class had to pay more in interest for both consumer goods and for housing, which inhibited long-term wealth formation. Partially cut off from the larger circulation of mortgage capital by racist investing processes, African Americans paid more if they could borrow at all. Still, the trade-off between material prosperity and long-term wealth must have seemed a vexing but easy decision to make. After a long road to the suburbs, middle-class African Americans must have wanted to enjoy cursing the crabgrass and the watching the second television just as much as their white neighbors; and like many of their white neighbors, they borrowed to do so.

The Early Failure of Bank Credit Cards

Businessmen did not matter nearly as much as suburban housewives in the creation of the credit card. While the bank credit card had been invented in the 1950s, its use was narrowly confined to traveling businessmen. America's shift to the credit card began with shopping at the local department store, not on a business trip. The mix of financing available to consumers had been changing since the 1920s, but merchants still overwhelmingly supplied consumer credit—not the bank. Asked as late as 1961 what kinds of financing respondents could use to shop at local retailers, 23 percent mentioned charge accounts, 14 percent mentioned installment plans, and 19 percent mentioned revolving charge plans. Only 1 percent of respondents mentioned bank charge plans.[54] The credit practices of department store consumers, not businessmen, drove the proliferation of revolving credit in the postwar period. The credit card, as we know it today, is modeled on this practice of credit, not bank cards.

Bank cards existed, but went largely unused. Combining the new debt practices that emerged from the wartime regulation, Diner's Club, along with now forgotten local bank charge cards, formed the first bank card systems in the early 1950s. Growing out of the personal loan department, these credit cards attempted to combine commercial banks' experience with personal loans with the demands of retail. Though experimented with by local savings banks, it would be national commercial banks, like Bank of America and its BankAmericard that truly realized the promise of this innovation, but not until consumers had learned to borrow at department stores, and not until the late 1960s.[55] The early experiment by major banks, like Chase Manhattan, shut down after only a few years.[56] Bank credit cards did not supersede department store credit cards until the 1980s, but their roots, like the department store plans, are to be found in the postwar. Throughout the 1950s, the most widely used charge cards were not from banks but from department stores and other retailers.

As the Charga-Plate revolving credit system spread across the country in the 1940s and early 1950s, banks began to offer other revolving credit systems, also relying on the Charga-Plate technology. These credit systems relied on the infrastructure that had been created through the expansion of the Charga-Plate charge account and the new practices associated with revolving credit. Innovations in consumer credit lending emerged wherever revolving credit took hold, but these experiments largely did not endure.

One such experiment began in Flatbush, Brooklyn, where a young banker named John C. Biggins, while working at his father's bank, noticed that the local cash stores lost customers to the department stores downtown that offered credit.[57] By the late 1940s, grocery stores, butchers, hardware shops, and other firms that until the 1920s operated on nineteenth-century-style open account credit, had become cash-only to compete with the lower prices of the cash and carry stores. But though the stores could not afford to offer credit, the customers still needed it. In this challenge, Biggins recognized an opportunity. The bank could offer credit directly to the customers of these cash stores. The bank could replace the shopkeeper as the main supplier of credit.

The "Charg-It" plan that Biggins envisioned was not a simple replacement of the old butcher ledger. He brought to bear all the modern credit systems popularized by department stores in the 1940s. Applications for the plan could be made at either the bank or a member store. Rather than the informal personal relationship of the older open book credit, the Charg-It plan investigated each applicant using a credit bureau. Successful applicants received a Charga-Plate for identify.[58] Using the Charga-Plate, the bank could exploit all the cost savings associated with centralized accounting, billing, and collections.[59] Daily, stores would send the bank a slip with the charges and the bank would, that same day, credit the store's account, even before the customer paid the bill. The bank then used a "National Class 31 (18) cycle billing machine," like the department stores used, to send notices to the customers.[60] Centralized, mechanized credit, pioneered by department stores using Charga-Plate in the 1940s, made the per transaction cost of the Charg-It system much lower and more reliable. Descriptions of the system explicitly stated that the "mechanics of the system parallel[ed] the system used in any department store."[61] The lax collection policies and accounting of small shops would be replaced by professional, mechanized collection systems of the bank. Capital, always short in retail, would be supplied by the bank as well.

The Charg-It plan required no personal relationship between retailer and consumer. Customers could use their Charga-Plate in any store that belonged to the plan, whether the owner knew them or not. Biggins based borrowers' limits on the credit bureau report, not on personal relationships. The shopkeeper would know nothing of his customers' finances, only their purchases. The Charg-It plan made charge accounts impersonal and institutional even at the neighborhood store. The local retailer could not use credit to bind customers to the store, but without the bank the retailer would lose the customer to the department store who could.

The neighborhood store, the thinking went, could better compete with downtown stores, and the banks made money from both the stores and the shoppers. The regular 30-day charge account had no fee, but Charg-It shoppers were charged 0.5 percent per month, or 6 percent annually, for the revolving credit account.[62] The bank, at the same time, charged retailers 8 percent of each purchase—an enormous cut of the revenue.[63] While they got immediate use of the funds, retailers also lost 8 percent of their sales revenue.[64] For the banks, 8 percent must have made for a tidy profit, but it fatally limited the number of retailers interested in such a program. Certainly department stores, with their own credit systems, wanted no part of it. Small retailers, already facing difficulties, must have been dubious, despite the opportunity to lure customers back in.

Such a novel program as the Charg-It system was not unique, but more of an incremental improvement over existing wartime department store practices that many banks were discovering.[65] Biggin's Charg-It system was not the only centralized, bank-run charge credit program independently created in the early 1950s, and all the rest relied on the same factors: offering department store credit techniques in exchange for hefty cuts of the revenue. Like the Charg-It plan, they were created for cash stores outside the downtown to compete with the large credit-granting department stores.[66] These credit programs, though resulting from innovative bankers seizing the opportunities of the moment, only became possible because of the spread of department store credit practices. But they did not take off.

When Biggins's father sold the small Flatbush National Bank to the large commercial bank Manufacturers Trust Co., shortly after Biggins had created the program, the new owners promptly shut the program down.[67] Biggins left Brooklyn for New Jersey, joining the Paterson Savings and Trust Company as the head of their personal loan department. Here Biggins made the Charg-It system work. The infrastructure of the personal loan department was set up for just this kind of processing; the department had experience with small loans and connections to credit bureaus. Moreover, if customers charged too much on their revolving or regular charge accounts, the bank, a reviewer noted, could easily "consolidate all their debts" as well as offer them loans for "other worth-while services."[68] Biggins ran his program in the New Jersey suburbs successfully for many years, and through its success, ended up as the bank's president.[69] Yet his program remained a novelty. His small bank did not have the capital to expand such a program. Moreover, the program was limited to smaller, independent stores. The major stores where people shopped—the department stores—would not take Biggins's cards or any other card offered by another financial institution. The long road to universal credit cards would take another twenty years, but in the interim Americans managed to borrow what they needed from department stores. While bank cards remained novelties, confined to particular local areas or to consumer niches, like traveling businessmen, mainstream America shopped at department stores on Charga-Plates.

The Success of Department Store Credit

Like any industry, department stores needed to constantly increase profits, but unlike many industries, there had been no noticeable increase in organizational efficiency, reflected in increased profits, since the mid-1930s. With the exception of World War II, gross margins on merchandise had stagnated since the Great Depression.[70] The cost of running a department store could not be further reduced. Only by increasing revenue could profits continue to grow. Retailers could either build more stores or sell more goods to each customer. Between revolving credit and suburbanization, it turned out that they could do both at once.

Federated Department Stores' postwar plan relied on intertwining suburban expansion and revolving credit. Federated had formed in 1929 as an alliance between local department stores to share capital and expertise, but before World War II the management of these stores remained relatively autonomous. Following the war, however, Federated transformed from a holding company with loose control over its original stores, which were based in the northeast, to an actual company focused on managing a national expansion. Abraham & Strauss, Bloomingdale's, and Filene's would maintain their unique brands but with greater merchandise, finance, and operational coordination. To maintain profits, Federated wanted to follow its customers and conducted detailed studies of where the American population was moving to gear its operations accordingly. Unlike before World War II, when Federated concentrated on the profitable operation of its downtown stores, in the postwar period it began to focus on building suburban branch stores of its well-known downtown brands and by expanding its operations into the booming Sunbelt. The first and biggest of its suburban expansions was the Abraham & Strauss store in suburban Long Island in 1951.[71] By 1953, Federated operated seventeen branch stores across the country. As Federated described in its 1954 *Annual Report*, "Abraham & Strauss is as much a part of Brooklyn as the Dodgers. When Brooklynites moved to the suburbs, they usually moved to Long Island." And like the Dodgers, Federated also moved its investments to Los Angeles, reflecting the shifts in the American population.

Not surprising, as American consumers moved to the mortgage-financed suburbs, so too did their locus of shopping. The auto literally drove this new model of shopping. New branch stores of the downtown department stores were built at the intersection of the highways. Federated built

Sanger's "Big Town" branch, for instance, seven miles from downtown Dallas at the intersection of highways 67 and 80 on the loop around the city, where parking lots for their customers could be more easily accommodated.[72] Parking lots for autos pulled the shoppers into the suburban stores. From 1945 to 1955, the parking lots of Federated Department Stores, the prominent nationwide retail chain, increased in area from 65,000 to over 2.5 million square feet. Branch stores had more space for parking than for shopping.

What made this expansion possible was the tremendous success Federated had in capturing the dollars of the postwar consumer. Using Federated's innovative credit policies, consumers spent more money than ever before. These profits borne of credit-driven sales allowed Federated to grow across the country.[73] Focusing on the population shifts of the postwar period, Federated sought to open new stores in the growth areas of the Southwest, like Los Angeles and Albuquerque, under the name Fedway, and by buying regional chains like Bullock's-Magnin in Los Angeles, Sanger's in Dallas, Goldsmith's in Memphis, and Burdine's in Miami.[74] In this expansion, Federated focused on three points: first, becoming the "dominant store"; second, providing the "service and merchandise" that its stores were known for elsewhere; and third, using "those techniques of operation" that had made Federated so successful in other markets.[75] In its suburban expansion, Federated Department Stores began to see revolving credit as one of its most effective techniques to expand sales.

Department stores expanded sales by building new stores in the suburbs and through revolving credit—both in terms of drawing new customers into the store and having them spend money. In 1955, half of new stores opened in suburbia.[76] Revolving credit was an important way to bring customers into these new stores and to build loyalty. When new stores opened they would send unsolicited plates to customers in the area. Of course the "area" was carefully considered to make sure it was, as one industry consultant, Howard Abrahams, called it, one of the "right neighborhoods."[77] Surprisingly, these stores reported there was no difference in rate of default between those customers who applied for an account and those who got them unsolicited in the mail.[78]

Getting those Charga-Plates into customers' pocketbooks even before the store opened made all the difference to sales. Americans loved their charge accounts and nearly three-fifths of all households had a store charge account. Since consumer credit came from these persistent relationships, shoppers could not, on a whim, drop into a new store and buy on credit. For a customer to shop at a retailer, that retailer needed to already have the Charga-Plate in the customer's hand. Stores vied to make sure their Charga-Plates, and not a competitor's, were easy to come by.

Still, even once a customer had a Charga-Plate, it was usually one of many. Eighty percent of charge account customers had accounts at more than one store.

Revolving credit was even more important in the suburbs than in the city. Two-thirds of white suburbanites shopped with revolving credit and monthly payment credit that was twice the rate of white city-dwellers.[79] Industry professionals reminded stores that though the suburban consumers tended to have a higher income than their urban counterparts, they also had more demands on their income.[80] Abrahams reminded credit managers that the "stressing of the revolving credit account appears very important" in capturing the business of these consumers.[81] Already in debt for their auto and their home, "the extended payment plan is very appealing."[82] Half of surveyed households had bought something on installment credit in the past two years at a department store and one-third of the households had used multimonth credit plans. Three-fifths of those who had bought on the installment plan, moreover, had also used a multimonth credit plan at a department store as well.

Consumers bought a variety of goods through these two forms of credit. Reversing conventional wisdom about credit buying, more consumers bought clothes than durable goods on credit, even though more respondents thought buying durables on credit (83 percent) was the "right thing to finance" rather than buying clothes on credit (32 percent). Those that bought on credit overwhelming paid on monthly terms, with 22 percent using revolving credit and 33 percent using unspecified "monthly payments." Only 14 percent of credit buyers used 30-day charge accounts. Of those that bought on multimonth credit plans, 35 percent bought clothes, 22 percent bought furniture and house furnishings, and 20 percent bought durable goods and household appliances. Revolving credit slowly overtook installment credit, not only for soft goods but for durable goods as well, even though respondents believed that they should use more structured installment credit for durables. As more consumers used revolving credit, they began to abandon installment credit for both everyday and long-term financing.

Retailers loved credit customers because they bought more than cash customers. Even 85 percent of consumers knew that someone with a charge account was "likely to make more purchases than a person who doesn't have a charge account."[83] Credit manager of The Fair in Fort Worth, Texas Dean Ashby, reported that "the average charge sale was three times the average cash sale."[84] Ray Johnson, the credit manager of The Boston Store in Fort Dodge, Iowa accounted in detail the differences in buying patterns between cash, 30-day, and budget revolving accounts customers. Per sale, the average 30-day charge customer bought 134 percent more than a cash customer, while the average revolving account customer bought 62 percent more.[85] Although the 30-day customer bought more per sale than the revolving account customer, the revolving account customer shopped more frequently—with an average of 3.8 transactions per month compared to 2.3 for the 30-day customer.[86] Over two-thirds of the revolving account customers shopped at The Boston Store each month, compared to about one-third of the 30-day customers.[87] The revolving account customer, on average, bought 107 percent more than the 30-day customer in a month.[88] Revolving account customers had higher store loyalty and spent more money than either 30-day customers or cash customers.

Retailers recognized that expanding the revolving credit customer base would expand sales. The desire for these types of customers was so strong that stores still sought the credit business of customers who had been laid off. Bessie Tearno, credit manager at The Wallace Company in Schenectady, New York—which at the time faced widespread industrial layoffs—worried that "many of our former charge account customers were reluctant to continue to use their account because of these reduced incomes."[89] The answer, for this credit manager, was not to restrict credit when there was a "decrease in take-home pay" but to convert her customers, and Schenectady's workers, to revolving credit, which would give them more flexibility in their repayment schedules. Converting charge customers who had difficulty making payments on the 30-day plan to revolving credit accounts, would help the customers more, Tearno believed, than cutting off their credit. The Wallace Company charged customers 1 percent interest per month, or 13 percent per year on their unpaid balances, unlike on the 30-day plan, which helped offset their expenses in carrying the account. While the credit manager was more responsible with his department's budget, the same could not be said for the consumer.

The older notion of the responsible credit manager looking out for customers' budgets appeared less important than helping them buy even when enduring reduced incomes. The customers, Tearno believed, "fe[lt] a certain satisfaction in knowing that they continued to maintain a high credit standing with the store" even in the face of "reduced work schedules." The customer could rely on the revolving credit to get them through the slow times and the store would win that customer's loyalty. During this charge campaign, Tearno was happy to report, The Wallace Company increased their accounts from 7,500 to 35,000.[90] Both customers and retailers alike assumed that slack industrial times like those of the early 1950s in Schenectady, could not last and credit could help retailers and consumers weather the ups and downs of the business cycle. While Tearno encouraged customers to borrow more money, the Wallace Company still imposed limits and hardly any of the accounts exceeded $90.

Though Tearno enthusiastically promoted the revolving credit, limits still existed.[91]

The limits at the heart of the revolving budget plan ultimately produced a contradiction that undermined its profitability. Credit managers had derived much of their self-satisfaction from their paternalism, helping consumers decide how much they "ought" to borrow. But credit limits, as they were designed to do, stopped the buying. Revolving credit customers bought more frequently, but could buy no more than their limits allowed. Unlike 30-day charge accounts, which had no limit, revolving budget accounts' limits constrained spending. The impulse to curtail unpayable accounts and paternalistically to supervise consumer borrowing ran up against the need to sell more merchandise in the competitive boom times of the early 1950s. Among larger retailers the moral strain was evident. As the credit manager at Federated's Lazarus & Co. remarked in 1954, "we try to control our revolving accounts, but we are more interested in increasing sales."[92] In the mid-1950s, however, most credit managers still clung to the importance of borrowing limits and maintaining low outstanding balances.[93]

Another problem also dogged the revolving budget account. While on average, the revolving patron spent more than the 30-day customer, not everyone was average. One credit manager at Ziesel Brothers Company in Elkhart, Indiana, Robert Calvert, felt that the limits of revolving budget accounts had actually hurt some of his sales potential by restraining higher-income customers' purchases. Wealthier patrons signed up for revolving accounts at the store and used them, but bought much less than they would on the 30-day accounts that had no limits. The novelty of the revolving account intrigued some wealthier customers and the store gave them the plan they wanted, but in doing so the store also sold them fewer goods. Calvert related the story of a "very well-dressed lady of neat appearance" who had recently moved to a "better section" of Elkhart.[94] Checking her records at the credit bureau and at the store, he found that she spent and paid for $15 worth of goods every month. Her credit bureau report revealed that in the city in which she previously had lived, she had had a 30-day account through which she spent nearly $300 a month. The budget revolving account, intended for the poorer customers, had migrated up the class hierarchy until it was actually constraining the purchases of well-off customers. "The cold fact" that the woman could buy more but would not because of the limit frustrated Calvert and every other credit manager.[95] As revolving budget accounts became more mainstream, limits intended to reduce the bad debts of low-income consumers actually hurt sales to middle-class consumers.

Part of this contradiction between expanding sales and revolving budget accounts also arose from the differences in sales logic between department stores and durable-good retailers, from whom the practice of installment credit had arisen. Revolving budget accounts followed installment credit's practice of limiting sales, but the soft goods that department stores mostly sold had a different time cycle than installment credit. In a durable goods store, like a furniture shop, households might buy a bedroom suite on installment, but rarely would they need to buy another bed anytime soon. For department stores, the picture was completely different. A customer might buy a shirt, but the next week he might need to buy pants. A store focused on sales and profit, and not a short-sighted concern with payments, would try as much as possible to keep a credit line open for the customer to buy as much as possible.[96] Quick, repeat business was at the heart of the department store, which offered a variety of goods for sale that wore out quickly. The logic that made sense with installment sales was fundamentally incompatible with a business model driven by repeated, small purchases.

As the pressure for higher sales and the realization that customers paid back what they borrowed set in, soft good retailers began to question their assumptions about credit limits. For many stores, the fears of the unpaying customer went unfulfilled. Almost everyone paid what they owed. A survey in 1954 showed that among stores with over $20 million in annual sales, there was a median loss of .14 percent in charge sales, .43 percent in installment sales, and .81 percent in revolving credit sales.[97] This survey was very small but the anecdotal evidence supports its main claim that under 1 percent of borrowers defaulted on their store credit accounts. Slowly credit managers began to warm to the idea of relaxing the limits and letting customers decide how much to borrow. The credit manager of St. Louis's Boyd's, Kenneth Oetzel, remarked in 1955 that the "best sales promotion idea" would be to tell customers that their credit department was not a "protective department."[98] Adhering to the initial limits on revolving credit, he believed, hurt sales. If departments "doubled or tripled" the limits, Oetzel thought they would "sell more merchandise."

Federated Department Stores agreed. After a year and a half study, Federated announced in 1955 that it was going to switch to a more "flexible" system of credit for its customers.[99] Always the innovators, Federated Department Stores by 1956 had begun to implement its experimental "flexible credit limit plan," which began the unraveling of the connection between budgeting and revolving credit.[100] Herbert Landsman, Federated's research director, explained that the goal of this new experiment was to tap into the affluence of the new suburbanites. Landsman believed that revolving credit was the best way to draw in the business of the "$3000 to $10,000 a year family income group[,] . . . many of whom are young, have established families and bought homes in the new suburban areas, and have all those needs which go with new homes and growing children."[101] In suburbia, Landsman believed, this income group was "the nucleus for the movement to the suburbs where new ways of living have been established." Revolving credit, Landsman held, was an important part of this new way of life.[102]

Federated's early innovation and promotion of revolving credit had led, Landsman believed, to fantastic "volume and profit growth of the company."[103] Unlike what detractors of the revolving credit plan had predicted at the outset, the problems Federated actually encountered had little to do with default. Customers, it seemed, always wanted to exceed their budget limits, and when special dispensations were provided, they paid Federated back. Federated, in Landsman's opinion, "regarded revolving credit customers as less able to spend and pay than was realistic under present economic circumstances." In Federated's credit policy lingered the class-biased perception that the revolving credit customer was less well-off than the charge account customer.

By the 1950s, however, even if this perception remained, the preference was for revolving credit, even among the middle-class. Special procedures did permit specific customers to exceed their budget limits, but such on-the-floor authorizations always created administrative complications for the credit department. Authorizations by floor managers could not be easily mechanized and they disrupted the efficiency gains of the automated credit billing and accounting systems. Floor managers scrawled authorizations onto account cards and ledgers, creating the possibility of easily losing track of who had borrowed what and whether the customer actually had the financial status to back up that borrowing.[104] What good was a limit if it had to be frequently broken? Moreover, the more responsible customers—who could probably be safely loaned more money—were exactly the kind of people who would not even ask to break their limits.[105] In the opinion of the charge sales manager at Martin's department store in Brooklyn, the customer who wanted to break their budget limit usually was "the poor risk who owes you two or three hundred dollars on a ninety dollar account and gives you a big collection headache."[106]

Federated needed to find a way to make this limit more flexible and contain the credit chaos. In doing so, however, Federated credit managers still could not bring themselves to abandon the idea of a proper limit for balances. Landsman reiterated that Federated still feared "over-buying" and the bloating of balances resulting in a "serious delinquent condition."[107] The new flexible credit limit program created a system for customers to exceed their budget limits, but still provided pressures to keep their balances under that limit. Like the postwar income tax system now widely experienced by consumers, the flexible credit limit was graduated.

The standard Federated limit on the revolving budget account in the mid-1950s was $120 and the flexible limit program maintained that limit, but allowed customers to go over it. As customers exceeded that limit, the amount they had to repay each month increased, from 8.3 percent for $120 to 25 percent when the balance was above $300.[108] With flexible limits, floor managers no longer had to decide on a case-by-case basis whether to allow customers to surpass their limit. The flexible limit resulted not only from the administrative problems of credit managers and the demands of consumers, but also from new billing machines that could be programmed to calculate, for each customer, the amount owed.[109] More flexible machines allowed more flexible billing. But it was the pressure of sales, the headaches of managers, and the desires of consumers that drove the innovation in credit limits to take advantage of the new machines.

With the flexible credit limit program, for the first time consumers—not credit managers—determined what their proper limit ought to be. The flexible credit limit program was an experiment not only in streamlining administration but in seeing how consumers would respond to unlimited credit. Unlimited credit payable over time was a possibility that no customer had encountered before Federated's program. The paternalistic credit manager limiting purchases for the good of the customer was no more. Would consumers run amuck? In this free-fall of choice, Landsman wanted to know "whether customers will, in fact, use this self-discipline."[110] The answer to that question would come quickly, as retailers adopted credit plans in the early 1960s that did away with credit limits entirely.

By the early 1960s, consumers' ideas also began to change about the class signification of stores that offered installment (lower class) or 30-day charge accounts (higher class). Whereas 30-day charge accounts had been associated since the 1920s with high-end stores, by the early 1960s the majority (61 percent) of those surveyed believed that there was no difference in quality between stores that offered revolving or installment credit and those that only offered 30-day charge accounts. Only 6 percent thought the 30-day credit store catered to "high-income people." The old-time charge account had lost its cachet. According to the interviewers, two-thirds of the sample exhibited no preference for either the "type of store" that had 30-day or revolving credit. The lower-class stigma of stores that offered revolving or installment credit had waned.

If the stigma had waned, opinions about those who borrowed was mixed. More than race or class, Americans' ideas about borrowing depended on their own habits.[111] Consumers who used charge accounts and installment credit disproportionately thought that credit users like themselves were "ordinary."[112] More tellingly, credit users also disproportionately thought that people who used credit were "well-to-do" and had "lots of money." Borrowing made these debtors feel affluent, even as it sapped their wealth. Consumers who did not borrow had sharply divergent impressions of debt. Survey respondents who did not use charge or installment credit thought that those who did were "spendthrift," "impulsive," and "unwise."[113] Ideas about credit use closely matched up with credit habits, even as they did not align with income. Once a consumer began to borrow, borrowing seemed more normal and ordinary, even a way to show that you had finally made it.

Mortgages, auto payments, and revolving credit began to make sense as part of a larger world of practices and opinions. Credit enabled households with limited wealth to live the lives of their more affluent neighbors. Shopping, however it was financed, provided both a social outlet and a consumer strategy for Americans looking to live the good life. It was on the suburban periphery—built out of mortgage debt, shopped at through department store revolving credit, and driven to on automobile loans—that the true promise, and hidden costs, of credit equality would be understood.

Option Accounts and the Contradictions of Sales and Capital

Beginning in 1958, the credit industry witnessed changes in practices that moved consumer credit from an adjunct to sales to a source of profit in its own right. The experiments with limits that had occurred through the middle of the decade were consolidated in a new type of revolving credit that was cumbersomely named the "monthly charge account with option terms," which was quickly abbreviated to the far simpler "option account." This new credit practice completely erased the credit limit. Instead of the graduated repayments of the flexible limit plan, a customer would pay a fixed percentage of the balance—1/2, 1/3, 1/6, or whatever the store deemed appropriate.[114] Interest would be charged on the remaining unpaid balance. It is at this moment that interest rates, which had still been at the breakeven rate of 1 percent per month, shifted to the profitable 1.5 percent per month or 20 percent per year.[115] The interest rate added to the store's service charge, which varied widely but usually amounted to a few dollars. The option account excited credit managers because it enabled them to earn profits on their departmental balance sheets. Retailers widely recognized that credit drove sales profits, but as credit managers politicked for power and recognition within their organizations, they rarely got the same status as the merchandise managers—largely because their departments only lost money or broke even. The option plan transformed the social and profit opportunities of the credit department and in doing so remade its role with the company, rapidly forcing companies to confront the limits of their own ability to finance consumer receivables. While immediately popular to consumers and successful in promoting sales, the option account also placed onerous demands on the capacity of retailers' capital, even as it presented the possibility of that capital earning profits by becoming consumer debt.

The option account put the decision to repay in the customer's hands. Either the customer could repay in 30 days and pay no finance charge, or repay over several months. For credit managers, combining the two kinds of accounts—revolving budget accounts and 30-day accounts—solved many problems at once. They would no longer have to hound their 30-day customers who missed a payment, which happened frequently and which alienated the delinquent customers.[116] The store would automatically begin to charge them interest and a service fee. Without limits, there would be no need for special, time-draining exceptions to the limit.

Rather than help consumers budget, the option account just helped them buy more. The option account inverted the moral justification for the revolving budget account. Whereas the revolving account was intended to help the customer stick to a budget worked out in concert with the guidance of the credit manager, the option account placed the choice with the customer. An assistant credit controller with Gimbel Brothers remarked that, "the approach is extremely logical to the customer because she becomes her own credit manager."[117] This logic was at odds with the logic employed fifteen years earlier, when women were assumed to be profligate and in need of control. The invariably female customer now enjoyed the empowering ability to choose how much to borrow, without consulting either her husband or the male credit manager. In face of the demand and need for the option account, the gender logic underpinning the credit relation shifted.

Because revolving credit was so much more profitable than 30-day credit, department stores promoted the use of revolving credit in numerous ways. In the store, credit managers pushed option accounts on young couples registering at the "Bride's Shop." Young couples had, in the words of one credit manager, "to furnish homes from top to bottom" and would need credit to do so.[118] Relying on the credit rating lists of credit bureaus, stores sent direct mailings to customers with good credit. One store found that 50 percent of this targeted audience opened accounts within three months.[119] Newcomers to town, whom stores found through their registration at the local credit bureau when they set up their gas, electric, and phone accounts, would be sent Charga-Plates in the mail.[120] The credit manager of Macy's bought new home owner lists and mortgage reports, believing that "no woman moves without wanting to redo her new house" and an option account would enable her to redo the house without worrying about the budget.[121]

Consumers generally responded enthusiastically to the option account. Some customers—mostly older customers habituated to the 30-day accounts—objected to the combination of the two systems. Mindful of a class distinction that was quickly eroding in the new suburban lifestyle, older customers clung to the signification of being the kind of person who had a 30-day and not a revolving account.[122] Invoking older meanings of privilege, one customer complained to a Detroit credit manager that, "If you are going to penalize me just because I was a little over 30 days paying my bill this month, well, you can close my account."[123] Another customer complained, invoking the budget justifications of the previous decade, that she had "paid $20 a month for years on my account, now you want $30 for the same outstanding balance. This completely upsets my budget, and I am sending you $20 as usual. If this is not acceptable, please close my account."[124] In the end, however, credit managers did find that "many former habitual delinquent 30-day customers now [paid] their accounts in full each month to eliminate [avoid] the service charge."[125] Such complaints, while exceptional, still exposed the discursive shifts between the older 30-day and revolving budget accounts and the new option account. The same Detroit credit manager who received these letters also emphasized that personal attention tended to smooth over the transition. All the customers who complained converted their accounts to the option plan and were not lost.[126]

As expected, customers bought more. Much more. As early experimenters predicted, the option accounts increased sales. Revolving customers bought more and now all customers had the option to become revolving credit customers at any time. On the option plan, one store increased its credit sales 20 percent. Another store doubled its accounts receivable in one year.[127] One credit manager reported that former charge account holders who would only buy "small purchases from time to time," "these same customers now consistently run sizable balances" with the option account. [128] The profit-oriented credit manager would become, as one credit manager insisted, "a zealot in the conversion of thirty day accounts to the newer forms of income-producing accounts."[129]

Some smaller department stores had resisted offering credit because of the expertise required in evaluating credit histories, but the option account required less expertise to administer than either the 30-day or budget revolving accounts. The option account could be easily and rapidly adopted, even by those stores with little credit experience. Unlike earlier credit plans, the option plan required less extensive expertise in setting appropriate limits, as the task of the credit manager as disciplinary figure largely had devolved to the customer. For instance, Garvin's department store in Lancaster, Pennsylvania, a city with a population of 70,000 in 1960, had three department stores. When Garvin's decided to move beyond 30-day credit, a field in which they had participated for only five years, they decided to jump immediately to option revolving credit.[130] All accounts were converted to the option account. Initially, the interest rate of 1.5 percent was higher than their competitors in Lancaster, but customers embraced the option plan anyway.[131] Sales increased 18 percent and new accounts increased 23 percent.[132] The two other stores in Lancaster quickly followed suit, adopting the option plan and raising their interest rates to 1.5 percent. When the option plan entered a market, consumer demand and firm competition quickly drove its proliferation.

As credit departments shifted from unprofitable consumer conveniences to profitable consumer necessities, credit managers changed the way that they understood their receivables. David Bollman, the credit manager of Pittsburgh's Joseph Horne Company, chastised the shortsightedness of the "many credit managers [who] take pride in the small losses they have. Yet with that low loss ratio, how much business are they turning away by being so strict?"[133] Despite the over-buying of merchandise that had to be marked-down, no one faulted the department store buyer. Customers bought more when they had more choice. The net result was more sales and higher profits. Yet the credit manager was encouraged to not allow any defaults. Perhaps, Bollman suggested, this was not the most profitable way to practice credit. Offering more credit, he also suggested, might sell more of those clothes that eventually had to be sold at a loss. The possible defaults would be more than offset by the greater sales.[134]

Unlike the credit manager of the 30-day account, who was focused on quick repayment and low outstanding balances, the profit-oriented credit manager of the option account needed long repayment periods and large outstanding balances. Gribbon instructed other credit men in the novel idea, at least in the early 1960s, that "if maximum income [was] to be achieved" the store must promote the "extending [of] the payment terms."[135] Longer periods lowered monthly costs, which made customers happier even as they paid more in interest. Relating the experience of Macy's, Gribbon noted that in 1958 installment accounts had a longer repayment period than revolving accounts—nine months versus seven months. In 1959, Macy's told its customers that longer periods had been arranged for both types. Customers responded "enthusiastically," while paying more in interest and service charges.[136] The consumers still eventually paid off their purchases, but Macy's "service charge income followed the upward course of sales and receivables."[137] Defying the "traditional view" about the longer-paying customer, which held that the longer a customer took to pay, the greater the likelihood of default, Macy's found it was more profitable to offer longer terms—longer terms that also did not increase the rate of default.[138] The option plan, moreover, did not restrict customers to budget limits that had to be repaid before more purchases could be made. Customers bought more and the credit department made more money.[139]

While the new option account drove department store sales and consumer balances ever higher, it also caused new financing difficulties for the stores. Even by 1958, R. H. Bulte, a credit manager at Stix, Baer & Fuller in St. Louis, remarked that "more money [was] invested in Accounts Receivable than in merchandise inventories."[140] Like most stores, more than 60 percent of his store's sales were on credit. Stores needed credit to meet their sales and profit goals. At the same time, however, stores needed more and more money to handle the ever-higher levels of consumer borrowing. Leondias Trotta, the manager of the NRDGA Credit Management Division, pronounced 1959 "an eventful year for the credit profession" because it was, he believed, the "year which will mark the turning point of concepts to the realization that credit can and should be a self-supporting function." Yet at the same time, Trotta noted that while credit had grown in importance and profit, "today credit receivables exceed the total value of inventories and represent the largest single asset of department stores except for land, building, and fixtures."[141]

In the early 1950s, Federated Department Stores, for instance, offered three kinds of charge accounts: installment, 30-day, and revolving budget accounts. In February 1952, consumers owed Federated about $60 million: half the money owed, $31 million, was in 30-day accounts; $24 million was in revolving budget accounts; and $16 million was in installment accounts.[142] Six years later, Federated had $136 million in outstanding accounts, of which two-thirds was revolving credit ($90 million) and one-third was 30-day credit ($43 million).[143] Two years later in 1960 balances reached $167 million. In 1960, Federated had net retail sales of $760 million for the entire year.[144] If at one moment in February it carried over 20 percent of its yearly sales in accounts receivables, the capital required to finance those balances was not inconsiderable.

Few credit professionals recognized, at first, how difficult it would be to scale their credit operations up, even as their sales growth depended on expanding their customers' debts. In 1959, Federated's John Lebor cautioned other credit managers about their calculations of profitability. Until the late 1950s, credit departments broke even or lost money, but overall they drove up the stores' profitability through sales. Some credit managers tried to calculate how much their credit expanded sales as a way to show higher management that their departments made money for the company. For these calculations, they relied on certain values of the "cost of capital," which they took to be the interest rate on a 90-day bank loan.[145] Lebor, sensitive to the institutional constraints that so strongly shaped their business, reminded other credit managers that "the facts of life are that not even one-half the capital we need to operate our stores can be borrowed." No bank would lend a department store all the capital it needed to finance their receivables. A department store's capital had to be primarily derived from internal profits and stock sales. The belief that a store could simply borrow from a bank, Lebor insisted, was "a serious fallacy that, if followed for a sustained period, can destroy a large part of the value of a business."

Despite his warnings, many credit managers continued to believe that they could expand their receivables and borrow money to finance their customers. Yet the structural limits to capital could not be avoided. To get more capital they would have to either divert working capital from other parts of their businesses or sell stock. Stock sales were always expensive and very inflexible. Though department stores needed to expand their credit operations to continue to expand their sales, internally and externally they would confront the limits of what they could actually finance. Economies of scale would not apply to department store credit operations. As their credit operations grew, the capital required would grow more expensive, not less expensive, as they ran out of available bank funds. Department stores faced a punishing feedback loop of credit, sales, and capital. To restrict credit would cut sales. To expand credit would require expensive borrowing. As department stores entered the 1960s, customers continued to increase their spending on credit and their accounts receivable swelled. Department stores, unbeknownst to their managers and owners, would soon have to decide whether they sold merchandise or credit.

The drive to cordon off credit from sales came also from the internal institutional aspirations within department stores. Beyond the internal contradiction of capital costs and credit expansion, there were always ambitious executives within firms who saw the option plan's profitability as the gateway to their own increased autonomy and power. John Gribbon, manager of the accounting department of Macy's, suggested the far-reaching implications of this revision in the role of the credit department. Calling for the credit department's separation from retail into an "autonomous entity," Gribbon the accountant envisioned the department through the lens of the balance sheet.[146] Imaging the columns of numbers, he saw the autonomous credit division having "two sources of income: the service charges paid by customers, and a commission on credit sales paid to it by the store." Charged for overhead and interest by its owning company, the credit division's "primary goal . . . would be to increase store profit," not just sales. The "Net Cost of Operation" would be the judge of its effectiveness. Service charges and profitability on its receivables would drive its profits. Separate and autonomous, its operations and incentives would shift.

For Gribbon, the profit-driven credit division would also increase the personal status of the credit manager. Rather than an adjunct or junior partner to sales, credit would become a source of profit in its own right. Gribbon suspected that, with a credit department driven by profits, "the credit manager would be treated on the same basis as the merchandise manager."[147] This profitable credit manager would "be paid incentive bonus, so his success or failure, as well as his earnings, would be determined by the net operating results of his department."[148] Along with status equality would also come income equality with the merchandise manager. To the ears of credit managers, this increase in status and income would have been a welcome one. The secret to this personal prosperity was credit department profits and the expansion of consumer balances. The option plan offered both. The expansion of accounts receivable would give credit managers the raw material to make profits. Drawing an analogy to the merchandise managers, Gribbon said that, "one can no more maximize profits while working with minimum receivable balances, than he could with minimum inventory."[149] To maximize the store's profits and their own status, credit managers had to grow the accounts receivable.

Of course once this credit unit became separate, it mattered little to the company who operated it, as long as the company got its share of the profit. The recognition of functional difference opened the door for other companies to come in and subcontract the credit operations of stores. Department stores, after all, primarily made their money on merchandising. In 1959, Macy's John Lebor had said, "fundamentally our business is selling merchandise. We make our profit from this function and not from the extension of credit." This belief drove the choices of department stores through the 1960s as they confronted the limits of capital.[150] Once credit was separated, it no longer mattered to the core retail business, nor did it matter socially to the executives who controlled the internal politics of the company. While some credit managers watched their departments grow into profitable subsidiary corporations, others saw their entire credit operation subcontracted out and their power taken away. Just as debt for the consumer had become separable from the products sold, debt had also become separable for the retailer. The constraints of capital and the demand for sales, however, drove the institutional transformation of consumer credit in many different directions.

How to Grow: Retailing, Manufacturing, or Financing?

Even as firms confronted similar capital shortages as they expanded their credit offerings, different firms found different solutions. Whether these firms were large retailers like Federated Department Stores and Sears, who formed their own finance companies, or smaller retailers like Wolff & Marx, who looked outside for financing or durable goods or manufacturers, like General Electric, who converted archaic installment credit subsidiaries into dynamic credit leviathans, all retailers had to find a solution to the capital scarcity created by the retail expansion of consumer credit. Since credit could not be constrained without tanking their core retail business, retailers had to borrow more funds or subcontract their credit operations. No profitable retailers actually tried to restrain their customers' indebtedness.

For the largest department stores, one option was the creation of their own internal, or "captive," financing company. In 1959, Federated, which had for the past decade looked outside the company to partially finance its growing receivables, organized a wholly owned subsidiary company to handle its consumer credit.[151] The Federated Acceptance Corporation began to handle the chain's consumer credit financing needs. Even long-time retailers with established banking relationships for financing their receivables formed finance companies to capture the profits of consumer credit. Other department stores, like Sears, Roebuck, confronted problems similar to Federated. Large retailers like Sears had financing options not available to smaller stores. Since the 1930s, Sears had offered installment credit to its customers, but since 1937 it had also sold these contracts to banks and finance companies outside the company.[152] Beginning in the early 1950s, Sears began to increase the amount of internal financing of installment accounts. According to its 1950 annual report, Sears had "an abnormally heavy demand for durable goods in the second half of the year" spurred by "the Korean fighting." Sears sold $360 million worth of consumer paper to banks and financed $87 million internally, which was 1.8 times the previous year's internal financing.[153] In just that year, Sears went from financing 23 percent to 30 percent. By 1957, credit sales accounted for 44 percent of total annual sales.

Recognizing the importance of credit and the profits it was forgoing to its financiers, Sears formed a subsidiary captive finance company to finance its customers' purchases—the Sears Roebuck Acceptance Corporation (SRAC). SRAC made its money by selling short-term bonds to institutional investors, who in turn financed the installment purchases of Sears's customers. The decision was profitable. In the first full year of operation, total installment contracts owned swelled to $289 million, with a new income of nearly $2 million.[154] The following year income doubled to $4 million and contracts grew to nearly $400 million. Through the early 1960s Sears continued to invest in SRAC, expanding the initial $50 million investment by $115 million from 1964 to 1966.[155] Sears could have invested in stores, inventory, or production but decided that the best investment was in growing its ability to finance consumer debt. The next year, in 1966, SRAC realized a net income of $31 million.[156] By 1967, SRAC earned over $100 million a year, which was comparable to other major finance companies like GMAC, CCC, and GECC.[157] Sears had successfully turned its small installment finance operations into a major financial firm.

Stores large enough to offer their own option credit plans but too small to form their own finance companies could look outside their organizations to national finance companies. For instance, San Antonio's Wolff & Marx turned to a national financing firm, the Commercial Credit Company. The story of Wolff & Marx appears typical in its intertwining of revolving credit, sales growth, and suburban expansion. Edward Sullivan, president of Wolff & Marx, remarked in 1961 that it had "been apparent to us for some time that we would need additional working capital by this year if expansion of sales and the consequent enlargement of receivables was to be continued." Like most department stores that had converted to revolving credit in the 1950s, their sales had grown, but as customers reached the limits of their revolving budget accounts they stopped buying. Sullivan lamented the stalling of sales growth as "many of our customers had bought their limit and we were in effect budgeting their charge purchases" and restraining their consumption.[158] To convert to the option account, however, would require vastly more financing, but to not convert would inhibit sales growth.

Though converting to the option plan "would strain [their] cash position," Wolff & Marx had to become "more progressive," Sullivan thought, to keep their sales growing. The demand for additional working capital when Wolff & Marx opened their suburban store pushed the company to look for new sources of capital. The store had borrowed "to the limit" at the bank to finance its revolving budget accounts and could not get any additional money.[159] Moreover, the bank demanded an onerous reporting on each account for which the store borrowed money. The bank tended to see each loan as for a particular set of goods or for an individual customer rather than a fungible blend of customers, goods, and accounts. A single default required reports and repayment. The bank was used to lending to businesses for singular investments, not volatile volume of revolving credit.

Turning to the Commercial Credit Company (CCC), Wolff & Marx found it could borrow the full volume of accounts receivable without the need for laborious paperwork.[160] CCC understood the ways of consumer finance from its experiences with automobile and durable contracts.[161] Wolff & Marx could borrow 30 percent more capital than at the bank and without the need for the large staff that the bank's report required.[162] With the influx of capital, the store could concentrate more on merchandising—building a more flexible and fully stocked inventory of clothes. Between the credit promotions and the larger inventories, sales at Wolff & Marx went up 42.4 percent over the previous year.[163] Turning to finance companies made borrowing, Sullivan said, "simple and pleasant."[164] CCC Executive Vice-President James Newman remarked that the "billions of dollars by which retailers' sales have swollen within the past few years, [have] strain[ed] the limitations of the conventional money arrangements that are readily available to the stores."[165] Newman and CCC observed that many stores confronting the limits of their capital had "become obliged to restrict their credit sales—the lifeblood of profit increases—for no other reason that that of obtaining funds to enable further growth."[166] Without the "convenient borrowing methods" that CCC and other finance companies could provide, department store growth would be choked off.[167] For smaller retailers, finance companies provided capital at a cost that allowed consumer debt to grow and retailers to profit off the ever-increasing sales.

Large manufacturing companies had different needs from retailers, but they also had different options. More than strict retail companies, manufacturers experienced the limits of capital through the dealers who sold their goods, though they were aware, more generally, of the shortage of capital among retailers. Like many other manufacturing companies in the 1930s, GE had set up a wholly owned subsidiary corporation to finance the installment contracts of its dealers—the General Electric Credit Corporation.[168] Like many other captive finance companies, GECC, originally named General Electric Contracts Corporation for its focus on installment contracts, expanded in the postwar period into retail finance related to GE products.[169] By 1960, GECC financed over $500 million worth of retail sales and nearly $250 million in wholesale inventories a year. But the growth of GECC's profits was threatened, Charles Klock, president of GECC wrote in its annual report, by the "increasing variety of revolving credit plans."[170] Revolving credit eased the purchasing of amounts both "large and small," enabling consumers to bypass the specialty financing of GE dealers.[171] At the same time, because of the "large number of low-balance transactions that must be financed," revolving credit seemed "unpromising" to GECC, but over the long term, because of its prevalence, Klock thought that "profitable methods must be found to meet the need for this type of credit."

At the same time, consumers who still shopped at specialty appliance dealers turned elsewhere for their credit. Though 1963 was a banner year for sales, credit sales at GE dealers had decreased, although credit extensions in general had increased. Consumers, the GECC believed, were turning to outside financers like small loan companies, which offered cheaper rates.[172] At the same time, consumers also used debt consolidation loans more frequently, decreasing the interest that GECC earned on its loans.[173]

Durable good retailers, by the early 1960s, began to look to alternative credit plans, like revolving credit, as installment credit's advantages for durable good sales—such as the possibility of repossession in case of default—no longer held as much sway. Installment credit of the sort that GE dealers offered had become less important by the early 1960s because of the decreasing prices of resale goods and changes in the legal relationship between finance companies and dealers. Repossession, by the early 1960s, was no longer a viable economic strategy for durable goods other than autos. By the late 1950s, many installment sellers stopped filing their contracts with the government, a necessary step in case repossession was needed. For instance, one refrigerator dealer sold over 20,000 units a year.[174] To file the contract at the courthouse cost $1 per contract, or over $20,000. In the last year he actually filed, he repossessed twelve refrigerators, which meant that he paid $20,000 for twelve used refrigerators that he might or might not be able to resell. It made no economic sense. E. O. Johnson, credit manager of Famous-Barr in St. Louis, reported that they sold between 25,000 and 30,000 installment contracts a year, and in their warehouse they had only "three pieces of repossessed merchandise" in January 1956.[175] Most people paid off their contracts, and for those that did not, it cost more to repossess than to write off the loss. When customers did not pay their debts, one credit manager asserted that the unfiled installment contract was "purely psychological" as "a good collection lever" because it cost too much to pick up and resell the goods.[176] While important perhaps as a threat to make sure that installment contracts were paid up, the goods, once repossessed, could not be easily resold. Intense manufacturing competition kept the prices of GE appliances and television sets relatively low. If consumers could buy new goods cheaply and with easy credit, why would they buy them used if they did not have to? The "major portion of credit losses" for GECC in 1963 was for repossessed and unsellable appliances. Without economically viable repossession, installment credit's advantages seemed unclear.

Moreover, because of a changing legal relationship between the installment finance company and the appliance dealers, dealers were no longer *required* to take repossessed stock and sell it. The relationship between the retailer and the contract holder had gradually shifted in the previous decade to a "non-recourse" relationship. If the buyer defaulted and the durable good was repossessed, the holder of the debt had no recourse to the dealer. The dealer was not obligated to resell the merchandise. For the debt holder, profits had to be made on the debt itself, independent of the value of the durable good. Without recourse, the installment debt became separated from the good itself. For installment financers, the lack of recourse pushed them toward new ways of thinking about consumer finance where they would not be left holding the bag if the consumer defaulted.[177]

Since by the early 1960s goods could not be profitably resold, the holder of the revolving debt cared less about repossession. The enforcement of the debt obligation, then, became more important than control of the merchandise. As John Lebor of Federated Department Stores noted in 1959, "customers feel a greater moral obligation to meet their general unsecured obligations than those secured by a specific merchandise item."[178] What made a loan a good loan was the borrowers "ability to pay," not the "replevin value" (the repossessed value of the goods).[179] Having the goods repossessed could no longer absolve the buyer of the debt. Revolving credit severed the connection between the goods and the money owed on the goods that had so defined the installment credit relationship. The separation of debt obligation and legal title that would have made financiers nervous in the 1920s created new opportunities for financiers' investment in the 1960s. Changes in the profitability of resale drove this transformation in debt investment.

Making the customer directly responsible for the money through revolving credit made profiting on the debt much easier. The decreased prices of durable goods in the early 1960s led, unintuitively, to the death of installment credit, not because people chose to buy these relatively cheaper goods for cash, but because these lower prices depressed the sale price of used goods. Astute credit professionals like Lebor recognized that "revolving budget accounts were a natural outgrowth" of this shift.[180] Under outside pressure from other finance firms and internal pressure from changes in installment contracts, GECC introduced an experimental plan in 1961 for revolving credit for its dealers, with tremendous long-term ramifications for both GECC and General Electric.[181]

By 1964, GECC found this revolving credit, without its complicated contracts, was drawing customers back to its appliance dealers. Moving to the new revolving credit rewarded GECC with greatly increased profits. Klock reported in 1964 that, "practically our entire increase in volume and profitability came from new types of financing we introduced in the last five years."[182] In other words, from 1960 to 1965 GECC reinvented itself from an installment contract finance company into a revolving credit finance company. The annual reports of this period reported enthusiastic forays into credit reporting, computer billing and collection, and other techniques required for revolving credit. With its deep pockets,

GE invested in large-scale credit processing facilities at regional computing centers.[183]

With the expansion of such capacity for evaluating revolving credit applicants and the ability to process its billing, GE now could extend its computing power beyond its own dealers. Though expensive, these systems enabled complicated billing schemes heretofore unknown to retail. Computers allowed firms to efficiently keep track of aging accounts. Option accounts, with their highly variable repayments, needed this more intensive data processing to work properly and their increased profitability and consumer desirability spurred companies to use ever-greater amounts of data processing equipment in their businesses. Imagine combing through stacks of paper to find which accounts were 90 days late and which ones had been paid. Imagine doing this for millions of dollars of sales.[184] Then imagine having access to a wondrous machine that, with a click of a button, would not only call up all the sales records but print out bills at the same time, and then one gets an idea of what possibilities computers allowed for the retail industry.

In 1966, GECC began to offer its revolving credit services to other retailers who could not afford to buy the expensive computer systems and also to provide the capital needed to finance revolving credit operations. Like installment finance companies had done in the 1930s, GECC offered "private label" credit to retailers unable or unwilling to finance their own revolving credit plans.[185] Retailers would maintain brand loyalty but use GECC's financing and machines.[186] Discount chains like Caldor's, for instance, could now offer their own "Caldor's Credit Card" like a more well-to-do department store.[187] Customers appreciated Caldor's trust in them and, like department store revolving credit customers, tended to shop more, but unlike at a Federated department store, GECC and not Caldor's would reap the profits on the debt. By 1968, over half of GECC's profits came from this relatively recent turn to revolving credit.

In less than a decade, GECC went from helping GE realize its profits on mass production of televisions to financing soft goods at Caldor's. By 1969, one in twenty-five households was using GECC credit, whether it recognized it or not.[188] While GECC's profits had stagnated in the postwar period, after 1961 when revolving credit was introduced GECC's net earnings increased, on average, 17 percent a year.[189] In 1969, recognizing the strength of its new financing schemes, GECC separated revolving credit off from its Home Products division. Consumer financing had become completely autonomous from GE's manufacturing wing. GECC's 1972 *Annual Report* noted that the company provided "personal credit card service to mass merchandisers of soft goods, housewares, cosmetics, luggage and just about anything sold by the average department store or discount chain."[190] GECC's revolving credit division had only a tangential relation with GE's core manufacturing business, and through its private label revolving credit business financed the purchase of goods manufactured by GE's competitors.

GECC had begun to move beyond the organizational scheme and profit logic of an economy based on manufacturing to one based on finance. Profits were reaped not through the expansion of GE sales but by financing the purchase of goods regardless of the manufacturer. In the expansion of GECC into these new arenas of consumer credit, GE's began its epochal transition from a manufacturing company to a finance company. While in the 1960s manufacturing still dominated the profits of GE, in the shifting investment priorities of large manufacturers the outlines of a post-Fordist economy in the making could be seen.

Credit's Future: The Return of the Bank Card

As early as 1959, John Lebor surveyed the retail field and noticed "more types of retailers adopting credit selling." Though department stores had led the way—habituating consumers to borrow on their cards and creating innovative organizational techniques to make revolving credit profitable—other firms took notice. At first, department store professionals like Lebor believed the bank credit cards would have little effect on their business. Such cards, they believed, would enable small stores to offer credit like the department stores, but the practice would not expand because banks' charges absorbed so much profit.[191] What this argument neglected was that by the early 1960s credit was not seen as a customer courtesy but as a customer necessity. Department stores had done their job well in convincing consumers of the benefits of revolving credit. Small retailers hoping to compete offered bank cards, whatever the cost. For department stores, however, there was no need to allow the use of bank cards in their establishments. In an informal survey of NRDGA membership, less than a quarter of stores allowed the charging of bank cards at their stores.[192] More important, only 1 percent of households knew they could even use a bank card at their local department store.[193] Lebor and most other credit professionals thought bank cards would "have no substantial effect on department store revolving budget credit."[194] Stores offered their own plans and resisted the incursion of outside creditors.

NRDGA, nonetheless, invited a group of representatives of the new bank card industry to their 1959 credit managers' conference. While there had been early forays into universal credit cards in the early 1950s, with rare exceptions like Diner's Club, most programs had been halted.

Chase Manhattan bank had unveiled a large program in the early 1950s only to close it three years later.[195] But by the dawn of the 1960s, commercial banks had rethought their assumptions about credit cards.

Witnessing the profitability and popularity of the department store cards, banks began their own programs. One of the speakers at the convention was Citibank's J. Andrew Painter, who had begun his career in consumer credit at the first personal loan department operated by a commercial bank in the 1920s.[196] While the "Citibank Ready-Credit Plan" was only three months old, Painter saw it as the natural extension of Citibank's "thirty one years of our personal credit" offerings.[197] In its first three months of operations, Citibank received over 40,000 applications for its bank card, of which they approved two-thirds—over $13 million in credit.[198] Charging 11.78 percent annually, its program was more expensive than conventional personal loans, but cheaper than the 20 percent then charged by department stores. Painter explained consumers' "great deal of interest in the plan" from the ways in which "people have been accustomed to thinking in terms of the availability of credit when they want it; and that is why all types of revolving credit plans have been so successful."[199] Citibank's bank card program relied on the shift in consumer practices learned at department stores.

Other company representatives speaking at the convention, like Joseph Garcia of the seven-month-old American Express Company, pointed to the range of stores without ready access to credit. American Express, Garcia explained, would focus on "service establishments" like "hotel charge privileges, motels, restaurants, auto rental, specialty store shops such as florists, candy stores, luggage shops, and so forth."[200] Specialty cards, like Carte Blanche, which had been in business for three weeks, hoped to replicate Diner's Club for specific markets. The Hilton Hotel chain, owner of Carte Blanche, intended its card to encourage brand loyalty and repeat business, like department store charge cards, among a core market of "eight million men and women of responsibility . . . who make $7,500 a year or more."[201] These new credit cards, whether narrowly focused or broadly conceived, all relied on the new habits of borrowing that American consumers had become accustomed to in the 1950s. Unlike retailers, these finance companies and banks did not have the limits of capital to restrain their financing of consumer debt. With their larger capital pools, banks, always searching for more marginal investments, would enable consumers to borrow even more. Though initially they did not threaten the ways in which most Americans shopped on department store cards, they portended the world of universal credit cards, owned by banks and large finance companies like Citibank and GE, in which we live today.

Conclusion: Institutionally Resolving the Contradiction of Capital and Credit

The suburban world of credit promised prosperity to many different kinds of Americans, who though they came from very different places in society could share a common material prosperity. Debt made this shared consumption possible. Was it more moral to spend only what was in hand, the popular personal finance magazine *Changing Times* wondered, than to borrow and give "children nursery school, music lessons, and travel" or "a better home and neighborhood"?[202] While "debtors" might have been popularly denounced as "a segment of society at the bottom of the income scale," as one senator said as he bemoaned the credit-driven economy, debtors were, in fact, not the bottom of the scale but the scale itself, against which the achievements of prosperity were measured.[203] Borrowing enabled the good life, not only for the earner but for the earner's family. The family was in debt but they also enjoyed all the modern amenities that the postwar consumer world offered.

Whether through internal or external financing, retailers found opportunities to access the capital they needed to expand their sales and consumers' borrowing, changing both the way they did business and the ways in which American consumers borrowed. Most retailers made the choice, as Lebor had predicted that they must, to be merchandisers. At the same time, that choice was not so resolutely made by large manufacturers like General Electric. Disconnecting its finance subsidiary from a direct connection to their manufactured goods, GECC began a long road to becoming GE Capital, one of the largest financial companies in the world today and one that has no privileged relationship with the products of GE, outside of the dividends paid to the shareholders who own both companies.

Consumers at the same time enjoyed the flexibility and empowerment that credit without limit provided. For the first time, consumers decided how much they should borrow. This new credit made sense to retailers and financiers because of the decreasing importance of repossession and property rights associated with the installment contract. Profits were still made on manufacture and sale, but the lower consumer prices of goods also made them more difficult to resell. Fordist manufacturing had created a world of material plenty for those who could pay for it. But the important point, for capital, was that the consumer paid—both through buying the goods and through interest.

With the option account, retailers and consumers had arrived at a new credit system that separated debt completely from the goods borrowed for, and which made the enforcement of the debt relation itself matter more than the recovery of the goods unpaid for. The economics of the low-cost manufacturing that was necessary but not sufficient for this new credit system did, nonetheless, support its proliferation once it came into existence.

The postwar economy began to change in the mid-1960s, as America's economy began its decisive shift from manufacturing to service—from a high-wage economy based on balanced growth and historically low levels of inequality to a world where inequality, so pervasive in pre–World War I America, once again began to emerge. At the center of this transition, consumer credit would both enable and constrain the political actions, economic choices, and survival strategies of working Americans. They were entering a world in which their existing habits, borne in a world of growth, did not prepare them. At the end of the postwar era, as we will discuss in the next chapter, those groups denied credit looked to the state for redress of their exclusion, seeing debt as the sure path to the good life. Even as the state began to guarantee that access, the wage growth upon which the virtuous cycle of debt depended, disappeared. No state policy could substitute credit for wages forever, and for those who began to borrow in the 1970s the economic commonsense developed in the postwar economy would no longer make any sense at all.

Chapter Six

Legitimating the Credit Infrastructure

RACE, GENDER, AND CREDIT ACCESS

BY THE MID-1960s, a two-tier credit system had emerged in the United States. The practices, technologies, and assumptions embedded in the credit practices of affluent and poor consumers could not have been more divergent. For middle-class Americans, credit had become an entitlement. Rather than a privilege, it was a right deeply imbricated with suburban material culture and everyday middle-class shopping habits. Home buyers borrowed their mortgages, financed their cars, and charged their clothes. To be denied credit went beyond an economic inconvenience; credit access cut to the core of what it meant to be an affluent, responsible adult in postwar America.

Even as poor Americans evinced consumer desires of the 1960s, their credit experiences remained more akin to the world of the 1920s. For poor African Americans in the cities, in particular, credit relations had toxically stagnated. Urban ghetto retailers kept their accounts in leather-bound ledgers and collected payments door-to-door every week, rather than on mainframes that billed automatically like suburban retailers. Credit cards were non-existent. Mortgages were hard to come by.[1] Less transparent and more prone to hucksterism, urban credit relations seemed to exploit poor consumers' limited geographical mobility, meager financial resources, and fear of impersonal institutions.

Affluent white women, despite their greater access to retailers, confronted inequalities in credit as well. In a world of retail set up for men or dependent married women, working married and divorced women struggled to acquire independent credit access. Credit scoring and rating systems, purportedly objective, were in practice based on the life patterns of men. Objective credit standards were geared toward affluent, white men. In a consumer society dependent on credit, even well-paid women could not borrow for cars, homes, or department store shopping, which curtailed their choices and insulted their sense of self-worth rooted in the consumer privileges of their class. Professional women wanted credit access concordant with their economic power.

Even as the credit problems of affluent, white women and poor, black Americans emerged for different reasons and with different consequences, credit reformers lumped both as discrimination. In the name of fairness and equality, activists, executives, and policymakers negotiated a series of laws in the late 1960s and early 1970s intended to promote credit "fairness" for all Americans—first for women and then for many varieties of discrimination. In attempting to end discrimination, Congress pushed businesses away from possibly prejudiced loan officers to more objective computer credit models, which legislators thought would remedy discriminatory lending.

Through these acts, the federal government grappled with the ubiquity and centrality of consumer credit in the economy, and with the fact that denial of access to credit, whether because of race, income, or gender, constrained the choices and quality of life available for consumers. Though critics attacked the particular ways in which the credit system was constituted, there was no longer a fundamental critique of the role of credit itself in the economy and society.[2] By the 1960s, credit access was deemed to be unequivocally beneficial. Credit use, far from marking one as immoral or unthrifty as it might have in the 1910s, denoted high social status and personal responsibility. In the 1960s, those without credit agitated for more "fair" or "equal" access. By the end of the decade, as access to credit became a social marker of independence and prosperity, various credit activists for women and people of color demanded access to credit. Those left out—middle-class women and working-class African Americans—wanted in.

Congress passed laws to guarantee impartial (which was equated with "just") access to credit. At the same time, these laws legitimated practices that would have seemed usurious two generations earlier. Despite the regulation, the mechanisms of debt enforcement and surveillance—credit rating agencies—remained outside federal control, which might have made the credit system truly transparent. Attempts to create a federal credit information agency failed and credit rating information remained the province of private corporations and not the government. By the 1970s, consumer credit, legitimated as fair through federal policy, grew to an unprecedented volume and creditors extended it, in the name of consumer equality, to all Americans with uncertain consequences for the country's economic future.

"White Man Ain't Milking Me No More": Ghetto Riots and Congressional Reactions

As Americans watched poor, black neighborhoods burn in April of 1968, the causes of the riots, which included widespread looting, it was commonly believed, went beyond a protest of Martin Luther King's assassination. For some, rioters had simply run wild, indulging themselves in the consumer goods that they ordinarily could not afford. For many white policymakers, however, a lack of ownership, rather than a lack of consumption, explained the riots. Since the neighborhood residents did not, for the most part, own the stores, rioters burned them. But for black leaders, as well as white intellectuals and politicians long involved in credit reform, the reasons behind the riots were more complicated and tied not only to the difficulties of ownership, but to the credit system poor Americans faced in a society defined by consumption.[3]

Even before King's assassination, in July of 1967 President Johnson had appointed the Commission on Civil Disorders to understand why poor, black residents of American cities had been rioting repeatedly for the past two years. That most stores in riot-torn areas were white-owned, the Commission found, led to "the conclusion among Negroes that they are exploited by white society."[4] While emphasizing unemployment and a lack of business ownership in black communities, the Commission also pointed to the "exploitation of disadvantaged consumers" as one of the causes of the riots. Rioters, protesting merchants "selling inferior goods" or "charging exorbitant prices," had lashed out against white merchants.[5] Poor families in the ghetto, after all, had the same postwar material desires as the affluent residents of the suburbs. Nearly all poor, black households, for instance, had televisions. The way that inner-city consumers purchased these televisions, however, could not have been more different than the way that suburban consumers bought theirs. Unequal debt and consumer practices were at the heart of the divide in the Kerner Commission's oft-repeated pronouncement that, "our nation is moving toward two societies, one black, one white—separate and unequal."[6]

Rather than just anonymously taking televisions, groceries, and clothing from stores, the actions of many rioters revealed deeper frustrations with their personal relation to retailers. The rioters exacted the vengeance of consumers repeatedly wronged as they looted stores. The perceived wrong was the selling of shoddy merchandise at high prices on credit with usurious interest rates. The rioters rebelled not only against the white ownership and the substandard goods, but also the draconian credit relations that compelled poor consumers to pay more, get less, and be publicly shamed when merchants repossessed the goods on default.[7] During the April 6th riots in Chicago, the *Washington Post* reported, a 72-year-old neighborhood man, "his deeply etched face illuminated by a blazing grocery store" chanted "burn, burn, burn. White man ain't milking me no more."[8] Credit structured the world of ghetto consumption and it was the structures of the credit system that drew the ire of rioters more than a lack of business ownership in their communities.

Since the early 1960s, a series of investigations, including the widely-read sociology study by Columbia professor David Caplovitz, *The Poor*

Pay More, showed that despite the lower income of ghetto inhabitants, they actually paid more for the same goods than wealthier consumers. A Federal Trade Commission report issued in 1968 detailed the prices that consumers paid in low-income area stores and middle-class stores in Washington, D.C.[9] Prices were much higher at the low-income credit retailer than in the general market. While at the general market store goods that sold for $100 wholesale cost $159, in the low-income store the same goods cost $255.[10] For instance, the exact same model of GE dryer that cost $238 in more affluent areas cost $370 in the poorer areas of Washington.[11] Despite the higher prices, poorer residents who wanted to buy a dryer tended not to leave the neighborhood for the cheaper stores. Local neighborhood merchants offered them credit that many poorer consumers could not get at the lower-priced downtown or suburban stores. Even though, as Caplovitz found in his New York study of low-income families living in public housing, three-fifths of those interviewed thought buying on credit was a "bad idea," these families bought on credit all the same.

Even in public housing, Caplovitz found that those who used credit had a better material standard of living and owned more appliances than those who bought strictly for cash. But that better life came at a cost.[12] The families who bought only on credit tended to stay more within the neighborhood than those consumers who at least sometimes used cash. Seventy percent of low-income consumers only had credit references with low-income retailers or no credit references at all, which meant that they could not get credit outside their neighborhood. Credit tied lower-income consumers to neighborhood merchants, who enabled them to buy more, but at higher prices.

Without credit references, much less credit ratings, downtown stores would not extend ghetto residents credit, confining them to neighborhood stores.[13] Paul Dixon, the chairman of the Federal Trade Commission, testified before Congress that, "the poor are poorly served when seeking to satisfy their wants for home furnishings and modern appliances, products which are part and parcel of an acceptable standard of living in American today." Dixon believed that "steps must be taken which will render unprofitable behavior which seeks to exploit the ignorance, immobility, or illiquidity of the poor." The necessity of consumer credit to buy modern merchandise on a limited income bound poorer consumers to local merchants, who charged higher prices and higher interest rates than the merchants in more affluent areas. Ghetto consumers comparison-shopped less than their middle-class analogues and did not search out the lowest possible prices, opting instead to shop locally. Dixon and other credit reformers thought that a lack of education caused these "buying habits of the poor." Educating shoppers to comparison shop would not, he acknowledged, "alleviate the misfortune of poverty" but would "work to assure that each member of our community regardless of income receives a dollar's worth of goods for every dollar spent."[14] But rather than *just* a failure of consumer education, ghetto consumers could not comparison shop because they could not get credit outside their neighborhoods. Lower-income consumers knew credit buying on such usurious terms was, as Caplovitz found, a "bad idea," but if they wanted televisions and other markers of modern life, they had no choice.

Middle-class conventions of credit lending failed ghetto residents, isolating them from the larger consumer market. Even relatively high-income ghetto residents had few accounts outside their neighborhoods. Fifty-seven percent of ghetto households with incomes over $500 a month either had no credit references or references only with local merchants.[15] One reason that even relatively high-income households from the ghetto had no outside credit was that local merchants actively sought to constrain the choices of low-income consumers. For instance, inner city residents would go to Sears, fill out a credit application, and put down other stores where they had credit. These ghetto retailers would shortly thereafter receive a call from Sears inquiring about the customer. The retailer would claim not to have ever heard of the customer, Sears would refuse the customer credit, and then the retailer would call the customer to tell them to "come on in, your credit is good with us even though not with Sears," as a legal aid lawyer testified in 1969,[16] More than consumer education, ghetto consumers needed a financial path out of the closed credit system of their neighborhoods.

In ghetto economies, the Federal Trade Commission discovered a world of installment credit that had been eclipsed in the revolving credit world of the postwar suburb. Installment credit, waning elsewhere in the economy except for in the purchase of automobiles and houses, remained the most frequent credit instrument of ghetto life. Revolving credit had not penetrated the economic world of the poor. Low-income area retailers charged interest rates whose distribution skewed higher than in affluent areas. While middle-class retailers in appliances and furniture only sold 27 percent of their sales volume on installment credit, in low-income areas retailers sold 93 percent of their sales on installment.[17] While many affluent and suburban stores no longer even offered installment credit, in poor, urban areas installment credit remained the only kind of credit to be had. At low-income stores, 7 percent of installment contracts charged 33 percent interest rates, while no middle-class stores charged so much.[18] Some ghetto merchants charged lower interest rates, but in turn, raised their prices. The FTC investigators found that instead of competing on price, like middle-class retailers did, lower-income merchants competed mostly on ease of credit terms. Whether in prices or in interest, poor consumers paid much more than affluent consumers for the same goods.

With installment credit came the possibility of repossession, which had largely disappeared in the revolving credit economy elsewhere in the United States. The income of ghetto residents, Dixon testified, was "low, irregular, and unreliable."[19] Even after consumers borrowed, disruptions in their income could make them unable to complete the payments on what they borrowed.[20] While repossession had become economically unfeasible for middle-class Americans, the enormous rate of default in the ghetto made it still necessary.[21]

Why was repossession so high in the ghetto? Beyond the irregularity of income, one of the senators involved in credit reform, William Proxmire, believed the "shoddy merchandise" poor consumers bought on time made them feel "taken" and "so many of them stop making payments."[22] Stopping payment, in his view, was an act of protest rather than an act of irresponsibility. Rather than reflecting the creditworthiness of the buyers, the high rates of default reflected the exploitive relationship between the buyers and the sellers.[23] But by breaking the contract, shoppers further eroded their perceived creditworthiness, which made them further "unable to get credit in downtown stores" even though the problem was not the consumers' inherent creditworthiness but the low-quality goods.[24] Small acts of consumer resistance only tightened the grip of ghetto financing structure.

Though the poor paid more, ghetto merchants did not profit more. These merchants charged their customers outrageous prices and grinding interest rates, but their return on investment was actually *less* than that of retailers in more affluent areas. With remarkable access to accounting ledgers, credit applications, and customer surveys, the FTC survey provided a picture of the complete relationship between ghetto merchant and ghetto customer that was lost in other consumer-oriented studies.[25] While the report affirmed the higher prices and shady sales practices found in other studies, it also found that these practices did not result in higher returns for retailers.

Consumers faced higher prices at low-income market retailers, but the sales and credit methods of the ghetto retailer quickly eroded this sales margin. The average gross profit margin at these stores was 61 percent compared to 37 percent at general market retailer, but the costs of the ghetto retailer were quite different from his counterpart in the suburbs.[26] Since nearly all the sales were on installment credit, merchants faced the greater bookkeeping and billing expense that had propelled more affluent retailers towards the advantages of revolving credit in the 1950s. Low-income consumers had higher rates of default and the installment contract, unlike revolving credit, allowed retailers to repossess goods and to take the defaulter to court. And ghetto retailers did.

Ghetto retailers used the courts much more frequently to enforce the debt obligations of their customers than middle-class retailers, obtaining one court judgment for every $2,200 in sales.[27] To put this number in perspective, the FTC pointed out that one large, middle-class department store—whose sales volume "far exceeded" the total volume of *all* low-income retailers in Washington D.C.—had only 29 judgments for the entire year.[28] If middle-class retailers filed suits at the same rate as low-income retailers, instead of 616 court cases a year, they would have had 55,000 judgments.[29] Repossession was a standard part of consumer life in the ghetto, but relying on repossession did not increase profits, it just lowered losses.

While retailers relied on the courts to enforce their debts, they did not rely on bank and finance companies to finance their installment contracts. Unlike middle-class stores, 80 percent of low-income retailers did not sell their installment contracts to finance companies or banks. Only 2 percent of general market appliance stores and 43 percent of general market furniture stores did not sell their finance paper.[30] In-house financing demanded more staff to handle all the accounting and billing for all those installment contracts, which for middle-class retailers were cheaply outsourced to a finance company.[31] Moreover, by not selling their installment paper, low-income retailers had to bear any debt loss directly and, unlike finance companies, could not diversify their risk across cities and companies.[32] For every dollar of merchandise sold by a low-income retailer, 6.7 cents went to bad debt losses compared to the 0.3 cents of a more affluent retailer's sales dollar.[33] With 22 times the bad debt loss per $1 of sales, ghetto merchants had to charge higher interest rates and prices. With such high rates of default, it is unclear whether any finance companies or banks would have purchased the contracts.

Instead of selling contracts to finance companies, ghetto retailers instead borrowed the capital directly from the bank and had to pay for the interest on the money borrowed as well as to repay that money to the bank whether or not customers paid them. By charging higher prices, merchants could not only raise their margins, they could also be more certain of avoiding losing the money they had already paid the wholesaler for the merchandise. If an installment contract ran twelve months, the low-income retailer recovered the wholesale cost, on average, in six months, while for the general market retailer it would take eight months. Anticipating a higher rate of default, the low-income retailer raised prices so that even if the customer stopped paying halfway through the contract, the retailer did not lose money.[34] Between bad debt losses, lawyers' collection fees, higher insurance premiums, more accounting staff, and higher sales commissions, the higher costs of ghetto retailers accounted for 94 percent of the difference in the gross margins.[35] While the ghetto merchant still made 6 percent higher net profits on sales than middle-class retailers, lower volumes, fixed costs, capital expenses, and higher debt losses led small, low-income retailers to make less money on their invested capital than the large middle-class retailers. The rates of return on capital invested showed that despite the higher net profits, low-income retailers actually had a lower rate of return (10.1 percent) than general market appliance stores (20.3 percent), furniture stores (17.6 percent), and department stores (13 percent).[36] The poor paid more, but the merchant did not profit. The credit system of the ghetto hurt both sellers and buyers.

Though the system hurt both ghetto retailers and consumers, it was the anger of consumers rioting in the streets that alarmed Congress and the nation. In addition to the higher prices, the frequent court decisions, wage garnishments, and repossessions that were the bread-and-butter of the ghetto merchant no doubt contributed to the antagonism of poor consumers. Repossessions were public affairs that everyone in the neighborhood could witness. Repo men would come and remove the family television, publicly shaming the family. The public methods of the low-income retailer fostered resentment in ways that the suburban revolving credit, whatever its drawbacks, kept more private.

By no coincidence, the stores that sold on credit, the *Washington Post* reported, were the "most popular victims of the riots."[37] When D.C. rioters broke into many stores, they burned the credit records before they took the merchandise.[38] Burning the records, they hoped, would erase the debts that many rioters had at their neighborhood stores. More than an opportunity to get free merchandise, the riot was a chance to start over. As an "easy-credit" clothing store burned, one man reportedly yelled in the street, "burn those damn records!"[39] In another widely republished account, a mother told her son as they looted a grocery near 7th and S streets, "don't grab the groceries, grab the book."[40] The book held the records of debts that she and her son, as well as many other people in the neighborhood, owed to the store. Burning credit records, it was hoped, would end the onerous interest payments.

The efficacy of this record-burning strategy remains uncertain because the newspaper accounts after the riots so directly contradict the investigations before the riots. According to newspaper accounts, outside of very old-fashioned neighborhood groceries, most stores that sold on credit kept copies of their records off-site. While their merchandise might have been lost, their accounts receivables were not. The *Washington Post* reported that furniture stores, for instance, kept copies of their payment records on microfilm off-site. For stores that used finance companies for wholesale credit or to rediscount their loans, the finance companies also had records. Most stores kept duplicates somewhere else in case of conventional fire, which in these cases also protected them against arson. A *Post* reporter noted that "their stores may not be in the best of shape, but their books look good."[41]

For stores that did not resell their debt, the situation for lenders was more dire. The positive spin in the *Post*, while no doubt true for some stores, was contradicted by the exhaustive Federal Trade Commission (FTC) investigation of the previous year. The FTC found that the vast majority of ghetto merchants, unlike their suburban counterparts, continued to keep their credit records on-site and did not resell them to finance companies or banks, as was the norm for retailers in more affluent areas.[42] If in-house financing had led to exploitation, it had also led to a possibility to resist that exploitation. While the *Post* reported the futility of burning the credit records, it seems entirely possible that many of the records were destroyed in the uprisings. For those retailers who had lost their credit records and along with them all their records of who owed them money, they must have been looking for a way to move those financing operations out of the store, where the records and the accounts receivable invested could be protected. Despite the failure of the rioters to destroy the debt record completely, the lesson of their actions was clear to community leaders and legislators reexamining credit policy—exploitative ghetto credit contributed in a significant way to the April rebellions.

Separating the role of creditor and retailer would have been a way to ameliorate tensions in riot-torn neighborhoods. The FTC report recommended that a clear way to help low-income consumers would be to encourage "local community efforts in the development of effective credit sources [that] could contribute materially to freeing individuals from dependence on 'easy' credit merchants."[43] Whether or not the merchants of the ghetto made excessive profits, the effect on poor consumers was still the same: they paid more than wealthier ones. If a way could be found to extend them credit to shop at stores that would not ordinarily grant them credit, they could spend less and stretch their dollars further.

As Congressional hearings, government investigations, and sociological studies confirmed after the riots, ghetto residents lived in a credit world unimaginable to suburban consumers. Emergent habits from middle-class institutions did not exist in the same way for poor, black Americans. This difference was not simply a gap in consumer education, as many critics suggested, but in how institutional practices constrained the choices of ghetto shoppers. While the financial rationality of the choices that many ghetto shoppers made have seemed illogical to economists and politicians, these choices were no less rational than those of middle-class Americans. The difference for ghetto shoppers was the fragility of their income, their relative lack of political power, and the differences between an installment credit and a revolving credit system.

Before the 1968 riots, credit reform to empower consumers had been largely unsuccessful. Some legislators, like Senator Paul Douglas from Illinois, had pushed unsuccessfully for credit reform throughout the early 1960s. Legislators intended to make all loans express their interest rates and charges in a uniform manner, known as Truth-in-Lending laws, as a way to empower consumers in their credit choices.[44] Knowing the true interest rates on loans, they thought, would allow consumers to choose intelligently from a range of lenders. Douglass and his allies proposed these laws year after year, only to have them stall in committee or lose a vote on the floor. Though the hearings on these bills revealed a great deal of credit trouble in American cities, it was not until the events of 1968 that sufficient political momentum thrust credit to the forefront of American politics.

In the aftermath of the riots, the liberal Wisconsin Senator William Proxmire led hearings that inaugurated a long series of influential credit reforms over the next decade. The assumptions held by policymakers about how to best resolve the problems of unequal credit access limited the scope of the reforms, even as they profoundly altered the American economy in often unexpected ways. Proxmire believed that to restore the political and economic stability of the American city required resolving the inequities of finance in the urban economy. As the witnesses and the legislators pondered the problem of ghetto credit they recognized, as did Betty Furness, the special assistant to the president for Consumer Affairs, that "the proof was right here in the streets 2 weeks ago . . . [in] the stores that were burned and looted."[45] Consumer credit, which had driven the expansion of the suburbs, needed to be found for the city as well. Opinions, nonetheless, differed widely over what aspects of ghetto finance most needed reform.

At Proxmire's hearings, the way in which expert witnesses envisioned this investment in the ghetto varied, but across the political spectrum all emphasized the importance of local control. Across the political spectrum, many of the legislators, bankers, and credit experts believed that to restore order, ghetto business would have to be controlled by African American businessmen and the profits reinvested in the neighborhood. Jacob Javits, the Republican senator from New York, believed that "the lack of involvement of the . . . poverty area resident in the ownership and management of the business community which serves him," led to the riots.[46] While "white-owned stores were burned and looted," Javits saw that the "'soul-brother' establishments were spared."[47] Black ownership, he reasoned, would lead to social stability. Walter Mondale, a liberal senator from Minnesota, believed that empowering the "people of the ghetto" was as important as their financial well-being. Mondale insisted that beyond lower interest rates, "community self-determination must be our goal." As Mondale remarked at one hearing:

> In the wake of riots and unrest, the relevant question is not "What is the return on investing in the ghetto?" The real question is "What is the cost of not investing in the ghetto?". . . . Can anyone really believe that he can insulate himself indefinitely from the problems and frustrations faced by black America?. . . . Of what benefit will higher yielding investments be if our Nation is wracked by social conflict and fear.[48]

Conservatives and liberals alike could agree that African American–owned businesses would stabilize the ghetto. Experts disagreed, however, on what policies could foster economic self-determination but would still be within the capacity of the federal government. For some, the government needed to direct business funds into poor neighborhoods to create jobs. For others, cultivating and mentoring local entrepreneurs would give residents ownership of their own communities. For still others, the key was control of locally supported financial institutions. For Proxmire, the key was to emulate the successful credit programs legislated during the New Deal, like the FHA, that did not abandon the private sector but found a way to guide its funds for the public good. While there were those who tried to find alternatives to mainstream capital, the solution, Proxmire felt, was to convince banks and finance companies to reinvest in the people of the city.[49] The alternative, he feared, was continued unrest.

Responding to the unrest, many well-intentioned bankers tried to find ways to support home ownership and African American–owned businesses in the ghetto, believing it was a lack of small business financing that had led to the riots. Consumer credit ranked lower in the discussions of economic development than the more respectable forms of investment. Giving people a stake in where they lived, through business and home ownership, seemed more logical to the bankers than providing consumer loans, even though it was the feeling of consumer exploitation that drove the riots. Bankers like George Whitney, who represented the Investment Bankers Association of America, recommended insurance programs for business ventures analogous to FHA housing insurance programs to lure capital into the ghettos.[50] Providing investment funds, even subsidized by the government, would not change the costs of real estate, of higher-priced post-riot insurance, and of unpaid debts. The higher risk default rates of ghetto consumers, FTC Chairman Paul Dixon cautioned, would inevitably lead to higher costs. Either there would need to be a "voluntary action" on the part of community-minded bankers or "some kind of a Government-guarantee program or some kind of subsidy" for credit to be extended to these borrowers.[51] Furness similarly believed that "the private sector has got to be encouraged to move into—not out of—the ghetto areas [and] banks and other financiers will have to find new ways of establishing criteria for credit, ways geared to the poor community."[52] The poor needed better access to credit if they were to become as economically stable as middle-class Americans. Banks would have to be encouraged by the state to enter these risky, marginal markets, but they would have to do so for the sake of political and social stability—if not for profit.

If it were so difficult to bring middle-class retailers to the poor neighborhoods in the cities, why not bring poor consumers to the middle-class stores? With ghetto consumers perceiving exploitation at every turn, Proxmire imagined that providing more credit options would enable ghetto consumers to buy outside the neighborhood, which seemed less daunting than attempting to regulate high-priced ghetto merchants. Market competition would do the rest and drive local merchants out of business. Senator Proxmire envisioned providing the poor with "more direct consumer credit" that sidestepped exploitative retailers. Consumer credit from "banks, credit unions, or other institutions . . . would permit ghetto residents to obtain their own credit on reasonable terms and thus shop in the more reputable stores which charge lower prices."[53] If consumers could use credit at department stores, then these marginal, exploitative retailers could be driven out of business. Proxmire believed it was "the failure of the large downtown stores to adequately serve the low-income market which permits high-cost merchandising practices of the ghetto merchant to survive." Firm competition would never allow "Sears, Roebuck [to] survive in the middle-class shopping centers," if it charged the higher prices of ghetto merchants.[54]

The clear solution to Proxmire was to reintegrate the ghetto and the market. While bringing the market to the ghetto would help many ghetto consumers, it would, at the same time drive under neighborhood businesses that already eked only marginal profits, further limiting local jobs to an already underemployed population. Nonetheless, credit that would come from financiers and that could be used everywhere, including retailers that would never extend credit to poor African American consumers, would alleviate much of the ghetto consumer's difficulties.

To create this flow of consumer credit would require giving up Mondale's dream of local control and self-determination. Existing ghetto financial institutions could not provide this service. Though many institutions and groups attempted to position themselves as creditor to the poor, for various structural reasons, they all failed. Black-owned banks were practically nonexistent. The largest one in the United States, Freedom National Bank in New York, according to Theodore Cross, the editor-in-chief of *Bankers Magazine*, was the 1734th largest in the country with only $30 million in deposits.[55] Black-controlled banks typically had higher costs and lower returns than mainstream, white banks. Ghetto banking costs were higher because so many more of the deposits were small savings accounts rather than large commercial checking accounts.[56] Avoiding the fees of checking accounts, even small businesses in the ghetto had savings accounts. All that extra work created greater labor and interest costs. The personal loans tended to be small and the commercial investments even smaller, which limited profits.[57] Freedom National Bank, with its $30 million in assets, had 85 employees for all its extra savings account work, nearly double the amount that would have been expected for a bank of its size, draining bank profits that limited the growth of its investment capital.

For any substantial amount of capital, then, black businessmen and consumers had to turn to white-controlled banks. Many states like Illinois limited the branches a bank could have. In Chicago, the large suburban banks could not open branches in the city.[58] Even states that did not limit branches had difficulties in ghetto neighborhoods not encountered elsewhere in the city or the suburbs. Ghetto banks had higher default rates than conventional banks. Banco de Ponce, a bank that operated in the Brownsville section of Brooklyn, had a consumer loan default rate three times higher than the average in Manhattan. To make up for this loss, Banco de Ponce charged 1.5 percent higher interest than the average Manhattan bank as well. The rate difference, driven by higher default rates, made it impossible for Manhattan banks to invest in ghetto consumer loans. As Cross pointed out, it would be "absolutely impossible for a bank such as the Chase bank downtown to establish a higher rate on its automobile loans in Harlem than the rate it charges in downtown areas."[59] A white bank, additionally, could not risk the public relations nightmare that would be created by charging higher interest rates at its ghetto branch than at its main branch. Even if an African American businessman came from Brooklyn to Manhattan to get a business loan, the "downtown banker," Cross believed, "often avoids taking the note of a Negro businessman, because the banker doesn't want the potentially bad publicity that may ensue 'pulling the strings' on a minority borrower."[60] To avoid the possible appearance of discrimination, ironically, bankers had to actually discriminate by not opening ghetto branches or lending to minority borrowers. Because the white banks could not themselves alter their rates and therefore could not invest directly, Cross suggested that the capital had to be moved into the ghetto by some other means.

Several federal agencies and community activists enthusiastically, and unsuccessfully, promoted other possible ways around this difficulty through the creation of alternative, local financial institutions. Despite the best of intentions, these alternatives, like credit unions, could not address the larger investment and credit needs of the ghetto. The Office of Economic Opportunity (OEO) and the Bureau of Federal Credit Unions, to take one of the largest programs, offered extensive consumer education through a plan called "Project Moneywise" that sought to show poor consumers how to use credit and give them, through locally-run credit unions, financing alternatives to those provided by merchants.[61] Like similar programs dating back to the 1920s, these hopeful educators of the 1960s believed that the difficulties in credit use stemmed from poor consumer education.[62] Unlike earlier credit educators, these programs emphasized shifting the control of banking to the local community. Credit union groups expressed hostility to national organizations, focusing on the importance of promoting community-run, community-owned banks. Between 1965 and 1968, Project Moneywise organized 218 credit unions across the country.[63] Growing out of the local control ideals of the left, community credit unions seemed to be a promising solution to the problem of credit for the poor. Training what the assistant director of the Bureau of Federal Credit Unions called "indigenous leaders" to go back to "their communities" and form credit unions, fit the self-determinationist model of local control.[64] Robert Levine, the assistant director for research at the OEO, envisioned "black power strengthened and directed constructively through green power" at these credit unions."[65] While Proxmire wondered, "How can we channel surplus funds from many of the credit unions in wealthy areas to poverty areas?," Project Moneywise advocates imagined a community-run, self-supporting program that drew on the "latent savings in the community" independent of larger financial institutions.[66] Community-run, such a program would have provided the needed services, and kept the profits, in the community.[67]

The problem with such plans, however, rested with the lack of "latent savings" that communities were able to deposit in the credit unions. Those 218 credit unions had a combined capitalization of only $2.2 million.[68] While the OEO paid for the initial setup costs, staff salaries, and space rentals of these credit unions, the actual capital to lend was extremely scarce.[69] Poor Americans had relatively little savings and larger credit unions would not put their capital at risk by investing in these well-intentioned banking projects.

The OEO and the Bureau of Federal Credit Unions could create offices, but they could not create capital. The OEO found that "in most cases capital accumulation among the poor is so slow that it takes years before a low income credit union can make loans that are meaningful."[70] Moreover, ghetto credit unions that did accumulate capital faced exactly the same choice as larger financial institutions: should they invest in the lower-risk mortgages of white subdivisions or in higher-risk urban areas? Why should credit union managers privilege the theoretical needs of the community over the very real investors who saved at their bank? Community credit union bankers made the same prudent decision that the national banks did. Federal Reserve studies had found that even ghetto credit unions reinvested funds in white suburbia.[71] While it was easy to provide an office, credit unions found it difficult to amass capital or even to keep that capital in the community when the risks and resources so favored the suburbs.

Additionally, the financial services of the federal credit unions involved with Project Moneywise were antiquated and did not address the needs of poor consumers. Project Moneywise's credit unions offered consumers old-fashioned personal loans for their consumption.[72] These programs clung to older models of personal loans rather than extending revolving credit cards to consumers. In the credit union model, lower-income consumers would have had to go to the credit union, get additional loan money, and then go to the retailer. These barriers to transaction that department stores had done away with in the 1950s were unnecessary in the late 1960s. Without credit cards, which would have enabled ghetto residents to shop in lower-priced middle-class stores, federal credit unions could do little to address the underlying credit problems of the urban poor.

Undercapitalized and antiquated, alternative financing schemes like Project Moneywise, while successful in a limited fashion, could not scale up or reach out to meet the needs of the ghetto. The small amounts that these credit unions commanded would not be able to fix cities, which was what Proxmire and the committee aimed to do. Proxmire did not want to wait for any "splendid pilot approach" to work out over twenty to thirty years.[73] Citing the Kerner report's five-year deadline for better housing, Senator Proxmire wanted results "in the next few years" akin to the dramatic reversal of the New Deal.[74] Other solutions, outside of state-subsidized credit unions, would have to be found.

While policymakers and businessmen focused on increasing the business credit of the black entrepreneur or offering alternative credit schemes through credit unions, other black leaders, more connected with the day-to-day needs of their poor, pushed for greater credit access.[75] John Jacob, who in 1968 was the acting executive director of the Washington Urban League, applauded the calls for business investment in the ghetto, seeing the hearings as "one of a number of growing indications that America has finally decided that it might be appropriate to begin to extend capitalism to black Americans."[76] While Jacob approved of "putting capital in the hands of Negro citizens [as] part of the answer to easing urban unrest," he also doubted if these business-oriented white policymakers truly understood the situation. Jacob wondered if white businessmen focused on the virtues of business ownership had learned the "lesson from our expensive history." If white American consumer life could not be moved to the ghetto, perhaps, some black leaders like Jacob suspected, could the ghetto consumer be moved to white America?

Rather than invest in the ghetto, Jacob called on Congress and bankers "to consider a concept that would extend the consumer credit system available now to most Americans," that is, "a credit card for the ghetto residents."[77] More than ownership, ghetto residents wanted what all other Americans wanted—to shop without feeling cheated. Jacob believed that credit cards would give ghetto consumers the choice to shop wherever they preferred. Consumers could shop at local stores run by proprietors they were familiar with, or if they felt cheated there, they could go elsewhere, either in their neighborhoods or in white areas.

Credit cards for ghetto residents were necessary, Jacob felt, because white institutions discriminated against black consumers. Whether because of racial prejudice or economic creditworthiness, 70 percent of ghetto residents still did not have established credit with what FTC chairman Dixon called "general market retailers."[78] The Urban League's program would remedy this deficiency. Jacob pointed to the main culprits in denying poor African Americans credit—credit bureaus, department stores, and financial institutions.

Jacob held that discriminatory lenders denied the credit because of their race. African American consumers could not get charge cards at the cheaper downtown stores. Credit bureaus automatically, he thought, downgraded their credit ratings. White banks, he believed, would not lend to them. Capitalism for Jacob was a consumer capitalism from which African Americans had been excluded. Credit cards would liberate the black consumer from "mainline credit bureau [that were] the end all in establishing credit" and from "the loan shark, to the pawnbroker, to the "credit advisers," or to the high-interest purchase plans." Cheaper credit would lower the overall costs of consumption for ghetto consumers. As Jacob reminded the committee, "black people in the ghetto buy television sets, washing machines, clothes, and toothpaste" just like white people in the suburbs, but they just paid more for them. Ghetto residents "buy them with borrowed cash that will cost them double or triple in the long run . . . [and] on installment plans that balloon prices so that they could have bought three items by the time they get through paying for one" durable good.[79] Credit would save ghetto residents money. If white policymakers and bankers were really concerned about increasing the stake of African Americans in capitalism, they would worry less about business loans and find a way to enable black consumers to affordably borrow to buy their homes, cars, and toothpaste just like white America. To deny black consumers credit was to continue to exclude them from the prosperity that defined what was best about the United States.

Jacob thought this plan was feasible because of the Urban League's experiences in running a credit union for ghetto residents in Washington, D.C. The Urban League apparently had different experiences with "low-income people" than most credit unions. In two years of operation, the credit union made 901 loans for over $100,000. Unusual among ghetto residents, the default rate at the Urban League credit union was low—only sixteen loans, or 1.2 percent of total loan volume.[80] "If credit can be extended without risk to ghetto residents in the form of loans," Jacob wondered, "why not also extend that great American tradition of 'buy now—pay later' to the ghetto consumer as well."[81] Jacob imagined expanding credit unions around the country that would provide credit services to the poor. Merchants would sign on to the program because credit unions would guarantee payments even if the consumers defaulted, like the FHA guaranteed housing loans. He believed that ghetto merchants would lower their credit prices in return for the increased debt compliance of African American residents.[82] These consumers would hopefully spend most of their money in their neighborhoods. While white bankers thought black ghetto residents needed to own the local business, Jacob believed they just needed access to cheap credit in their neighborhood to feel like they had a "stake" in it. Consumer choice, not business ownership, resided at the heart of the ghetto unrest.

Revolving credit cards would best serve the flexible credit needs of ghetto residents. The unyielding fixed repayment plans of installment credit frustrated ghetto consumers, whose paydays could be as irregular as their debt due dates were regular. Unlike department store credit, borrower interest rates could vary by "degree of delinquency and/or defaults."[83] For Jacob, the key to success for the program was avoiding strict repayment programs for a population with irregular work. Through guaranteed payments for merchants and flexible credit for consumers, Jacob hoped that credit prices would fall and ghetto consumers would be given readier access to the goods that they wanted.[84]

Investment in these credit unions, Jacob imagined, could come either from the private sector or the government, and the credit company could be operated on a profit or nonprofit basis.[85] Jacob thought that most ghetto residents cared more about their own access to flexible credit than whether the lender was black or white. Jacob's novel departure from most of the other business-oriented testimony that the committee heard attracted Proxmire's imagination. While other witnesses conveyed the trickery of merchants and the importance of black entrepreneurship, Jacob offered a different way to quell black consumers' rage—provide them with choice.

While Jacob and the committee debated the riskiness of lending to ghetto residents, with their high default rate of nearly 14 percent,

Proxmire suggested that perhaps the solution lay not in government subsidized credit unions but by encouraging existing companies, like American Express, to offer their credit services to ghetto residents. Proxmire wondered if Jacob thought it "feasible for commercial banks to organize this service as opposed to starting new companies?"[86] Rather than see credit cards as another way for white institutions to exploit black consumers, Jacob thought the ghetto residents would welcome it and it might engender "a new attitude toward the whole banking institution," making banks seem more a part of the community.[87] In general, Jacob suspected banks would be unwilling to provide such services because of their traditional discrimination against black borrowers. Remedying racial discrimination in lending practices would almost, by itself, solve the problem of credit in the ghetto. The director of the Urban League agreed that ending racial discrimination, either by legal fiat or a shift in banker culture, would enable credit cards to reach the ghetto residents who needed them and ameliorate one of the primary sources of urban unrest.

While Congress did not fund the programs, over the next few years Jacobs' vision and Proxmire's hope for the dissemination of credit cards in the poor neighborhoods of the American city would nonetheless become a reality, but not in the way that they had imagined. In 1968, following the hearings, Congress passed the Consumer Credit Protection Act, which mandated uniformly calculated interest rates on all credit transactions. Consumers could now make informed choices in their credit and compare deals between different lenders more easily. The Act empowered consumers who had the option to make rational choices between several options, but in the late 1960s many poor Americans' credit choices remained limited. The credit card was still not in the ghetto. Despite the push for reform coming from the ghetto riots, the new law did nothing to extend credit to poor African Americans. As the president's special representative on Consumer Affairs, Betty Furness, remarked in the aftermath of the 1968 riots, "this nation long ago extended a promise to all its citizens—a promise of [e]quality [*sic*] and justice and freedom. It is time that promise was fulfilled."[88] To fulfill the consumer promise of postwar America to everyone, credit would have to be guaranteed to everyone. But the road to rebellion-quelling credit cards in the ghetto would emerge not from well-intentioned banks, credit union activists, black entrepreneurs or even moderate black leaders, but unexpectedly through the legislative lobbying and street protests of predominately white feminist groups. Credit equality for women would open the door to legislation and practices ending all forms of credit discrimination, including against ghetto residents, even though everyday problems facing affluent, white women could not have been more different.

Women, Credit, and Discrimination

While poor, black Americans confronted the limits of their credit options and turned, unsuccessfully, to the state for redress, another group, much more affluent but still constrained in their credit access, began to lobby Congress for credit equality. For upper-middle-class women in the late 1960s and early 1970s, credit formed an indispensable foundation of their economic and social lives, yet the ability to use credit remained contingent on a man's creditworthiness or even his permission. Unlike today, when microfinanciers win Nobel prizes for recognizing the higher creditworthiness of women over men, in the 1960s and 1970s lenders considered women of all marital statuses poor credit risks. Single women, married women, and divorced women all encountered barriers in their access to credit, but for different reasons and with different effects. Marital, parental, and employment statuses all shaped women's need and demand for credit, and why creditors denied them that credit. While women enjoyed greater liberties in divorce and coverture law at the end of the 1960s than earlier, they also found that everyday credit practices and retail policies had not kept pace with the statutes. Affluent white women who explicitly juxtaposed their class-based "right to credit" against welfare subprime mortgage programs for poor blacks, demanded credit in the name of ending discrimination—a rhetorical move that ultimately and unintentionally aided poor, black consumers as well.

The Consumer Protection Act of 1968, whose passage was strongly aided by the ghetto riots of that year, even while not redressing the root causes, had also, in addition to the Truth-in-Lending provisions, mandated the creation of the National Commission on Consumer Finance. The Commission existed only for a few years, from 1970 to 1972, but its hearings and its recommendations had an important effect on federal policy. While it examined many aspects of consumer credit, one of its primary roles was to investigate whether lenders discriminated against women, and if so, how. As during the hearings on credit in 1968, the commission articulated the centrality of credit to the promise of American life. Representative Ira Millstein, who chaired the hearings, believed that "credit has been and continues to be the cornerstone upon which our enviable U.S. standard of living rests."[89] Like the authors of the Consumer Credit Protection Act, the commission believed the key to a just credit economy was not direct federal regulation but making borrowing transparent to consumers as they decided between credit options.

At the heart of this investigation, however, rested a contradiction that repeatedly surfaced throughout the credit reform of the 1970s, but was ultimately addressed, though unsuccessfully: the appropriateness of real categorical discrimination in a credit system based on profit.

Discrimination might, it was argued, reflect actual differences in borrowing behavior. Group A might be charged higher premiums because they, as a group, could be riskier borrowers than Group B. If lenders were to profit from lending to Group A, then they would need to charge Group A higher interest rates or refuse them credit at a higher rate than Group B to have the same rate of profit. The third-rail question of the hearings was: If Group A is riskier than Group B, can the higher rates of interest and refusals be considered unjustifiably discriminatory? As Representative Ira Millstein and Senator William Brock asked many witnesses about the possibility that women actually were poorer credit risks than men, the witnesses stammered and then claimed, like Betty Howard of Minnesota's Department of Human Rights, that "anything that stereotypes an individual . . . is discriminatory. You cannot judge an individual by grouping characteristics."[90] As testimony to the entrenched belief that discrimination, ipso facto, was wrong, even if possibly actuarially justified, few witnesses seemed to even understand the question and repeatedly returned to the importance of the individual.

Even as Millstein asked this crucial question, however, he woefully misunderstood how credit systems worked at the beginning of the 1970s. Actuarial science and statistical analysis had little bearing on whether lenders extended credit to women—or any other group. While limited numeric systems existed, these were rarely based on detailed statistical analysis. Loan officers' everyday prejudices and assumptions more decisively determined credit eligibility. Creditors, or rather their low-level evaluators, did not deny women credit or charge them higher premiums because of their unflinching loyalty to statistical regressions but because they believed in a certain set of assumptions about the proper relation of men, women, and credit.

For both the witnesses and the commission, the solution to discrimination against women lay in greater transparency of credit evaluation and increasing automation of decision making, moving credit evaluation out of the hands of discriminatory loan officers and into the algorithms of objective quantitative credit lending models, which they believed would end discrimination. Senator Leonor Sullivan, one of the driving forces behind the 1968 act, saw the hearings' purpose as discovering if "discriminations against women in the extension of credit are based on real or imagined creditor problems or on old laws which may or may not still exist."[91] Sullivan was less agnostic than Millstein about discrimination. She "notice[d] that many millions of women, American women, obtain credit today without any difficulty, . . . but those women who encounter difficulty in obtaining credit often are penalized for no other reason that the fact that they are women and that is wrong."[92] Making credit evaluation objective would help women get the credit that they deserved.

While many industry and government representatives testified before the commission, women's groups as well as professional women constituted the bulk of the witnesses. These self-selected voices of women were not average women. They were affluent, mostly white women who were for the most part lawyers practicing in Washington. They were the exact opposite in most ways from the ghetto rioters of a few years earlier, save for the fact that they too lived in Washington, D.C. Yet they also felt discriminated against by retailers and banks. Affluent, married women's frustrations were political—retailers wanted to extend credit only in the name of the husband and these women wanted to be recognized autonomously from their husbands. For divorced women the discrimination was more economic—for a variety of institutional reasons, retailers resisted giving divorced women credit, despite their incomes. Unlike many ghetto rioters, these women had large amounts of money at their disposal, which ultimately retailers wanted spent at their stores. Between organized protests, political lobbying, and firm competition, professional women were able to convince Congress and retailers to change their practices and the law.

The existence or lack of individual credit histories for women drove many of the differences in credit access between single, married, and divorced women. Single women, ironically, had the easiest time establishing a credit identity, but lenders' limited their credit access in ways that they did not for single men. Department stores, since the 1920s, had readily provided single women with sufficient income charge cards. Nonetheless in the early 1970s, even after the ostensible end of coverture, when a woman married creditors merged her credit identity with that of husband. As National Organization for Women (NOW) representative Lynne Litwiller testified, "in a country where credit is more important than money . . . women are summarily excluded, at best tenuously eligible conditioned upon remaining forever single. Any woman who is married, has been married, or who may ever get married, 90 percent of all women, will find that credit follows the husband."[93] Even in the late 1960s and early 1970s, as so many middle-class married women entered the workforce, women still depended on their husbands for their economic identity. For feminists, credit dependency on their husbands was a tangible reminder of how institutions defined them as an economic appendage of their husbands. Much more so than single women, married women confronted challenges in acquiring credit if they wanted it independently from their husbands. While married men could easily make credit choices affecting their households, women who tried to do the same met consistent and obdurate obstacles. At the intersection of the feminist desire for economic independence and the middle-class performance of consumption, credit access contingent on their husbands' approval focused the exasperation that many professional women felt about the limits of their economic freedom. Government studies, Congressional hearings, and women's letters revealed the pervasive and infuriating difficulty women had in contracting credit without men.

The department store provided the largest source of frustration to affluent, married women partially because these women had so easily acquired credit there before marriage. Middle-class and professional women, forced to get their husband's approval to shop even when they spent their own hard-earned money, became furious. Most department stores forced newly married women to close their accounts and reapply for credit in their husbands' name. Women's credit history prior to their marriages had no bearing on their credit as married women and credit access depended on her husband's credit history. For women who had shopped at these stores for years, dutifully paying their bills every month, the demand for reapplication did not seem like due diligence but a gross insult to their personhood.

Jorie Friedman, for instance, had worked as a well-paid newscaster for Chicago's NBC affiliate for many years before meeting her husband and had had credit accounts at most major department stores, always paying her bills on time. Through her large salary as a newscaster, she never had any trouble getting credit, that is, as she testified, "until [she] got married."[94] Friedman recalled that, "the response of the stores was swift." One store closed her account immediately and all the rest sent her applications to reapply, asking for her husband's name, bank accounts, and employer. Friedman's own name, accounts, and employer no longer mattered. The stores all claimed that they were forced by the law to close the accounts, but using her investigatory skills as a reporter she quickly discovered that there were no such laws in Illinois. Retail credit practices, not the law, created the situation.

Unfortunately for both Friedman and her husband, her husband had been unemployed when they were married since his unsuccessful bid for mayor of Chicago. With a husband out of work, the well-paid newscaster could not get credit. Applying for a charge account at "one of the world's largest department stores," Friedman was asked for her husband's employer. As he was unemployed, she offered her own employer and her bank. The credit officer told her that, "we don't care about the women, just the men" and refused her an account. To Friedman, this experience summed up the credit problems of married women: "in the eyes of a credit department, it seems, women cease to exist, and become non-persons, when they get married."[95]

Credit represented more than a simple extension of payments for these professional, independent women; credit access reified both their middle-class consumer power and the gender limits circumscribing that power.

To be confined to the limited economic and social role of "wife" as dependent, to be as Friedman said, "treated like a child," abrogated professional women's public achievements. All over, professional women found they could not shop without their husband's authorization, even if they paid the bills. For Friedman, Campbell, and other professional women, being denied credit was a violation of their consumer freedom.

For women who were the primary household earners, such a husband-centered credit system made their lives even more difficult. Josephine McElhome, an economist with the Federal Home Loan Bank Board, testified that "in general, it seems that unless a married woman of childbearing age has a long work history and can produce a doctor's certificate stating that she cannot bear children, her income will be largely disregarded."[96] Similar medical information was never required for men. Sharyn Campbell, a lawyer with NOW's Women's Legal Defense Fund, recounted the story of a married woman who, upon applying for charge card with a "major chain store," was told that her application could not be accepted unless her husband was listed as the head of the household and she as a dependent.[97] The outraged woman, who was a "practicing attorney earning the same salary as her husband," went to the Fund for legal redress when the credit officer told her that she "might have children and then become dependent on [her] husband."[98] Lenders took the greatest possible care to establish the probability of a wife's possible pregnancy, including requiring in many cases a letter from her doctor that she was either infertile or on a well-regulated birth control program. No similar inquiries were made, Campbell pointed out, about "the effect that unforeseen illness or physical impairment would have on [the husband's] earning capacity."[99] No medical examinations or doctor's letters were ever required on behalf of the man. Pregnancy was seen as an inevitable interruption in payments. Working mothers were not conceived as part of the credit system.

Usually lenders only counted the husband's income in determining how much credit the couple was good for; if they counted the wife's income, lenders only included a fraction thereof. In Minnesota, the state Department of Human Rights received repeated complaints of sex discrimination in credit access. To investigate discrimination, the Human Rights department had two investigators—a man and a woman, each earning $12,000 and each the sole supporter of a family—go to twenty-three banks to borrow $600 for a used auto. More than half the banks refused the woman credit without the husband's signature, or "approved the loan only as an exception to their usual procedures." Some, suspecting her marriage was in trouble, referred the female investigator to marriage counseling. The same banks, denying the woman a loan, waived the co-signer requirement for the man.[100] The St. Paul's study showed, as its published form was titled, that women could not easily borrow money for an auto, even though a husband could easily borrow without his wife.

Lenders defended their policies in several ways, all of which resulted from the absence of a married woman's independent credit history from her husband. At Sears, Roebuck, women regularly had difficulty gaining independent credit without the assistance of men. Mildred Hagen, a credit executive with Sears, testified that accounts defaulted to the husband unless the wife requested special treatment. The Sears manual allowed special treatment if "her circumstances qualif[ied] her as acceptable according to Sears *normal* standards" [emphasis in text].[101] Hagen insisted, however, that accounts defaulted to the husband in an effort to "avoid confusion of misapplied payments, misapplied sales, etc." rather than an intentional desire to affirm patriarchy.[102] Male authority, however, riddled the Sears credit training manual. The manual required that a married woman's name be prefaced by "Mrs.," and that the remainder of her name be that of her husband, as in "Mrs. John Smith." Again Hagen explained this procedure as a simple artifact of bookkeeping. The Sears witness claimed that "these instructions help to prevent mistakes on credit reports" and that "without this information it is possible for erroneous reports to be made if there are a number of individuals with the same common name in file." Sears justified its denial of women independent credit in an effort to keep the files straight with the credit bureau, even as this denying of credit kept their identities *out* of the credit bureau, which in turn demanded that women not have independent credit identities! In keeping a family's, that is, the husband's credit rating straight, women were denied an economic existence. With all credit transactions in her husband's name, a married woman could not have a credit history.

Many lenders also erroneously pointed to state laws that made the husband responsible for the wife's debts, which they claimed forced them to check with husbands before extending their wives credit.[103] Yet the reverse was not true. If such laws had still existed—which, by 1972 they did not—the wife would have also been responsible for her husband's debts. Yet these same responsible lenders never thought they ought to consult with the wife before extending the husband credit. Moreover, such national firms, such as the department store J.C. Penney, often had common credit applications for their stores across the country, undercutting the state-specific requirements that they used to defend their credit policies.[104]

Bank credit cards, like BankAmericard, treated women largely the same as the department stores. Creditors resisted giving wives autonomous credit identities from their husbands. BankAmericard policy was to issue cards only in the name of the husband. Credit card companies and department stores typically assumed that the husband headed the household and could, at his leisure, extend credit cards to other members of a household including his wife. For a woman to apply for a Diners' Club card, for instance, required a husband's authorization, whereas a husband's application did not require a wife's authorization.[105] Wives could receive a "supplemental" Diners' Club card with the written permission of her husband and $7.50.[106] The additional card asked only for the wife's first name and middle initial—there was no way to indicate if a wife had a different last name from her husband. Treating women as appendages to their husbands could be bad for business. A Chicago woman, for example, wrote Congresswoman and feminist activist Bella Abzug about her frustrating experience with BankAmericard. In May 1970, when her bank switched over from a regional credit card network with First National Bank of Chicago to the national BankAmericard network, all earlier cards were canceled and replaced for members in "good standing."[107] But as this female cardholder noticed, all the customers in good standing "must be standing in a Men's room somewhere."[108] All her male acquaintances received their cards, as did her husband, but she only received an application. After repeated calls and letters to First National Bank, where she had a savings account of over $2 thousand and a history of prompt payment, a credit manager, who tried once again to have her fill out an application, assured her that she would have her credit card by January. By March of 1971, when her credit card still had not arrived, she closed out both her and husband's accounts with the bank. More than the loss of convenience was the outrage at being treated differently than her husband. Swearing that she would "never willingly put another penny in your bank" in a letter she wrote to the bank, she hoped that other women, "treated in this same high-handed fashion," would also someday withdraw their money to the bank's regret.[109]

Separate credit histories were possible, to establish in theory, but for most married women the institutional and financial barriers were insuperable. Homer Stewart, who was senior vice-president of consumer loans and credit cards at Dallas National Bank and a spokesperson for the American Bankers Association, affirmed that in his bank a woman upon marriage would have to reapply for her bank credit card, which at Dallas National was "Master Charge." Stewart claimed the reapplication was to find out if she would continue to work. If she continued to work, the bank would continue the plan, but if she stopped working to "settle down and raise a family," the bank would insist in putting the card in "papa's name."[110] It was possible, Stewart explained, for women to create autonomous credit identities even while married, but it was neither standard nor easy. Credit bureaus, at least in Stewart's home state of Texas, could establish a separate identity for the married woman, but she had to make a special request at the local credit bureau "at her request." While men automatically acquired a public economic identity, married women with public economic identities were special cases.[111]

Additionally, the merger of identities had tangible economic benefits for most couples, which prevented many women, even if they were frustrated by the merging of their identities, from establishing separate credit histories. Most married women, Stewart testified, wanted their income lumped with their husband's in their credit applications so that the household could borrow more.[112] Only in couples where the wife earned enough by herself and had feminist political beliefs did women want, and could financially afford, separate credit accounts. Women could be identified separately but at the cost of a reduced ability to borrow. For professional women or for women who earned substantially more than their husbands, this choice could make sense either politically or economically, but for many middle-class and working-class women, the desire for greater credit limits constrained their abilities to assert autonomous credit ratings while married, even if they knew that creating a separate credit rating was an option.

Such asymmetry of economic identity, as representative Martha Griffiths noted, gave "the husband control of the couple's finances, of course, and prevents the wife from ever establishing her own credit record."[113] Without a credit record, the annoyances faced by a married woman multiplied into serious problems if she was divorced, abandoned, or widowed. For women whose husbands left them, credit became a nightmare. Abandoned women, who may or may not have worked, suddenly became responsible for all the bills of the house. If the household owed money, she was responsible for paying the debts. Yet, even if she managed to pay off these debts, she would be ineligible for additional credit without her absent husband's signature.[114] Without a divorce, her situation was dire.

Even for divorced women, who were becoming increasingly common in the early 1970s, credit difficulties increased.[115] Because husbands were expected to approve credit for their wives, divorced women who wanted credit at department stores were compelled, sometimes, to produce a divorce decree or even have their ex-husbands sign for the account.[116] Divorced men, who still retained the family credit rating, did not need their ex-wives' signatures for anything. Part of the reason for these refusals was that companies did not consider alimony and child support payments as income. For many of these women who had small children to care for, however, alimony and child support were their primary source of income. Even if their lenders ignored their income, many women, such as Sandra Reinsch, a divorced Virginia woman, remained surprised at their credit refusals since she "had paid all [the] bills promptly for years."[117]

Lenders' refusal of credit despite a good repayment history astonished these divorcees, but their so-called repayment histories were in their husbands' names, and not their own. Divorced women, to creditors, had no history. Having submerged their credit identities throughout their marriage, women found that now divorced they did not have a shared credit record with their ex-husbands, but rather had a gaping hole in the records for the entirety of their married lives. While divorced men continued to enjoy the creditworthiness their record provided, divorced women were effectively unknowns, and were treated as such by lenders.

Of course women, single, married, or divorced, who did have separate credit identities and who were "acceptable according to Sears' *normal* standards," could have independent lines of credit. But as Hagen, the Sears credit executive, testified, Sears did not grant credit to those who were "unemployed or working part-time and cannot show sufficient regular income to meet the payment," or when credit information was "insufficient."[118] Either not having enough "income" or being outside of the credit bureaus' reports was enough to be denied credit, which was the case for almost all divorced women. Sears would give divorced women credit but only if they had, as Hagen said, "the ability to pay and the willingness to pay . . . [as] evident through past credit history."[119] But of course, divorced women often did not have a credit history. For married women and divorced women, either of these conditions was often enough to deny them credit independent of their husbands or ex-husbands.

The "normal" policy for Sears, and similar retailers and creditors, was geared to a world of social relations becoming increasingly abnormal in the early 1970s. The "unusual circumstances" of working and divorced women rapidly was becoming more commonplace. The "marriage in which the 'responsible' member is the wife," but the husband has a bad credit record, was rectifiable only through the special intervention of the credit sales manager. Similarly, a businesswoman who wanted to have credit in her maiden name would also face obstacles, although they were not insuperable. Sears did not believe that a contract with a woman under her maiden name, which was no longer her legal name, would be valid or enforceable.[120]

Sears considered divorced women "unusual." For Sears, the lack of a credit record for these divorced women made a general "policy position" impossible since every situation was "individual." Yet Sears managed to extend credit to young men and women without previous credit histories all the time, and this was not considered an unusual circumstance. The Sears manual encouraged the interviewer to have a "friendly, businesslike approach employing a liberal amount of tact" but also emphasized the "thoroughness [that was] essential in obtaining *all* the information needed to facilitate a prompt investigation and sound credit judgment decision."[121] Hagen remarked, in response to pointed questions, that divorced women without credit records would need to be interviewed and counseled by the credit officials, which as so many witnesses testified, they found demeaning since their husbands had to undergo no such travails. The ex-husband's credit record, often spotless through the ex-wife's careful management of their finances, guaranteed him easy credit, while guaranteeing her a series of impertinent interviews. Beyond the inequities of gender, consumers deemed the credit manager's interview insulting even though such interviews had been a standard part of the credit process throughout the 1950s. Filling out a form and checking with a computer record was considered the polite way of lending money. Not only who was borrowing, but who—or what—was deciding to lend was changing by the early 1970s.

For Sears, these "unusual cases . . . represent[ed] only a very small number of the transactions Sears handle[d]," but for the women whose lives it circumscribed, the experience was both infuriating and degrading.[122] Whether the number of Sears's divorced customers was small was due to the hassle that these "unusual cases" encountered or because this group was naturally small and/or did not want credit remains indeterminable. It seems more likely, judging from the larger demographic statistics, as well as the other witnesses at the hearings, that it was not that they did not want credit but that Sears and other retailers made it difficult for them to acquire it.

Though lenders commonly discriminated by sex and marital status, such practices began to change in response to agitation from both above and below in the early 1970s. At the local level, independent feminist groups as well as those associated with national organization like NOW organized locally to petition their city and state governments for changes in their laws. For instance, after the failure of the Minneapolis government to pass an antidiscrimination law, an official with the Department of Human Rights reported, a "west suburban female liberationist group" organized "protest marches, rallies, had confrontations with department stores and credit bureaus, demanding that women be able to establish their own credit."[123] Eventually such protests forced the city government to change the law.

Despite the local patchwork of legal changes across the country, discrimination persisted. While the suburbs of Minnesota erupted in protest and the laws were changed, the St. Paul's study, which took place six months after the passage of the antidiscrimination law, revealed the persistence of practices and assumptions among loan officers that hampered the ability of women to borrow, even as higher-level policies attempted to stamp out gender discrimination as a way to reach out to female consumers.

The culture and practices of low-level loan officers, more than the law itself, engendered discrimination. Betty Howard, of the Minnesota Department of Human Rights, believed that despite the law, the formal antidiscrimination policies of banks "[did] not appear . . . to be filtering down to the middle and lower level of credit interviewers."[124] Howard testified that despite the law, most interviewers, with whom credit control rested, believed "anatomy is destiny." An attractive woman of childbearing age, "regardless of her employment record or good credit references," would have difficulty in getting credit, one credit bureau head told Howard, because "they are very likely to get pregnant and are considered bad credit risks."[125] Similarly, department store credit officers had similar difficulties implementing higher-level directives. Even after official Sears policy changed to count alimony and child-support as income, the actual employees did not always do so. Hagen referred a "problem of communication" to the lower-level credit employees whose decisions reflected "society and circumstances" rather than corporate policy. With such "radical changes" under way in society, Hagen argued, it would take time for the corporate policies to be truly understood by employees.[126]

At the executive level, lenders, even in companies where informal discriminatory practices persisted, tried to change the direction of their companies to increase profits. More than any law, the potential profits of lending to affluent women provided a tremendous incentive for feminists to fight for change. At the same time as organized women protested discrimination, some lenders who saw a tremendous market opportunity in appealing to affluent, creditworthy women, began actively to try to alter their lending practices. "Our policy," Sears credit executive Mildred Hagen stated, was "to adjust to . . . consumer needs." Joseph Barr, president of American Security and Trust Company and former undersecretary of the treasury, testified and believed that "profit is still a more powerful motive than discrimination, especially in public institutions."[127] Contradicting the testimonies and letters from women who encountered discriminatory lenders, he believed from his experiences as a banker that most women were good credit risks, but most importantly he thought that if women were good credit risks, and bankers discriminated against them, they would lose good profits. Market pressures would solve credit discrimination if women were good loan candidates.[128]

Homer Stewart, American Bankers Association representative, emphasized that women with their higher earning power could make good loan candidates, but that they had to "meet the qualifications for credit" just the same as the "male borrowers."[129] These standards, according to Stewart, include "good character, vocational stability, financial capacity to repay, considering continuity of income and availability of assets, personal qualifications, such as an age commensurate with the maturity of loans, and a purpose for the loan."[130] Stewart did not believe there was "widespread discrimination against women simply because of gender" but because, according to his figures, women's median 1969 income was $5,080 compared to $8,670 for men. It was the difference in income, rather than discrimination, that led women to be rejected for credit.[131] On the surface, this argument seems sound and makes sense, yet when considered alongside the actual experiences of high-earning women, the social practices of credit belie this simple argument. For instance, Stewart pointed to the reason for the co-signing of a woman's automobile loan—as a guarantee in case the woman died someone would be responsible for the loan. But on men's loans, no such requirement was made.[132] Yet men who owed money on cars died every day. Stewart's qualifications were based on male borrowers, male life patterns, and male credit histories. Women, particularly married and divorced women in the late 1960s and early 1970s, could not, because of marriage, meet these requirements. Single women were easier to lend to, Stewart noted, because they had a credit rating.[133]

If profits could be made, it was believed, banks would lend. The market would correct itself. Some banks did seem to be following this logic, like National Bank of North America, a New York–area bank owned by the finance company C.I.T., which ran advertisements proclaiming that they, unlike their competitors, did not discriminate: "whether you're a Miss, Mrs., or Ms., we make loans to all creditworthy people."[134] In the advertisement, an attractive blond woman, who carries department store boxes under her right arm and holds her left fist up—signifying both greeting and solidarity—unites consumer credit with feminism. For women who faced challenges because of their marital status, reading that "married, single or divorced . . . none of that matters" must have mattered a lot. Despite these gestures toward credit equality from bankers, the market incentives for lending to women had *already* existed and had *already* failed to erase discrimination. National Bank of North America's advertisement was unique enough to warrant winning a "positive image award" from NOW.[135] The market alone would not completely change lender discrimination. Loan officers whose judgments were based on inherently discriminatory information, were embedded in a bureaucracy and a culture that did not always respond to market pressure.

Many of these bankers had no problems, at least publicly, in supporting legislation to erase sex discrimination in lending. John Farry, president of the U.S. Savings and Loan League, stated that he would be "willing to accept and promote such an amendment." These bankers who already tried to maximize their profits from lending to well-paid women had no problem helping the market along with some antidiscrimination legislation. Yet legislation, even they acknowledged, might be necessary to hurry along cultural changes that market forces could apparently reform only slowly.

Across the country, local chapters of NOW organized "credit task forces" to gather information and organize on the local level, while coordinating with the national offices in Washington. Following the hearings, Sharyn Campbell, who had become the national coordinator for the NOW Task Force on Credit, reiterated in a letter to the membership the organization's belief "that all people should have equal access to credit privileges provided they are creditworthy."[136] The National Commission on Consumer Credit hearings had spurred NOW into action. Campbell told the membership that the hearings had "established that a nationwide pattern of discrimination against women [did] indeed exist in the various elements of the credit industry. At the local and state level, Campbell encouraged local chapters to "conduct studies to document discriminatory activities," as well as protest discrimination from retailers and lenders, and to support legislation to end "the denial of credit on the basis of sex or marital status." The local legislative campaign was very successful. By 1974, half of the states had laws prohibiting discrimination against women.[137] At the everyday level, however, women still needed to confront the assumptions of employees, which was necessary, as NOW Vice-President Gene Boyer thought, "to help make feminist credit policies a reality by whatever means possible."[138]

Some banks attempted to use feminism to sell their financial services and to take market share from discriminatory lenders. Though drawing on the language of black radicalism, feminist credit activists reaffirmed the primacy of income as the justification for credit access and, while certain that gender discrimination was unjustifiable, offered contradictory positions on racial discrimination. Class prerogative structured feminists' notions of women's liberation.[139] Many of the testimonies centered on the outrage that middle-class, professional women felt at being able to have careers as independent women and still be treated like dependent homemakers. More than the amount or type of credit, these critics, like NOW's Lynne Litwiller, seemed more bothered that a "woman achieves the use of credit only as an appendage of the husband," than that women in general were ever denied credit. Credit for these professional, married women was not a strategy of survival but an expression of class privilege, economic independence, and pride.[140] To struggle for equality and respect in the workplace and then be denied the consumer benefits of that achievement in the marketplace just reinforced how undervalued professional women were. "While it might seem [that] the refusal to grant credit to married women is a trifling matter," as Equal Employment Opportunity Commission lawyer, Sonia Pressman-Fuentes saw it, "to women and to blacks such conduct is devastatingly symbolic of their second-class status in American society."[141]

At root, however, much of the anger expressed at the hearings was the class outrage of being treated like a poor person. Feminist critics both identified with and distanced themselves from the poor. As Faith Seidenberg of the American Civil Liberties Union, and past president of NOW testified, "all women are poor, even those who work . . . because they have no access to credit."[142] Though she intended it as a statement of solidarity, the implication of Seidenberg's statement was that being a woman made even a rich person be treated like she was poor person, which was wrong. Denying poor borrowers credit was justified, but denying the wealthy was not. Yet in her testimony she also asserted the shared experience of "poor women, middle class women, and even women with wealthy husbands" to get credit.[143] In New York, Seidenberg remarked, it was "almost impossible to open an account in a department store under her own name, even though she [was] a professional and [was] gainfully employed."[144] While feminist critics wanted credit to be available to all women, they also wanted their occupational and class status to count when it came to consumption. When questioned about the legal right to credit, Seidenberg agreed that while borrowers could be turned down for financial reasons, they ought not to be turned down because they were "black or because they are women or because they are Italian or something."[145]

At the national level, NOW intended to continue to gather evidence of discrimination and push for the passage of Congresswoman Bella Abzug's antidiscrimination bills in Congress.[146] Responding to the testimony as well as letters written to her about women's experiences, Abzug called for the end of credit discrimination based on sex. Whatever the cultural and social roots of discrimination, she saw the law as the final arbiter of what was allowed. Credit discrimination against women was possible because "all credit institutions, whether they were banks, department stores, mortgage companies are able to do this because at present, neither the United States nor the individual states have passed legislation to prohibit credit discrimination based upon sex."[147] Abzug called for "viable and vigorous legislation . . . to correct this incredulous and dehumanizing practice against women."[148]

Again and again, different witnesses asserted that loans should be made on the basis of personal credit histories, not demographic categories. Abzug, like most of the other witnesses, denied the possibility of valid discrimination based on gender or marital status, pointing to the cultural underpinnings, rather than the actuarial underpinnings, of the discrimination.[149] And also like many of the other witnesses, Abzug drew an analogy to racial discrimination, pointing out that "historically efforts made in our society to make it tough for people to participate equally economically in connection with race."[150] The torrent of antidiscrimination legislation to help black Americans get credit ought to be passed for women as well. As professional women confronted a credit system that made it difficult at every turn to get credit, the language and policies of the civil rights movement and Great Society program were both used and attacked to justify greater credit access for women.

Unlike credit discrimination against women, however, Abzug believed that some discrimination against black borrowers might be justified statistically. This was possible because she believed the statistics showed that with black borrowers there were "greater risks" because they were more frequently of a "lower economic level" than whites.[151] This belief about African American income was never far from the surface of the witnesses' testimonies and indeed from the comments of the legislators themselves. While white women could be wealthy and thus deserve credit, the federal government had helped blacks, who tended to be poor, get credit. The federal government provided access to credit where the market, by itself, could not justify it. To be clear, Abzug did not think the federal government had done wrong by legally mandating access to credit for poor, black Americans. Indeed, she believed that they should be given credit even if the statistics showed that they were higher risks. But she also believed that women should be guaranteed credit access as well and she thought that they as a group, unlike blacks, were not worse risks. In her view, the federal government had a moral imperative to step in and guarantee access to credit whatever the riskiness of the borrower. Giving credit to women was a necessary step toward "women exercis[ing] their right to rake part in all aspects of American economic life." Credit for African Americans and women helped integrate and elevate women into productive economic roles.

In many companies, the push for ending gender discrimination from above was undone by the embedding of low-level employees in sexist and racist cultures. But applicants could not be judged one by one. The call for judging individuals on their own merits went against fifty years of lending practices. Categories were necessary to lend at the volume required in a debt-driven economy. Credit scoring, while not statistically derived in 1970, offered an opportunity to undo unjustifiable discrimination. Deciding between credit applications, whether by sex, telephone ownership, or shoe size, was a necessary component of the system. What could be done, however, was to make sure that discrimination based on cultural assumptions and habits be replaced by scientific discrimination based on data and evidence. Discrimination could be made transparent and objective. Congress could insist that such discrimination be grounded in evidence and not anecdote. In doing so, feminist activists believed that gender discrimination could be eliminated, even if racial discrimination might not be.

The difficulty with this position, of course, is that it required information on every single individual. If a person was not tracked throughout their economic life, credit could not be had. Avoiding discrimination gave a moral underpinning to expanded surveillance. For instance, NOW's press release during the hearings called on "Congress [to] amend the fair credit reporting act to require such [credit bureau] agencies to maintain individual files on all consumers without regard to sex or marital status."[152] Progressive groups like NOW promoted universal credit surveillance to insure equal credit access for all. Women—single, married, or divorced—would all have credit ratings to insure fairer access to credit. Universal credit access would require individual credit records for all citizens and so would bring additional complications to the push for credit equality.

Surveillance, Computers, and the Fair Credit Reporting Act

Like the other credit reform bills, the Fair Credit Reporting Act, first passed in 1970 and amended in 1973, sought to restore fairness to the credit industry. In this case, Congressional policymakers sought to make credit reporting "fair," by which credit reformers meant "accurate." The bill's aim was not to restrain the operation of credit agencies but to make them accurate. Consumers could not opt out of their files, but they would be able to contest the information contained. While policymakers expressed anxiety over so much information in private hands, they also recognized the importance that such a system had for the economy.[153]

Confidentially and accuracy concerned everyone. But for a credit agency to work, information had to be shared. As Senator Charles Goodell (R-NY) insisted, "access to such [credit] information [should] be limited to those individuals who have a specific, immediate, and relevant need for such data." Goodell, like many others, pointed to the "rights of an individual to his privacy," but the legal privacy rights against unwarranted state intrusion did not exist for private corporations.[154] Giving information only to those who "needed" it was an ambiguous goal that was difficult to implement and legally suspect. While a government-run credit data system had been debated and defeated in the previous year, the government's role in regulating the credit reporting industry was still undecided.[155] In 1969, a consumer had no legal standing to challenge an error on a credit report, much less find out if an error existed in a credit report. While some voluntary guidelines had been adopted by the Associated Credit Bureaus in the previous year, many policymakers remained suspicious of the power and secrecy of the credit reporting companies. As

Virginia Knauer, President Nixon's representative on consumer affairs, remarked, "too many consumers feel that information fed to credit reporting agencies is not always full information, and sometimes not even correct information." To Knauer, the credit databanks constituted "almost a privately run spy network."[156] For Paul Dixon, the chairman of the FTC, the framework set by this bill would set the stage for the next era of capitalism. Dixon saw this legislation as important because "the rapid growth of interconnected credit bureaus tied in with computer centers and telephone lines constitutes an agglomerate growth pattern which will likely parallel, in ultimate significance, the history of the railroad and telephone systems."[157] Credit reporting would form the infrastructure of the computer-age economy, as the railroad and telephone had made possible the industrial-age economy. To Dixon and the authors of the bill, the fairness of the Fair Credit Reporting Act (FCRA) was in preserving the accuracy of information. Dixon saw "the two words as synonymous in this bill. Fair and accurate."[158] These two issues, privacy and accuracy, drove the debates surrounding the FCRA, and how to resolve them would shape the future of the credit reporting industry, which, outside of legal questions, was under other pressures as well.

By the late 1960s the credit reporting industry issued 97 million reports but even as it expanded it was transforming under new demands from technological change and firm competition. While the most rapidly growing and most profitable credit bureaus were computerizing, the majority of credit bureaus, even in 1969, were not updating their methods. And though at the end of the 1960s a few credit agencies like the Retail Credit Company overshadowed many smaller bureaus, these local credit bureaus still existed and constituted the bulk of bureaus in the United States. The older, local model of credit reporting, while still dominant and which relied on local informants, card catalogs, and telephones, only slowly gave way to objective accounting data, computer data bases, and modems. Computerization changed credit reporting not only quantitatively in terms of speed and volume, but qualitatively by transforming the kinds of data reported and the companies that controlled the information. Credit reports in the late 1960s and early 1970s were in a transitional moment between filing cards and data banks. While credit bureaus standardized information, it still was stored in old-fashioned ways, containing qualitative personal information.[159] Today's standardized credit scores had not yet been popularized. Information remained detailed, personal, and prone to error.[160] As Congress wrestled with regulating credit information, legislators were caught between old and new, making policies suitable for neither.

Retail Credit Company was first organized in 1899 in Atlanta by two brothers, Cator and Guy Woolford, who had experience in the grocery business. Initially, the company provided consumer credit information for local grocers and other retailers who extended open-book account credit.[161] The company expanded into insurance, personnel, and automobile reports, so that by the 1960s consumer credit reports made up less than 20 percent of the company's business.[162] In the early years of credit bureaus, information came from local informants who were paid by the report. Lawyers and bartenders alike informed on fellow citizens. By the early 1960s, however, Retail Credit Company brought this paid informant network in-house and full-time inspectors wrote 98 percent of all reports.[163] Credit bureaus, who now paid these inspectors full-time salaries, pressured investigators into producing many reports per day, with the expectation that a certain percentage of those reports would be negative. At the Retail Credit Company, for instance, investigators produced an average of 11½ reports a day or, in an eight-hour day, a report every forty minutes, with no lunch break. Such time pressure precluded the cross-checking of information.

These inspectors pressed the boundaries of privacy, reporting a hodgepodge of personal information to retailers, who then decided in idiosyncratic ways on whom to lend to. As Erma Angevene, executive director of the Consumers Federation of America, noted, credit reports moved beyond the financial into "value judgments on our marital relationships, our personal habits and morality, how well we maintain our households and a countless number of other intimate details."[164] One widespread system of finding out information about a newly arrived household was called, depending on the city, either "Welcome Wagon" or "Welcome Newcomer."[165] When a middle-class family moved to a new place, the credit bureau would employ one of these two services, which would send a respectable middle-class woman to the new house to call on the woman of the house. Accounts varied on what happened next. According to critics, the Welcome Wagon employee would welcome the newly arrived wife into the neighborhood and present her with complimentary gifts from local merchants.[166] Dissimulating herself as a friendly neighbor, the employee would accept the inevitable invitation in to have a cup of coffee. As one unguarded housewife remarked, "Here comes a nice lady with nice little gifts. You sit and tell the nice lady these things."[167] Over coffee, she would casually ask about the recently arrived woman's family: her husband's line of work, their religion, where they had lived before, how many children she had, what kind of car she drove, and on and on. While many women found this line of questioning a bit too familiar, for the sake of propriety they answered the questions.

After the employee left, the inspector entered all this information into a credit bureau report and moved to the next address, which she gleaned from the credit bureau's records of new utility account openings. These reports would include all the information from the conversation as well as a description of how well kept the house was and what furniture needed to be purchased, which then was sent to local merchants. Finding out where the family used to live allowed the local credit bureau to forward that information from the previous credit bureau. According to the credit bureaus, these employees were instructed to present themselves honestly as representatives of the local credit bureau. Presenting surveys of visited homes, credit bureaus claimed that over three-fourths of households remembered that the visitor was from a credit bureau.[168] Moreover, 91 percent of those surveyed thought, "there [was] advantage in having credit record transferred here." While the reliability of the survey was suspect since it was taken after the disparaging reports in the local newspapers, it also revealed that many thought there was an advantage to having a continuous credit record, pointing to the pride in, and importance of, a credit history. As these employees were paid to find out information, like other investigators at the credit bureau, Welcome Wagon employees who did not produce information could lose their jobs. All credit bureau employees felt pressure to dig out information. Even if the bureaus were clear in their instructions, there would no doubt have been incentive on the part of the Welcome Wagon employee to obscure her origins.

Such intrusions affected more than shopping. Whereas earlier one needed a good job to get credit, by the end of the 1960s one needed good credit to get a job. Credit bureaus' power went beyond consumption into the workplace since employers frequently consulted credit reports when someone applied for a job. Both small credit bureaus and national ones, like Retail Credit Company, used their data for purposes other than credit. Alan Westin, a Columbia University law professor and well-known privacy advocate, believed that for the unemployed, the credit report could have what Westin called a "self-fulfilling prophecy."[169] Negative information about a person's work habits or personal finances, possibly biased or incorrect, could prevent future prospective employers from hiring that person. The bureau reported the same information as in a credit report, but instead of denying someone a loan, the report denied him or her a job.[170] And every inquiry into the credit record was recorded, leading future prospective employers to see a long history of rejected job applications.

For the misrepresented, even finding out that a credit report maligned their reputations proved challenging. The contracts between the potential employers and the credit bureaus forbade telling denied workers about the report at all, much less the source of the negative information in the report.[171] Even by the late 1960s, consumer activists believed, many consumers did not know the importance of their credit record in shaping their public and private lives.[172] Cloaked in secrecy, these bureaus wielded a tremendous amount of power over people's consumption and work lives, but with very few avenues of recourse for the misrepresented.

W. Lee Burge, president of the Retail Credit Company, defended the investigatory model of credit reporting. The information they found, he claimed, helped the economy function efficiently. Protecting their sources kept the information free-flowing and honest. Burge thought that, "the confidential treatment we have accorded over the years to the sources of our information, as we have to the individual reported on, is vital to the continuance of the smooth flow of business information."[173] If consumers knew the identity of the informants then they would harass them, especially when the information was accurate and damaging. Revealing informants would not increase accuracy, Burge insisted but, because of fear of harassment, "sources [would] alter their stories."[174] The intensely personal information revealed through investigators and services like the Welcome Wagon were important because Burge believed that "the care with which a person exercises the premises of his home seemed to be carried over into other habits of his life."[175] Despite his claims to the contrary, the Retail Credit Company manual instructed investigators "to investigate in such a manner that the applicant or insured will not learn of the investigation."[176] The decentralization of the information in card files and 300 branch offices offset, Burge felt, the Orwellian possibilities of the information's misuse. The very inefficiency of the qualitative, noncomputerized systems made Retail Credit Company's services not nearly as sinister as detractors like Westin claimed.

The older filing systems still allowed for privacy breeches, however, even without being centralized. Credit information could be accessed either by paper requests, or more frequently, it was obtained over the phone. Subscribers to the credit bureau service would receive an identification number and when they needed information on someone would call the bureau and give the identification number. But, as William Willer, critic of the credit reporting industry and director of the National Consumer Law Center, there was no telling who had that number, or even whether they were using it only for work-related purposes. In December 1968, an investigation by CBS News found they could get ten out of twenty randomly chosen names from a credit bureau.[177] Information was restricted to credit bureau members, who may or may not be creditors. The FBI, while not a provider of personal loans, credit cards, or mortgages, nonetheless was the largest single user of credit bureau services.[178] Rather than conspiratorial and Orwellian, however, the credit bureaus should be understood as just negligent and profit-oriented. Only after the media and governmental backlash against the ease with which anyone's information could be had, did they begin to restrict access. But by 1969, even voluntary industry guidelines on privacy were insufficient to quell the rising call for regulation.

While lawmakers debated the privacy concerns created by the networked power of computers, to capture the efficiency gains of computerized credit systems reporting agencies moved away from the most invasive breeches of privacy. Policymakers agreed with industry that someone's debt record and income could be reasonably used to predict their future behavior. While opinions over the relationship of drinking, divorce, and household cleanliness with creditworthiness persisted, after the FCRA they became largely irrelevant, not by legislation but by changes in the credit information industry itself. The turn to strict financial data, practiced by new companies like Credit Data Corporation (CDC), largely erased the privacy concerns over personal information created by investigative credit reporting.

CDC, founded only a few years earlier, represented a different model of centralized, anonymous, computerized credit reporting. In the words of its founder and CEO, Harry Jordan, "Credit Data is the first on-line computerized credit reporting agency in the United States."[179] By 1969, CDC had 27 million people on file and was adding a half-million people a month.[180] Each customer had computers installed on-site. Credit Data's cutting-edge system allowed access to a borrower's credit information in less than three minutes over a direct teletype connection to the corporate mainframe. Jordan's privacy concerns structured the organization of the CDC. He believed "that if data banks of the sort that we operate are to survive without creating a mechanism for a police state or for an entirely different sort of society from what we have lived in the past, they must be very carefully insulated from access for purposes other than the announced intended one."[181] Jordan claimed, as well, that CDC was less prone to hoaxes than other organizations because the information was accessed by dedicated computers and not by telephone. While anybody could steal an identification code and phone-in, computers that could dial-in to the mainframe were much harder to come by in 1970. CDC did not release information to the government, and through the late 1960s and early 1970s was embroiled in litigation with the IRS for refusing to release consumer information.[182]

Accuracy in its data, moreover, was much higher than in traditional credit bureaus. CDC data did not come from police reports or consumer interviews like Retail Credit Company, but from the accounting data bases of its subscribers. Such accounts were, of necessity, more accurate than the hearsay reported by inspectors. As Jordan noted, "it is in the subscriber's own interest to keep his books in balance and he takes stringent measures to reduce the errors in his accounting system."[183] Financial data obtained in this way was cheaper to acquire and more accurate than investigative reporting. If their clients were content with just financial data, why should a credit rating agency find out if someone had a bad driving record or a drinking problem when such information could open them to potentially expensive libel suits? Converting handwritten data to computer data opened the possibility of typing errors.[184] CDC's computer-to-computer data transfer created no such errors. Harassment issues had less meaning when there was no individual informant but an anonymous magnetic tape containing a company's financial data. Between the new laws and the new data systems, the companies that practiced old forms of credit reporting either began to lose ground to the new companies like CDC or adopt their methods.

Credit bureau companies like Retail Credit, which had the organizational wherewithal and capital to adapt to the new system, continued to prosper. Small town credit bureaus that eked out marginal profits with expensive, manual card catalogs were trapped in legacy organizational systems and did not have the money to computerize.[185] In 1973, Associated Credit Bureaus reported that 20 percent of its membership had an average gross income of only $10,500 a year. Only 80 of its 2,100 members had computerized, which left a gigantic market niche to fill for TRW and other large computerized credit agencies with consumer reports that were cheaper to produce and that would quickly obliterate the smaller companies. As Retail Credit Company used its large capital to become Equifax in the mid-1970s, it changed more than its name—it changed the way it did business. The older, inaccurate, expensive investigative reports gave way to the new methods. The profitability of the new credit methods led to Credit Data's acquisition by the large conglomerate TRW in the early 1970s.[186] Following the efficiencies of the computer age, TRW abandoned investigative reports on consumers and had no information about habits, moral character, driving record, or health in their records, just financial data on outstanding debts, income, and payment histories.[187] Rather than relying on investigators, TRW relied on accounting books. The information was cheaper, more reliable, and easier to quantify and to store on a computer's magnetic tape. Using this new information, TRW quickly caught up with its competitors.

Character, the old cornerstone of the four C's, which formed the basis of lending, no longer mattered. A new "C," computer, had taken its place. The long shift from qualitative to quantitative credit information had been completed. In the end, legislators and consumer groups feared the inaccurate and personal information of the older system more than centralized computer information. Consumer groups like the National Consumers League were willing to cede the existence of such data bases in return for citizens' ability to correct inaccurate records.[188] The credit data could exist but only if it were true. Credit reporting agencies could wield the power of information but it had to be used in a fair manner.

While the new laws fostered greater transparency and reduced credit discrimination, they also created a much more complicated environment in which to lend. For smaller retailers, the red tape was too much. By the late 1970s, Congressional researchers believed that the "trend for retailers to eliminate the use of in-house credit and to rely instead on bank credit cards such as Master Charge or BankAmericard," was in part driven by the "amount and complexity of Federal regulations."[189] Most importantly, the computerized credit report encouraged the movement away from humans judging other humans to a credit system based on computerized information analyzed by computer models. Computerized credit reporting moved the industry away from hearsay, moralizing, and discrimination toward a more impartial and financial basis for its judgments. At the same time, computerized credit reporting further consolidated consumer finance operations in large banks and finance companies outside the hands of retailers.

Unexpected Statistical Reasoning and the Equal Credit Opportunity Act

The fight for credit fairness as understood in expanded credit access, begun with the Consumer Credit Protection Act, culminated with the Equal Credit Opportunity Act (ECOA) in 1974 and its subsequent amendments. Emerging from the recommendations of the National Commission on Consumer Finance's final report, and reflecting the nationwide surge of feminist activism on credit issues, ECOA initially focused on the experiences of women. ECOA, as passed, forbade only discrimination on the basis of sex and martial status.[190] Banning one form of discrimination made banning other forms politically easier. Congress quickly expanded the antidiscrimination protections of the ECOA with amendments passed in 1976 to prohibit discrimination by race, religion, national origin, or age.[191] As President Ford signed the amendments into law, he remarked that it promoted "equal opportunity in all aspects of our society" and the shared commitment of Congress and the administration to "achieve goals of fairness and equality in a broad range of business transactions [that] millions of American consumers engage in every day of every year."[192] Under ECOA and its amendments, credit discrimination through so-called "protected categories" became illegal. The suspicions of a private information data base on every American and the lingering doubts about borrowing—fears still prevalent in the 1960s—were overcome and resolved in the notion of fairness and accuracy. Universal information was legitimate as long as it was accurate, and enabled every American had the right to credit regardless of race or gender.

As late as the early 1970s, race had remained a standard question on many credit applications. The FTC conducted a study of the lending practices of a major consumer finance company in 1970 and 1971. Collecting racial information remained a standard practice. At the individual level, Sheldon Feldman, an FTC official said, whether an applicant was white, black, or "of Spanish origin" was noted on every application. The credit applications were all given a point score of which white borrower got seven points, a "person of Spanish origin" four points, and a black borrower no points at all. Loan officers inspected minority applications more attentively than white applications. Applications from "racially mix marriages," Feldman noted, "were automatically rejected because of what was considered to be the inherent instability of such marriages."[193] As with mortgages, this major consumer finance company made no loans in "blacked out" areas that were, Feldman found, "largely black, low income neighborhoods in large cities." Even if reliable customers had lived there before the finance company imposed the blackout, they received no more loans.

By the late 1970s, in an effort to eliminate any possibility of lawsuit, many creditors completely eliminated loan officers in evaluating applicants, accelerating the shift to computer-based credit models.[194] The "traditional credit manager," Richard Cremer, a Montgomery Ward's credit executive, remarked, "emphasized his face-to-face contact with the credit applicant," which allowed non-relevant qualities of the applicant to cloud the loan officer's judgment.[195] "Biases, prejudices, and even mood" could affect the loan officer's evaluation, Cremer felt, and this hurt revenue. The credit score, according to Ward's policy, "encourage[d] a decision motivated by economics alone" and was the "only available method that [met] the criterion of fairness."[196] Race, marital status, and other "protected categories" were easily removed as variables from the models as creditors moved from human "judgmental systems" to computer credit models. Without these discriminatory categories in the models' variables, any hint of illegality could be easily disproved. Creditors could point to their models—which had no variable for gender or race—and say that they did not discriminate. The computer model offered creditors the appearance of non-discrimination by eliminating human prejudice. Applications became more consistent and less subject to the whims of a particular loan officer. In computer models, feminist credit advocates believed they had found the solution to discriminatory lending, ushering in the contemporary calculated credit regimes under which we live today.

Yet removing such basic demographics from any model was not as straightforward as the authors of the ECOA had hoped because of how all statistical models function, but which legislators seem to not have fully understood. The "objective" credit statistics that legislators had pined for during the early investigations of the Consumer Credit Protection Act could now exist, but with new difficulties that stemmed from using regressions and not human judgment to decide on loans.

In human-judged credit lending, a loan officer who knew the race and gender of an applicant would be *more* discriminatory, whereas in a computer credit model, knowing the applicant's race and gender allowed the credit decision to be *less* discriminatory. The dilemma in completely excluding race, as well as other protected categories, was that if these variables actually did predict whether a borrower would default and if they correlated with anything else, then the correlated variable would acquire the predictive power of the protected category. Women would not have to be biologically less creditworthy than men for this to occur. Women could simply be more vulnerable to unemployment, which caused income interruption. If women tended to disproportionately own high-heeled shoes, then the variable in the dataset for high-heel ownership would also reflect women's job volatility, since gender would have been eliminated from the regression. Without gender in the data set, the spurious relationship between shoe ownership and creditworthiness could not be mathematically eliminated. The collision of statistics with racist and sexist labor markets, not culture or biology or shoe ownership, could produce discriminatory credit scores. But with credit scores, what had once appeared discriminatory now seemed objective. In passing legislation geared to a world of prejudiced loan officers, Congress made the newer computer-driven credit models actually more discriminatory.

In real life, zip codes, not shoes, came to be at the center of a renewed credit debate. Zip codes, developed for the efficient distribution of mail and not economic demography, began to be heavily used by credit-scoring companies. Zip codes, in some areas, also tended to loosely reflect racial and economic geography. For instance, if race actually did help predict the default rate of borrowers and did correlate with zip code, however loosely, then a zip code variable, in the absence of a race variable in the model, would acquire race's predictive power, which in turn, correlated with a more volatile labor market.[197] In the late 1970s, lawsuits were brought against Amoco, Mobil, and Diner's Club for racial discrimination by their use of zip codes in their credit models. Critics, like Massachusetts Senator Paul Tsongas, correctly saw the use of residential location as a proxy for race in these credit models. A study conducted by the Massachusetts Attorney General's office found that 43 percent of African Americans in the state lived in zip codes that hurt their credit scores. They were six to seven times as likely as whites to live in such neighborhoods, making it more difficult for them to get credit.[198]

Rather than address race directly, and the greater difficulties that African Americans had in holding onto a job in the tough economy of 1970s Boston, Tsongas only sought to add geography to the long list of other protected categories.

By sidestepping the more fundamental question of how economic structures, not individual character, made borrowers creditworthy, the anti-discrimination legislation was rendered less important than it needed to be. The desire to render two borrowers otherwise the same except for race and gender ignored a fundamental reality of the American labor market. Race and gender did affect the ability of men and women to find and keep employment. While Congress might pass a law to help guarantee access to credit, the labor markets continued to pay women less and fire African Americans more frequently. Without remedying the underlying differences to secure the ability to pay back debt—good jobs at good wages—the law only encouraged overlending to borrowers. In a sexist and racist labor market, otherwise the same women and African-Americans were frequently less creditworthy—not from any intrinsic untrustworthiness or lack of desire to pay back their debts, but from the very precariousness of their position in the workplace.

While firms could not explicitly use race and gender in their lending models, lenders found ways to sneak them in, like through zip codes. Such sneaking, it turned out, proved nearly impossible to avoid by the very nature of the mathematics that they used, if race and gender turned out to affect default rates, which, given the racist and sexist nature of labor markets, would have been unthinkable. Every time a variable was excised from the model, any other variable, if it correlated with gender or race, would then pick up the effect. If liberals wanted to rectify the financial condition of poor women and minorities, rather than focusing on credit access, they would have had to remedy the core inequalities of the labor market. Credit access could not recreate the white middle-class prosperity, which relied as much on credit as on good jobs.

As William Fair, the founder of Fair, Isaac & Company, the foremost developer of credit models in the United States, remarked, if Congress wanted to exclude race as a matter of social policy, then it should pass a law implementing that vision, but to exclude race from the credit models did not, and could not, accomplish that goal.[199] Simply disallowing a category made it impossible for it to be statistically separated off from other correlated variables. Geography and race were correlated, but without knowing the race of borrowers, it became impossible for geography not to include the effect of race.[200] Divorce, for instance, was such a strong predictor of a borrower default that Citibank struggled in the 1980s to make its credit models predict default and not just marriages breaking up.[201] If creditors could ask for race and martial status, actual discrimination could have been eliminated, rather than just the appearance of ending discrimination.[202]

At the same time, however, of all the credit card providers in the United States by the late 1970s, only two oil companies and Diner's Club were called to task for such discrimination. Most credit card companies had already voluntarily removed zip codes from their credit models, for fears of these accusations. The discrimination against minorities and women, so pervasive only a decade earlier, seemed to have been largely eliminated from public view, legitimated by the apparent absence of gender and race from creditor's computer models. Master Charge and VISA were no where to be found. Diner's Club was singled out, but it was alone among the large universal credit card systems. The credit card industry upheld the letter of the ECOA by expanding its credit offerings to inner-city Americans, no doubt replacing much of the older, expensive credit systems. While formally eliminated, however, racial and gender discrimination persisted through the transition from human- to computer-based evaluation methods. The commonsense reasoning of ECOA could never be fulfilled in a computer credit model world, where statistical reasoning held sway. The "social evil of stereotyping," as Tsongas termed it, had been ostensibly eliminated from the world of credit. The reality of credit lending remained less certain. Lenders had less information on which to lend, which raised default rates, but that did not seem to restrict their lending, which grew throughout the 1970s to ever-greater amounts.

Conclusion: Fair Credit for All

Early calls for an actuarial basis for credit scoring had, in some ways, been achieved. The seemingly arbitrary discrimination of possibly sexist and racist loan officers had been computerized. Prejudice was no longer part of the credit system. But the third rail question of credit lending remained: Is it discrimination when there is a statistically significant difference between populations? While Congress passed legislation to maintain the appearance of fairness and prohibited discrimination, William Fair's honest rejoinder to the public-relations-oriented retailers and voter-oriented politicians remained. In the creation of these discrimination-free models, Congress legislated away their ability to fully eliminate the effects of race and gender. Transparency was attained. The credit system, mysterious and arbitrary in the mid-1960s was, by the late 1970s, legible and mechanistic. In an effort to end credit discrimination and give more Americans the opportunity to enjoy consumer prosperity, liberal politicians remade the legal context of indebtedness.

The credit reform laws made credit easier to acquire for many consumers. In return, under this mantle of fairness, accuracy, and transparency, new creditor and credit rating firms rapidly expanded their operations across the country, further nationalizing, centralizing, and computerizing the credit industry. While lenders initially turned to computer credit models to avoid paying for credit reports, as credit reports themselves computerized, the two systems integrated. William Fair's company went on to create the well-known FICO score—Fair, Isaac Corporation score—that is today synonymous with credit score and is generated for every American by the big-three credit agencies, two of which descended from Retail Credit Company (Equifax) and Credit Data Corporation (Experian). "Fairness" in lending, defined as objective and widespread, seemed to have been achieved, but the earlier lingering question of whether people ought to borrow, and did borrowing actually help consumers when their incomes were uncertain, remained unanswered. In a time of rising unemployment and deindustrialization, the logic of borrowing from a future income—which underpinned the postwar growth economy—began to unravel. Credit cards for all emerged at the exact moment when the future had become less certain than ever before.

Membership, nonetheless, had its privileges. For women, as an American Bankers Association representative testified, the "the only way we can tell sex right now including our credit scoring system . . . is by her name."[203] Individual credit records created the possibility of individual interest rates. The creation of individual interest rates allowed banks to extend credit in ghetto markets without the appearance of discrimination. Unlike retailers tied to the 1.5 percent per month, new individual interest rates could vary freely with credit scores. Credit had become a right because credit had become a necessity. Only when it was optional could it be seen as a privilege. If consumer credit became a necessity in participating in the modern economy, as both a worker and a consumer, then it started to become a right. Of course, credit was a right for which everyone had to pay.

The onerous experiences of credit and the poor in the 1960s, rather than being obviated by the consumer credit acts of the late 1960s and early 1970s, instead coincided with a new age of post-growth economic volatility in which the middle class began to experience the uncertainty, unpredictability, and sudden losses of income that had previously only characterized poor, urban life. Though revolving credit, which was better suited for varying incomes, increasingly replaced installment credit, working Americans overall had a more difficult time repaying their debts, even with the credit card's flexibility. Easing the access to credit for millions of Americans and legitimating its expansion, the credit acts helped put all Americans into the position of the indebted poor, and in the face of economic uncertainty, even once stably employed Americans, once again, experienced the vicissitudes of capitalism. Outstanding debt levels, growing gradually since the World War II, exploded as consumers borrowed as they had for generations, but, for the first time, found themselves unable to pay back what they borrowed. While the amount of outstanding debt tripled from 1970 to 1979, the gap between what was loaned and what was repaid increased seven times, to $35 billion a year.[204] Everywhere, in the face of uncertainty and declining real wages, Americans indebted themselves to maintain the life they had once been able to afford.

Chapter Seven

Securing Debt in an Insecure World

CREDIT CARDS AND CAPITAL MARKETS

IN 1978, DONALD AURIEMMA, then the vice-president of Chemical Bank's personal loan department, doubted the wisdom of Citibank's aggressive expansion into the credit card business that had begun a few years earlier. Auriemma expected that the expansion would not pay off for Citibank since he believed that "the credit card business is marginal, [and] it'll never make big money for banks."[1] Yet within a few years, these marginal profits on credit cards would become the center of lending. By the early 1980s, credit cards metamorphosed from break-even investments to leading earners. With much higher profits than commercial loans, financial institutions began to lend as much money as they could to consumers on credit cards. By the early 1990s investments in credit cards were *twice* as profitable as conventional business loans. Drawing on newfound ways to access capital markets, lenders borrowed funds from the markets, supplemented by their own money, to fund consumer debt rather than business investment and remake the possibilities of the American economy. Using new mathematical, marketing, and financial techniques, issuers tipped the scales of capital allocation in the U.S. economy toward consumption over production. For banks to lend, consumers had to borrow. And borrow they did—in record amounts on their credit cards and against their homes. In 1970, only one-sixth of American households had bank-issued revolving credit cards, compared with two-thirds of households in 1998.[2] Increasingly the now plentiful credit cards allowed consumers to borrow more money and with greater flexibility than they had before. For home owners, home equity loans also offered a new way to borrow by tapping into the value of their homes. Like credit cards, home equity loans allowed borrowers to pay back their debt when they wanted, without a fixed schedule.

Credit cards and home equity loans—though both revolving debts—still appeared quite distinct from one another in how consumers used them and thought about them. Credit cards bought pants, dinners, and ski vacations. Mortgages bought houses. Credit card debt was unsecured by any claim on real property, while the installment debt of mortgages was secured by a claim on unmovable property. While these two different financial practices—borrowing against a home's value and borrowing on a credit card—appeared very different for consumers, the business logic and financial practices that underpinned them both grew more and more similar over time. By the late 1980s, these two different debts converged and become financially indistinguishable in how they were funded—by asset-backed securities. By the mid-1990s, even consumers began to use home mortgages and credit cards interchangeably, consolidating the debt of credit cards into the debt of mortgages. How the mortgage and credit became indistinguishable defined a key aspect of the financial transformation of this post-1970s world, reshaping the relationships of lenders and borrowers.

As lenders sought to expand their loans, consumers had new reasons to borrow. While protestors demanded fair credit access for all Americans, innovations in basic financing and lending techniques enabled lenders to profitably extend that access. Home equity loans enabled home owners to borrow against rapidly inflating values of their houses. Credit cards, using new statistical credit scores, allowed more Americans access to plastic than ever before. Mortgage-backed securities, created in the Housing Act of 1968 to fund development in the inner city, paved the way for the easy resale of debt as a financial investment, even as the original development intentions were forgotten. All forms of personal debt became sold as securities, allowing the world to invest profitably in American debt. As wages fell, Americans continued to borrow ever-greater amounts, making up the gap between incomes and expectations. Through home equity loans, consumers could easily turn their rising home prices—growing even faster than the inflation that eroded their wages—into money to pay off their credit card bills. Historians who have seen the increase in debt outstanding in the 1970s as a result of increased borrowing, rather than a decrease in ability to repay, have interpreted this rise as a strategic response to inflation. Borrow today and pay back tomorrow when the money is cheaper. Yet few borrowers self-consciously responded to the rise in interest rates. While inflation did not have this strategic consequence for borrowers, it did have an important strategic consequence for lenders, who, in their fixed-rate portfolios, felt the rising interest rate most keenly as they watched their profits fall. Lenders' business responses to inflation, more than consumers, pushed household debt in new directions that previously, in the most literal sense, had been impossible.

Personal debt after the 1970s was made possible through the global connections of capital that arose after the fall of Bretton Woods. The story of high-flying finance divorced from the everyday lives of Americans, a viewpoint through which financial history is too commonly told, makes as little sense as telling the story of the 1970s only from the viewpoint of consumers. Borrowing and buying, after 1970, took place in a

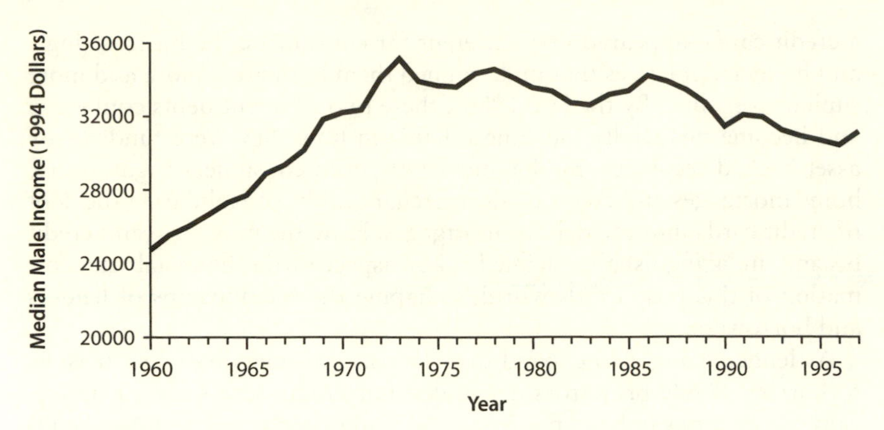

Figure 7.1. Median Male Wages. Source: Robert A. Margo, "Median earnings of full-time workers, by sex and race: 1960–1997," Table Ba4512 in *Historical Statistics of the United States, Earliest Times to the Present: Millennial Edition*, eds. Susan B. Carter, Scott Sigmund Gartner, Michael R. Haines, Alan L. Olmstead, Richard Sutch, and Gavin Wright (New York: Cambridge University Press, 2006). In 1994 dollars.

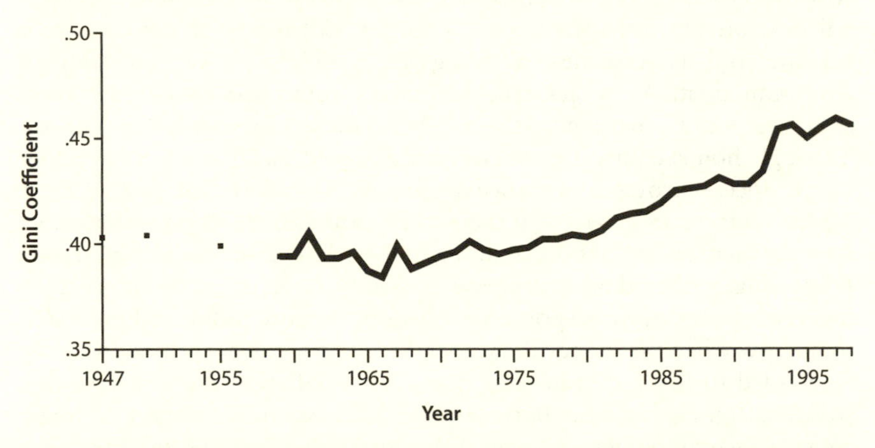

Figure 7.2. Income Inequality. Source: Peter H. Lindert, "Distribution of money income among households: 1947–1998," Table Be1-18 in *Historical Statistics of the United States, Earliest Times to the Present: Millennial Edition*, eds. Susan B. Carter, Scott Sigmund Gartner, Michael R. Haines, Alan L. Olmstead, Richard Sutch, and Gavin Wright (New York: Cambridge University Press, 2006).

very different world than that of the postwar period, a world where employment and prices were more volatile, where median real wages had fallen for thirty years, and where wealth inequality, which had contracted in the postwar period, had once again began to widen. The aberration of postwar prosperity had ended and the true face of American

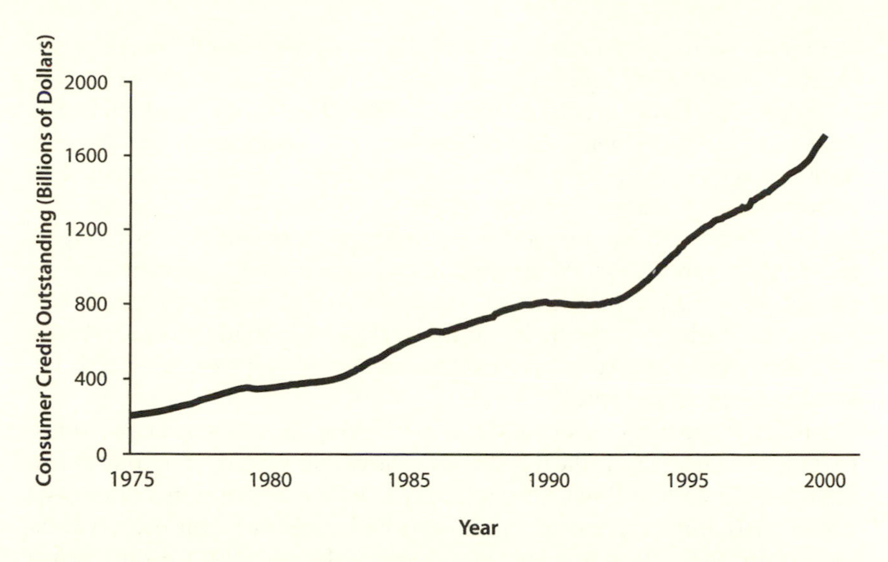

Figure 7.3. Consumer Credit Outstanding. Consumers of the 1970s continued to borrow as they had since World War II, but as inequality widened they were increasingly unable to repay what they borrowed. Repayments, not borrowing, were what changed in the 1970s. To fund this borrowing, financiers developed new ways to invest in debt. Source: Federal Reserve, "G. 19, Consumer Credit, Historical Data," http://www.federalreserve.gov/releases/g19/hist/cc_hist_sa.txt, accessed December 2009; in billions of seasonally adjusted dollars.

capitalism—unequal and volatile—had returned with the vengeance of the repressed. The proliferation of revolving credit and home equity loans, as well as securitization, reflected, and to some degree enabled, this changing economic order. While the expansion of debt occurred because consumers were less and less able, on average, to pay back what they borrowed, the massive investment necessary to roll over that outstanding debt required lenders to use capital markets in innovative ways. Moving beyond the resale networks of the mid-twentieth century, new ways to sell debt anonymously on national and even international capital markets inaugurated a new relationship between consumer credit and investor capital. In an insecure world, unsecured debt came of age.

Mortgage-backed Securities and the Great Society

The financial innovation that ultimately allowed capital markets to directly fund any form of debt began with the federal government, not business. In the late 1960s, the federal government sought a way to channel capital into America's rioting cities. Capital would make possible the Great Society ambitions of saving America's cities and the newly rising pension funds needed to invest. Ironically, pension funds borne of strong union movements helped provide the justification for policies based on remedying poverty through better access to capital, rather than better access to wages. For Great Society policymakers and promoters, the problems of inequality were framed as a problem of credit access rather than job access. More credit, and not higher wages, would be enough to solve the problems of America's cities. Toward that end, federal policy fashioned the financial innovation that made possible America's debt explosion—the asset-backed security—that expanded well beyond its original purpose.

Solving the urban crisis would require solving the housing crisis. But to fix the housing crisis, radical financial innovation would have to occur to maintain the capital flows into mortgages. As the urban riots became the urban crisis, however, mortgage markets had a crisis of their own. American mortgage markets had abruptly frozen—the so-called Credit Crunch of 1966—as investors rapidly withdrew their deposits from banks and put their money in the securities markets. Stocks and bonds offered greater returns than the Federal Reserve–regulated rates available at banks[3] Without these deposits, banks could not lend mortgage money. FHA Commissioner Philip Brownstein believed that "our innovations and aggressive thrusts against blight and deterioration, our massive efforts on behalf of the needy, will be lost without an adequate continuing supply of mortgage funds."[4]

In a novel move, policymakers seeking a way to fund an expansion of stabilizing home ownership in the cities turned to those same securities markets for new sources of mortgage funds.[5] Using markets as sources of capital defined the Great Society approach. Rather than distributing existing mortgages through resale networks as New Deal–era institutions did, markets would guarantee that credit crunches would not interrupt urban development. With the mortgage-backed security, Great Society policymakers tried to harness changes in capitalism to fit its programs rather than trying to regulate capitalism to fit its agenda.

Beyond the immediate crisis of the Credit Crunch of 1966, the old system of buying and selling individual government-insured mortgages through personal connections had already begun to break down over the 1960s. The instruments and institutions through which Americans saved had changed. Beginning in the late 1950s, the big growth in American savings was through pension funds. Pension funds, unlike insurance companies, had little interest in buying mortgages. Whereas insurance companies had large mortgage department staffs whose job was to buy, sell, and collect on mortgages, pension fund managers preferred to invest in stocks and bonds, which could be easily tracked and managed. In 1966, pension funds held $64 billion in assets, according to the Federal Home Loan Bank Board, 60 percent of which were invested in stocks and 25 percent in corporate bonds.[6] While pension funds did not have the mortgage departments of insurance companies, they shared the insurance companies' interest in safe, long-term investments like bonds. To create a new flow of funds, a new financial instrument would have to be fashioned to meet the needs of large institutional investors without the desire or capacity to oversee the collection of a mortgage. If mortgages could be fashioned into an easy-to-invest-in form such as bonds, then pension funds, policymakers believed, would flock to mortgages, which promised a slightly higher return. Making mortgages bond-like, bankers and policymakers realized, would radically expand their investor base, which would have been the goal of such an instrument.

President Johnson announced that to fulfill the aims of his urban housing agenda, he would "propose legislation to strengthen the mortgage market and the financial institutions that supply mortgage credit."[7] Government studies in the aftermath of the "deplorable" credit crunch insisted, in the words of Senator John Sparkman, chairman of the Senate Committee on Banking and Currency, that action be taken to "insure an adequate flow of mortgage credit for the future."[8] The solution, Sparkman asserted, lay in "correcting deficiencies in our financial structure."[9] FHA officials, like Philip Brownstein, believed the mortgage-backed security "may very well be the break-through we all have been seeking for many years to tap the additional sources of funds which so far have shown little interest in mortgages."[10] Disparate groups, from bankers to unions, demanded Congress fashion a "new security-type mortgage instrument" to channel the money invested in the securities markets into mortgages.[11] With the support of the mortgage industry, as well as politicians, this mortgage instrument encountered few obstacles. Even the Fed, whose authority would be hampered by such an invention, encouraged Congress to consider creating debt "instruments [issued] against pools of residential mortgages" to "broaden [the] sources of funds available for residential mortgage investment," so as to "rely less on depository institutions that tend to be vulnerable to conditions accompanying general credit restraint."[12] Creating such instruments would undermine the Fed's ability to affect mortgages through its monetary policy, and in turn weaken its control over the money supply, but quarantining mortgages from the rest of the economy would also put the Fed, if need be, beyond public blame.

The Housing Act of 1968, which implemented this vision, remade the American mortgage system in a way that had not been done since the New Deal. Congress privatized the Federal National Mortgage Association

(FNMA) and created its signature financial instrument—the mortgage-backed security.[13] At the same time, the Housing Act inaugurated a short-term program, called Section 235, which used these mortgage funds to loan money to low-income borrowers, whose interest would be directly subsidized by the government.[14] Through mortgage-backed securities and these low-income loans, policymakers hoped to stabilize the unrests of the American cities.[15]

These Section 235 loans allowed low-income buyers with little or no savings to buy new and pre-existing homes. The program provided billions of dollars in financing for millions of homes during its operation. The federal government's role in housing in 1971, when federal programs subsidized 30 percent of housing starts, was shockingly higher than in 1961, when only 4.4 percent did, with "much of the increase in housing units . . . occur[ing] in section 235," according to Nixon administration officials.[16] Government-sponsored mortgage debt accounted for 20 percent of the overall increase in mortgage debt in 1971.[17] While in operation, the Section 235 marshaled new financial instruments to transform hundreds of thousands of Americans from renters to owners. Section 235 created such an upswing in housing that by 1972 the president of the Mortgage Bankers' Association could pronounce it the "principal system" for low-income housing.[18] One prominent mortgage banker declared that Section 235 "answered the cry, 'Burn, baby, burn' with 'Build, baby, build!'"[19] Eighty percent of the funds were earmarked for families at or near the welfare limit. A home buyer who qualified for the program would receive an interest-subsidy every month such that the government would pay all the interest above 1 percent. Sliding scale down payments, which reached as low as $200—two weeks' income for the median Section 235 buyer—would enable even the very poor to own a house.[20] If the borrower defaulted, the government would pay off the balance of the loan. Home buyers could borrow up to $24,000 as long as FHA house inspectors declared the property to be in sound condition. Having bought a home, their monthly rent payments would become equity instead. Section 235 would build wealth. FHA administrators like Brownstein believed the Section 235 program "[broke] down the remaining barriers to the fullest private participation in providing housing for those who are economically unable to obtain a decent home in the open market."[21] By definition, Section 235 lent to borrowers who could not get a mortgage from conventional lenders. The program intentionally sought out the riskiest borrowers that Brownstein described as "families who would not now qualify for FHA mortgage insurance because of their credit histories, or irregular income patterns." Section 235 buyers had no normal access to home financing. The program offered them their only chance for home ownership. The Section 235 program lasted only a few years, eventually bought down by scandals eerily reminiscent of today's subprime crisis, as realtors, builders, home inspectors, and mortgage bankers colluded in unsavory ways to defraud trusting first-time buyers without alternatives for home ownership.[22] Nonetheless, the mortgage-backed security invented to fund the program persisted, and in the long-run, exceeded the reach of its original purpose, enabling new sources of mortgage capital for home buyers of all incomes.

While in theory the mortgage-backed security allow borrowers to bypass financial institutions and borrow directly from capital markets, in practice, a long chain of financial institutions still mediated the connection between borrower and lender, and it was the way in which the mortgage-backed security fit those institutional needs that made it such a success. Making the mortgage-backed security work required adjusting the financial institutions that constituted the mortgage market—mortgage companies, institutional investors, and the FNMA. The FNMA existed before the credit crunch, but the Congressional response to the credit crunch remade FNMA into a new kind of institution, even more privatized and market-oriented—with a new kind of financial instrument containing great possibilities. Created in the New Deal to buy and sell government-insured mortgages across the country, FNMA had forged a national secondary market for mortgages offered through the FHA. During the 1960s, however, the federal government had created more and more socially oriented, specialized housing programs that relaxed the FHA's lending requirements, especially in the inner city. FNMA had resold these mortgages alongside the other mortgages. Many policymakers believed that the "credit requirements" used by federal lending programs were "too stringent," overlooking potential borrowers' "true merits."[23] Only "liberalized" mortgage financing, which relaxed the FHA's strict standards, would provide financing to low-income buyers or in low-income neighborhoods.[24] Though mortgage officials at the FHA were critical of this policy, loose lending policies found support across the aisle in Congress.

Though privatized, the Housing Act still provided extensive federal oversight over FNMA, explicitly ruling that the secretary of the Department of Housing and Urban Development (HUD), even after FNMA's privatization, could still require FNMA to purchase low-income mortgages.[25] Internal matters to FNMA would be private, but larger market actions would remain partially under government control. The Act spun off a new agency, the Government National Mortgage Association (GNMA or Ginnie Mae), which would handle all the subsidized mortgage programs. Splitting FNMA into two organizations—FNMA and GNMA—would cordon off the welfare programs from the market programs, and privatization would take the welfare expenses, to a large degree, off the federal budget because mortgages bought and sold would not look like a government expense on the accounting sheets, enabling the expansion of federal mortgage lending. Only the subsidies to GNMA, and not the total mortgages bought, would go on the books as a federal expense.[26]

Mortgage-backed securities initially came in two forms: the "modified pass-through" security and the "bond-like" security. Both forms gave the investor a claim on the monthly principal and interest payments of a large, diversified portfolio of mortgages. Both forms rendered the investor's connection to the underlying assets completely anonymous and secondhand. The differences between them initially irked the mortgage banking industry, however. The pass-through security delivered the real monthly principal and interest payments of the portfolio, minus a servicing fee, to the investor. The bond-like security provided a steady, even payment of principal and interest to the investor. The monthly variance for the pass-through security made it different than a normal bond, which mortgage bankers thought would reduce demand. The pass-through security could vary because of mortgage prepayments, defaults, and any of the other risks incurred with a mortgage. The bond-like security hid those events. While the pass-through mortgage-backed security provided new opportunities for tapping new institutional investors, mortgage bankers remained disappointed.[27] What they had wanted was a true bond, guaranteed by GNMA, with fixed guaranteed payments, not a bond-like pass-through instrument, in which they doubted investors would be as interested. Mortgage bankers had envisioned trading their mortgages for a bond, which would be sold at auction. Such a bond, with its underlying assets completely hidden to the buyer, would make mortgage reselling truly competitive, that is to say interchangeable, with other forms of bond issues.

In August 1969, the newly founded GNMA announced that it would be offering mortgage-backed securities for the first time.[28] After receiving suggestions from financiers, policymakers, and potential investors for the regulations surrounding the securities, GNMA, in association with FNMA, issued the first mortgage-backed securities on February 19, 1970. Three New Jersey public-sector union pension funds bought $2 million worth of pass-through securities from Associated Mortgage Companies, a sprawling interstate network of mortgage companies.[29] Soon thereafter, in May 1970, GNMA had its first sale of bond-like mortgage-backed securities, selling $400 million to investors.

While at first the bond-like mortgage-backed securities outweighed the pass-through mortgage-backed securities, the tables quickly turned. Within the year, in 1971, GNMA and FNMA sold over $2.2 billion in pass-through mortgage-backed securities and $915 million in bonds.

Within a few years, in fact, GNMA stopped offering the bond-like mortgage-backed securities entirely. For the bond-like mortgage-backed securities to work, the pools had to be enormous, at least $200 million, and the mortgage company had to have enough capital to guarantee the payments in case of default. Few private companies sold so many mortgages and none had the requisite capital. The pass-through mortgage pools could be much smaller—only $2 million. Private mortgage companies had to content themselves with pass-through mortgage-backed securities, and the mortgage companies could more easily acquire and bundle mortgages than GNMA or FNMA.

The drawbacks that mortgage bankers initially feared turned out to matter little. In many ways how the mortgage-backed security fit the institutional needs of investors mattered as much as the rate of return. While not a true bond, the pass-through security completely hid the hassle of mortgage ownership—the paperwork and collection—while still providing higher returns than government securities, and unlike corporate bonds, the mortgage bonds had foreclosable assets backing the debt. The market mediation that made the mortgage-backed security easier for mortgage companies—No personal networks! No salesmanship! Just buy a typewriter and some GNMA application forms!—made even the pass-through security much more appealing to investors than directly owning the underlying mortgages. Investment required no specialized knowledge of mortgages or even housing—the mortgage-backed securities could be compared to other bonds, whose safety was rated by Standard & Poor's. The mortgage-backed security eliminated the need to know about the underlying properties or borrowers. As Woodward Kingman, president of the GNMA noted, "this instrument eliminates all the documentation, paperwork problems, and safekeeping problems that are involved in making a comparable investment in just ordinary mortgages."[30] Institutions, big and small, did not need a mortgage department to track payments, check titles, or any of the myriad other details involved in mortgage lending. The institution just needed to file the security. Instead of tracking fifty individual $20,000 mortgages, an investor could just buy the mortgage-backed security for $1,000,000. The mortgage-backed security lowered the accounting costs by making the investments enough like a bond to attract the notice of institutional investors.[31] Investors embraced the new securities, although not always the investors that the creators of the mortgage-backed securities had originally intended.

At first, surprisingly, the biggest buyers of mortgage-backed securities were not pension funds but local savings and loan banks. Mortgage-backed securities turned out to be a great way for local banks, legally limited in their geographic scope, to invest in distant places.[32] Many states forbade local banks from lending money beyond a certain distance, but had no such provision against the buying and selling of bonds. Mortgage-backed securities allowed capital mobility for all financial institutions, but in allowing savings and loan banks such access, they did not increase the net available funds for mortgages as a nation, since savings and loan banks already invested in mortgages. Such purchases could, however, move funds to capital-poor areas.

With the declining investment in FHA loans in the 1960s, local home buyers outside of the capital-rich east found it harder to find funds for a mortgage since there was no comparable national market for conventional mortgages as there was for federally insured mortgages.[33] Every house was unique, which made reselling mortgages difficult. FHA loans had established a secondary market and national lending for distant mortgagees because, through its guarantee and its standards, the FHA created a homogeneity that allowed those loans to be sold as interchangeable commodities.[34] All loans that were not federally insured, so-called "conventional mortgages," had no such secondary market. No conventional mortgage, by itself, could be so homogeneous as to be traded across the country. Mortgage lending, for the conventional market, required local knowledge that no distant mortgage banker could have.

While FNMA could resell federally insured mortgages, such loans grew less important each year in the 1960s. Though the mortgage banking industry had flourished through its ability to originate FHA and VA loans, and then resell them on the secondary markets through FNMA, this reselling could not be done for conventional loans. While federally insured mortgages made up a large portion of American borrowing, it was a good business model, and helped move substantial amounts of capital across the country. After World War II, the use of conventional mortgages had fallen as Americans turned to FHA and VA mortgages to finance the suburban expansion. Around the late 1950s, however, the use of conventional mortgages stabilized at about half of all mortgages issued, and then began to grow again. By the mid-1960s, conventional mortgages accounted for two-thirds of all mortgages. In 1970, conventional mortgages—though double the volume of federally insured mortgages—had no national secondary market. For mortgage companies, this rise in conventional mortgages was dire. While mortgage companies originated 55 percent of federally insured loans, mortgage companies originated only 5 percent of conventional loans.[35] And with fewer investors buying federally insured mortgages, demand fell along with supply. The possibilities of a mortgage-backed security for conventional mortgages excited mortgage bankers, because as American consumers moved away from federally insured mortgages their core business shrank.

To create a secondary market for conventional mortgages, Congress, in the Emergency Home Finance Act of 1970, authorized the creation of the Federal Home Loan Mortgage Corporation (FHLMC or Freddie Mac), which drew on the mortgage-backed security financing techniques developed in the Housing Act of 1968. Like FNMA, FHLMC could buy and sell mortgages and issue mortgage-backed securities. Unlike FNMA, Congress intended FHLMC to buy its mortgages primarily from savings and loan banks rather than mortgage companies. Otherwise, the two corporations were largely identical. By this point, mortgage experts, like FNMA executive vice president Philip Brinkerhoff, recognized that finding new sources of capital could "be accomplished more efficiently through the issuance and sale of mortgage-backed securities than through direct sale of mortgages."[36]

FHLMC learned from FNMA and, in November 1970, almost immediately after its inception, issued mortgage-backed securities. While this first group of loans was federally insured and not conventional, FHLMC demonstrated to skittish investors that it could buy mortgages and issue mortgage-backed securities. Having its first portfolio insurable guaranteed that existing mortgage-backed security investors would buy the first issue. Thereafter, FHLMC began to transition into conventional mortgages, developing innovative methods to standardize conventional mortgages. Even if the home differed, standardization of information helped their commonalities come to the fore. FHLMC developed a national computer network called AMMINET to provide up-to-the-minute information on mortgage-backed security trades and issues, creating a real national "market" with national information.[37]

By 1972, FHLMC, with established procedures for credit evaluation, loan documents, appraisals, mortgage insurance, and mortgage originators, began to issue completely conventionally backed, mortgage-backed securities—creating the first national conventional mortgage market. More than just standardization, however, conventional mortgages could be traded because they were issued through mortgage-backed securities and not the old assignment system of the 1950s. While the FHA mortgage reduced investors' risk by homogenizing standards, the FHLMC reduced risk by heterogeneous diversification. The mortgage-backed security came with a pre-diversified portfolio for a given interest rate, so that the investor did not need to cherry-pick mortgages across regions and neighborhoods. The risk of one bad loan could be diluted across many good loans in a mortgage-backed security's underlying portfolio. Mortgage portfolios backing the securities brought enough diversification, it was believed, to overwhelm any outlying bad loan. For investors who would never see the property, such risk-reduction was essential.

FHLMC substituted risk-reducing portfolio diversification for risk-eliminating federal guarantees.

For GNMA and FNMA, the federal government lent its authority to their operations, and FHLMC, in mimicking them, acquired their patina of government insurance. Beyond the portfolio diversification, as a last resort, the Housing Act of 1968 had also authorized the Treasury Department as a "backstop," or buyer of last resort to the market, enabling them to buy up to $2.25 billion of FNMA mortgage-backed securities if they could not be sold.[38] Otherwise, FNMA was considered to be private—paying taxes and earning profits.[39] But this amount the Treasury could "backstop" was more important symbolically than practically, as it amounted to only about half of FNMA's annual mortgage purchases in 1972. Investors wanted the reassurance that the unlimited tax-collecting resources of the federal government stood behind the securities, even if, legally, there was not an unlimited backstop. While GNMA and FNMA announced in their publications that the "full faith" of the U.S. government stood behind their issues, the reality fell far short of the promise—but for investors, it was close enough. Dangling promises, diversified portfolios, and foreclosable houses convinced many investors.

The mortgage-backed security had come into its own and quickly began to define how mortgage funds flowed in the United States. By 1973, FHLMC was buying three times as many conventional mortgages as federally insured mortgages—nearly $1 billion in conventional mortgages.[40] The next year, 1974, FHLMC further doubled its conventional mortgage activity to nearly $2 billion and shrunk its purchases of federally insured mortgages to $261 million.[41] This rapid expansion into an uninsured market was made possible through FHLMC's assiduous mimicry of the debt instruments of GNMA and FNMA, which continued through 1972 to deal primarily in federally insured mortgages. By the end of 1973, FNMA was, next to the Treasury, the largest debt-issuing institution in U.S. capital markets.[42]

Mortgage-backed securities rescued the mortgage banking industry and preserved the easy access to mortgage funds that middle-class Americans had come to expect. Capital markets became a central source of funds, as the older institutional investor and small depositor arrangements had collapsed in the face of rising interest rates and shifting savings practices. By 1970, withdrawals at savings and loan institutions exceeded deposits nearly every month.[43] The president of the Mortgage Bankers of America, Robert Pease, declared at their annual convention that, "except for FNMA, there is almost no money available for residential housing. We are in a real honest-to-goodness housing crisis!"[44] On average in 1971, $50 million worth of mortgages flowed from the capital markets through mortgage-backed securities into American housing each month.

In both the cities and suburbs, mortgage-backed securities provided new sources of mortgage funds. While direct mortgage assignment collapsed, mortgage-backed securities provided the financing to dramatically increase the new housing programs in America's cities. Federally subsidized mortgages, resold as FNMA mortgage-backed securities, propelled the American building industry in 1970, accounting for 30 percent of housing starts (433,000) and 20 percent of the mortgage debt increase.[45] In the first year of sales, GNMA issued over $2.3 billion in mortgage-backed securities, funneling money backwards into federal housing programs.[46] Typifying the connection in many ways, the first company to bundle enough mortgages for resale, as discussed earlier, was Associated Mortgage Companies, Inc., whose advertisement for its pool of mortgages, "Ghetto ready,/ghetto set,/ go!," illustrated the explicit connection between funds for inner-city America and mortgage-backed securities.[47] Mortgage company lending surged as well, providing 90 percent of FNMA's purchases.[48] By January 1973, mortgage companies originated more conventional mortgages than FHA or VA loans.[49] Moving away from a reliance on bank deposits, the mortgage industry had been rebuilt atop a new foundation of securities.

The mortgage-backed securities also promoted the lending of mortgage dollars even further down the economic ladder, to those borrowers outside the federally subsidized programs. By November of 1972, FNMA had begun to emulate FHLMC and began to buy mortgages that covered up to 95 percent of a house's price.[50] FHLMC had offered them earlier, but for two firms created and privatized to compete with one another and to service different kinds of financial institutions, competition drove them both to similar lending programs. Mortgages with as little as a 5 percent down payment could now be repackaged and sold as a security. FNMA actuaries calculated that the rate of default on a 95 percent mortgage was three times higher than on a 90 percent mortgage. The higher risk required a higher yield, but investors trusted the U.S. government to make good on the payments, even when the American borrowers could not. Yet, the assurance of payment was not sufficient to draw pension funds to invest in the mortgage-backed securities in the amounts that the creators of the securities had imagined they would.

Mortgage-backed securities, by the mid-1970s, sold in great numbers, but not exactly as the framers of the instrument had intended. While pensions bought over half of the bond-like mortgage-backed securities (52.72 percent) within a few years, such bonds were not sold any longer and pension funds resisted buying the far greater volume of pass-through mortgage-backed securities, bought by the savings and loan banks.[51] As Senator Proxmire remarked in Congressional hearings on the secondary mortgage markets, the increase in mortgage-backed security buying by pensions, while "commendable," was still a low relative share of the market.[52] Pension funds, intended to be the primary source of investment for mortgage-backed securities, accounted for only 21 percent of FNMA mortgage-backed security ownership.[53] Though GNMA actively sought investment from pension funds, as late as 1975 such funds accounted for only 8.29 percent of 1975's purchases of pass-through mortgage-backed securities. Savings and loan institutions bought 41 percent of the pass-through mortgage-backed securities. Pension funds' share of purchases rose, but did not take on the leading role policymakers had hoped for in providing a new source of mortgage capital. FNMA and FHLMC did, however, provide leadership to the U.S. mortgage market. With the creation of mortgage-backed securities, FNMA's centrality to American mortgage markets increased, sometimes supplying by the mid-1970s as much as half of all new mortgage funds in a given quarter.[54]

Mortgage-backed securities offered institutional investors stable, bond-like investments in mortgages and provided American borrowers a growing source of mortgage capital. Low-income mortgage lending, funded through those mortgage-backed securities, contained the possibility of giving inner-city renters a stake in their cities to quell, as legislators hoped, the urban unrest. While low-income mortgage lending, in the Section 235 program, quickly fizzled in scandal, not to return in great numbers again until the end of the century, mortgage-backed securities equally quickly assumed a central role in the economy. Savings and loan banks bought these early mortgage-backed securities, substituting their easy administration, low risk, and higher yields for their own mortgages, which did not add, on net, to the level of available mortgage capital. Pension funds—the investors for whom the mortgage-backed security was constructed —still remained minority buyers, but through changes over the next few years would find other ways to invest in American mortgages.

Home Equity Loans and Adjustable-rate Mortgages

While critics gaped at the rising levels of outstanding debt in the late 1970s, economists and social critics always seemed to exclude mortgages from these calamitous computations. These numbers were supposed to reflect the dangerous debt, not the responsible debt. Mortgages, after all, were good debt, helping Americans "own" their homes. Home owners "built equity" by repaying their principal—along with the interest on the debt—every month. And if the value of the home rose, which they had in every year since the Great Depression, then home owners would reap 100 percent of that increase. Houses were the easiest way for people to leverage their equity—multiplying the reward on an increasing value of an asset. Though home owners paid interest on the mortgage, they could get the entire increase in house price. While borrowing on the margin to buy stocks was seen as risky, buying a house with a mortgage was seen as prudent. Homes, for most Americans, were the only kind of financial leverage to which they could have access. For many, such leverage paid off handsomely in the late 1970s. While the average price of houses doubled between 1970 and 1978, the overall consumer price index rose only 65 percent.[55] Equity owned nearly doubled from $475 billion in 1970 to $934 billion in 1977.[56] Housing prices rose faster than other consumer goods. The inflation-driven rise in house prices provided a broad spectrum of home owners a lot of equity. This paper wealth of equity, however, mattered little since home owners of the 1970s could not use it without selling their home.

Bankers first offered home equity loans in the 1970s to fill just this need. Home equity loans made the value of a home owner's house more accessible. The equity could be spent while still living in the home. Second mortgages had existed since the nineteenth century—though they became less common with the expansion of FHA loans, which forbade such "junior mortgages"—but home equity loans were more like credit cards than a junior mortgage.[57] Home owners could arrange a line of credit and then borrow up to that limit as they liked, repaying the debt irregularly. With flexible access to the credit line, home equity allowed consumers to move money in and out of their house as they saw fit. Easy access to home equity meant that home owners could use the equity of their house to consolidate their other debts, and unlike credit cards, if the borrower did not repay the debt, the lender could foreclose on the house.

The artificial distinction between non-mortgage and mortgage debt, underpinned by this idea of inevitably rising house prices, obscured the ever-growing equivalence between these forms of debt, and legitimated home owners' borrowing against the value of their houses. Borrowing against a house, on some level, required less financial reasoning than comparing two credit card offers. Comparing interest rates required mathematical skills to calculate the costs and benefits of switching, and the answer was strictly numeric. Borrowing against a house was rooted as much in ideas of ownership as in cold calculations. Home owners already "owned" the equity. It was theirs to spend. The feeling of ownership allowed the choice to be easier than the choice between credit cards, and non-numeric. Yet, the danger of foreclosure remained. Even in 1983, a banking journal wrote that, "the public hasn't taken too kindly to resales, refinancings, and second mortgages."[58] Caught between "the conflicting desires of minimizing taxes and owning their homes outright," many debtors resented the home equity loan, even as they took greater advantage of it.

These home equity loans were unlike traditional fixed rate mortgages in other ways too. At the center of lenders' innovations in the late 1970s was the floating interest rate. In an era of stable, low-interest rates, like the postwar period, lenders could comfortably extend credit at a fixed rate of interest. The sharply rising interest rates of the 1970s, however, made many banking practices unprofitable. Lending long-term mortgages at a low rate and forced to borrow from depositors at high rates, bankers sought out a new way to lend money. A floating interest rate solved their problem. Mortgages with adjustable rates allowed banks to lend money without incurring interest rate risk. Such adjustable rates shifted the risk of a rising interest rate to the borrowers, who, also with fixed incomes, would be even more unable to weather such a shift in their payments than institutions.

In the early 1980s, adjustable rate mortgages (ARMs) and secondary markets made commercial banks' re-entry into mortgages profitable again—and easier.[59] If banks wanted mortgages in their portfolios, ARMs allowed them to do so without interest rate risk. If they wanted a quick resell, secondary markets, including mortgage-backed securities, were deep and easy to use, which was necessary if banks were to lend money for mortgages. While bankers embraced the variable rate mortgages, relatively few borrowers did. Attempting to switch borrowers from fixed to variable rate mortgages, banks offered introductory teaser rates, as much as 5 percent lower than the market fixed rate mortgage.[60] Despite teaser rates, ARMs comprised only 11 percent of all mortgages in 1984.[61]

Fixed rate mortgages continued to be the most popular mortgages for borrowers, but presented unacceptable risks for lenders. While it was possible for bankers to offer fixed rate mortgages and hedge the risk of interest rate changes through derivatives, such hedging was outside the skills of most bankers. Even the slightest miscalculation or misunderstanding of how the derivatives functioned could expose a bank to serious losses. Few commercial bankers could carry out a complex hedge strategy against interest rate fluctuations. While mortgage companies with limited capital had securitized mortgages since the early 1970s, banks increasingly used mortgage-backed securities to reduce their interest rate risk. By securitizing the mortgages, banks could collect a steady, interest-rate-independent stream of servicing income and leave the risk of interest rate fluctuations to someone else.[62] Once banks began to resell loans, the advantages were overwhelming. Only a third of commercial banks, in 1984, resold mortgages to the secondary markets.[63] But those that did sell, sold nearly all—90 to 100 percent—of their mortgages.[64]

If banks sold off fixed rate mortgages whenever possible, they held onto home equity loans. While lenders struggled to move borrowers into variable rate mortgages, only 4 percent of creditors offered fixed rate home equity loans.[65] Forty percent of creditors even offered interest-only loans, unheard of at the time in standard mortgages, because the principal was never repaid.[66] As one banker in Fort Lauderdale remarked, "the yield is so good on these [home equity] loans that my parent company doesn't want to sell any."[67] More than half of all bank advertising dollars were directed at home equity loans by 1986.[68] Eighty percent of home owners knew about home equity loans and 4 percent of home owners had them.[69] Large consumer finance companies as well, like Household, began in 1980, "redirecting assets from less profitable areas into more profitable activities[,] in particular, real estate secured loans."[70] In the next two years, home equity loans, with variable rates, rose from 34 percent of Household's portfolio to 50 percent. Household's reallocation of capital is understandable since it realized a return on its loans of 5.6 percent.[71] By the early 1980s, faced with a rising cost of funds, variable rate home equity loans appeared ideal, even for the larger banks. In a joint interview with leading bankers, the consensus on the great challenge to consumer banking was the same: the cost of funds. George Kilguss, senior vice-president of Citizens Bank, remarked that "unless you have variable-rate installment loans, you run into a problem."[72] Kilguss expected Citizens would begin to offer an "open-end credit line with a variable rate in 1983. Equity mortgages will secure these lines, which we expect to be large." Home equity loans offered banks a way to offer consumers variable rate credit, which solved their cost of funds problem, and offered banks more secure collateral. While banks explored the possibilities of secured lending, they also expanded the boundaries of unsecured lending through innovations in credit card lending.

Collateralized Mortgage Obligations, Tranches, and Freddie Mac

Extending the pass-through mortgage-backed security into other forms during the 1980s, financiers opened up the financing of consumer mortgages. While pass-through mortgage-backed securities offered investors a more bond-like investment, they were still not bonds. And the mortgage-backed securities still had other drawbacks: time and risk. Not all investors wanted a long-term investment over the life of the mortgages, yet they wanted the security and return of investing in house-backed securities. In June 1983, FHLMC, in association with the investment banks Salomon Brothers and First Bank of Boston, issued the first collateralized mortgage obligation (CMO).[73] The CMO worked just like a mortgage-backed security of the 1970s except that instead of a single kind of bond, each mortgage pool was split up into several different kinds of bonds. These kinds of bonds were called "tranches," from the French word *tranche,* meaning "slice." Rather than a mortgage-backed security having a single maturity and interest rate, the CMO sliced the mortgage-backed security into multiple bonds, each with a different maturity date and interest rate. The first CMOs offered by FHLMC had three tranches, arbitrarily named A-1, A-2, and A-3, each of which had a different maturity and interest rate.[74] The first tranche had a five-year maturity, the second a twelve-and-a-half year maturity, and the third a thirty-year maturity. All tranches received interest payments, but principal payments only went to the tranche with the shortest maturity.[75] The shortest maturities have the lowest risk of default or prepayment, since they received the principal payments, and they also received the lowest interest rates.

Tranches made investing in mortgages, especially the short-term tranches, a more certain investment. Early prepayment risk, when interest rates fell and borrowers refinanced, upset the calculations of investors, as did the uncertainty of defaults. The longest maturities, with the highest risk of default or prepayment, commanded the highest interest rates. In CMOs, investors could find what they needed to match their investment needs. The CMO allowed the staid mortgage to split into a variety of securities, each with a unique rate of return different from that of the original mortgage. A mortgage could be a high-risk, high-return investment. A mortgage could be a quick-paying, low-risk investment. With the right math, a mortgage could be turned into anything.

Slicing the mortgage-backed security into tranches expanded the potential investor pool. Institutional investors wanted investments that came due when their obligations came due, like an insurance company paying death benefits or a pension fund beginning to fund a retirement.[76] Mortgages and mortgage-backed securities had only long-term maturities. With different maturity dates, the tranches allowed investors to match the dates of their obligations with the maturity of their investments. Insurance companies, for instance, would statistically know what fraction of their life insurance policies would come due, hypothetically, on January 3rd, 1987. The company would want enough of its investments to come due on that day to cover those expenses, but not more and not less. If the investment matured earlier, then the insurance company would have to find another investment, which cost money. If the investment matured later, then the insurance company would not have the cash to meet its obligations. Different investors—insurance companies, pension funds, banks, etc.—all had different time frames and the tranches enabled mortgage investments to fit these time frames, from just a few years to several decades, rather than the real timeframe of mortgage repayment.

Tranches allowed a wide spectrum of investors to put their money in mortgages and tested the limits of the charters of the government-sponsored enterprises that created them. FHLMC President Kenneth

Thygerson, upon his retirement in 1985, proudly claimed to have "tried to extend the barriers to the limits of the corporation's charter. Future opportunities will require an act of Congress, so this is the time for me to look to the private sector."[77] These limits could only be extended by using the most recent technologies. Slicing mortgage-backed securities into tranches required elaborate payment calculations—not only for Freddie Mac, but for investors as well. As Dexter Senft, a First Boston investment banker who worked on the first CMO, remarked, "these products couldn't exist without high-speed computers. They are the first really technologically-driven deals we've seen on Wall Street."[78] Pricing all those tranches, and paying them, required computing power unavailable only a few years earlier. Innovations like the CMO gave Freddie Mac access to new sources of profit as well as new investors. In the three years Thygerson was with Freddie Mac, its portfolio increased four-fold from $25 billion to $100 billion, as its profits increased nearly five times. In the private sector, the rules governing Freddie Mac would not apply, allowing Thygerson, and others like him, to extend the boundaries of finance to places unimagined. The next appointed president of Freddie Mac, Leland Brendsel, who had been directly responsible for the first CMO as Freddie Mac's CFO, reflected the importance of the CMO to Freddie Mac's future.[79] Other financial institutions began to offer CMOs, substituting the government's backing for their own, or their credit insurance companies. Citibank, for instance, offered its first CMO in 1985—using its large resources to smooth out the repayment schedule—by providing minimum guaranteed principal and interest payments.[80]

For the home owners financed through mortgage-backed securities and CMOs, however, the complex debt instruments remained largely opaque, and unimportant. When John and Priscilla Myers of Lancaster, PA, bought their $47,000 two-bedroom split-level in 1984, they went to their local savings and loan for a fixed mortgage.[81] Since their local savings and loan, like all banks of the 1980s, feared holding onto fixed rate mortgages, the mortgage was resold and pooled into a CMO. For John Myers, the actual owner of the mortgage did not "make a difference . . . as long as Priscilla and I were able to get the money for the house." The flood of money from pension funds and other nontraditional investors into mortgage-backed securities gave the Myers the ability to buy their home. While CMOs transformed the mortgage industry, and the amount of capital available to borrow, they also opened the door for turning any other kind of steady stream of income into a security. This alchemical science of turning assets into securities, after it had been perfected with the CMO, underpinned the expansion of many other debt instruments of the 1980s, such as credit cards. Soon the Myers family, and millions of other Americans, would be able to borrow much more than just a mortgage from capital markets.

Credit Cards in the 1970s

Despite their high interest rates, the profitability of credit cards has fluctuated over the past thirty years, sometimes eking out only marginal profits. While Americans always paid a higher interest on credit cards than any other form of debt, the credit card companies—"issuers" in the industry-speak—faced many challenges: the cost of funds, borrower default, finding new creditworthy borrowers, and firm competition. Making credit cards profitable required clever business strategies that challenged conventional ideas of creditworthiness as much as conventional understandings of capital. During the 1970s, those who had access to revolving credit shifted their debts away from installment credit.[82] But only the most creditworthy households (35 percent) had bank cards in 1977—double the number in 1970 but still not a majority of American households. Before 1975, retailers continued to serve as the primary source of revolving credit, but such credit was limited in its use to individual stores.[83] Only ten of the one hundred largest department stores in the United States took bank credit cards before 1976, continuing to rely on retail credit cards to maintain store loyalty.[84]

Universal credit cards that could be used anywhere had existed in various guises since the 1950s, but were not widespread until the late 1970s. In the early 1960s, merchant billing networks were proprietary—Diner's Club and American Express each billed merchants for their own cards. In 1966, banks set up two separate networks that separated the billing of merchants from the lending of consumer credit. Bank of America, in 1966, began to allow other banks to use its billing system—BankAmericard. Also in 1966, another group of banks started the Interbank Card Association, which became MasterCard in 1980, in a bid to share the costs and difficulties of expanding merchant participation. Bank of America spun off BankAmericard in 1970 to the banks that used the system, eventually rebranding itself by 1977 as VISA. These two systems standardized merchant fees, but allowed issuers to charge borrowers whatever they liked, which allowed banks to focus on lending to consumers and not selling their card systems to merchants.[85] At first member banks could only use either VISA or MasterCard, but by 1975, after a lawsuit, such restrictions were dropped.[86] The proliferation of VISA and MasterCard allowed credit cards to be used by more merchants, which in turn made them more useful for consumers.

In the late 1970s, bank cards were issued only to the most creditworthy borrowers, who tended to repay what they borrowed, and consequently banks' profits were meager. The primary challenge for credit card issuers was that the borrowers least likely to default also tended to pay off their debt every month—denying the creditors any interest income. These "non-revolvers," who did not revolve their debt from month to month, treated credit cards like mid-century charge cards. In contrast, borrowers who might not pay off their debt every month had a higher chance of not paying at all, leading to "charge-off" or a complete loss on the loan. Between the non-revolver and the defaulter was the much sought-after "revolver," who paid the interest every month but not the principal. This sweet spot of revolving debt promised the highest profit rates for credit card companies, but differentiating the revolver from the free-loading non-revolvers and defaulters was extremely difficult. For the credit card companies of the 1980s, revolvers were profitable but lending to them went against the easy risk management models based on guaranteed repayment developed in the era of installment credit.

Issuers also faced the challenge of consumers' expectations of how they should behave. Unlike department stores, where most consumers used revolving credit until the mid-1970s, credit card issuers sold no goods. The income from the cards was the only income. Consumers had always been told by retailers to pay their charge account bills on time, which generalized a particular connection between profit and repayment into a more general moral principle. What these credit card companies called "revolvers" had historically been called "slow-payers" and had been the bane of all earlier creditors. Slow-payers tied up retailers' expensive capital. Though borrowers who paid their debts on time still thought of themselves as "good customers," the logic of revolving credit was different—profitable customers revolved their debt. In 1980, 37 percent of VISA customers, accounting for half of VISA's credit volume, paid their bills in full and thus incurred no finance charges.[87] Consumers believed they were good customers when they paid their bills, but they actually were bad customers, at least from the perspective of the lender.

Proper consumers, but not profitable ones, resisted the idea that they were doing something "wrong." Non-revolvers abided by the compact created through generations of credit use, now firmly inscribed in common sense. But these proper customers lost money for the d issuers and the easiest way to rectify that was simply to charge them a fee for their unprofitable behavior. Citibank in April 1976, for instance, attempted to charge a 50 cent fee to customers that did not maintain a balance.[88] Incensed that good customers were charged fees, the House Consumer Affairs Subcommittee conducted investigations, at which William Spencer, the soon-to-be president of Citibank told the committee, "you obviously do not believe that we are, in fact, losing money on this portion of the business. Let me assure you the contrary."[89] Whether because of threatened legislation or "competitive pressure," as a Citibank spokesperson claimed, the fee stopped in December 1976. Even the possibility of a fee, it turned out, was struck down two years later in 1978 by the New York Supreme Court, and Citibank was forced to return the fees to its customers.[90] The business solution, in the 1970s, to non-revolvers could not simply be a fee, but something that satisfied both the bottom line and the moral expectations of customers. Rather than charge fees afterwards to those who were not revolvers, credit card companies would have to find the revolvers ahead of time. The entire system by which lenders conceived of "creditworthiness" was geared, however, to screening out revolvers. To make revolving credit more profitable for bank lenders, new criteria would have to be developed.

Discrimination and Discriminant Analysis

The Equal Credit Opportunity Act implemented through the Federal Reserve's Regulation B pushed lenders toward more "objective" models of lending that excluded race, sex, and other protected categories—defined by the Fed as "demonstrably and statistically sound" models. These statistically sound models were required to avoid any inkling of sex or race discrimination. Understandably, lenders quickly developed in-house models, subcontracted them, or bought them from third-party companies, in an effort to avoid legal tussles. The credit scoring system offered by GECC, for instance, promised to be "discriminating enough to accurately determine credit worthiness, yet objective enough to avoid discrimination."[91] While these models were kept secret from the public—though not the Fed, which required proof of their objectivity—academics attempted to develop their models using the same available techniques. If academic and commercial credit systems were similar, which the academics at the time certainly thought they were, then the problems facing academic systems would also be in the commercial credit scoring systems.[92] Of course, while the corporate models were secret, the academic models were not. And neither were their shocking findings.

If the antidiscrimination laws of the 1970s hoped to guarantee women and African Americans access to credit, the models developed in the early 1980s confirmed that not only would be this possible—it would be profitable. The models relied on a statistical method called "discriminant analysis" that, despite its exceedingly confusing name, grouped potential lending populations on the factors that distinguished them—without human prejudice. Using discriminant analysis, statisticians could group borrowers into good and bad default risks based on observable characteristics (like phone ownership or income) using data provided by lenders or credit bureaus.[93]

The great challenge, of course, was not just finding defaults and non-defaults, but revolvers and non-revolvers. These models, while better than random guessing, were not nearly as accurate as the imposing mathematical apparatus might lead one to expect. An academically constructed multidiscriminant model correctly placed 67 percent of the sample into the correct groups of revolver and non-revolver. While 17 percent more correct than a random 50-50 guess, one-third of the sample was still incorrectly placed.[94] Unlike a human loan officer, such models could be objective, and ostensibly ignore protected categories. But in general, these models worked no better, and often less well, than human loan officers in differentiating between borrowers—with or without prejudice.[95] A lender could still not afford to trust these kinds of models to find the sweet spot of revolvers. The risk of default remained too high.

The very groups that credit cards tended to lend to—affluent households—turned out to be the worst revolvers. The higher the level of education and income, the lower the effective interest rate paid, since such users tended more frequently to be non-revolvers.[96] The researchers found that young, large, low-income families who could not save for major purchases, paid finance charges, while their opposite, older, smaller, high-income families who could save for major purchases, did not pay finance charges. Effectively the young and poor cardholders subsidized the convenience of the old and rich.[97]

And white.[98] The new statistical models revealed that the second best predicator of revolving debt, after a respondent's own "self-evaluation of his or her ability to save," was race.[99] But what these models revealed was that the very group—African Americans—that the politicians wanted to increase credit access to, tended to revolve their credit more than otherwise similar white borrowers. Though federal laws prevented businesses from using race in their lending decisions, academics were free to examine race as a credit model would and found that, even after adjusting for income and other demographics, race was still the second strongest predictive factor. Using the same mathematical techniques as contemporary credit models, the academic models found race to be an important predictor of whether someone would revolve their credit. But while politicians of the 1970s worried that black Americans would be denied credit on account of their race, if creditors, desperate to find revolving borrowers, read academic papers, they found exactly what they needed. Based on the data, the most profitable group to lend to, if a bank were maximizing finance charges, would be black Americans. According to research done with Survey of Consumer Finances in 1977, black borrowers were three times as likely as white borrowers to revolve their debts.[100] While non-white, nonaffluent borrowers held out the promise of the greatest profit, even though the models circa 1980 remained inaccurate enough to base a lending program upon them. The interest rates available to lenders simply could not cover the losses that would be incurred by such lending.

For every loan, except those that will always default, there is a price that can be charged to make that loan profitable. The profit on a loan is determined by subtracting the cost of lending the money to the borrower from the price of the loan. Lenders of the late 1970s were squeezed from below by the rising cost of funds, and above by state-regulated caps on interest rates. Before lenders could pursue the sweet spot of revolving credit, lenders would have to find a way to address this squeeze. In 1978, lenders would finally have their chance.

End of Rate Caps and the *Marquette* Decision

Part of the reason that bankers were loathe to lend to the less creditworthy borrowers, and those more likely to revolve, was that many states capped the interest rates at too low a level to overcome the costs of default. For unsecured lending, the risks were much higher than for secured mortgage and installment lending, for which the caps had been established. The rate caps established for secured lending precluded all but the most creditworthy of borrowers from getting credit cards.

Economists of the 1970s, and today, have found it difficult to understand the appeal of interest rate ceilings. For economists, the interest rate contained no moral overtones, but was simply the price of borrowing money, taking into account the risk of the borrower and the relative demand for that money. Money was like any other commodity, and its price ought to have been set by supply and demand. For many people, however, high-interest lending smacked unethically of getting something from nothing. Profit without production seemed profoundly unnatural, as it had for centuries. But profit—not production—continued to be the ambition of the capitalists. In 1979, James Roderick, the chairman of U.S. Steel—the company most aligned in the American consciousness with real production— famously pronounced that "the duty of management is to make money, not steel."[101] If that was true for U.S. Steel, it was certainly true for Citibank. The repeal of interest rate caps, which would allow interest rates to rise to the level set by supply and demand in the market, came not from the state or federal government but from the Supreme Court—refashioning the scope of the credit card.

In 1978, in a seemingly insignificant case—now called the *Marquette* decision—the Supreme Court ruled that interstate loans were governed by the bank's home state rather than the borrower's home state.[102] A Nebraska bank had been soliciting credit cards in Minnesota with interest rates above the state's cap. The Court, in a unanimous decision, ruled that since residents of Minnesota could legally go to Nebraska and borrow money there, the residents of Minnesota should not be penalized, as Justice William Brennan wrote, for "the convenience of modern mail."[103] The National Bank Act had long allowed the interest rate to be determined by the regulations of the state where a bank was located, rather than the home state of the borrower. As the case was decided by an interpretation of federal law, rather than constitutional law, however, Justice Brennan emphasized that Congress had the power to alter the law if it desired.

In 1980, a Chase Manhattan banker predicted that the credit card, for the foreseeable future, would have a "low margin that slips back and forth between profitability and unprofitability."[104] Though the high interest rates of 1980 legitimated high interest rates on credit cards, profits were decimated by the comparably high costs for that debt, both from operations and from the expense of capital. A Federal Reserve study in 1981 found that operating costs were 46 percent of the total costs for consumer credit operations compared to 16 percent of commercial credit operations.[105] If banks were paying 8 to 10 percent for deposits in the new money market accounts, as Chase Manhattan's Paul Tongue suggested, then banks could not reduce their interest rates much further than 19 percent and still be profitable.[106] As one Minneapolis banker, who ran his bank's credit card division, remarked, "the cost of money is going nowhere but up." For commercial banks, the problem was finding a lower cost source of funds than consumer deposits. Between the credit controls and the negative yields, many banks sold off their credit card operations to other banks, with hundreds of thousands of accounts and millions of dollars of outstanding debt.[107]

For every credit portfolio sold for fear of losing money, however, that same portfolio was bought. Bankers who were bullish believed that economies of scale and correct pricing could make cards profitable. While small banks, with less than $25 million in assets, averaged 203 loans per credit employee, banks with more than $500 million averaged 1,702 loans per credit employee—or eight times as many loans, substantially lowering labor costs.[108] By the early 1980s, the top fifty issuers owned 70 percent of the outstanding balances. With these savings, the largest d companies could offer interest rates 4 percent lower than their smaller competitors.[109] Smaller banks could do little to compete with the interest rate difference or the lower operating costs.

But even the big banks continued to lose money because of the high costs of funds. Competitive, yet profitable, pricing—fees and interest—would be the key to making credit cards profitable, but that relied on knowing the risk potential of a borrower and finding a cheaper source of capital than savers' deposits. Citibank's earnings fell by one-third in the first quarter of 1980, largely from negative yields in credit cards that stemmed from the high cost of funds.[110] Despite 18 percent credit card interest rates, a Federal Reserve Study in 1978 found that Citibank's woes were widespread in the credit card industry. Small banks, with deposits under $50 million, actually lost money equal to 1 percent of outstanding debt, and the largest banks, with deposits over $200 million, had net earnings of only 2.9 percent of outstanding debt. As the cost of funds increased even more in 1979, analysts expected disastrous losses and for small banks to retreat from the bank card business.[111]

While the *Marquette* decision made relocation to other states possible, the rising cost of funds made it compulsory. After the decision, large credit card issuers relocated to South Dakota and Delaware, states that lacked interest rate caps, where they could issue cards across the country. The rewards of deregulation for Delaware and South Dakota were considerable. Card receivables in Delaware grew 24,375 percent. In South Dakota receivables grew a staggering 207,876 percent. More importantly, perhaps, tax revenues grew as well, from $3 to $27 million in South Dakota and from $2 to $40 million in Delaware.[112] The states acquired a new tax base, and every other state saw their sovereignty undermined by their inability to regulate credit card companies in their borders. Uber–New York Citibank moved its credit card operations to Sioux Falls, South Dakota under duress. Moving credit card operations to another state cost money. Staff had to be trained; buildings had to be found. Such moves were limited to only the largest firms, who could afford to uproot or branch their operations across the country. Smaller banks, still constrained by usury laws, in turn, felt pressure to sell their operations to larger, more efficient banks. Local politicians and customers could and did protest such moves, but without federal support were effective only for a short time. Banks like Minnesota's First Bank System, for instance, a bank holding company of ninety-two subsidiaries, planned to consolidate all of its credit card operations in a South Dakota affiliate.[113] But between bad publicity and the threat of legal action by the state's attorney, the bank stopped. Such political and consumer pressures, however, could not end the appeal of a lack of usury rates or curb the cost of funds.

Despite scattered counterexamples, like Minnesota's First, states were largely unable to stop the movement of big banks to deregulated states. During the next five years, two-thirds of states, including Minnesota, removed their interest rate ceilings or raised them far above market levels. Following Citibank's move, New York, no doubt fearing the loss of other major banks, removed its usury laws. As expected, in states without ceilings, where risk and return could better equilibrate, charge-offs rose alongside interest rates. In 1984, states without interest rate controls had a charge-off rate of 1.38 percent compared to 0.85 percent in states with strict interest rate controls, as lenders sought out riskier customers.[114] Consumers also equilibrated their use of credit card debt and home equity debt, as higher interest rates pushed consumers from credit cards to home equity loans. Though such practices were still not common, economists found that in states that did raise their interest rate caps, home equity borrowers tended to use more of their borrowing to purchase consumer durables, since mortgage credit was cheap relative to credit cards.[115] Rate deregulation gave millions of Americans access to credit who otherwise would have been denied, but this access came at a higher price. Without rate caps, issuers could explore new, riskier markets for credit cards and Citibank, now in South Dakota, expanded its credit card operations to thirty-five states.[116]

Credit Cards and Class Performance in the 1980s

One of riddles of credit cards is how they fell from the height of exclusivity at the beginning of the 1980s to the depth of opprobrium by the middle of the 1990s. To have a credit card defined what it was to be rich. Take, for instance, the film *Trading Places* (1983), where Dan Aykroyd, as the commodity trader Louis Winthorpe III, is turned out from high society and a high-paying job after his bosses, evidently amateur sociologists as well as commodities brokers, offhandedly bet whether Aykroyd would descend to crime when deprived of his money and his social networks. After he has been turned out of the Heritage Club, arrested for drug possession, and humiliated in front of his prim fiancée, his last-ditch attempt to show that he is wealthy and upstanding is to show his credit cards to a recent prostitute acquaintance ("You don't think they give these to just anyone, do you? I can charge goods and services in countries around the world!") in an attempt to borrow money from her. When the cards are taken from him minutes later by a bank employee ("You're a heroin dealer, Mr Winthorpe. . . . It's not the kind of business we want at First National"), the last vestige of his class identity is taken away. Credit cards were the most basic tool in his performance of wealth, something without which Aykroyd most certainly could not be who he wanted to be any longer.

Credit cards in the 1980s symbolized the care-free consumption of the affluent. Instant gratification became possible on plastic. More than symbolic, however, affluence was the reality of who owned credit cards in 1980. In the early 1980s, as economist Peter Yoo points out, a household in the top decile was five times as likely to have a credit card as a household in the lowest decile.[117] Today, credit cards have acquired an air of the disreputable, associated with the broke and irresponsible, but that shift occurred rather quickly during the late 1980s and early 1990s. Before its loss of status, however, credit card companies trucked on their exclusivity to expand their market shares.

In the 1970s, it was easy to market cards. Without fees and with relatively few households having cards, the plastic marketed itself. By the 1980s, however, the most reliable borrowers already had them.[118] And it was hard to attract new customers because of the fees. As bank card profitability fell as the interest rate rose, banks looked for ways to increase their revenue, including raising the annual fees charged. Borrowers, it turned out, were far more attuned to fees than interest rates. The annual fees, while accounting for a much lower share of the bank's revenue than the interest on the revolving debt, were far more noticeable and to the customers, objectionable. A MasterCard survey in 1981 found that in response to higher fees, 9 percent of cardholders canceled at least one card. In contrast, while 54 percent of cardholders had their interest go up, only 19 percent noticed. Raising annual fees simply encouraged borrowers to have only a single card, on which they borrowed more.[119] As the credit card industry concentrated and the cost of funds began to wane, credit cards expanded through the middle and upper class, relying on annual fees and a wide spread between interest rates and funding costs to provide profits. And profits for banks more than doubled from 2 percent to 5 percent.[120] By the beginning of 1983, as the prime rate fell from 20 percent to 10.5 percent, and credit card rates remained high, the profitability of credit cards returned and issuers began to aggressively expand.[121] Despite the desire for revolvers, credit card issuers, fearful of defaults, did not lend to riskier borrowers. Some bankers believed that the credit card market had achieved saturation in 1984, with 53 percent of households. The remainder, a banker writing in the ABA Journal, noted that "the remaining households do not qualify for ownership."[122] Getting those who qualified for ownership to use a particular issuer's card became the challenge of the mid-1980s. In some ways, the credit card business in the mid-1980s was a zero-sum game: either you used one particular card or another. With rising fees, consumers tended, more and more, to consolidate their cards.

Convincing creditworthy borrowers to get another card required more than just offering a slightly lower interest rate or fee. A creditworthy household would be besieged by solicitations, and soon they would not accept additional fee-issuing cards. Luckily for credit card issuers, credit cards were as much social performance as financial tools for consumers. Issuers looking to expand their market share had to rely on the social meanings of credit cards. Whipping out the right credit card after a business dinner or in front of "frenemies" at the mall enabled consumers to display their social position. Credit cards operated doubly as financial tools and social tools, enabling the performance of class-as-wealth—the prestige card—and class-as-occupation—the affinity card. The social performance of credit enabled credit card companies to overcome the apparent market saturation of creditworthy households in the early 1980s.

The performative affluence of credit cards helped make them desired across all economic strata. And as credit cards became more commonplace, credit card companies used evermore exclusive cards—gold, black, platinum—to wrest market share from their competitors and higher fees from their borrowers. In the early 1980s, credit card issuers decided who would receive the cherished plastic, and then gave those who were the most creditworthy a way to show it off. The emergence of revolving credit "prestige" cards in 1982 marked a turning point in credit card usage, as MasterCard and VISA card issuers sought to displace American Express from the lucrative travel and entertainment segment.[123] While a "gold" AmEx had existed since 1966, VISA and MasterCard credit cards had not distinguished between borrowers.

The prestige cards were more than just branding. Borrowers had higher minimum limits (at least $5,000) and sometimes ridiculously high limits of $100,000. Banks aimed the cards at individuals with high incomes and hoped that with higher income would come higher balances—and they were correct. Many bankers found that prestige cards carried double the balances of conventional cards, as their users moved their travel expenses onto the cards. Many bankers shared the feelings of Florida banker Michael Clements: "the premium cards have exceeded all our expectations so far."[124] Clements observed that, "we are dealing with a far different market than that in standard bank cards. Most of the premium cardholders have solid banking records and they aren't afraid to spend." These higher-income consumers paid up to $45 a year for the prestige cards, getting the travel and entertainment (T&E) services that traditionally only American Express and Diner's Club offered, as well as the prestige of having a gold credit card.[125] Providing many of the travel services that American Express traditionally provided, but with more participating merchants, the new prestige cards worked just as their issuers hoped. Merchants embraced the shift, since VISA and MasterCard charged them less than AmEx.[126] Between the higher balances and the fees, the prestige cards could be very profitable. One banker calculated that his customers were earning the bank a gross margin of 23 percent.[127]

Such affluent customers were relatively indifferent to changes in interest rates. Though the prime rate fell by 14 percent from 1982 to 1987, credit card interest rates remained steady. The falling cost of funds would seem to allow a competitive firm to offer a lower interest rate and steal market share.[128] In 1987, American Express attempted just such a move, fighting back against the revolving credit offerings of VISA and MasterCard, with its first revolving credit card, the Optima. With only a 13.5 percent interest rate, the Optima carried an interest rate far less than the national average, which was closer to 18 percent. Yet consumers proved shockingly insensitive to interest rates. Non-revolvers did not care what the interest rate was. A quarter of cardholders did not even know their interest rates, and 60 percent believed that most rates were about the same. Even banks that attempted to charge less, like the medium-sized Central Bank of Walnut Creek, California, found that customers were indifferent. When Central Bank promoted its 18 percent card, which was 3 percent less than the average California credit card, with $250,000 in advertising, it increased its accounts only from 24,000 to 26,000. In the end, Central Bank simply sold off its portfolio. In 1986, Manufacturer's Hanover Bank, one of the largest issuers, cut its rate to 17.8 percent from the standard 19.8 percent. Other banks, except Chase Manhattan, simply ignored the move, and within three years, both Chase and Manufacturer's went back to the standard 19.8 percent.[129]

Americans, it turned out, were insensitive to relatively small differences in interest rates, if they already had a card and were not worried about repayment. American Express researchers found that the hassle of switching credit cards was offset when there was a difference of at least 4 percent. Though the Optima won customers, it did not overtake the revolving credit market of Visa and MasterCard. Indeed the customers most sensitive to interest rates seemed to be the riskiest, whatever their other characteristics. Optima, with its lower interest rate, reported twice the default rates of VISA or MasterCard.[130] By 1992, American Express had lost over $1 billion on the card. Only those worried about paying back their debts switched for less than 4.5 percent.

While prestige cards captured the American Express and Diner's Club T&E market, card companies invented a new way to sell credit: occupational and, its close-kin, educational identity. Beginning in 1982, Maryland Bank, N.A. (MBNA) pioneered the marketing of so-called "affinity cards" to sell credit cards to self-identified professional groups.[131] In a little over a year, MBNA had $230 million in outstanding balances and over 200,000 accounts. By aiming high—75 percent of professionals, the average income was $75,000—MBNA enjoyed the high profitability that prestige cards afforded. MBNA prestige cards were used twice as frequently as regular cards and carried balances 70 percent higher.[132] Identity and institutions converged in the affinity cards. Professional groups, from dentists to soldiers, enthusiastically embraced affinity cards.[133] A New York bank, for instance, had a 32 percent response rate to a solicitation to military officers, many times higher than the typical credit card solicitation. College students, despite their current lack of income, emerged as a growth market as well. Anticipating higher income after graduation, issuers, with the assistance of the universities, began to offer credit cards to students. The card programs, compared to today, appear shockingly conservative. A Milwaukee banker wrote of how he captured the "attractive market segment" of college graduates in his state. A college student would receive a solicitation, and if that graduate had secured a "career-oriented job paying $12,000 or more a year," possessed a "permanent Wisconsin home address," and attended a Wisconsin school, then the bank would give that student a credit card, even though the student did not "qualify for credit under [the] usual criteria."[134] The alma mater frequently got a cut of revenue from such cards for providing access and mailing lists.[135] While class identity flagged, perhaps, as a way to organize labor, it rejuvenated the organization of capital among the professional classes.

1986: Tax Reform and Securitization

In 1986, two events made debt more expensive for consumers to borrow and cheaper for banks to lend. While these two events, the Tax Reform Act of 1986 and the first credit card asset-backed security, had nothing to do with one another, they both pushed all forms of consumer debt, in unexpected ways, toward complete interchangeability. Though the Tax Reform Act sought to differentiate credit card debt from mortgage debt, market forces and financial innovation like asset-backed securities pushed them back together.

By the middle of the 1980s, credit cards and other non-mortgage debts were starting to be seen as something not to be encouraged. Owning a house, arguably, served a valuable social function by rooting home owners in a community, but auto loans, much less credit cards, did not. Yet taxpayers could deduct the interest that they paid on any and all consumer debt. The mortgage deduction on the income tax, commonly believed to have been intentionally invented to encourage home ownership, existed more as a residual of an older nineteenth-century idea of borrowing than an intentional policy. When Congress created the U.S. income tax in 1913, borrowing and interest were conceived as strictly business activities. For small businesses, the personal and entrepreneurial were indistinguishable. Borrowing was done for investment—like buying property or inventory—and this interest could be written off as a business expense. As debt became legal and widespread for personal consumption, rather than business consumption, this aspect of the tax code remained unchanged. Borrowing for cars, as well as houses, remained deductible throughout the postwar period. The interest on credit cards, when they became widely available, could be deducted as well.

Until 1986, that is. Congress passed a tax reform law that phased out the interest deduction on all forms of consumer borrowing except for mortgages. Wrapped up in the tax reform act that Ronald Reagan called the "second American revolution," was a provision to end the long-standing interest deduction for nearly all types of consumer credit.[136] Other features of the Tax Reform Act of 1986 received more attention at the time—the top marginal tax rate was dropped from 50 percent to 33 percent while the lowest tax rate increased from 15 percent to 18 percent—but leaving consumers only able to deduct the interest on their home borrowing, radically altered the terrain of consumer credit, transforming the relationship between home equity loans and other forms of consumer credit, as well as making debt absolutely more expensive.

Still seen as a good form of debt, mortgage interest deduction could continue, but other forms of unsecured debt would lose their protected status under the tax code. Actively discouraging credit card borrowing through the Tax Reform Act, policymakers provided home owners with a strong incentive to remove the equity from their homes to pay off their other debts. In theory, this should have lowered their interest payments on their credit cards and given them tax-deductible and lower interest payments on their home equity loans. In practice, however, many borrowers found it difficult not to run up the debts on their credit cards again.

Debtors used the equity from their houses to pay off their credit cards. While some politicians pushed for restrictions on the mortgage deduction for expenses related to housing, such constraints were ultimately dropped, as enforcement would be impossible.[137] While maintaining the deduction on home equity was justified through the American dream of home ownership, consumers in practice could use home equity loans for anything. Though in 1986, home equity lines were only a tenth the size of the second mortgage market, lenders expected that home equity loans would grow quickly in the aftermath of the Tax Reform Act.[138] Not until 1991, however, would the deduction for all non-mortgage interest be fully phased out. The interest deduction, of course, only mattered to those who paid interest on their consumer credit debts—installment borrowers and credit card revolvers. For those who paid off their cards every month, there would be no interest deduction. For those who paid, however, the interest rate deduction would push them toward a new way of thinking about their home finance.

While the Tax Reform Act caused borrowers to think in new ways, lenders were also thinking in new directions in securitizing debt. More borrowers rolling over their debt meant lenders needed more capital to finance it. While the cost of borrowing funds had abated somewhat by the mid-1980s, the bottleneck of capital had not been fully solved. The lack of new sources of capital constrained lenders' expansion and they searched for alternatives to the traditional saver's deposit. Banks mostly lent money from these deposits, which continued to decline as savers put their money in pension funds, money market accounts, and mutual funds instead of the traditional savings account. Commercial banks' share of deposit assets had fallen from half in 1949 to one-third in 1979.[139] Finance companies, in contrast, could issue short-term bonds, called commercial paper, to fund their credit card operations, accounting for up to half of the lent capital of the larger firms.[140]

Some commercial banks, in an effort to remain competitive, mimicked the finance companies by opening non-consolidated subsidiary corporations.[141] Not officially part of the bank, its operations would not be part of the bank's accounting reports. Rather than depend on high-interest certificates of deposit (CDs) to attract more savings, banks could create a subsidiary corporation that would buy the consumer debt from the bank. This subsidiary, in turn, would issue commercial paper and use this money to pay the bank for the debt. The subsidiary would then use the consumer debt to pay off the commercial paper. This paper would be at a lower-interest rate than the CD, which would increase profits overall and skirt the reserve requirements faced by the bank. In Nebraska, for instance, First National Bank of Omaha created First National Credit Corporation in 1980, moving its credit card debts to the subsidiary. Though First National Bank of Omaha was only in the top 300 banks for its size nationally, it was in the top 20 banks nationally in terms of outstanding credit card debt, growing from $40 million to $110 million in only three years.[142] Capital markets and commercial paper could finance expanding consumer demand in ways that traditional bank deposits could not.[143]

Structured finance innovations in 1986 ended the last bottleneck on funding consumer credit by providing the last direct connection from capital markets to lenders. Between the cost of funds, experience with securitized mortgages, and the growing profitability of credit cards, banks tried to develop ways to securitize credit card debt. While other forms of consumer credit had been securitized earlier, the backing assets of these other consumer debts were all installment credit with fixed repayment schedules similar to mortgages. Mortgage repayments had nowhere near the volatility of credit cards, where payments in any given month could vary from nothing to everything. A mortgage could be prepaid, but that occurred from observable changes in falling interest rates, and when a mortgage wasn't refinanced, borrowers rarely paid more than the minimum. The ability to securitize the irregular repayment schedules of consumer credit to appear like a regular payment of a bond represented a breakthrough in finance.

The conditions for the invention of credit card securitization had existed for a few years—the rapidly growing demand for revolving credit and the example of collateralized mortgage obligations—but it was a mistake, not a deliberately successful act that made the invention of credit card securities necessary. In 1984, Columbus-based Bank One had paired with a television shopping channel to provide credit to its clientele. The charge-off rates for this portfolio were expected to be 5 to 6 percent, with an initial crop of high charge-offs. A high default rate followed by a decline was common in all forms lending and older, stable accounts called "seasoned" accounts could be expected to be significantly more reliable. In this case, however, the fall-off never came. Charge-offs remained high (around 11 percent) and with $2 billion invested in the portfolio, executives at Bank One were desperate to find a way to find another way to fund this portfolio.[144] As William Leiter, who headed the project at Bank One, stated, "our credit card portfolio was growing more rapidly than we felt comfortable funding."[145] Leiter's public statement was, to some degree, an understatement, but Bank One figured out a way to fund that debt outside the bank, by passing the portfolio's risk to an investor outside the bank.

When Bank One securitized $50 million in credit card receivables in 1986, a new era in consumer credit opened.[146] Pricing and structuring these irregular payments had taken Bank One two years to figure out, but at the end of those two years they had found a way out of that particular situation, and more generally the capital bottleneck for credit card issuers. Securitizing credit card debt moved the debt off the books of the bank, treating the credit card debt like a sold-off mortgage, forgoing the need for new deposits. Securitization allowed banks to expand their lending much faster than their capital, ordinarily, would allow, and doing so without putting their own money at risk. The Bank One securitization augured another aspect of credit card funding that went unreported in the trade press.

The securitization of this credit card debt allowed Bank One to fund this risky portfolio from capital markets, retaining the profitable fee income for itself. Risky lending and securitization demanded one another. Letting capital markets fund the deposits instead, and take on the risks of default, allowed Bank One to focus on servicing the cards and rapidly expanding their customer base. While banks had expanded their deposits since the 1960s by selling negotiable CDs, securitization allowed them to directly sell assets. Though investors in the security would get the interest and principal payments, the bank would still receive servicing income.

Within a year, other card companies issued their own credit card–backed securities, or "card bonds," and brought closer the relationship between investment banks, which facilitated the issue of stocks and bonds, and commercial banks, which lent money to businesses and consumers. Banking institutions formally separated since the Glass-Steagall

Act of 1933, began to work ever-more closely together. The credit card–backed security required the skills and assets of both commercial banks and investment banks, in this case Bank One and Salomon Brothers. Not to be outdone, by January of 1987 MBNA securitized its first pool of credit card receivables through the investment bank Morgan Guaranty.[147] Unlike Bank One's security, which paid a fixed rate, MBNA's security paid a floating rate pegged to the London Interbank Offered Rate—a standard internationally recognized interest rate. Such a feature eliminated the interest rate risk in such a security, something that could threaten the value of a fixed rate security like a traditional mortgage. But the riskiness of unsecured debt, compared to the secured debt of mortgages, made the card bonds look for ways to decrease the risk of investments. The tranches of collateralized mortgage obligations were not enough to get the card bonds to AA or AAA investment-grade ratings. Credit insurance made up the difference in risk, and in turn, made securitization possible. Insurance companies insured the portfolio against calamitous default. Only by insuring the security against loss could banks get the necessary AA or AAA credit rating that most institutional investors needed.[148]

For the largest holders of credit card debt, securitization offered an easy way to expand their lending. Citicorp, by the mid-1980s, was by far the largest holder of bank credit card debt, with more than $10 billion in receivables—double the holdings of runner-up Bank of America.[149] Through a securitization deal with Goldman Sachs, Citicorp could move some of those billions off its books and into the market, freeing up capital for other investments.[150] Securitization could also increase income. First Chicago began to securitize its credit card receivables more frequently through the late 1980s and increased its operating earnings by 22 percent in just one quarter of 1989. Credit card fee revenue increased, in one quarter, from $54.4 million to $82.7 million.[151] Securitization offered higher income and freed up capital, allowing credit card issuers to finance ever-higher levels of outstanding debt. While at first the investors were "leery of these assets," as the Morgan Guaranty treasurer who headed the issue remarked, investors soon learned to overcome their initial hesitation.[152] Though the debt was unsecured, the repayment proceeded steadily.

While securitization expanded, subsidiary banks, developed in the early 1980s, persisted. In 1988, Bank One that had pioneered securitization, still resold $1 billion of its credit card debt to a subsidiary, Banc One Funding Corp, which issued short-term commercial paper to finance the debt.[153] Credit card securitization was created to solve that one particular problem, but commercial paper remained the solid standby. Commercial paper, though it did not transfer the risk of default to market investors, remained cheaper and more flexible than securitization. Commercial paper markets were deep, allowing the commercial paper issues to be easily resold, which gave investors the liquidity that they prized. Without that liquidity, card bonds commanded a premium. Banks could move large or small amounts of receivables off their books to the subsidiary, which could flexibly issue paper against the receivables. Securitization, with a shallow market and higher transaction costs, still posed obstacles. But that would change quickly, as a recession collided with changes in banking regulation to make securitization come to the fore of consumer debt financing.

While in the late 1980s securitization offered a clever maneuver to find additional funds, by the early 1990s securitization became necessary for banks' profitability if banks were to comply with the new regulations resulting from the Basel Accord.[154] Securitization was not required by Basel, but to comply and to profit, securitization was necessary. The Basel Accord, an international banking regulation agreement between the G-10 under negotiation for most of the 1980s, required banks to hold enough capital to secure their loans, but with a twist: the amount of capital a bank would have to hold depended on the riskiness of its loans, so-called "risk-weighted capital." Like the risk models developed for consumer lending, banks would hold different amounts of capital for different default risks of loans. The capital ratio would be determined not by the absolute ratio of capital to loans, but by the weighted ratio. Loans were multiplied by their riskiness. Buying a U.S. treasury bond would have a zero weight, as it is considered the safest of bonds, while lending to a corporation would have a 100 percent weight.[155] The full range of investments all had risks defined by the agreement, but the risk weights did not reflect an objective reality. Was a business loan exactly double the risk of a home mortgage? Moreover, if a loan was deemed riskless—with a zero weight—then there would be no need to hold capital. Banks could buy, for instance, as many treasury bonds as they wanted without consequences for their capital requirements.

With a required capital-to-asset ratio of 8 percent, the largest banks in the United States and throughout the world would require much more capital to meet the new standards.[156] Reallocating a bank's loan portfolio to comply with the Basel Accord meant searching for ways to get as much return out of those low-risk assets as possible. Securitizing credit card loans gave the bank an effective risk weight of zero, since it no longer "owned" the loan. Similarly, banks faced 50 percent risk-weighted loans if they extended mortgages. Mortgage-backed securities also offered a zero weight, which freed banks from the capital ratio. Securitizing the debt allowed banks to make as many credit card loans, or mortgage loans, as they possibly wanted, as if they were treasury bonds[157] The capital requirements meant to hedge risk simply pushed banks toward securitization rather than reducing their lending.

In contrast, off–balance-sheet entities such as nonincorporated subsidiary corporations like Banc One Funding Corporation would have a risk weight for their lending that would have to be capitalized against. The risk weight for these loans would be 100 percent. The new capital rules made securitization the clear winner over subsidiary corporations, despite the higher costs. Instead of acquiring new capital, or restricting lending, securitizing debt allowed banks to comply with the new requirements. Federal accounting regulations, still sovereign in the United States, could have been even stricter, but they were not. Pushing loans off the books into securities, according to Generally Accepted Accounting Principles (GAAP) accounting conventions, lowered the required capital ratio. The confluence of GAAP and Basel made greater securitization for banks necessary. By increasing capital requirements, the regulation unintentionally accelerated and solidified the shift to securitization for banks. Instead of locking up 8 percent of their capital, banks could avoid locking up any capital since securitization required none. Increasingly common, the now-deep card bond markets transformed the American debt industry in other ways as well.

After the tumultuous years of the late 1970s and early 1980s, when revenues hovered around zero or less, credit cards had become breathtakingly profitable. Between 1983 and 1990, according to a Government Accounting Office (GAO) study, the average return on assets—which for banks are primarily loans—was 0.57 percent.[158] The return on credit card loans was 4.68 percent—or 8.2 times as great! While credit card loans generally had higher operating costs than conventional business loans, with 8.2 times the revenue they more than made up the difference. Banks frantically sought new sources of capital, like the card bond market, because the profits of credit cards were so much higher than their other investments. Such profits, as always, lured in new competition, who could also rely on these new methods of securitization to fund their loans. As conduit for capital, rather than sources of capital, such lenders no longer faced the greatest barrier to entry in lending—money to lend.

The Rise of Pure Play Credit Card Companies

With the expanding market for securitization, credit card banks with no other business—so-called "pure play" or "monoline" issuers—found their business model worked and expanded rapidly. Securitization lowered, if not eliminated, the capital to lend barrier.[159] Fast-growing issuers like First USA, Advanta, and Capital One, all used securitized receivables to fund their growth, rather than internal capital. Such pure play companies, unlike commercial banks, did not have access to deposits; they had no other source of funding. Credit rating agencies rated them BBB, which, if they had not used tranched securitization, would have made their funding prohibitively expensive.[160] Tranched securities were the only way that these companies could get AAA ratings on at least part of their securities. First USA, for instance, securitized two-thirds of its debt, according to its CFO Peter Bartholow. In 1994, as First USA's portfolio doubled to $11 billion, its securitized debt rose from $2.6 billion to $7.2 billion.[161] With tranches, First USA's rival Advanta could offer a tranche of its security as a AAA bond and pay only 0.18 percent more than London Interbank Offered Rate (LIBOR). Advanta would have to pay a much higher rate to its last tranche, and use credit default insurance, but for the other tranches the rate was very low. Instead of not being able to sell any of its debt as a BBB bond, it could sell nearly all of its debt with an AAA rating. Compressing the bulk of the risk to the last tranche and then using insurance to offset that risk, companies with few assets could sell AAA bonds. Card bonds could get higher ratings than an issuer's own debt ratings.[162] Investor demand for high-quality bonds outstripped supply, said Murray Weiss, senior vice president at the investment bank Lehman Brothers, leading many investors to "cross-over buy" similarly rated credit card receivables. High investor demand kept the price of the securities high. The risk premium over treasury securities fell to an all-time low, as investors began to believe in the AAA ratings accorded such debt and the spread narrowed between corporate AAA bonds and credit card AAA bonds.[163] Advanta, using such cheap funding, securitized all of its new debt in 1994—$2 billion.[164] Without securitizing their debt, these companies could never have expanded so rapidly.

By 1995, a quarter of all credit card receivables were securitized.[165] The new pure play companies, relying on securitzation to fund their expansion, grew much faster than the rest of the credit card industry, with a 32.6 percent growth in receivables in 1995, accounting for more than half of the growth of the entire industry ($31.5 billion of $56.5 billion total growth in receivables outstanding).[166] In 1990, MBNA was the first pure play credit card issuer to go public and within a few months its stock price doubled.[167] While these firms grew quickly, they also realized lower profits, receiving only 10.9 percent interest income compared to the industry average of 12.3 percent. Relying on securitization rather than deposits cost the new companies 1.5 percent more in funding costs than the banks.

With securitization, capital—that rarest of decidedly unnatural resources—suddenly became plentiful. In 1990, 1 percent of U.S. credit card balances were securitized. By 1996, 45 percent were securitized.[168]

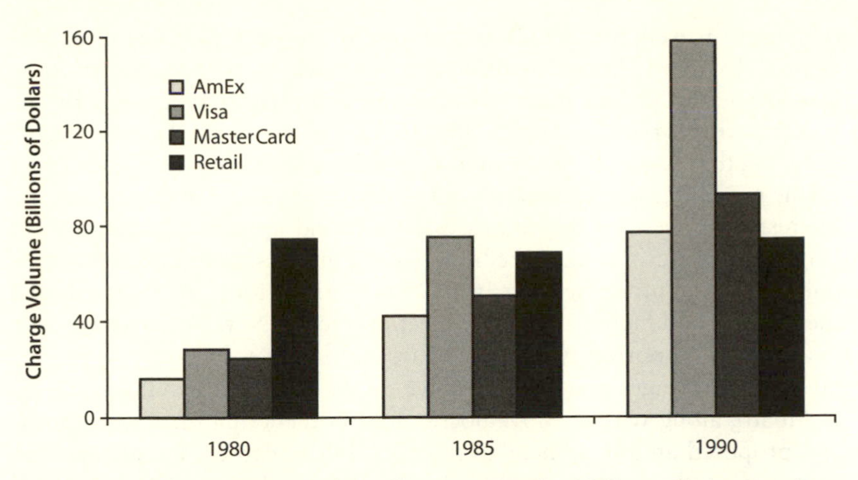

Figure 7.4. Charge Account Volume by Year. Even by 1980, retail charge volume still outstripped charges on American Express, Visa, or MasterCard. By 1985, retail charge cards had lost their dominance, and by 1990 even American Express had a greater charge volume. Source: Wertheim Schroder & Co., "US Credit Card Industry: Second Annual Review-Industry Report," 9–10. In billions of dollars.

Of the increase in balances from 1990 to 1996, from $165 to $395 billion, securities funded 77 percent of the difference. Without card bonds, credit card debt could never have grown to the scale it achieved in such a short time. By 1997, 51 percent of credit card debt was securitized, marking a turning point when more debt existed in capital markets than on bank's balance sheets.[169] Americans charged three times as much in 1998 as in 1988. Investors, not bankers, lent Americans this money. Unlike traditional investments, however, the borrowed money created no additional production, only additional demand. Capital invested in card bonds was not turned into shoe factories, but shoes. Card bonds necessarily crowded out productive investments. Every dollar funding a credit card was, literally, a dollar not funding a new factory—or any other productive investment. At the same time, card bonds created a supply of capital for consumer credit that allowed lenders to lower interest rates and exacerbated firm competition, enabling evermore marginal borrowers to have access to greater amounts of credit.

D'Amato's Gambit

In 1991, the economy was once again in recession, and while no decisive policies were implemented, politicians still, nonetheless, had to eat, preferably at well-connected fundraisers. At one such fundraiser, on November 13, 1991, President Bush was speaking to an audience of New York Republicans and made an off-hand comment, unapproved by his speech writers, that he would "like to see the credit card rates down," believing that lowered rates would help the economy recover.[170] This economic reasoning was, at best, obscure, but the vague sense that these high interest rates were to blame possessed a broad appeal, as the recession heightened the criticism of credit cards as unnecessary and expensive indulgences. The junior senator from New York, Alfonse D'Amato, heard the remark, and facing a tough re-election race in New York, seized on it as a political opportunity. The next day, as the houses of Congress negotiated the final stages of a bill to resolve the savings and loan (S&L) crisis, D'Amato, along with then Democrat Joseph Lieberman from Connecticut, proposed an amendment to the S&L bill to cap credit card interest rates nationally at 14 percent.[171] In the Senate, the amendment passed quickly, 74 to 19. Lowering credit card rates seemed to fit the political calculus of both Democrats and Republicans.[172]

While the measure passed quickly, as the reality of what was about to happen sank in, pundits, lobbyists, and policymakers just as quickly denounced the move. Treasury Secretary Nicholas Brady cautioned that cutting back credit access, since issuers would no longer be able to lend to riskier borrowers, would reduce consumer demand exactly when it was needed to strengthen the economy.[173] Such a cap, Brady claimed, would result "in credit cards which are elitist."[174]According to the American Bankers' Association, restricting lending to customers who would be profitable to lend to at 14 percent would have eliminated between $60 to $150 million, or 26 to 66 percent of the outstanding credit card debt. Such a violent reduction in outstanding debt would have, according to industry spokespeople, collapsed the profits of leading banks and pushed the United Sates further into recession. The *Wall Street Journal* estimated that such a cap would have changed Citicorp's $1.50 per share earnings into $0.58 losses per share.[175]

Issuers would have also been forced to unsecuritize their debt, nightmarishly bringing the debt back onto their books. Citibank, for instance, would have found itself 0.75 percent below its capital requirement. Such a cap would have destabilized capital markets as well as issuers. For pure-play issuers who used securitization more heavily, the cap would have spelled their demise. Recognizing the danger of destabilizing the banking system, already weakened from the S&L crisis, House Speaker Thomas Foley, through procedural adeptness, managed to split the measure from the larger banking bill, which allowed it to die in the House. That allowed the session to end without a vote, which was, by then, seen as the sensible thing to do. While lower interest rates might have pleased many cardholders, reducing the number of Americans with credit cards by two-thirds would certainly have offset the political gain from reducing interest rates.

Such high rates, D'Amato and his allies surmised, could only be possible in the absence of competition. If an industry was competitive, it was deemed efficient, and therefore fine. Only monopoly, evidently, could justify regulation. While 6,000 firms issued credit cards, 57 percent of the balances were controlled by the top ten firms. Citicorp alone had 18.3 percent in 1992.[176] The exact same rate—19.8 percent—at seven of the largest ten banks, D'Amato asserted, was damning evidence of oligopolistic collusion, demanding, at the very least, an extensive investigation.[177] Chuck Schumer (D-NY) pushed for an 18-month study period, which the banking industry opposed, since the uncertainty surrounding the outcome of the investigation would make securitizing debt, in the meantime, much more difficult. Nonetheless, the GAO launched an investigation whose results were published in April 1994.[178] The credit card industry, it found, was competitive despite the stability of its interest rates.[179] With six thousand issuers nationwide, it was hard to imagine coordination.[180] The seemingly collusive interest rates belied a frenzy of competition.

The low barriers to entry fostered by securitization allowed competition between issuers, despite the apparent staggering sums required to achieve economies of scale. To be profitable, the industry had to be concentrated, but a company could easily be dislodged by an upstart with easy access to capital and new ways of lending. The credit card industry in the early 1990s was competitive but concentrated. Though the largest lenders controlled the bulk of the industry, they could not easily dictate prices like an oligopoly. Ironically, the threat of a cap actually made the industry less competitive, since securitization became harder during the 18-month investigation. Investors were afraid that the United States would legislate a lower interest rate, threatening the interest rates on the underlying portfolios behind their card bonds. Securitization, in early 1992, was at one-third the level of a year earlier, with only $1 billion in securities issued compared to $3 billion.

While the interest rate cap failed, the threat of such a cap pushed banks to find ways to lower their interest rates. In 1992, the percentage of credit accounts with interest rates of 16.5 percent or less grew from 9 to 39 percent.[181] Credit card accounts with interest rates of 18 percent or more fell from 69 percent of all cards to 43 percent. D'Amato did not get his ceiling, but he fashioned a new discourse critical of credit cards that shifted the focus away from yuppie-era affluence to recession-era indebtedness, and the threat of government regulation was sufficient to push issuers to lower their rates. While the legal cap failed, a new "moral cap" was successful, according to the head of AmEx's Optima card division.[182] Citicorp, in

1992, began to offer a variable rate credit card, which, with its market-driven, rather than monopolist-chosen, prices up or down, would seem to placate policymakers.[183] The securities that funded these cards were also variable rate. With a variable rate credit card, Citicorp issued a massive ($1.33 billion) offering of floating-rate credit card securities—nearly doubling the global volume of such securities and the first to be backed by variable rate credit cards.[184] By 1993, market fears of a rate cap had abated, but the variable rate cards rapidly took over the industry.[185]

If securitization underpinned the cheap capital that allowed for a competitive market, perhaps more consequential than D'Amato's failed attempt to cap the interest rate was the failure of the Financial Accounting Standards Board (FASB)—the group that sets the generally accepted accounting principles (GAAP)—to put securitized debt back on the books of issuing companies. In November 1994, a new FASB director proposed to change the way banks accounted for the securitization of revolving credit. Issuers would have had to hold capital against possible losses. The measure was voted down 6 to 1.[186]

If this measure had passed, securitization would have died. With such an accounting change, issuers could not have sold off debt as quickly as they lent it, since issuers would have had to grow their capital at the same rate as their loans. While doubling loans was possible, doubling capitalization was considerably more difficult. If the measure had passed, the pure play companies would have gone out of business. No alternative source of funding for their portfolios existed. The continued expansion of securitization came about, in part, because of an obscure accounting trick. This FASB ruling, as much as D'Amato's interest rate cap, could have squashed the expanding levels of consumer credit in the 1990s.

D'Amato's push for a cap reflected a greater cultural ambivalence toward credit cards. By the early 1990s, credit cards were no longer seen as the playthings of the glamorous, but the trap of the profligate. The short-lived *Debt* game show, hosted by the iconic Wink Martindale, showed how differently credit card debt was viewed by the mid-1990s. While in the mid-1980s, credit cards marked high social status, by the mid-1990s credit cards had acquired a patina of desperation and bad choices. Paying off one's debt seemed impossible, except for the deus ex machina interventions of game-show hosts. Produced by the Walt Disney Company, *Debt* envisioned a world where a tuxedo-clad Wink Martindale descended from the heavens to erase one's debt, as fantastic a tale as Cinderella herself.[187] Though credit card companies and consumer advocates condemned the show as irresponsible, 5,000 soon-to-be bankrupt debtors clamored for the show's four hundred spots. The show was canceled after only a few seasons. Americans evidently wanted their own debt divinely erased, but did not want to watch it on television.

Reshuffling Prime and Profitability Models

If D'Amato and the FASB failed to change the rules governing lending, the recession nonetheless changed the ways different classes of Americans borrowed. While banks discovered new sources of capital to fund credit cards, Americans faced the first national recession in a decade. Higher charge-offs cut into the banks' rate of return, with the return on credit card debt falling by a quarter to 3.55 percent in 1991.[188] Unemployment rose again, as it had not since the 1982 recession, triggering a wave of defaults, but also other changes in debt practices as well. While unemployment rose, most Americans surprisingly cut back on their debt. Credit card companies feared that Americans' prudent use of credit—not borrowing more while in recession—was a dire predictor of things to come. Was the recession a return to frugality?[189] Payments were up, but volume was up as well. While consumers continued to spend more on their credit cards—Visa spending grew 7.6 percent in 1991—consumers paid off this increase. Unlike during the recession of 1981, the average borrower did not increase his or her debt load.[190] And according to a senior vice president at First Union Bank, "it's getting worse."[191] Revolving debt grew 15.5 percent per year in the late 1980s, but its growth slowed to 5.1 percent in 1991.[192] Balances did not grow at all in 1992.

Meredith Layer, a senior vice president at American Express, lamented that "an anti-materialism movement is forming. Some call it the New Frugality."[193] The head of AT&T's credit card operation claimed, "the age of Yuppiedom is gone."[194] "In the '80s, interest rates were not the topic of cocktail conversation," the president of a credit card research firm noted, but instead "what they were spending money on with their cards."[195] While credit card executives saw a possible decline in consumption, Americans as a whole felt less prosperous. A lifestyle survey conducted by a prominent advertising company found that between 1975 and 1992, households felt that the ability of their incomes to satisfy "nearly all our important desires" fell from 74 percent to 60 percent.[196]

The new frugality, though true at an aggregate level, broke down when examined by income level. Economists found that during the 1980s, poor households had expanded their access to credit, but did not expand their debt.[197] During the expansion, these poorer households reduced their debt, even as the more affluent expanded their debt. While average card balances for all households doubled from $751 in 1983 to $1,362 in 1989, poor households halved their balances from $723 to $352, using the expansion to reduce their debt burden.[198] Fed economist Peter Yoo explained that the growth in credit card debt from 1983 to 1992 was from "households with previous credit card experience and with above-average incomes, not [from] inexperienced, low-income households."[199] The poor were the most prudent users of credit. Middle-class households expanded both their access to credit and their debt burdens. More than simply an increase in the number of households with credit cards, the rising debt was the result of households borrowing more intensely—average household debt rose 117 percent.[200]

During the recession of 1991, however, the behaviors of the poor and middle class switched. Middle-class households cut back on their debt while poor households used their newly available credit lines to increase their debt burden and weather the recession. Poor households increased their debt burden, on average, to $917, while households overall remained unchanged ($1,366). The number of poor households revolving their credit card debt increased from 54 to 72 percent. After the recession ended, behaviors across income groups converged as poor households continued to expand their debt burdens like middle-class households, rather than reducing their debt burden as during the 1980s expansion. Credit card issuers, in the end, had nothing to worry about with the "new frugality." The 1992 recession marked a changing point in the credit card borrowing habits of poor Americans, bringing their borrowing more in line with the more affluent—at least in terms of debt burden. The numbers, however, reflected the considerable stringency with which the poor were given credit cards. Only the most prudent were given cards, since their income was so much lower. It makes sense, then, that such borrowers would not run the higher balances of the more lax, more affluent borrowers. All that would change in the 1990s, as seen not only in the labor market pressures of the recession but in the increasingly relaxed lending standards following the recession. While debt practices of the poor and affluent differed in the 1980s, issuers tried their best not to repeat that mistake in the 1990s—all classes would revolve their debt.

In the early 1990s, credit card issuers faced a greater challenge than potential regulation: running out of borrowers. New creditworthy—or "prime"—borrowers were in short supply by the early 1990s. Rejections fell among prime borrowers in the 1990s, from 18.5 to 7.9 percent, as lenders competed keenly for their balances.[201] By the mid-1990s, Americans with good credit records had credit cards—the market was saturated. With the advent of prime market prescreening software, credit card companies had completely saturated creditworthy borrowers, as computers quickly told lenders who would be a good credit risk. Seventy-four percent of households had credit cards in 1994. More credit cards (313 million) existed in the United States than people.[202]

Running out of prime customers, credit card companies aggressively targeted other firms' best customers, luring them away with introductory teaser rates to transfer balances. Offering low interest rates and no fees, balance transfers could quickly erode a lender's portfolio. Competition for balances, even before the recession, had been fierce. Beginning with AT&T, in 1990, credit cards rolled back the fees on which they had depended since their inception. AT&T boldly expanded its market share with its Universal Card by being the first issuer to offer no-fee credit cards.[203] Other card companies had to drop their fees or lose their customers to AT&T. In the midst of the recession, as balances stagnated, the competition grew even more intense. Bank of America, slow to catch on to the no-fee card, lost 11 percent ($955 million) of its balances from 1992 to 1993 to competitors.[204] Issuers resisted dropping their fees, attempting to offer increased benefits in exchange for annual fees, such as GE Capital's rewards card in September 1992.[205] GE's card flopped and it was forced to continue offering benefits but without a fee.[206] Companies that did not eliminate fees saw their balances flee. The dropping of fees and the creation of teaser rates did not stop the consumer capital flight from card to card. So-called "card surfers" shifted their balances from one card to another, following teaser rates.[207] The easy movement of revolving balances only hurt profits. Citicorp, for instance, only lost 2 percent of its customers in the fourth quarter of 1997, but lost 26 percent of its revenue, since those lost were revolving balances.[208]

Though balance transfers seemed an easy way to expand, balance transfers were a lose-lose proposition. The "musical chairs" of balance transfers, as one bank executive termed it, created a game that few companies could win.[209] While balance transfers rapidly grew receivables, they were not the best way to sustain long-term growth. Balances transferred under introductory teaser rates could be just as easily transferred again six months later to another card. Even worse, if a borrower could never repay the debt at a higher rate, and could not find another card to transfer the balance, the creditor would be stuck with a massive default. If the customer had a choice, the balance would simply leave after an unprofitable six months and if the customer had no choice, the balance would be defaulted on.[210] Such gains were short-term at best. Either way, the card company would lose.

Banks created clever promotions to hold the balances, offering declining interest rates on greater balances and increasing rebates if borrowers deferred their redemption. Rebates on credit cards, where borrowers would get a percentage of their spending back, had emerged during the late 1980s. Mellon Bank took the rebate to a new level, offering a d that if borrowers did not claim their rebate would get an additional 5 percent of their interest back every year. After twenty years all of their interest would be returned! Such schemes neglected a fundamental truth: customers who intensively managed their balance transfers were already financially precarious. Unfortunately for Mellon, its card attracted precisely the revolvers who believed they would never be able to pay off their bills—for whom the 100 percent rebate was attractive. Despite their prime credit ratings, borrower defaults reached 27.6 percent of receivables, compared to a normal 4 percent charge-off for borrowers with similar FICO scores.[211] Mellon Bank lost nearly 30 percent of the money it lent. Revolvers who revolved for convenience made for good business. Revolvers who borrowed because they spent more than they earned—persistently—made for bad business. No model could screen for these kinds of revolvers. But computer models, in general, had begun to acquire an accuracy that was impossible only a decade earlier, and it was on the basis of these models that lenders delved further down the risk/return curve, relying on their ability to transfer that default risk to the holders of the credit card securities and, ultimately, the insurance companies that backed those tranches.

The Seduction of the Risk Model

Beginning in 1987, Household Finance Company, by now one of the largest credit card issuers in the United States, began to segment its existing portfolio ever finer, building on the discriminant analysis techniques of the 1970s. Carefully raising credit limits and lowering pricing to encourage high-revolving but low-defaulting borrowers, Household grew more profitable.[212] But such partitions were based on past behavior and with existing customers. The question remained: how to predict future behavior, especially the behavior of non-customers? In the late 1980s, credit card and credit rating firms attempted to develop software that would better predict the borrowing behavior of debtors than the slightly-better-than-coin-flipping models of the late 1970s. Not until 1992 could commercially available software accurately predict the future profits of a borrower well enough to make a lending decision. Armed with such models, however, lenders could rely on securitization to provide all the capital they would need.

These models possessed a variety of names: behavioral models, risk models, profitability models. At the center of all these models was an attempt to maximize profits, by lending to revolving customers, while avoiding the losses of defaults. The revolving customer inhabited a narrow band between defaulter and non-revolver. Finding that sweet spot of revolving balances for each customer was extraordinarily difficult—much harder than just avoiding defaults. Behavioral models, the first to be widely used, focused on avoiding default. Fair, Isaac, the company that created the FICO score and foremost credit model firm, estimated that while in 1989 issuers used such models on only 14 percent of credit card accounts, 75 percent did by 1992.[213] To a large degree, this timing was technologically determined. In only a few years, computing power doubled, software prices fell by half, and data availability grew, allowing the vast majority of issuers to employ such techniques. Companies frequently developed their own software, often in concert with outside advisors. Banc One, for instance, turned to Andersen Consulting for help developing its proprietary system, Triumph, which used the latest data-mining techniques to price risk. But software developed outside a company was often superior. Credit rating agencies had an advantage over individual lenders; they knew all of a debtor's history. TRW, for instance, developed its own in-house probability models that generated repayment probabilities based not only on one particular debt, but on a borrowers' entire portfolio of debts—information that individual lenders did not always have. The challenge with such software was that if one lender knew that information, then every lender could, leading to excessive lending to a borrower. Fair, Isaac, not to be outdone, released PreScore in 1992, to prescreen credit bureau data to find prospective borrowers.[214]

When a borrower missed a payment, behavioral software calculated the probability that a borrower would resume payments or whether the missed payment was an aberration. Rather than waiting 180 days before referring an account to a collection agency, risk models helped debt collectors spot accounts far earlier than ever before.[215] A good model could help a lender collect the debt before any other lenders. By focusing on risk rather than time overdue, collections could be more efficiently conducted. Rather than call clients who would probably pay anyhow—and potentially lose their business by offending them—collectors could focus on the clients who would not.

Behavioral models allowed credit card companies to be stricter with those likely to default and appear laxer to those who would have paid anyway. This balance of strictness and laxness was necessary to maximize the profitability of revolvers. Credit card issuers conducted in-house experiments with control and test groups to find out how their collection techniques affected repayment. Too harsh methods resulted in repayment, but with subsequent lower balances, which lowered profits. Retaining the revolvers, who might miss an occasional payment, and keeping a watchful eye, helped boost profits.

Calculating the expected future profit of an account depended on more than just the likelihood of default. Risk, after all, was not the same as profit. Software had to know a particular company's costs and prices. The commercial release of software to calculate the potential profit of a borrower, rather than simply the probability of default, took until 1992.[216] So-called "profitability scoring" required computer resources and data that most companies did not possess. Companies needed at least three years of detailed credit data and the computing power, data, and software to do that kind of analysis. It did not exist before 1992, when MDS Group, the second largest credit scoring company behind Fair, Isaac, offered the service for $40,000 to $60,000. Mark Argosh, a vice-president at the consulting company Mercer, estimated that profit-per-account rose 2.5 times by using such techniques.[217]

Profitability was not just about potential defaults but also potential attrition. Lenders normally lost between 10 and 20 percent of their cardholders each year to competing firms.[218] Knowing in advance what the warning signs of such losses were, and which borrowers to hold on to, would save lenders a great deal of money. Keeping a customer was always cheaper than finding a new customer. Such profitability models helped lenders decide where to aim their retention efforts. Retention efforts cost money, however, and selectively aiming efforts at the most profitable could help the bottom line. While lenders and credit rating companies developed these models to handle the risk of the prime market, the models would prove to be essential after the 1992 recession and in the subsequent expansion of the credit card industry to those with less than perfect credit.

This riskier market would prove, through changes in law and technique, to be the most lucrative during the recovery. The death of the fee card forced issuers to use the profitability models to make better choices in lending. By 1996, only 2 percent of bank card revenue came from annual fees compared to 76 percent from interest income.[219] GE, for instance, provided a 2 percent rebate against charge volume. Without finance charges, such a rebate quickly became a loss. In 1996, GE instituted a "maintenance fee" for customers who had less than $25 in finance charges annually. When issuers offered to waive fees for revolvers, consumers in focus groups took it badly. Such a move appeared "self-serving" for the issuer—which it was. The pure play, securitization-driven issuers like Advanta, which was the tenth largest issuer by 1996, opted for a more focused approach than that of GE. Using profitability modeling, Advanta attempted to increase the profits on its non-revolving accounts—resorting to fees only as a last step.[220] First USA did the same. A former account-acquisition specialist with First USA claimed that while 60 percent of new accounts began as non-revolvers, First USA was "very good at turning convenience users into revolvers." Profits from revolving credit seemed fair while punishing those borrowers who paid on time seemed unfair. Fairness and profitability dictated that the sweet spot of revolving debt be made rather that just discovered. One credit card consultant opined that "the challenge is to instigate, accentuate, and accelerate desirable behavior."[221]

Subprime Lending after the Recession

As the economy recovered, the business of credit cards looked very different in the mid-1990s than it had in the mid-1980s.[222] While credit card debt's relative profitability fell from the heights of the late 1980s, such debt continued to be much more profitable than other commercial bank investments, leading banks to continue to throw as much money in their direction as possible.[223] Larger organizations had greater resources and expertise to devote to the risk management necessary for continued expansion. Over the late 1990s, balances continued to concentrate in fewer and fewer lenders. But, at the same time, new risk models made these large lenders confident that they could safely lend to ever-riskier borrowers.

The pure play companies had come of age. What the Federal Reserve called a "credit card bank"—a bank with its assets primarily in consumer loans and whose consumer loans were 90 percent or more in credit card balances—accounted for 77 percent of all balances in 1996. These banks, in 1996, reported net earnings of 2.14 percent of outstanding balances, below the peak of 1993, but still higher than the average return of 1.86 percent on all commercial bank assets.[224] The credit card in the post-recession world functioned differently than it had in the 1980s. Issuers estimated that 80 percent of new accounts were variable rate.[225] In 1991, 23 percent of cards floated; by 1998, 68 percent did.[226] No-fee cards were now standard.[227] Though the cost of funds fell 1 percent in 1993, the average margin on interest income fell only 0.5 percent. Market competition drove borrower interest rates down. Market competition also drove borrowers to the highest efficiency lenders, who could cut interest rates the lowest, further concentrating the industry. Attrition rates continued to be 11 to 13 percent, despite all the attempts to stanch balance transfers and canceled cards. Continued expansion meant that new markets would have to be conquered.

If prestige cards had targeted the wealthy or soon-to-be wealthy, other bankers were beginning to discover how to lend to the other half. The cost of finding new borrowers had grown immensely. One direct-mail credit card vendor, marketing to prime customers, recounted that while he had gotten a 6 to 7 percent response rate in the 1980s, he now got 0.02 percent.[228] The market was saturated. With such low response rates, costs per new prime customer grew incredibly.

Controlling the risk of lending to less sound borrowers—the other 26 percent without credit cards—meant relying ever-more on risk models. To keep growing, lenders had to make riskier and riskier loans. By 1995, 58 percent of households earning under $20,000 received credit card offers in the mail each month, up from 40 percent in 1993. Edward Bankole, vice-president in Moody's structured finance group, said that "more and more of the new wave of cardholders tend to be the ones who are on the low end of the credit risk spectrum."[229] By 1998, with average losses of 6 cents on the dollar, risk management was essential to a successful business. At the same time, however, card companies keenly felt competitive pressure on interest rates and special promotions from other lenders. These twin challenges of risk and return were answered by expanding into the terrain of more risky borrowers—the so-called subprime market. Willing to pay higher fees and interest rates for credit access, those who were traditionally denied appeared to offer a lucrative opportunity when viewed through risk models, and lenders believed they could lend profitably to such borrowers.

The models made possible the expansion of lending to minority groups, for both financial and legal reasons. Lending to minorities was at the center of the subprime expansion, since this group tended to have no prior relationship with a bank. One-fifth of Americans had no relationship with a bank, the so-called "unbanked," and that one-fifth overlapped strongly with the 26 percent of American households without a credit card. Only 45 percent of lower-income families had a credit card in 1995.[230] Unbanked Americans were disproportionately African American and Latino.[231] Convincing these groups to apply and then to correctly screen them for risk would provide immense profits for the firm clever enough to figure out how to do it. The "uncarded ethnics," as an article in *Credit Card Management* referred to minorities without credit cards, were seen as a risky, but lucrative growth field.[232] Lending to such groups heavily relied on the computerized risk models, but these groups were not like previous populations without credit cards who already had other forms of credit. While traditional credit card holders developed their credit histories at department stores, these populations did not have credit histories at such stores. Lenders looked to nontraditional credit records, based on utility payments and phone companies, rather than retailers.[233] Such "thin file" customers, minority or not, made issuers rely on factors other than individual credit histories. As many as 20 percent of applicants had thin-file histories and would have been denied credit in the 1980s, but with the new models these thin-file applicants could receive credit as well. With "behavioral models and other risk-management tools," lenders could take a "calculated gamble" on these thin-file borrowers, *Credit Card Management* reported.

Defaults could still be terminal for issuers, however. Every potential borrower could not be given a card, no matter how great the returns on fees. Accessing riskier customers—who were more likely to pay late and more likely to revolve—required the most cutting-edge risk management tools. The risk models allowed borrowers to anticipate when a borrower would default. A better prediction model would enable the lender to get to that borrower before the other 4.5 creditors to whom the average defaulting credit cardholder owed money.[234] Firms like Baltimore's Neuristics, which grew out of Johns Hopkins University research in artificial intelligence, combined all the varieties of risk modeling into one product designed for subprime lending. Eight of the top 25 credit card firms used the product, Neuristics Edge, to send preapproved solicitations to potential borrowers with FICO scores under 650—the boundary between prime and subprime.[235] The CEO of Neuristics, Richard Leavy, explained, "25 percent of the people in that population are 'bad,' but that means 75 percent are good." Finding that 75 percent would "eliminate most of the fat and deliver the profitable customers." But if a company lent to that 25 percent, it would no doubt take devastating losses.

What made borrowers a good credit risk—income, job stability—was homogenous, while what defined a bad credit risk was heterogeneous.[236] The subprime market was made up of two groups: emerging credit and recovering credit. Emergers had little credit history, whether because they were students or simply unbanked. For recent immigrants and racial minorities, who because of discrimination or of preference did not shop at the stores where transitionary forms of credit were offered, like store charge cards, lenders had little data for their models to rely on. Recovers, in contrast, had an extensive, but bad, credit history. Some bad credit histories, though, resulted not from bad choices but from cataclysmic events outside the borrower's control like illness or job loss. These borrowers, now healthy and employed, could actually be good candidates for credit, despite their poor repayment histories. Still, while some borrowers had fallen on hard times, others were simply unable to manage their finances, moving in and out of bankruptcy multiple times. These borrowers would always be a credit risk. Differentiating that heterogeneous risk would be the source of all subprime profits.

Pattern recognition in these models grew more complex, aggregating data from a variety of sources. New transaction models examined what a customer purchased, and based on that data, predicted bankruptcy. Many cash advances late in the month, for instance, could indicate a borrower was running out of money before payday. Meals charged at casinos could indicate gambling. Put together, this borrower's riskiness looked very different than one who just bought meals and got cash advances.[237] Such analysis probed deeply into the everyday buying patterns of borrowers, something that creditors never had full knowledge of before. While cash loans were fungible, credit on plastic was not. The loans were always for specific ends. While creditors gave credit card holders greater freedom in their borrowing, their knowledge of what was actually bought by borrowers expanded. The appearance of freedom was deceiving, however, since credit lines could be revoked at any point.

The models enabled more inexperienced lenders to be overconfident, taking the model for reality. Modelers expected smooth continuity, not abrupt discontinuity. While such models took account of individual account demographics and history, they did not take account of future economic forecasts or unexpected population differences. Lending in an expanding economy is always less risky. Perhaps the marginal borrower would be more susceptible to downturn than the traditional borrower. If the data used for the model were less than the length of the business cycle, the lender would not have a stress-tested portfolio.[238] The senior project manager for Fair, Isaac's Horizon system explained that the challenge of risk models was that "the borrowers who tend to go bankrupt look just like a lender's most profitable customers."[239] And the markers for default for subprime borrowers might be different than those of prime market borrowers. As the vice president of a subprime credit card issuer remarked, "the customers are different (from the traditional market) and the customer's behavior is really different."[240] If this was true, then the risk models developed with the data of prime market borrowers would fail.

The models used data borne of a long period of falling interest rates. While interest rates had changed since the early 1980s, they had steadily fallen. As one credit card banker remarked in 1995, "the fundamentals of the business are being sustained by the Fed, not by the underlying consumer proposition."[241] Interest rates had fallen since the 1970s, so when then Chairman of the Federal Reserve Alan Greenspan briefly raised rates in 1995, credit card issuers were uncertain what would happen. Issuers feared a backlash from the public, who, by then, commonly switched cards for small interest differences.[242] Though consumers had enjoyed the downward flexibility of floating rate cards, their response as rates went up was more uncertain. More important, for the issuers, was how other issuers would respond. A rising cost of funds could allow companies with deep pockets to subsidize their borrowers, and watch the balances flow in as customers switched to their lower rates. Issuers like GE, Capital One, and NationsBank all offered teaser rate cards with fixed rates 3 percent below prime, to encourage just such movements.[243] Interest rates, despite up's and down's, continued to fall until the early 2000s, when they could fall no further, effectively driving the real cost of borrowing to less than zero. The reality of floating rates was, however, much more volatile for the economy as a whole than just a shifting balance of market share among credit card companies.

Collective hazards resulted as well from the automated screening systems pitching cards to the same marginally creditworthy borrowers. The aggressive expansion campaigns netted issuers with even riskier customers than they had anticipated.[244] Because so many issuers competed simultaneously for the same clients, borrowers had accepted multiple cards at the same time. Unbeknownst to other lenders, borrowers went from zero to many credit cards all at once. As Robert Hayer, a director at Smith Barney, explained, "You [the borrower] may be able to handle what I gave you from a credit perspective, but that doesn't protect me from X-Y-Z bank down the street issuing more credit to you."[245] Issuers, like Capital One, sometimes nearly doubled the interest rates of customers who opened additional credit lines. . .[246] Customers complained that they paid their bills on time and ought not be charged more, even though the risk model predicted a higher rate of default. Nigel Morris, president of Capital One, defended the practice, suggesting that "the credit card business [of the future] will look more like the insurance business, with pricing based on likely outcomes instead of one price for everybody." Yet while death was a certainty for everyone, catalogued on tables with billions of data points, the economic futures of borrowers were far more unique and less susceptible to the prognostications of actuaries.

More broadly, though, Capital One recognized the danger that expansive access to credit could pose for a household. Smaller regional banks took more time than large banks between mailing and approving credit, leading to serious lags in credit information, which left them overexposed to a decrease in creditworthiness. These issuers could not handle the risk of these new borrowers and began, in 1995 and 1996, to sell off their receivables as they had during the consolidations of the late 1980s.[247] Larger issuers, with cheaper collection mechanisms, could then profitably buy the distressed portfolios of these smaller banks. For the larger issuers, who then securitized their expanding portfolios, the models seemed to work. Losses on securitized credit card debt had fallen, by 1996, to a six-year low.[248] Lenders that tried to set aside capital, like Bank of New York, were punished as their stock prices fell. Investors presumably believed that capital would be better invested than conserved against possible loss, believing in the validity of the lending models.[249] Subprime lending, relying on ever-more clever models, underpinned by securitization of debt, drove pure play stock prices and American indebtedness ever-higher.

The *Marquette* decision of 1978 had allowed credit card companies complete freedom with interest rates, but interest rates, while not subject to regulated caps, were still subject to market competition, much to D'Amato's chagrin. With so many issuers, and such liberal access to securitized capital, interest rates were very competitive. Set too high, a rate and a borrower would jump ship. Fees, however, were harder to compare between lenders. Unfortunately for credit card companies, fees, unlike interest rates, were still regulated by individual states, until 1996 that is. In 1996, a Supreme Court decision, *Smiley v. Citibank*, extended the *Marquette* decision to allow banks to charge late fees if the card was issued in a state that allowed such fees.[250] Barbara Smiley, a California homemaker, had two credit cards through Citibank, in South Dakota.[251] In 1992, she brought a class action lawsuit against Citibank on behalf of California borrowers charged $15 late fees, which she saw as illegal under California law. The Court upheld the position of the Comptroller of the Currency, that fees were simply another form of interest. While this might seem like a broad interpretation of the word "interest," such reasoning unpinned all the usury laws of the twentieth century, which had treated fees as a surreptitious form of interest that drove up the real cost of borrowing. If fees were a form of interest, then the *Marquette* decision held that individual states could not regulate issuers in other states. While such flexible definitions made sense to lawyers, for consumers the difference between fee and interest was more than financial. Interest rates were very public and perceptible, while penalty fees were more clandestinely concealed in the fine print of contracts, making it harder for consumers to compare credit offerings. In practice, *Smiley* undid thirty years of truth-in-labeling legislation for consumer credit. Consumers, moreover, generally expected to pay on time and tended not to include fees in their comparisons. Credit card companies, hamstrung by competition on interest rates, began to focus on maximizing fee income.

The *Smiley* decision came just in time for the credit card industry. As the profitability of interest income fell through the mid-1990s, penalty fee income had risen, but was still subject to state laws. By the late 1990s, profits in the credit card industry, while still higher than commercial loans, continued to slide. By 1996, after-tax return on assets was at 1.2 percent, nearly half of what it was in 1993.[252] The low barriers to entry and the frenzied competition had driven profits down. A senior analyst at Moody's remarked that the "competition of the past five years has changed the nature of the industry."[253]

What profits remained were sustained by the increased interest and fee income derived from subprime lending, lower charge-offs derived from home equity loans, and higher fee income from penalties and merchant fees.[254] One-quarter of all customers paid their bills late and issuers happily charged them an industry-average $26 fee.[255] As customers used their cards for more mundane spending, income from merchants rose, enabled by the *Smiley* decision.[256] While many credit card analysts were ambivalent about the subprime expansion, credit card issuers had little choice if they were to grow. While bond rating analysts might argue that the issuers who are "moving down the credit spectrum . . . are moving too far down," the prime customer market was saturated and issuers took what was left.[257] For subprime borrowers, issuers began to offer interest rates less than a borrowers' actual riskiness justified, to act as loss-leaders for the more profitable fees.[258] Lenders lost money on the interest rates, but recouped those losses with fees. Effective interest rates, therefore, were much higher, even if the borrowers believed they were paying only a few percent more than prime borrowers. With fees, the effective interest rates on lending could be much higher, and more difficult to compare for borrowers, allowing even riskier lending.

While D'Amato had been concerned about interest rates being too high at the beginning of the 1990s, after *Smiley* he should have been concerned that rates were too low! By the end of the 1990s, interest rates, especially for subprime lenders, were mere loss-leaders for the more lucrative fees. As consumers loaded up on credit, many debtors turned to debt consolidation offered by home equity loans to get them out of their situation.

Home Equity Loans Revisited

In 1991, a frustrated wife wrote a letter to Leonard Groupe, a financial advice columnist with the Chicago *Sun-Times*, a tabloid daily in Chicago. After her husband had attempted to convince her to take out a home equity loan to consolidate their debt, she had remained skeptical. Though the home equity interest would be deductible and have a lower interest rate, the thought of a home equity loan still "scare[d]" her. Home equity, in the 1990s, had begun to be used more frequently to consolidate credit card debt. The four-year phase out of deductible credit card interest, authorized by the Tax Reform Act of 1986, culminated in 1991—leaving only the interest on mortgages and home equity loans deductible. Debt consolidation did not become the leading use of home equity loans until 1991, when the tax deduction on other forms of debt was fully eliminated. Unlike second mortgages, home equity loans revolved, making them easier to add to, even though many had minimum borrowing amounts. Once the paperwork was finished, borrowers could borrow more or less against the house.

The columnist's advice to this fearful wife echoed that of many consumer advocates. Though the interest is deductible, a home equity loan carried other dangers. An auto payment might be more expensive, but defaulting on an auto loan only ended with the auto being repossessed. If payments were missed on a home equity loan, borrowers would have their homes foreclosed. In the short-run, such a foreclosure was unlikely, since the payments would be reduced from what the husband and wife currently paid. More dangerous, the columnist wrote, in keeping with the standard advice, was that "people like your husband, who apparently has grown accustomed to accumulating installment debt, probably lack the discipline to genuinely profit from a second mortgage home-equity debt-consolidation loan." The couple would probably run their credit card debt back up, and then be stuck with that debt on top of their increased mortgage. Consumer rationality and spending habits rarely go hand-in-hand.[259] Incurring more mortgage debt was difficult, but charging was even easier. If the debt could be easily shifted, hard-won equity could be easily depleted. Paying off the credit cards might have been a good idea, but doing so left home owners with tempting lines of unused credit on credit cards. Credit counselors saw that may of their customers who paid off their credit cards with their home equity also found that they soon had to pay for a "transmission" or "battery" that went out and they did not have the cash.[260]

Despite the advice of this columnist, and nearly every other popular writer on the subject, from 1996 to 1998 four million households paid back $26 billion in credit card debt from their homes' equity.[261] Forty percent of home equity loans were for debt consolidation—nearly twice the percentage of the next most frequent use, home improvement.[262] The advantages of home equity loans over credit card debt were clear. In addition to the tax incentive, the interest rates on home equity loans were considerably less than those for credit cards. In 1997, the average home equity loan charged 1.27 percent over prime or 9.77 percent—much less than even the lowest credit card rates, and home equity interest was deductible. Even subprime home equity lenders, like Household and The Money Store, offered home equity interest rates less than the average credit card.

The transubstantiation of credit card debt into home equity debt, which resulted in few charge-offs, made card bonds appear to be better risks than they actually were. In 1998, consumers increased their credit card repayment rates but did so largely by using the equity in their homes; borrowers increasingly relied on this equity rather than their income to repay their debts. Eventually, however, home equity runs out. While home equity made credit card borrowers appear to be better risks, bond ratings experts at Moody's attributed the drop in charge-offs to tighter underwriting standards and accurate models.[263] Sapping the equity savings of America made the models appeared more reliable than they actually were. While credit card lending was intended to rely only on income, it actually relied on asset appreciation.

These home equity loans went well beyond traditional first or even second mortgages. Lenders began to provide extremely high loan-to-value mortgages. While FHA lenders of the 1930s winced at the idea of lending more than 80 percent to a borrower, some lenders provided 100 percent, 125 percent, even 150 percent of a home's value. The "equity" being borrowed against served only as a pretense of collateral. By definition, home owners could not have more equity in a house than it was worth.[264] The average home equity borrower, like the ideal credit card borrower, had income but not too much. The average home equity household earned $62,664, had children (2.6), a steady job (7.6 years), a steady address (7.6 years), and was relatively young (35–49 years old). In 1997, this average home equity borrower accessed his or her account 4.4 times over the course of the loan for an average withdrawal of nearly $30,000.[265] While credit card companies jockeyed to avoid being the unused "fifth card in a wallet," home equity lenders had no such problem.[266] With high up-front fees, 75 percent of home equity borrowers tended to use the line. Home equity loans, which had no grace period, also offered lenders a way to avoid the punishing non-revolver problem of credit cards. As soon as the money was lent, interest began accruing. Still, if a bank sold home equity loans to its own customers, the loan would eliminate the most profitable segment of its portfolio—the revolvers. If the bank refused to consolidate the loans of the revolvers, however, another bank would step in. Market competition drove banks to consolidate their own credit card customers, and with a lower interest rate the bank would actually lose money through loan consolidation.[267]

Credit card issuers, especially commercial banks, noticed the resurgent interest in home equity loans. While these loans accessed through credit cards had flopped in the 1980s, banks again began to experiment with such novelties following the recession.[268] Interest rates on such cards were much lower. Los Angele's Sanwa Bank, for instance, offered a Visa Gold card with a variable interest rate of 6.38 percent. Credit cards were also so much easier to use by the 1990s; retailers preferred cards to checks, which was an obstacle during the 1980s. By the end of the 1990s, larger and larger banks attempted to combine home equity and credit cards. In April 2000, Washington Mutual (WaMu) offered its "On the House" card with a teaser rate of 5.99 percent, as well as a picture of a generic house.[269] The credit limit was constrained only by the value of the borrower's house. Consumer advocates, like Stephen Brobeck of the Consumer Federation of America, continued to question the ease of borrowing inherent in such a card, since consumers could so easily "spen[d] the hard-earned savings that [they had] accumulated in [their] home, savings that most people need for their retirement years."[270] But for consumers living through the late 1990s, house prices seemed to go in only one direction—up. In 2000, 44 percent of credit cardholders paid their bills in full, compared to 29 percent in 1991, mostly not out of their paychecks but their home equity.[271] While home equity loans and credit cards could still appear different, in the capital markets the two became ever more indistinguishable.

Many home equity lenders, like The Money Store, operated similar to pure play credit card companies, lending to home owners and then securitizing the loans for sale in the market. By 1996, home equity securities overtook auto loans, to be the second largest volume of asset-backed securities, behind credit cards.[272] The big issuers in the home equity securities market were subprime lenders, like Household Finance, which by itself was one-quarter of the market, followed by the Money Store, Oldstone, Alliance, and Advanta.[273] Like credit cards, insurance and the tranche structure made these securities possible. The high ratings of the bonds came not from the inherent credit quality of the mortgages but from the insurance underpinning the issues. As the managing director of Moody's structured finance group said in 1996, "most transactions in today's market are rated AAA because they are insured by one of the major bond insurance companies."[274] Bond insurance companies made the securitization of these loans possible, which, in turn, made the expansion of home equity debt possible. Home equity loans and credit cards, available to consumers on plastic and funded by securitization, became ever-more indistinguishable.

In turn, the boundaries between the institutions that made this profitable convergence possible—insurance companies, commercial banks, and investment banks—were blurred as well. Ratifying this fact in law, the Gramm-Leach-Bliley Act of 1999 removed the official boundaries between these types of firms that had been put in place during the Great Depression to prevent excessive speculation, but had through numerous exceptions broken down over the 1980s and 1990s. Commercial bank Citibank joined with the insurance giant Traveler's Group to become Citigroup. The financial services industry could now formally consolidate itself—issuing, underwriting, and insuring all the debt Americans could possibly borrow.

Conclusion: To Float and To Fall

By the end of the 1990s, credit cards and mortgages alike had floating interest rates. Both credit cards and houses were financed by capital found in securities markets. Flexible, adjustable, and managed with the most cutting edge of risk management tools, credit card debt and mortgage debt were predicated on models purporting to accurately reflect reality. And yet those models depended on data collected for only a few years—considerably less than the shortest business cycle, and much less than the long-term oscillations in the economy. Indeed, even the terms "cycle" and "oscillation" imply a certainty to the motions of the economy more appropriate to the motions of the heavens. At least astronomers' models have billions of years of data.

The convergence of different kinds of credit and the fluid transfer of capital from markets to consumers presented an unprecedented danger for the economy. While there had always been doomsayers surrounding credit and the economy, the debt economy of the 1990s was something new. Pushing capital from across the world into the sweet spot of revolving credit allowed no wiggle room, and few lenders appreciated how aberrant the data were on which they based their models—just the past few years. These relatively new loan types, as well as laxer lending practices, put both subprime and prime borrowers at increased risk in addition to lenders. In an era of variable rates, a sudden rise in interest rates in 1995 would have a much more dire effect than it would have had in 1975. American households could now finance all their major borrowings with a floating rate—cars, houses, home equity loans, credit cards—and a rise in interest rates would hit all of their debt obligations at once. While floating rate loans made sense to individual lenders concerned about the cost of their funds, as a collective policy floating rates could lead to calamity. All debts would rise at once. Rather than reducing interest rate risk, variable rates increased it—for both borrowers and lenders.

The instruments of debt changed after 1970, but the more essential difference for borrowers was their place in the productive economy. While critics of the credit card industry have pointed to the *Marquette* decision as harmful for consumers, the decision allowed a more competitive industry to develop that ultimately lowered interest rates for consumers. The balance of power in capitalism was not determined by the interest rate caps for consumers, but whether they were able to pay back what they borrowed. Thirty years of wage stagnation made paying back those debts through anything but accidental asset inflation—homes and home equities—impossible. In the 1990s, the full flower of deindustrialization pummeled not only blue- but white-collar America as well.

While a generation of postwar consumers could safely borrow against rising incomes, the promise on which American prosperity had been built now cracked. The evanescent promise of getting a good-paying job that a generation earlier would have been seen as a sure path to upward mobility, only led in the 1990s to increased debt and certain bankruptcy after that job was downsized.[275] Even those with college educations found themselves downsized in the 1990s as information technology increased the efficiency of office work, and their wages converged with high school graduates. The only educational group that received a substantial increase in income during the 1990s was those with graduate degrees. These best-educated workers, who could multiply their efforts through the new information technology of models and data, produced tremendous profits for their firms, and were amply rewarded.[276] If their models put others to the brink of bankruptcy, for those who created them the models produced untold fortunes.

Credit issuers may have found the revolvers, and even pressured them to borrow, but the labor markets kept them in debt. While issuers struggled to push and to prod borrowers into not paying their bills, capitalism did their job for them—and did so effortlessly. Consumers borrowed more because their lives were more volatile and because more credit was made available to them. More credit was made available because credit card debt, on average, was a more profitable investment for banks than other investments. The same banal and brutal process of allocating capital that had made postwar America prosperous had come to undermine its long-term viability.

Epilogue

Debt as Choice, Debt as Structure

Fortune magazine, in an alarmist series of articles in 1956, declared that the "abnormally fast" rise in consumer credit since World War II would soon come to an end, since consumers "loading up heavily with fixed payments" and could afford no more debt.[1] Americans' "debts increase[d]" while their "liquid assets . . . decline[d]," therefore, *Fortune* concluded, "everything portends a downturn in the long-term rate of debt increase." Borrowing could not continue forever. Rarely has *Fortune* magazine been so wrong. The postwar rise in indebtedness inaugurated a long-term trend of credit expansion in which we still live. *Fortune*'s cautionary imagining of the end still looms over us. When this abrupt end to the "credit binge" came, *Fortune* foretold that "industries depending on it would be hard hit."[2] The sudden contraction of spending would undo all the thousands of factories, the tens of thousands of shops, and the millions of workers depending on borrowed money to drive the businesses that employed them. The American economy had grown dependent on credit to sustain itself, and if the credit stopped, no one knew what would remain.

This dependence on credit was the creation, intentional and unintentional, of the sometimes unlikely choices of government, business, and consumers. Over the first half of the twentieth century, government and business fashioned a new legal network of credit institutions and offered most American consumers a choice of whether or not to use this debt in their daily lives. By the end of the century, however, the choice to opt out of the credit system no longer remained. Three corporations assigned every American a credit rating. Their opinions governed consumers' ability to rent and to buy housing, to afford an education, to shop for clothes and food, to commute to work, and even to receive medical care—that is, the basic materials of daily life. Even to get a job, a worker needed good credit. The choice of whether or not to use credit ceased to exist for the American consumer.

Americans had to use credit and develop a "good" credit identity if they were to take part in mainstream commercial life. The Household Finance Corporation, reflecting this shift in thinking, issued an instructional book in 1971, *Children's Spending*, for parents and teachers to help inculcate the virtues of this credit world and illustrate "the problems that can result from a poor credit rating."[3] Parents who were befuddled on how to deal with the deviant thrifty child who "hoard[ed] money and refuse[ed] to spend it for the things he want[ed]," could learn ways to reeducate their child by setting up a "realistic repayment schedule."[4] Being "good" and maintaining a good credit rating had become synonymous, and certainly more virtuous than saving. *Children's Spending* argued that "saving for its own sake, dropping pennies in a toy bank which has no key, is outdated."[5] Saving could not provide evidence of character nearly as much as borrowing and repaying the debt. Such credit histories would prove necessary in this credit world, as credit rating became the key number to represent trustworthiness not only for borrowing for consumption but for all aspects of life.

While at earlier moments consumers could have lived without credit, by the 1970s it was no longer possible to be without credit and live in mainstream American society. Consumers denied credit in the 1960s had fought for greater access, not only because of credit's convenience but because of its perceived necessity in achieving the American dream. Consumers' achievement of the middle-class dream in the 1950s had been enabled by debt. Debt policies and practices underpinned a consumer order by the 1970s that made it difficult for consumers to extricate themselves from indebtedness even if they had wanted to. The lifestyle of debt was as inscribed in the built environment as it was in the habits of the shopping public. As the economy began to erode in the early 1970s, just after the federal census announced that the majority of Americans then lived in suburbia, the debt requirement of suburban living began to take its toll. Even if people wanted to reduce their borrowing, the very environment in which they lived made reduction difficult. Consumers needed mortgages to buy houses, and they needed installment credit to buy the cars required to travel the unwalkable distances created by suburban living.

While borrowing became more compulsory, paying back what was borrowed proved more difficult. The 1970s, while not the first time Americans worried about consumer debt in American history, was the first time that households became unable to repay their debt. The post-1970s debt expansion of unpaid debt differed from those that preceded it because late twentieth-century debt was borne not of business cycles but of unexpected structural changes. Although credit institutions continued to change, as they had for half a century, in response to the demands of capitalism and the state, the growth of debt in the 1970s resulted more from Americans' decreasing ability to pay back what they borrowed than from an increase in borrowing. Instead of seeing extravagant spenders in debt, we should see underpaid workers trying to keep up.[6] Americans' personal debt problem resulted not from a choice to borrow but from the rising inequality of income and wealth that had occurred since the 1970s, even as capitalist expansion relied on increasing consumption in an era of declining wages. Personal debt was no longer a private choice, but a structural imperative.

For those who control and regulate these structures today, the choices remain as they always have—within limits. The state has the power to make markets and guide the profitable flow of capital, as has been shown throughout this book. When policymakers acknowledged this flow, their policy ambitions have been successful. In the 1920s, small loan reformers helped channel capital to the working poor, to give them cheaper, yet still expensive, access to credit. In the 1930s, federal policymakers channeled this capital to create the suburbs, surpassing even the most grandiose of tax-funded programs. In the 1960s, Great Society reformers created mortgage-backed securities that expanded the lending pool for American home owners. Yet, when policymakers sought to dam the river of capital, to push back against it, to pretend it was something other than the callous miracle it is, they have realized only failure. Regulation cannot substitute for market discipline—all it can do is imitate market opportunity. Sticks without carrots do not work. Regulations need profits as much as rules to accomplish their goals. During the 1940s, Regulation W failed because it did not provide a profitable alternative for business, pushing the American economy toward the hybrid revolving credit. During the 1960s and 1970s, the Housing Act of 1968 provided new sources of mortgage funds, but it could not make the investment of those funds in the inner city profitable. Intervention is neither doomed to fail, nor is it guaranteed to succeed. Only by recognizing the limits of government's administrative capacities, and the realities of capital's tendencies, can government make successful and necessary interventions in the economy.

Even as legislators made policies to alter capitalism, the full consequences of these policies in an untidy market were not always understood at the time. Legalization of small loans drove out loan sharks, but expanded the numbers of Americans in debt and legitimated borrowing as an alternative to saving. Mortgage loans may have expanded available housing, but they also taught consumers to owe vast sums of money to impersonal lenders, to say nothing of the long-term devastation exacted on many American cities as whites fled to the subsidized suburbs. During World War II, policymakers sought to restrain consumer credit only unintentionally to promote a new form of credit—revolving credit—which ultimately enabled consumers to increase their spending to limits never before seen. Legislators of the Great Society program sought to help welfare recipients gain a stake in owning their housing, only to inaugurate the era of subprime mortgage loans. In the 1970s, seeking to end discrimination, state policies accelerated the creation of a centralized, privately-held credit information system with unforeseen consequences for American privacy rights. Most importantly, perhaps, in promoting credit for everyone, Congress never stopped to consider whether everyone *ought* to have credit. As the economy became more volatile and more unequal, the credit provided for everyone caused more problems than it solved. Instead of addressing the core problem of widening income disparities, legislators and businesspeople pushed consumer credit to rectify income inequality. Credit appeared to close the material gap between the American reality and the American Dream, but without rising wages the debts remained.

As the era of postwar growth ebbed, the consumer habits and business institutions predicated on growth led Americans down a path that none could have imagined and whose final consequences are still unknown. Born in a Fordist age of manufacturing, consumer debt remained for a post-Fordist age of service and finance. The credit regime that emerged from a time of stability persisted for a time of volatility. But many times in the past, as this book has shown, the alarm bells have rung out over a potential crisis of overextended consumers—and have always been shown to be in error. Perhaps doomsayers today are no different than those of earlier periods, but credit's profits today are closer to the heart of capitalism itself than ever before. The relative danger of relying on consumer credit to drive the economy remains a macroeconomic puzzle to be solved. The increased demand caused by credit stimulates the economy, producing jobs along with all those borrowed-for goods and services. The long-run consequence of credit is not in the borrowing but in how the profits from that economic activity are invested. Invested productively, the wonder of capitalism continues its expansion. Invested unproductively, potential production is lost, never again to be regained. Whether capitalism, through its operations, contains the seed of its own destruction, or if its economy can grow forever, is the central question in the history of capitalism, debated by economists since Marx first popularized the question in the nineteenth century. Both sides of the debate agree, however, that to continue, capitalism must locate new places for money to be invested profitably.

The current financial crisis, rooted in those credit instruments, occurred not because capitalism failed, but because it succeeded. For the past forty years, profits for the owners of capital have soared while wages for most workers have stagnated. This is not a deviation from capitalism, but how capitalism operates. To expect otherwise is naïve and dangerous. Inequality, whatever its social justice problems, hampers economic growth because of an imbalance between the supply of capital for investment and the demand of income for consumption. These owners have accumulated vast savings, but with limited investment options. Workers can only buy so much without higher wages. Without greater consumption, savings cannot be invested in more production. Yet savings must be invested somewhere. Economic inequality ultimately hurts investors as much as workers by limiting productive investment opportunity. Without possible productive investments, investors, who still need to put their money somewhere, are drawn into asset-bubbles and speculations. Capitalism's efficiency has wildly increased in the last thirty years, but the returns on that efficiency have gone to those at the top. Lending those returns to workers—by investing in credit card and mortgage asset-backed securities—rather than directly paying the workers, has caused our current crisis.

Investors in debt, whether loan sharks, banks, or bond holders, are always looking for a good return. The choice to lend was at the same time a choice to invest, and that choice was determined by a combination of risk and return. While new ways to make credit profitable appeared at various points in the twentieth century, credit's profitability was always, as in all economic matters, relative. Relative to manufacturing, credit in the first third of the twentieth century was unprofitable, and undeserving of the monstrous capital that was required to fund its expansion. Only in the midst of depression, when deprived other more virtuous, more lucrative, more productive business opportunities, did bankers for the first time dip their fingers in the credit pie, and only through the encouragement of the federal government. Through the option account and then the universal credit card, retailers and financiers discovered ever-more profitable ways to lend to consumers and to borrow from investors. Always the choice to lend was at the same time a choice to borrow, and that choice was determined by a combination of risk and return—that is, yield on the investment. This process of investment is not unique to debt, it is the foundation of our capitalist system.

The current financial crisis stems from the same source as the large capital poured into consumer credit: a frantic drive for yield. Capital sloshed about in the past few years from the technology bubble to the housing bubble, as investors sought safe (but always better than average!) returns on their money. Money poured into the riskiest tranches of mortgage-backed securities, not from malice, but for a simple increase in return over a treasury bond. As this book goes to press, the world's great capital reserves have fled the equity markets for American federal debt. If this crisis is going to end, there must be more productive places to invest than in the U.S. federal government's debt. Not only Chinese factories, but economies the world over, are hungry for capital to invest. Too much capital and too few places to put it, productively, is what classical economists called an overaccumulation crisis. Before the twentieth century, most economists believed that such an overaccumulation was inevitable, and in a sense they were correct. Economies with a stagnant level of technology eventually have too much capital and nowhere to put it.

Luckily for us, for at least the last five hundred years, as these cycles of overaccumulation have played out, this doomsday scenario has not occurred and for one reason only: innovation. Innovation, whether in new places, technologies, or ways of organizing labor and capital, has allowed us to harness the baleful overaccumulation of capital into growth. World War II did not get us out of the depression, having the ability to invest profitably in suburbia, aerospace, and electronics did. These investment opportunities were made possible by government-created investment opportunities. Productive and profitable investment is the only way to stem these crises. Regulating them out of existence is impossible, since wild profitability is capitalism's strongest attribute. Again, this financial crisis occurred not because capitalism failed, but because it succeeded in doing what it does best: profits and inequality.

Helping capitalism succeed in ways that benefit the American people is the proper role of regulation. Using regulation to open up new industries, as in the New Deal and World War II, resolves these accumulation crises and allows the blockages of private capital to loosen. While innovation is clearly the only way out of such crises of capitalism, it is far less clear what industries and places should be invested in. Should we—the American government and its citizenry—create incentives to build electric automobiles the way we incentivized building suburbia? I must be agnostic regarding the best investments to make, but it is clear that an investment crisis is at the center of both the rise, and recent fall, of the credit economy.

The same financial innovations that brought this crisis to a head could also help us. If instead of directing investment to nonproductive assets, securitization could help us invest in new industries, like green technology, which like aerospace in the 1940s now seems to offer new opportunities to soak up tremendous amounts of capital, produce profits for business, and jobs for workers.[7] The financial system coordinates the flow of capital, and as long as it coordinates it in a way that is both profitable and productive, the virtuous circle of capitalism continues. The diversion of capital into nonproductive investments is necessary for consumer capitalism to function, but it cannot be the central motor of the economy in a long-term, sustainable fashion. Housing markets must be liquid. Consumers ought to be able borrow against their incomes to buy that washing machine today. But the financial system loses its purpose when it attains mastery over the real, productive economy. Finance must help us work, not work us over.

Scandal and deceit were only superficially the cause of the financial crisis of the early twenty-first century. There were, no doubt, frauds and fabulists but, I would think, no more than in any other pursuit. Today's financial crisis was not caused by a few con artists and cheats, but by lack of profitable opportunity. Had the investors desperate for yield been able to invest in anything that returned slightly more money, they would have. The more difficult truth is that it was not one individual that made this happen, but the collision between a hundred small decisions, often for other purposes, and one unstoppable river of capital, whose direction could be channeled, but desired or not, had to flow.

The current credit crisis is not really, at root, about credit at all, but about the opportunities for capitalist investment. Find a new industry as deserving of American ingenuity as the automobile or the internet. Use public policy, as the FHA did to create millions of modern houses, to align the interests of capitalist investment and public need. Channeling capital for the social good is not only possible, it is the best way to solve the distressing failures of the market economy. The choice is not between the government or the market. The only choice is how to use government to control the market for social good. Profit, prosperity, and policy are not incompatible. While making policies that actually accomplish these aims is challenging, this book has shown that government possesses the biggest levers of control over how capitalism actually works on the ground—and usually operates without spending any taxpayer money. Not everyone will be helped by these methods. There is no universal solution and for those left out we need to continue to have direct spending, but in the main, market solutions guided by public policy can work to transform the most basic aspects of our material lives. Credit will, necessarily, be part of future piecemeal solutions to the challenges of capitalism, whose basic operations tend to divide people and classes from one another, increasing inequality and friction. Recognized for what it is and what it does, however, capitalism can be controlled, as it has been successfully in the past. Credit itself depends on its economic context for meaning, whether in ancient Babylonia or contemporary America, and fashioning that context is the choice that we make together. American capitalism is America, and we can chose together to submit to it, or rise to its challenges, making what we will of its possibilities.

Acknowledgments

THE ONLY REASON I am not overwhelmed by debt is because of the financial support of many institutions that have underwritten this book. While a graduate student, I received funding from the U.S. Department of Education (Jacob Javits Fellowship), the Center for American Politics at Harvard (Dissertation Fellowship in American Politics), the Newcomen Society (Dissertation Fellowship in Business and American Culture for Excellence in the Study of the History of American Free Enterprise), and the Charles Warren Center for American History at Harvard (Dissertation Completion Fellowship). A post-doctoral fellowship from the American Academy of Arts and Sciences was invaluable in providing the time to turn my rough-hewn dissertation into a polished book.

Archives are at the center of any historical project and at the center of those archives are hard-working librarians and archivists who provide guidance into their stygian stacks. At Harvard, I would like to thank the staffs of Historical Collections at Baker Library, the Littauer library, the Harvard-MIT Data Center, the Special Collections Division of Gutman Library, and the Manuscript Division of Schlesinger Library. Barbara Burg, Laura Linard, and Meghan Dolan, in particular, who made this project possible. Outside of Harvard, I benefited from generous archival access to the collections of the American Collectors Association and Citigroup provided by Tim Dressen and Patricia Bouteneff, respectively. John Reed, the former CEO of Citigroup, kindly allowed me to interview him for his perspective on the early history of the credit card. The staff of the Library of Congress and the National Archives, in College Park, made possible the dusty work of reading manuscripts.

While this book may have been about financial debt, what made it possible were all the intellectual debts I have incurred in writing it. At Princeton University Press, I found the most wonderful place for a young scholar to publish his first work. The close attention of two anonymous reviewers contributed in substantial ways to the revision of the manuscript from the dissertation, making the arguments clearer and the chapters more concise. Gary Gerstle's singular focus on the big picture helped me cut the fat and speak to the biggest questions. Dale Cotton painstakingly copyedited the final draft with an eye for detail that I truly envy. Most of all, I would like to thank my editor, Clara Platter, who shepherded the manuscript from dissertation to book, answering the seemingly endless questions of a beginning author with endless patience and wisdom.

Before Princeton even saw the book, however, was the long road of writing the first draft—the dissertation. I would also like to thank the advisors who ably steered me to the end of the PhD. Betsy Blackmar gently put up with naive questions from a bewildered undergraduate and encouraged me to consider the history of capital alongside the history of labor. Niall Ferguson offered fresh perspectives that deepened and complicated my analysis in ways that I never would have thought of on my own. Sven Beckert's excitement for the history of capitalism is infectious and his suggestions about how to write it invaluable. My advisor Lizabeth Cohen believed in this project from the outset, and her rigorous guidance over the years allowed this project to reach its full potential. Without her stewardship, this book never would have been possible. I could not have asked for a better-rounded group of scholars with whom to think through the history of capitalism.

Friends and colleagues provided equally valuable intellectual support through this long process, reading drafts and talking about capitalism even when they had better things to do: Mike Bernath, Kevin Birmingham, Saul Blecker, Kathryn Boodry, Lauren Brown, Alfred Chandler, Nico Carbellano, Christine Desan, Walter Friedman, Mike Godwin, Connie Goodwin, Will Heinrich, Evelyn Higginbotham, Chris Hilliard, Eric Idsvoog, Simone Ipsa-Landa, Andrew Kinney, Nadine Knight, Kelley Kreitz, Sonia Lee, Marc Levinson, Ken Lipartito, Lisa McGirr, Rebecca McLennan, Bethany Moreton, Ginger Myhaver, Julia Ott, Brian Pellinen, Sarah Potter, Bill Rankin, Mark Rose, Rachel St. John, Bruce Schulman, Laura Serna, Kimberly Sims, David Singer, Mark Stickle, Tara Smith, Weston Smith, Thomas Stapleford, Raphaelle Steinzig, Michelle Syba, Joseph Tohill, Dan Wadhwani, and Ben Waterhouse.

My family endured endless meandering conversations about the history of debt, for which I am extremely grateful. My in-laws George and Katherine Howe provided love and support as if I were their own. My sister Rachel Hyman helped in ways that she cannot know, through her enthusiasm for the project even when I doubted that it would ever end. My much younger brothers Noah and Eli Hyman perhaps only recently found out I was even working on this, and mostly just wanted to hang out, which was a welcome distraction. My stepmother Brenda Hyman insisted that I go to graduate school in a difficult moment when I considered doing something different with my life. Without my stepfather Greg Kuzbida's love of history, I never would have become a historian; it is because of many spirited debates about history across the kitchen table that I studied history at all. Though he passed away before I went to graduate school, I would also like to acknowledge my father, Joel Hyman, for instilling in me a dogged faith in working hard and pursuing one's goals even when they seem out of reach. My mother, Patty Kuzbida, always had words of support during the daily trials of writing, insisting that this work could have a larger purpose. I will always be most grateful for the curiosity that she encouraged in me, and which, more than anything else, has made me the person I am today.

When we first met in a crowded former tenement-turned-dorm in New York, I do not think Kate Howe ever could have imagined that she would have had this many conversations about FHA loans, much less with that red-headed boy from her German philosophy class. Every day I am amazed by my dumb luck in finding her. Though this book argues that we can, above all else, make choices to determine our future, meeting her made me believe in fate. And even if I had a choice, I would choose her again, every time.

Abbreviations

Abraham & Strauss (A&S)
adjustable rate mortgages (ARMs)
American Bankers Association (ABA)
collateralized mortgage obligation (CMO)
Commercial Credit Company (CCC)
Credit Data Corporation (CDC)
Equal Credit Opportunity Act (ECOA)
Fair Credit Reporting Act (FCRA)
Fair, Isaac Corporation (FICO)
Federal Emergency Relief Administration (FERA)
Federal Home Loan Bank Board (FHLBB)
Federal Home Loan Mortgage Corporation (FHLMC or Freddie Mac)
Federal Housing Administration (FHA)
Federal National Mortgage Association (FNMA or Fannie Mae)
Federal Trade Commission (FTC)
Financial Accounting Standards Board (FASB)
General Electric (GE)
General Electric Contracts Corporation (GECC); later General Electric Credit Corporation
Generally Accepted Accounting Principles (GAAP)
General Motors (GM)
General Motors Acceptance Corporation (GMAC)
Government Accounting Office (GAO)
Government National Mortgage Association (GNMA or Ginnie Mae)
Home Owners Loan Corporation (HOLC)
Department of Housing and Urban Development (HUD)
Inter-University Consortium for Political and Social Research (ICPSR)
Maryland Bank, N.A. (MBNA)
Motor Dealers Credit Corporation (MDCC)
National Negro Insurance Association (NNIA)
National Retail Dry Goods Association (NRDGA)
National Organization for Women (NOW)
National Recovery Administration (NRA)
Office of Economic Opportunity (OEO)
Office of Price Administration (OPA)
permanent budget accounts (PBAs)
Public Works Administration (PWA)
Retail Credit Institute (RCI)
Russell Sage Foundation (RSF)
savings and loan (S&L)

Sears Roebuck Acceptance Corporation (SRAC)
Security Bankers' Finance Corporation (SBFC)
travel and entertainment (T&E)
Veteran Administration (VA)

Notes

The following abbreviations will be found in the Notes:
BAK—Baker Library, Historical Collections, Harvard University, Allston, MA
CITI—Citigroup Archives, New York City, NY
RSF—Manuscript Division, Library of Congress, Washington, D.C.
NARA—National Archives, College Park, MD
NOW—Schlesinger Library, Historical Collections, Harvard University, Cambridge, MA

An Introduction to the History of Debt

1. William R. Hayward, *Money: What It Is and How To Use It* (Cambridge: Houghton Mifflin, 1917), 20.

2. Fannie Mae, more officially known as the Federal National Mortgage Association (FNMA), was created by the federal government in 1938 to buy and sell federally insured mortgages. The importance of FNMA in forging American mortgage markets will be discussed beginning in chapter 3.

3. See Martha L. Olney, *Buy Now, Pay Later: Advertising, Credit, and Consumer Durables in the 1920s* (Chapel Hill: University of North Carolina Press, 1991) for an insightful discussion of the growth of installment credit. This argument may seem functionalist on first glance, but the chapter elaborates the unexpected ways in which this outcome occurred contingently.

4. Robert M. Collins, *More: The Politics of Economic Growth in Postwar America* (New York: Oxford University Press, 2000), 38. As Collins has shown, above all else, the postwar economy was based on an assumption of growth. What Collins has not shown was how this intellectual framework translated into the real-world, everyday institutions under which people acted out their economic lives.

5. Elizabeth Warren, Teresa Sullivan, Jay Lawrence Westbrook, *The Fragile Middle Class* (New Haven: Yale University Press, 2000); Elizabeth Warren, Teresa Sullivan, Jay Lawrence Westbrook, *As We Forgive Our Debtors: Bankruptcy and Consumer Credit in America* (New York: Oxford University Press, 1989).

6. Much of the literature on consumer credit has focused on a cultural or inflationary explanation of the rise in consumer debt in the 1970s. See, for instance, Daniel Horowitz, *The Morality of Spending: Attitudes toward the Consumer Society in America, 1875–1940* (Baltimore: Johns Hopkins University Press, 1985); Robert Manning, *Credit Card Nation* (New York: Basic Books, 2000); Bruce Schulman, *The Seventies* (New York: Free Press, 2001); Juliet Schor, *The Overspent American* (New York: Basic Books, 1998); Lloyd Klein, *It's in the Cards: Consumer Credit and the American Experience* (Westport, Conn: Praeger, 1999); Brett Williams, *Debt for Sale* (Philadelphia: University of Pennsylvania Press, 2004); David Evans and Richard Schmalensee, *Paying with Plastic: The Digital*

Revolution in Buying and Borrowing (Cambridge: MIT Press, 1999); and Joseph Nocera, *A Piece of the Action: How the Middle Class Joined the Money Class* (New York: Simon & Schuster, 1994).

7. For a critical, yet less historically grounded view, see Williams, *Debt for Sale*. Similarly, Robert Manning refers to the "architects of the Credit Card Nation" as if the decades of long-term planning finally came to fruition in the 1980s (Manning, *Credit Card Nation*, 86.) I find the unintended nature of the economy both more believable and more terrifying than any plot.

8. Historians, sociologists, and economists refer to this process by any number of different labels such as "financialization," 'post-Fordism," "postindustrialism," and many other neologisms. I have attempted as much as possible to keep these terms, with all their accumulated debates, out of the text. Scholars have tended to focus more on describing this transition's effect on people rather than explaining why and how this transition occurred. I hope, in some partial way, to contribute to an explanation of personal debt's role in this change.

9. Lendol Calder's *Financing the American Dream* (Princeton: Princeton University Press, 1999) stands out as the foremost history of credit in the twentieth century, and even it ends in the 1930s. His self-described intention was a "cultural history" not a history of the "growth of certain industries," so it is somewhat unfair to criticize him for not producing the book he did not intend to write. Profit and production drive capitalism and to neglect them, even intentionally, I think overlooks key causal transformations in consumer credit, distorting the logic of its rise and the magnitude of its change. The social and cultural history of debt cannot, I think, be divorced from the business and politics of debt.

Other important books are Horowitz, *The Morality of Spending*, and Olney, *Buy Now, Pay Later*. Horowitz makes broad claims concerning moral thinking about debt but relies on a very narrow source base of a select few intellectuals and regionally specific budget surveys from the industrial North. Olney's arguments are very persuasive but focus primarily on the household installment buying decisions in the 1920s. I agree with her findings, but think that to understand the history of debt in the 1920s we need to look beyond the household to the firm. Like Calder, however, they both end before the World War II. Lewis Mandell's *The Credit Card Industry: A History* (Boston: Twayne Publishers, 1990) neglects the larger institutional, economic, and political context of the origin of the credit card, misattributing the origins of its practices with the bank and not the department store.

10. Cultural studies, of course, emerged as field deeply enmeshed with economic questions, most importantly with questions of class and control. As critic Terry Eagleton has noted, there has been a drift away from the material in the past thirty years within cultural studies, diluting the original importance of the field. See Terry Eagleton, *After Theory* (New York: Basic Books, 2004).

11. The history of American capitalism has witnessed a surging interest in the past few years. Important books of the 1990s, like William Cronon's *Nature's Metropolis* (New York: W.W. Norton, 1992), William Leach's *Land of Desire* (New York: Pantheon Books, 1993), and Thomas Sugrue's *The Origins of the Urban Crisis* (Princeton: Princeton University Press, 1996) began to synthesize

capitalism and the new social history, but the past few years have witnessed a true renaissance in the history of American capitalism. Sven Beckert's *The Monied Metropolis* (New York: Cambridge University Press, 2001), Lizabeth Cohen's *A Consumers' Republic* (New York: Knopf, 2003), Jefferson Cowie's *Capital Moves* (Ithaca: Cornell University Press, 1999), David Freund's *Colored Property* (Chicago: University of Chicago Press, 2007), Alison Isenberg's *Downtown America* (Chicago: University of Chicago Press, 2004), Meg Jacobs' *Pocketbook Politics* (Princeton: Princeton University Press, 2007), Robert Johnston's *The Radical Middle Class* (Princeton: Princeton University Press, 2003), Jennifer Klein's *For All These Rights* (Princeton: Princeton University Press, 2003), Shane Hamilton's *Trucking Country* (Princeton: Princeton University Press, 2008), Marc Levinson's *The Box* (Princeton: Princeton University Press, 2008), Bruce Mann's *Republic of Debtors* (Cambridge: Harvard University Press, 2003), Bethany Moreton's *To Serve God and Wal-Mart* (Cambridge: Harvard University Press, 2009), Stephen Mihm's *A Nation of Counterfeiters* (Cambridge: Harvard University Press, 2008), just to name a few, have all attempted to put labor and business back at the center of modern American history, but have not emphasized financial history.

12. For a few examples, see Rose-Maria Gelpi, *The History of Consumer Credit: Doctrines and Practices* (New York: St. Martin's Press, 2000); Ralph Harris, Margot Naylor, and Arthur Seldon, *Hire-Purchase in a Free Society* (London: Hutchinson & Co., 1961); and Victoria De Grazia, *Irresistible Empire: America's Advance through Twentieth-Century Europe* (Cambridge: Harvard University Press, 2005).

13. See Gunnar Trumbull, *Consumer Capitalism: Politics, Product Markets, and Firm Strategy in France and Germany*, Cornell Studies in Political Economy (Ithaca: Cornell University Press, 2006).

Chapter One
Making Credit Modern

1. Charles de B. Claiborne, "Finance Companies—The Banker's Viewpoint" (speech given at the annual meeting of the National Association of Sales Finance Companies, December 6–8, 1932, Ninth Annual Meeting), *Addresses at Annual Meeting, 1927–1937*, National Association of Sales Finance Companies, Baker Old Class Collection, Historical Collections, Baker Library, Harvard University, 2, BAK.

2. The tax code reflected the idea that all consumer borrowing was for convenience, in that it assumed that all interest-rate borrowing must be a business loan. All forms of interest—assumed to be only for business loans—were deductible. Today's mortgage deduction is but a residual of this older conception of borrowing. Not until 1986 were nonhousehold mortgage debts excluded from deductions.

3. Important exceptions to this assertion existed in rural areas, particularly in the sharecropping South, where profitability mattered less than social power.

4. "Mackey: Early History," folder "1917 Mackey Syndicate," box 123, Russell Sage Foundation Papers, Manuscript Division, Library of Congress,

Washington, D.C., 1–3. Hereafter I will refer to the Russell Sage Foundation collection as RSF.

5. Ibid., 3.

6. Ibid., 3–4.

7. "Loan Shark Tells Business Tricks; Foiled By Bureau," *Tribune* (Chicago) February 8, 1912, folder "1917 Mackey Syndicate," box 123, RSF Manuscript Division, Library of Congress, Washington, D.C.

8. Roy Rosenzweig, *Eight Hours For What We Will: Workers and Leisure in an Industrial City, 1870–1920* (Cambridge: Cambridge University Press, 1983), 53; Lizabeth Cohen. *Making A New Deal* (Cambridge: Cambridge University Press, 1990), chapter 2.

9. L. C. Harbison, "This List Shows 430 Occupations in which 6710 Borrowers Are Engaged," folder "1917 Mackey Syndicate," box 123, RSF.

10. L. C. Harbison, "Loans Made in Eight Offices in Illinois," folder "1917 Mackey Syndicate," box 123, RSF.

11. L. C. Harbison, Loan #6510, "No. 1," 1916, folder "1917 Mackey Syndicate."

12. Ibid., No. 1, Loan #6513.

13. Ibid., No. 1, Loan #6517.

14. Ibid., "No. 1" through "No. 6.".

15. Ibid., No. 2, #7143; no. 6, #14036.

16. L. C. Harbison, untitled table of profits for offices, folder "1917 Mackey Syndicate."

17. Harbison, "Loans Made in Eight Offices in Illinois."

18. "Mackey to Fight Usury Case" *Tribune* (Chicago), March 4, 1910, folder "1917 Mackey Syndicate."

19. Ibid.

20. Erd obituary, *Journal* (Chicago), folder "1917 Mackey Syndicate," box 123, RSF.

21. "Fattens on 'Loan Trust,'" *Journal* (Chicago), February 18, 1910, folder "1917 Mackey Syndicate," box 123, RSF.

22. Ibid.

23. Ibid.

24. He was accused of usury for the owning of Fidelity Trust Company, which lent money to borrowers but took a chattel mortgage in return. Jennie Nicholson borrowed $50, which in return she gave a chattel mortgage on her piano and other household goods. Six months later, Fidelity demanded $89 from her, which she did not have. They repossessed the piano and sold it for $200. She demanded the difference and was ignored. She sued for the difference. Ironically, this very problem of the difference between amount owed and recouped was the crux of the issue for installment sellers in the 1920s as well. However, by the 1920s such schemes, though not that rate of interest, were legalized. In this particular suit, the case was settled out of court. Nicholson received $110. "Mackey to fight Usury Case," folder "1917 Mackey Syndicate," box 123, RSF; "John Mackey, Society Man, Hushes 'Loan Shark' Suit," folder "1917 Mackey Syndicate," box 123, RSF; For a discussion and definition of chattel mortgage please see note 146.

25. "Mackey Sees No Stigma On Loans," *News* (Minneapolis), March 5, 1910, folder "1917 Mackey Syndicate," box 123, RSF.

26. This account of the origin of the small loan reform movement is drawn directly from Calder's *Financing the American Dream*, 124–35; Calder, 125 quoted in Glenn et al., *Russell Sage Foundation*, 1:3–11.

27. Calder, *Financing the American Dream*, 126.

28. Report of the Special Committee of International Government Labor Officials on the Enforcement of Laws Against Loan Sharks, (n.p., 1940), folder "Law Enforcement," box 1, RSF, Part 1, 1.

29. Calder, *Financing the American Dream*, 127; Wassam retreated to the academy and though active academically on these matters did not possess the public political presence that Ham did.

30. Ibid., 130.

31. Ibid., 134.

32. Ibid., 133.

33. Ibid., 4.

34. Ibid.

35. Ibid., 13.

36. Ibid., 143.

37. Ibid., 134.

38. Bankers Capital Corporation, *Industrial Banking: Its Contribution to Modern Business* (privately published, 1928), folder "General," box 147, RSF, 19.

39. Calder discusses, at length, the pains that these small loan lenders took to differentiate themselves morally from loan sharks. See Calder, *Financing the American Dream*, 135–47.

40. Joseph Budnowitz, "Pawnbroking: A Treatise on the History, Regulation, Legal Decisions, and a Comparison with Other Small Loan Agencies" (law thesis, Columbia University, 1931), folder "Levine: *The Law of Pawnbroking*," box 1, RSF, 25.

41. Budnowitz makes the argument that pawnbroking is the only universal, sound system of lending for the truly poor who are either unemployed, without furniture for collateral or friends who can co-sign. Because pawnbroking never leads to the mainstream of lending, I haven't discussed it very much. It is important to note that before the small loan reforms, pawnbroking, as well as loansharking, were very widespread in industrial America. See chapter 1 of Calder, *Financing the American Dream*, for more on pawnbroking.

42. Budnowitz, "Pawnbroking," 25.

43. Ibid., 29.

44. Calder, *Financing the American Dream*, 147. Though Calder mentions the charity and profit motives of lenders, I am making a sharper and more pointed distinction. He does not drive home the point about the importance of ample capital.

45. *Profits of Licensed Small Loan Companies,* folder "Profits," box 2, RSF.

46. "Mackey: Early History," 4.

47. P. E. Leake to C. M. Hindall, March 30, 1929, folder "P. E. Leake–J. H. Taylor Correspondence," box 124, RSF.

48. Ibid.

49. "Rufus DeWitt King, Booster of Georgia," *Atlanta Constitution*, April 24, 1933, folder "R. Dewitt King–Geo. H. Rosenbusch," box 123, RSF.

50. Untitled spreadsheet, folder "R. Dewitt King–Geo. H. Rosenbusch," box 123, RSF.

51. "Big Four Loan Sharks Launch Chain System," *New York World*, September 25, 1927, folder "R. Dewitt King–Geo. H. Rosenbusch," box 123, RSF.

52. Security Bankers Finance Corporation, 1928 Annual Report, folder "R. Dewitt King–Geo. H. Rosenbusch," box 123, RSF, 4.

53. Ibid.

54. Ibid., 7.

55. "Two Loan Sharks Coming to City," *New York World*, September 26, 1927, folder "R. Dewitt King–Geo. H. Rosenbusch," box 123, RSF.

56. William Shepherd, "They Turn Your Promise into Cash," *Collier's*, February 19, 1927, 52.

57. Ibid.

58. Ibid.

59. General Motors, Annual Report 1922, Historic Corporate Reports Collection, Historical Collections, Baker Library, Harvard University, 5–6. All General Motors and General Motors Acceptance Corporation annual reports are from the Historic Corporate Reports Collection at Baker Library.

60. Ibid., 5.

61. A similar transition happened in Europe with the introduction of the automobile. European finance companies modeled themselves on the American example. See Ralph Harris, Margot Naylor, and Arthur Seldon, *Hire-Purchase in a Free Society* (London: Hutchinson & Co., 1961), 23–24.

62. Martha Olney, "Credit as Production-Smoothing Device: The Case of Automobiles, 1913–1938," *Journal of Economic History* 44 (June 1989): 377–91.

63. Henry Hodges, "Financing the Automobile," *Annals of the American Academy of Political and Social Science* 116 (November 1924): 52.

64. Ibid.

65. T. E. Courtney, "The Future of Independent Finance Companies" (speech given at the annual meeting of the National Association of Sales Finance Companies, sixth meeting, 1929), *Addresses at Annual Meeting, 1927–1937,* BAK, 3–5.

66. General Motors, Annual Report 1924, 9.

67. Ibid., 2.

68. Ibid.

69. Milan Ayres, "Diversification and the Future of Financing," (speech given at the annual meeting of the National Association of Sales Finance Companies, fifth meeting, 1928), *Addresses at Annual Meeting, 1927–1937*, BAK, 4.

70. C. D. Rasp, "Rebates to Dealers" (speech given at the annual meeting of the National Association of Sales Finance Companies, sixth meeting, 1929), *Addresses at Annual Meeting, 1927–1937*, National Association of Sales Finance Companies, BAK, 2.

71. T. E. Courtney, "President's Address" (speech given at the annual meeting of the National Association of Sales Finance Companies, eleventh meeting, 1934), *Addresses at Annual Meeting, 1927–1937*, BAK, 5.

72. Arthur Newton, "Relations of Banking and Installment Sales Financing" (speech given at the annual meeting of the National Association of Sales Finance Companies, sixth meeting, 1929), *Addresses at Annual Meeting, 1927–1937*, BAK, 1.

73. Phillip Haberman, "The Finance Company: A Discussion Of Its Purposes And Functions:An Address Delivered Before Forum Of Philadelphia Chapter American Institute Of Banking" (speech given to the Philadelphia Chapter of the American Institute of Banking, April 1928), *Pamphlet Collection of the Sales Finance Association*, BAK, 3.

74. Ibid., 4.

75. Newton, "Relations of Banking," 1.

76. Victor Brown, "Operating a Successful Independent Finance Company" (speech given at the annual meeting of the National Association of Sales Finance Companies, sixth meeting, 1929), *Addresses at Annual Meeting, 1927–1937*, BAK, 2

77. Duncan, "Finance Companies from the viewpoint of the company," 1.

78. Haberman, "The Finance Company," 3.

79. Ibid., 3.

80. Ibid., 3.

81. Newton, "Relations of Banking," 1.

82. General Motors, Annual Report 1926, 10.

83. General Motors, Annual Report 1924, 5. Calculated by author.

84. General Motors, Annual Report 1919, 13; General Motors Acceptance Corporation, *Ninth Annual Report,* Annual Report 1928, 1.

85. General Motors, Annual Report 1923, 7.

86. General Motors, Annual Report 1925, 9.

87. General Motors Acceptance Corporation, Annual Report 1927, 1.

88. Shepherd, "They Turn," 53.

89. Ayres, "Diversification and the Future of Financing," 1.

90. General Motors, Annual Report 1926, 7.

91. General Motors Acceptance Corporation, Annual Report 1927, 2.

92. Ibid.

93. Ibid.

94. Ibid., 6.

95. Ibid.

96. Shepherd, "They Turn," 53.

97. Federal Trade Commission, *Report of the Federal Trade Commission on the Household Furnishings Industry*, vol. 3, *Kitchen Furnishings and Domestic Appliances*, October 6, 1924 (Washington: GPO, 1925), 38., 270.

98. R. Schuppe, "Standardization in Financing Commodities Other Than Automobiles" (speech given at the annual meeting of the National Association of Sales Finance Companies, sixth meeting, 1929), *Addresses at Annual Meeting, 1927–1937*, BAK, 4.

99. Federal Trade Commission, *Household Furnishings*, 38.

100. Ibid.

101. Ibid., 39.

102. Ibid.

103. Ibid.

104. Ibid.

105. Ibid., 40.

106. Other examples of this exist as well. Commercial Investment Trust, for instance, had arrangements with Hoover for vacuum cleaners and Landers Frary & Clark for washing machines. Most large commercial credit companies seem to have aligned themselves with large manufacturers, from whom they could make the most money. Smaller manufacturers were left to their own devices. See ibid., 40–41.

107. Ibid. These motors were not for automobiles, but other motor-driven durables.

108. Ibid., 38.

109. Ibid., 272.

110. Ibid. This analysis combines information from the table on 270 with the information from the finance company "prospectus" on 272–73. I have inferred that the unnamed company referred to is the Purchase Corporation since the numbers used on 272–73 are identical to those on 270. In any case, it does refer to a finance company, if not the Purchase Corporation, as I have inferred, then another one that the Federal Trade Commission investigated.

111. Ibid., 273.

112. Ibid., 271.

113. "Terms of typical installment illustrations advised by finance companies with implied rates of interest paid by purchasers," Table 76 in ibid., 270.

114. Ibid., 2.

115. Newton, "Relations," 3.

116. Ibid.

117. General Motors, Annual Report 1929, 1.

118. "Display Ad No. 55," *New York Amsterdam News*, November 29, 1922, 10.

119. GMAC v. Weinrich, 218 Mo. App. 68; 262 S.W. 425 (Mo. App, 1924).

120. Federal Trade Commission, *Household Furnishings*, vol. 1, 3.

121. Ibid., Vol. 1, "Table 48—Shares Of The Consumer's Dollar," 137.

122. Legal Aid Society (LAS, AR) (New York, NY), *Forty-eighth Annual Report for the year 1923*, Annual Report 1923, 50.

123. Ibid.

124. Ibid., 51.

125. Ibid.

126. Ibid., 50.

127. Ibid., 101.

128. Ibid., 102. It is impossible to know whether this higher fraction reflects the higher prices charge by installment houses or an actual higher volume of goods sold. Since the non-installment or lesser-installment houses turned over

their inventory more frequently than the installment houses, it is an uncertain figure at best.

129. Legal Aid Society (New York, NY), *Fiftieth Annual Report for the Year 1925,* Annual Report 1925, 56, 58.

130. Ibid., 56.

131. Ibid.

132. Ibid., 57.

133. Ibid. See also a description of this as a general industry practice in Federal Trade Commission, *Household Furnishings Industries,* vol. 1, 17.

134. LAS, AR 1925, 57.

135. Ibid.

136. Federal Trade Commission, *Household Furnishings*, vol. 1, 17.

137. LAS, AR 1923, 51.

138. Ibid., 52.

139. Federal Trade Commission, *Household Furnishings*, vol. 1, 129–30.

140. This argument runs counter to those made today by credit reformers, who believe that when loan originators hold on to the debts they will be more scrupulous in their lending practices. Clearly an incentive to avoid overlending is necessary, but removing the ability to resell debt can be pernicious as well.

141. Ronald Ransom, "Notes of Meeting with Association of Credit Apparel Stores," June 2, 1942, folder "(Apr–Jun 10, 1942)," box "502.3 – Installment Sales Credit," RG 82, National Archives, College Park, Maryland, 7.

142. Calder, *Financing the American Dream*, 151.

143. Archie Chadbourne, "Debt is the only adventure a poor man can count on," *American Magazine*, (December 1927), 44.

144. Ibid., 45.

145. Gene Smiley, "A Note on New Estimates of the Distribution of Income in the 1920s," *Journal of Economic History*, vol. 60, No. 4 (Dec., 2000): 1120–28.

146. Charles Hanch, "Should We Stop Installment Buying?: The Case for Installment Buying," *Forum and Century* 77 (May 1927): 651.

147. Ibid., 665.

148. Samuel Crowther, "We're Going to Stay Rich Now," *Collier's,* (January 30, 1926), 29.

149. See Calder, *Financing the American Dream*, 181, for his discussion of the "image of the female credit abuser" which does not as explicitly discuss the idea of guidance, control, and marriage, but does trace out a longer genealogy.

150. Anonymous, "Please Remit," *Saturday Evening Post.* (November 11, 1922), 22.

151. Ibid.

152. Ibid.

153. Nancy Cott, *Public Vows: A History of Marriage and the Nation* (Cambridge: Harvard University Press, 2000), 167. Cott discusses how "marriage and motherhood were assumed to be every woman's hope" and despite some vocal opposition from political activists, most women continued to see marriage and employment as mutually exclusive, with marriage being the preferred state, both economically and socially.

154. Albert Gregg, "People Who Are 'Slow Pay,'" *American Mercury*, March 1920, 48.
155. Ibid., 105.
156. Katherine Sproehnle, "You Furnish The Girl," *Collier's* 77 (February 20, 1926), 30.
157. Ibid.
158. Ibid.
159. Ibid.
160. "Please Remit," 88.
161. Samuel Reyburn, "Charge It," *Collier's*, (October 31, 1925), 25.
162. Gregg, "People Who Are 'Slow Pay,'" 105.
163. Ibid.
164. Arthur Little, "Getting On In the World." *Saturday Evening Post* 200 (December 24, 1927), 28.
165. Anonymous, "Debtor's Cowardice," *Saturday Evening Post* 194 (February 11, 1922), 23.
166. Ibid., 23.
167. Ibid., 23, 89.
168. Ibid., 89.
169. Ibid., 94.
170. Ibid., 93.
171. Ibid., 90.
172. Shepherd, "They Turn," 9.
173. Ibid., 52.
174. William Shepherd, "People Are Honest," *Collier's* 80 (November 21, 1927), 32.
175. *Collier's*, 77 (June 12, 1926), 20.
176. Ibid.
177. Ibid.
178. General Motors, Annual Report 1925, 9.
179. Couzens, "Installment Buying," 81.
180. This finance system, historians have argued, helped turn all those European immigrants into "white" Americans. While I do not explicitly engage the history of race construction, I hope that the effects of this literature on my work are evident. See, in particular, Matthew Jacobson, *Whiteness of a Different Color: European Immigrants and the Alchemy of Race* (Cambridge: Harvard University Press, 1998), and George Lipsitz, *The Possessive Investment in Whiteness* (Philadelphia: Temple University Press, 1998).

Chapter Two
Debt and Recovery

1. Franklin Roosevelt, "Second Fireside Chat—'What We Have Been Doing and What We Are Planning To Do," May 7, 1933, *The Public Papers and Addresses of Franklin D. Roosevelt*, vol. 2 (New York: Random House, 1938), 160.
2. Franklin Roosevelt, "Inaugural Address," March 4, 1933, ibid., 11–13.

3. Leon Henderson, "Small Loan Companies in Depression Periods," *The Robert Morris Associates* (May 1932), Folder "Abuses," Box 106, RSF, 240.

4. Roosevelt, "Second Chat," *The Public Papers*, 165.

5. Though, of course, FDR did not have the easy access to data that we enjoy today. Our statistical rendering of the economy was itself a by-product of the New Deal.

6. Franklin Roosevelt, "Three Essentials for Unemployment Relief. (CCC, FERA, PWA)," Speech to Congress, March 21, 1933, *The Public Papers*, vol. 2, 80.

7. *Economic Report of the President 1969* (Washington: GPO, 1969), 228. Recalculated from 1958 dollars to 2004 dollars.

8. Personality conflicts and internal politics no doubt mattered, but as I am more concerned with outcomes, I have focused on the intellectual history of the different positions and institutions.

9. Before the federal intervention in mortgage markets "the average family went along, budgeting for the interest payments on the mortgage, subconsciously regarding the mortgage itself as written for an indefinite period, as if the lender was never going to want his money back but would just be content to keep it out at interest forever. This impression, which the home owner built up when things were going fine, was strengthened by the fact that lenders most frequently did renew the mortgage over and over again when money was plentiful. They usually charged a fee for the renewal, which added to the high cost of financing, but even this did not give the home owners then any notion of the real dangers to their own financial stability to which this procedure could give rise in time of stress. " Federal Home Loan Bank Board, *The Federal Home Loan Bank System, 1932–1952* (Washington: GPO, 1952), 3.

10. To amortize a loan means that every month the borrower pays back both the interest on the loan as well as some fraction of the principal. "Un-amortized" means that there is no structured way for borrowers to repay the borrowed funds. Borrowers have to exert discipline and save up the principal. It is standard today, but in this period was primarily found in installment purchasing plans, as made clear in chapter 1.

11. By the end of the decade, there did exist some mortgages amortized over ten years. But these mortgages were in the extreme minority. Overall, terms on mortgages were highly variable.

12. Congress, Senate, Committee on Banking and Currency, *National Housing Act: Hearing on S. 3603*, 73rd Cong., 2nd sess., May 16–24, 1934, 198.

13. Miles Colean, *The Impact of Government on Real Estate Finance in the United States*, Financial Research Program IV: Studies in Urban Mortgage Financing No. 2, (New York: NBER, 1950), 81.

14. Leo Grebler, David M. Blank, and Louis Winnick, *Capital Formation and Residential Real Estate: Trends in Prospects*, Studies in Capital Formation and Financing (Princeton: Princeton University Press, 1956), 163.

15. Carl F. Behrens, *Commercial Bank Activities in Urban Mortgage Financing*, Studies in Urban Mortgage Financing (New York: H. Wolff Book Manufacturing Co., 1952), 18–19.

16. Grebler et al., *Capital Formation*, 202.
17. *New York Times*, June 17, 1934.
18. Federal Housing Administration, *Bulletin for Manufacturers, Advertising Agencies & Publishers* (Washington: GPO, 1934), 5.
19. Ibid.
20. Ibid.
21. Ibid.
22. Congress, *National Housing Act: Hearing on S. 3603*, 217.
23. Franklin Roosevelt, "A Message Asking For Legislation to Save Small Home Mortgages From Foreclosure," April 13, 1933, *The Public Papers and Addresses of Franklin D. Roosevelt*, vol. 2 (New York: Random House, 1938), 136.
24. The HOLC issued bonds to the original creditor in exchange for the mortgages. The HOLC then extended the terms of the mortgages.
25. C. Lowell Hariss, *History and Policies of the Home Owners' Loan Corporation*, Studies in Urban Mortgage Financing (New York: H. Wolff Book Manufacturing Company, 1951), 17. Table 1.
26. Ibid., 21–22, Table 2.
27. Ibid., 23, 29.
28. Ibid., 31.
29. Ibid., 17, Table 1.
30. Ibid., 1, 10.
31. Ibid., 75, 101.
32. *New York Times*, December 16, 1934.
33. "Ickes Corporation To Rebuild Slums," *New York Times*, October 29, 1933.
34. Ibid., 101.
35. *New York Times*, October 29, 1933.
36. Federal Emergency Administration of Public Works, *The American Program of Low-Rent Public Housing* (Washington: GPO, 1934), 4–5.
37. "PWA Funds Build 'Useful Projects," *New York Times*, December 1, 1933.
38. *New York Times*, October 29, 1933.
39. Gail Radford, *Modern Housing for America* (Chicago: University of Chicago Press, 1996), 91; See chapter 4 for the best examination of the origin and collapse of the PWA housing program. Whereas Radford's book sees the battles surrounding public housing as the most important aspect of the New Deal housing system, I focus on how New Deal housing policies remade private financial systems.
40. "Ickes Urges Billions For Larger PWA Plan," *New York Times*, November 15, 1934.
41. Radford, *Modern Housing for America*, 91.
42. "Slum Aid Interest Declared Too High," *New York Times*, January 28, 1934.
43. "7 Slum Projects Rescinded By PWA," *New York Times*, March 11, 1934.
44. Harold Ickes, "2,886 Million Hours' Work Provided by PWA Program," *New York Times*, June 17, 1934.

45. Ibid.

46. Like most Fed economists in the 1920s, Riefler held that during a recession the Federal Reserve ought to extend less credit because member banks would have fewer investment opportunities. While counterintuitive today, this seemingly baffling theory, called the Real Bills doctrine, grew out of the longstanding belief that the proper role for federal credit was for productive business investment and not macroeconomic control. Some economists have blamed Riefler, as a key proponent of this doctrine, for the contractionary monetary policy that contributed to the Depression. Reversing his 1920s outlook, Riefler's advice to Roosevelt's inner circle encouraged the expansion of credit in a daring new way. (Allan H. Meltzer, *A History of the Federal Reserve* [Chicago: University of Chicago, 2004], 271–75.)

Allan Meltzer blames the "Riefler-Burgess doctrine" for the Fed's policy in the late 1920s and early 1930s. In contrast, David Wheelock's view is the Fed, instead of consciously pushing for a contractionary policy, misunderstood increased member borrowing as a sign of a *expanding* rather than a *contracting* economy, leading to fewer open market purchases. Confusion over information, rather than confusion over monetary theory, in his view, led to the contractionary Fed policies. (David C. Wheelock, "Member Bank Borrowing and the Fed's Contractionary Monetary Policy During the Great Depression," *Journal of Money, Credit, and Banking* 22, no 4 (1990): 411–14.)

47. Congress, *National Housing Act: Hearing on S. 3603*, 49.

48. Ibid., 50.

49. FHA, *FHA Story in Summary, 1934–1959* (Washington: GPO, 1959), 4.

50. Ibid.

51. FHA, *Architects, Contractors, Building Supply and Other Merchants* (Washington: GPO, 1934), 4.

52. While Title I and Title II were implemented quickly, Title III of the National Housing Act, which authorized the FHA administer to charter private National Mortgage Associations, was not used until 1938. Private investors did not want to enter this field of buying and selling. Not until 1938 did Roosevelt request the Reconstruction Finance Corporation to provide the capital and management for a government-sponsored Federal National Mortgage Association (FNMA). (Federal National Mortgage Association, *Background and History of the Federal National Mortgage Association* (n.p., 1969), 4–7.)

53. FHA, *Mutual Mortgage Insurance: Administrative Rules and Regulations under Title II of the National Housing Act* (Washington: GPO, 1935).

54. Ibid., 3.

55. The lender paid 0.5 percent of the principal into the fund on the first day the mortgage took effect, and every year thereafter until the mortgage was paid off. The FHA classified mortgages into risk groups with similar maturity dates, so that excess fees paid into the fund could be returned in timely fashion and a fair manner. Everyone got all their money back if there were no defaults. (Ibid., 8–9).

56. Congress, *National Housing Act: Hearing on S. 3603*, 50.

57. "Sees 'Rent Dole' In Public Housing," *New York Times*, October 28, 1934.

58. FHA, *Architects, Contractors,* 4.

59. Congress, *National Housing Act: Hearing on S. 3603*, 162.

60. Ibid., 157.

61. Ibid.

62. *New York Times*, August 20, 1934. That is, individual loans could be reimbursed for 100 percent of losses, as long as those loans were no more than 20 percent of total loan volume.

63. *New York Times*, June 17, 1934.

64. The first foreclosure was reported in September of 1935.

65. *New York Times*, June 17, 1934.

66. *New York Times*, November 2, 1934.

67. *New York Times*, November 2, 1934; $16,000 in 1934 is $225,552 in 2004 dollars.

68. "Revival Due in Home Construction As a Result of 5% Interest Rate," *New York Times*, November 4, 1934; John M. Gries and Thomas M. Curran, U.S. Department of Commerce, Bureau of Standards, Division of Building and Housing, *Present Home Financing Methods* (Washington: GPO, 1928), 10.

69. Gries and Curran, *Present Home Financing Methods*, 9.

70. *New York Times*, November 2, 1934.

71. In contrast, HOLC mortgages permitted junior loans as long as they did not exceed the HOLC appraisal price. FHA practices really were a decisive with past banking practices. *History and Policies of the Home Owners' Loan Corporation*, 35.

72. Hariss, *History and Policies of the Home Owners' Loan Corporation*, 7.

73. FHA, *Here is the Housing Market* (Washington: GPO, 1941), 62.

74. Ibid., 58.

75. For a principal of $5,000, and assuming a fixed interest rate of 3.5 percent, each additional five-year period reduces the monthly payment, but increases the interest payment. Eventually, the rise in interest, which is amortized, offsets the decreased monthly payment, which is why, after twenty-five years or so, additional time does not really lower the monthly payment. But to increase the mortgage from three to ten years certainly makes a big difference in the monthly payment.

76. "President Orders 5% Interest Rate on Housing Loans," *New York Times*, November 2, 1934.

77. "Home Rehabilitation Loans," *New York Times*, August 17, 1934.

78. *New York Times*, November 2, 1934.

79. "Prepare To Insure Home Mortgages," *New York Times*, October 14, 1934; *New York Times*, November 2, 1934. This interest rate of 6 percent becomes important because it is deemed the fair rate by the government, which shapes how borrowers, in other kinds of loans, think about what they should pay for money; also remarkable was the plan that if the defaults were low enough, that money would then be used to pay off the mortgages themselves.

80. FHA, *First Annual Report* (Washington: GPO, 1935), 19. This separation of funds becomes important in the creation of a secondary mortgage market, discussed later.

81. "Banks and Trade Praise Housing Act," *New York Times*, July 23, 1934; "Vast Federal Housing Program Set Out," *New York Times*, August 5, 1934.

82. Harold Ickes, *The Secret Diary of Harold Ickes* (New York: Simon and Schuster, 1953), 234.
83. "Housing Chief Links Homes to Recovery," *New York Times*, October 7, 1934.
84. FHA, *How Owners of Homes & Business Property Can Secure the Benefit of the National Housing Act* (Washington: GPO, 1934), 7.
85. FHA, *Architects, Contractors*, 20.
86. FHA, *How Owners*, 7–9.
87. Ibid., 8.
88. FHA, *First Annual Report* (Washington: GPO, 1935), 1.
89. *New York Times*, October 6, 1934.
90. *Wall Street Journal*, November 3, 1934.
91. "Sees FHA Restoring Faith in Real Estate," *New York Times*, December 8, 1934.
92. "Bankers Urged To Aid FHA in Mortgages," *New York Times*, December 24, 1934.
93. FHA, *First Annual Report*, 11.
94. This plan is in stark contrast to the conflicts surrounding PWA housing programs.
95. Field Division, FHA, *Better Housing* 1, no. 5 (1934): 1.
96. FHA, *Local Chairmen of Better Housing Committees, Appointed and Reported to March 19, 1935* (Washington: GPO, 1935), 86.
97. FHA, *Better Housing* 1, no 8 (1934): 1.
98. FHA, *Bulletin for Manufacturers*, 4.
99. FHA, *Architects, Contractors*, 4.
100. FHA, *Bulletin for Manufacturers*, 4.
101. FHA, *First Annual Report*, 11.
102. FHA, *Better Housing* 1, no 8 (1934): 1.
103. Ibid., 3, 8.
104. "Lumber Head Asks PWA Housing Halt," *New York Times*, November 26, 1934.
105. FHA, *First Annual Report*, 2.
106. "33 Northern Cities Break Deadlock in Winter Work," *Better Housing* (December 1934): 1.
107. "Large Manufacturers Report Gains in Volume up to 500 percent," *Better Housing* (December 1934): 2.
108. *Better Housing* (December 1934): 7.
109. FHA, *First Annual Report*, 12.
110. Franklin Roosevelt to James Moffett, March 6, 1935; folder "Correspondence between state governors and Pres. Frankling D. Roosevelt concerning FHA legislation 1934–35," box 1. Records of the Federal Housing Administration, NARA.
111. Federal Housing Administration, *Underwriting Manual: Underwriting and Valuation Procedure under Title II of the National Housing Act* (Washington: GPO, 1936), preface.
112. FHA, *Third Annual Report* (Washington: GPO, 1937), 16.
113. *New York Times*, November 4, 1934.

114. FHA, *Underwriting Manual*, ¶304 (3)

115. This idea was the bedrock of 1920s and 30s installment financing theory. At any point, the value of the good would be at least equal to the amount it could get if resold. Theory is the important word here. Goods obviously depreciated at different, and often nonlinear, rates. But the good was expected to maintain some value over time, hence the anxiety surrounding lending for soft goods, like clothes, which could not maintain their resale value like furniture or automobiles.

116. FHA, *What is the FHA Plan?* (Washington, GPO, 1938), 2.

117. Refinancing existing mortgages under FHA was possible. There was a small premium of 0.5 percent above the normal rate. Still, this was only for refinancing already owned housing, not for the purchase of previously built housing. It still drove potential home owners to new housing stock.

118. FHA, *Underwriting Manual*, Part II, ¶133.

119. Ibid., ¶135.

120. Ibid., ¶136.

121. Ibid., ¶244.

122. Ibid.

123. Ibid.

124. Ibid., ¶236.

125. Ibid., ¶234.

126. Ibid., ¶266.

127. Ibid., Part I, ¶306 (2); Part II, ¶228.

128. Ibid., Part II, ¶208.

129. Ibid., Part I, ¶305 (1).

130. Ibid., Part I, ¶305 (2).

131. FHA, *Third Annual Report*, 17.

132. FHA, *Planning Neighborhoods for Small Houses*, Technical Bulletin No. 5 (Washington: GPO, 1936), 1.

133. Ibid., 3.

134. FHA, *Underwriting Manual*, Part II, ¶210 (d).

135. *New York Times*, December 30, 1934.

136. Thomas Sugrue, in *Origins of the Urban Crisis,* provides the best analysis of how government-insured financing co-created the suburb and the ghetto. Where his work looks at the racial consequences of FHA financing for the city, I focus more on how this form of financing shaped other fields of debt in the suburbs.

137. *New York Times*, October 29, 1933.

138. Congress, *National Housing Act: Hearing on S. 3603*, 179.

139. "Federal Housing Called Unsound," *New York Times*, May 20, 1934.

140. Donald B. Thorburn, "Bank Credit Goes on a Retail Basis," *Burroughs Clearing House* (October 1936), 10–11.

141. Federal Home Loan Bank Board, *The Federal Home Loan Bank System, 1932–1952* (Washington: GPO, 1952), 8.

142. Participation certificates were, in many ways, the earliest forms of mortgage-backed securities. After the passage of Glass-Steagall, they were suppressed as a financial instrument until their resurrection in the 1960s, as described in chapter 7.

143. Ernest Fisher, *Urban Real Estate Markets: Characteristics and Financing*, Studies in Urban Mortgage Financing (New York: 1951), 78; see also Hariss, *History and Policies*.

144. *New York Times*, November 2, 1934.

145. For more on the history of commodification and market-making, see Cronon, *Nature's Metropolis*.

146. *New York Times*, November 2, 1934.

147. FNMA, *Background and History*, 6.

148. Leo Grebler, *The Role Of Federal Credit Aids In Residential Construction*, Studies in Capital Formation and Financing (New York: National Bureau of Economic Research 1953), 42.

149. Known trading partners with repeated interactions exchanging federally tracked mortgages, differ substantially from what would evolve after the breakdown in the FHA mortgage system around 1970. See chapter 7 for details on the transformation to a true mortgage market.

150. Letter from James Moffett to FDR, October 30, 1934; Letter from FDR to James Moffett, November 1, 1934, reprinted, *New York Times*, November 2, 1934.

151. Grebler, *Capital Formation*, 229. The remaining difference can be explained through local variation in risk, not market imperfections. (A. H. Schaaf, "Regional Differences in Mortgage Financing Costs," *Journal of Finance* 21 (March 1966): 85–94.)

152. *New York Times*, November 2, 1934.

153. Ibid.

154. FHA, *Here is the Housing Market*, 11.

155. Willis Bryant, *Mortgage Lending: Fundamentals and Practice* (New York: McGraw Hill, 1962), 9.

156. Grebler, *Capital Formation*, 198.

157. Bryant, *Mortgage Lending*, 8.

158. FHA, *Third Annual Report*, vii–viii.

159. Ibid., 10.

160. FHA, *Sixth Annual Report* (Washington, GPO, 1940), 2–3.

161. FHA, *Third Annual Report*, 4.

162. Ibid., 7.

163. "Ickes Defines Aim Of Housing Funds," *New York Times*, November 24, 1934; "President Forces Accord On Housing," *New York Times*, November 25, 1934.

164. "PWA Pushes Ahead To Spend Millions," New *York Times*, November 27, 1934.

165. Radford, *Modern Housing for America*, 91; FHA, *Sixth Annual Report*, 30.

166. *New York Times*, November 27, 1934.

167. Grebler, *Capital Formation*, 29.

168. Ibid., 162.

169. James J. O'Leary, "Postwar Trends in the Sources and Uses Of Capital Funds," in *Proceedings of the Conference on Savings and Residential Financing, 1958* (Chicago: United States Savings and Loan League, 1958), 19.

170. At this point, it is important to remember for the contemporary reader that these mortgages were directly owned, whole mortgages, and not securitized mortgages. The investors owned the mortgages directly; they were not a claim on the mortgage. Indirect ownership of mortgages would not come until 1970. See chapter 7 for a length discussion of the origin of the mortgage-backed security.

Chapter Three
How Commercial Bankers Discovered Consumer Credit

1. J. Andrew Painter to Howard Laeri, August 16, 1976, folder "J. Andrew Painter," "Naetzker – Reichers," Oral History and Employee Memoirs, RG 12, Citigroup Archives, New York, NY, 2. Henceforth, references to the Citigroup corporate archives will be referred to as CITI. Painter was employed in the personal loan department on the first day of its creation and in 1952 took over after Steffan retired. This narrative, written as a letter by Painter in the late 1970s, recounts his life-long career at National City Bank.

2. Ibid., 3.

3. Ibid.

4. "Personal Credit Makes History in 10 Years," *Number Eight Magazine* 32 (May 1938), CITI, 2. *Number Eight Magazine* was the employee magazine of National City Bank.

5. "Our Entry Into Personal Loan Field Is Acclaimed By Nation's Press," *Number Eight Magazine* 23 (April/May 1928), CITI, 12.

6. Ibid, 12.

7. Bankers also commonly believed, as discussed in chapter 1, that loans ought to be invested in productive rather than nonproductive loans. The money invested from a business loan created more money, while the money spent through a consumer loan only purchased a commodity. While macroeconomically these two aspects might be entangled, well-trained bankers cared more about having their loans repaid with interest than sustaining consumer demand.

8. Painter to Laeri, 3.

9. Roy Rosenzweig, *Eight Hours For What We Will: Workers and Leisure in an Industrial City, 1870–1920* (Cambridge: Cambridge University Press, 1983), 53.

10. Frequently in this chapter I refer to bankers and borrowers alike as "he." This gender specificity is intentional as both bankers and prospective borrowers were usually men. Women could usually only borrow under their husband's names at personal loan departments.

11. Quoted in Thomas C. Boushall, *Bankers Monthly* (April 1935): 223.

12. *First Wisconsin Personal Loan Plan: Detailed Procedure with Forms* [1930], Box 92, Russell Sage Foundation Papers (RSF), Manuscript Division, Library of Congress, Washington, D.C.

13. "Our Entry," 25.

14. Dirk DeYoung, *Bankers Monthly* (May 1934): 278.

15. *First Wisconsin*, 3.

16. Quoted in Boushall, *Bankers Monthly* (April 1935): 223.

17. Irvin Bussing, *Report on Some Important Aspects of the Personal Loan Business From the Savings Bank Point of View to the Investment Committee of the Savings Bank Association of the State of New York* (1937), Folder "Savings Banks," Box 99, RSF, 2.

18. A. Cornelius Clark, *Bankers Monthly* (November 1932): 671.

19. Ibid.; as late as 1936, Bank of America advertisements for its personal loans explicitly connected establishing "valuable bank credit relationship" under the guise of personal loans and the ease of future business there (*Los Angeles Times*, February 18, 1936.)

20. Clark, *Bankers Monthly*: 671; this unintuitive computation confused people at the time as well. The reason for the 16 percent interest rate is the difference between being charged interest on the total or on the declining balance. If the loan was for a year, the average money loaned would be equal to half the initial loan, since at the beginning of the year the borrowed money would be $100 and at the end of the year it would be $0, with an average balance of $50. Eight divided by 50 is 16 percent. How to calculate interest rates was surprising controversial, running, as a side argument, through nearly all the scholarly and critical work on debt through the century.

21. Ibid., 672.

22. Quoted in Boushall, *Bankers Monthly*, 223.

23. Clark, *Bankers Monthly*, 672.

24. Chapter 2 focuses on the intended effects of the National Housing Act, describing how it nationalized and standardized mortgage practices in the United States. I argue that the specific ways in which home mortgages were remade set the stage for the expansion of other postwar consumer credit. Chapter 2 also discusses how Title I and Title II loan programs affected the housing industry and the American economy, as well as the process by which they were widely adopted.

25. Consumers could not use the program for movable durables like refrigerators.

26. FHA, *How Owners of Homes & Business Property Can Secure The Benefit Of The National Housing Act* (Washington: GPO, 1934), 7–9.

27. David C. Barry, "Consumer Financing And Its Relation To The Commercial Bank," *Journal of the American Statistical Association* (March 1938): 51.

28. J. H. Perkins to A. P. Giannini, March 13, 1934, National City Bank of New York – Bank of America Correspondence, 1929–1951, CITI, 1.

29. Lewis H. Kimmel, *The Availability of Bank Credit, 1933–1938*, conference board studies number 242 (New York: National Industrial Conference Board, Inc, 1939), 54.

30. *Economic Report of the President 1969* (Washington: GPO, 1969), 228.

31. John B. Paddi, "The Personal Loan Department of a Large Commercial Bank," *Annals of the American Academy of Political and Social Science* (March 1938): 135–41.

32. Kimmel, *Availability*, 52.

33. J. P. Huston, "Personal Loan Departments in Country Banks," *Mid-Continent Banker* (October 1935), Folder "Operating Techniques," Box 92, RSF.

34. Joseph D Coppock, *Government Agencies of Consumer Installment Credit,* NBER Studies in Consumer Installment Financing, vol. 5 (Camden: Haddon Craftsmen, 1940), 30. Table 3.

35. Painter to Laeri, 6.

36. "Steffan Made Director," *New York Times*, August 10, 1934, 2.

37. 'Resigns Housing Post," *New York Times*, December 21, 1934, 45; "Roger Steffan, Banker, 62, Dead," *New York Times*, December 28, 1955, 23.

38. Roger Steffan, "How Modernization Loans Benefit Property Owners, Business, and Banks," folder 001.401 – Steffan, Roger, box 4. "001.401 Russell, Horace to 001.411 Clayton, Lawrence," RG 82 Records of the Federal Reserve System Board of Governors Central Subject File, 1919–1954, National Archives, College Park, MD, 1.

39. Steffan, "How Modernization Loans," 4.

40. Painter to Laeri, 6.

41. Ibid.

42. Ibid.

43. Steffan, "How Modernization Loans," 5.

44. FHA, *First Annual Report*, 9.

45. The racial and gender limits of that new middle class limited access to the personal loans as well. On the social and economic origins of the new middle class please see Oliver Zunz, *Making America Corporate, 1870–1920* (Chicago: University of Chicago Press, 1990).

46. By the end of 1934, 72 percent of Title I loans had been made by commercial banks, compared to 22 percent for finance companies and 4 percent for industrial banks. FHA, *First Annual Report*, 9.

47. Ibid., 1.

48. Bussing, *Report on Some Important Aspects*, 2.

49. Paddi, "The Personal Loan Department," 136.

50. Bussing, *Report on Some Important Aspects*, 6.

51. Ibid., 2.

52. Ibid., 6.

53. See chapter 1 for a lengthier discussion of this convergence of small loan lending and the installment plan.

54. D. J. Defoe, "Helps Them Get On Their Feet: Five Per Cent Personal Loans With An Optional Savings Plan That Converts the Borrower Into a Saver and Investor," *Burroughs Clearing House* (September 1927), Folder "Operating Techniques," Box 92, RSF, 16.

55. "Gang Tactics Scored In Debt Collection," *New York Times*, January 8, 1940, 3.

56. During repossession, the borrowers lost the goods and all the money that had been paid for the goods. Equity loss in repossession, as explained in chapter 1, was the main threat to guarantee repayment.

57. Paddi, "The Personal Loan Department," 140.

58. "Depression Has Proven Harvest For Loan Shark," *Iron Mountain Michigan News* (September 1932), Box 106, RSF.

59. Bussing, *Report on Some Important Aspects*, 2.

60. Ibid., 3.

61. Painter to Laeri, 5.

62. "Bank Lowers Rate On Personal Loans," *New York Times*, May 12, 1936, 33.

63. Barry, "Consumer Financing," 53.

64. Paddi, "The Personal Loan Department," 136; Barry, "Consumer Financing," 54.

65. Paddi, "The Personal Loan Department," 136.

66. Ibid. John Paddi was, at the time, assistant vice-president of Manufacturer's Trust Company of New York and in charge of its personal loan department.

67. Barry, "Consumer Financing," 53; *Burroughs Clearing House,* "The Small Loans Setup" (January 1936), "Operating Techniques," Box 92, RSF, 12.

68. "Drop in Small Loans A Sign of Recovery," June 24, 1934, *New York Times*, XX2.

69. Rolf Nugent, *Banking* (December 1937): 26. These numbers are uncertain since the data is actually for those departments still existing in 1937. If a substantial number of departments folded from the early 30s, then these numbers would be more inaccurate the further into the past they went.

70. These numbers should be used as estimates since they were collected from a survey mailed to banks by Nugent when he worked for the Department of Remedial Loans of the Russell Sage Foundation. More accurate than the absolute numbers, I think, is the rate of change of loan balances and number of departments organized. Nugent felt that the loan balances probably reflected 90 percent of the actual total number, while the number of loan departments was probably only 75 percent of the actual number. See *Preliminary Report of the Personal Loan Department Study* (1937), Folder "Loans Receivable by Year," box 99, RSF.

71. FHA, *First Annual Report*, 1.

72. "To Extend Small Loans," *Burroughs Clearing House* (August 1936), Folder "Operating Techniques," Box 92, RSF.

73. Frank R. Sage, "Ideas for Building Small Loan Volume," *Burroughs Clearing House* (April 1940), Folder "Operating Techniques," Box 92, RSF.

74. "Personal Loan Business," *Wall Street Journal*, June 30, 1936, 7.

75. "Personal Loans Add to Revenues, Bankers Testify," *Wall Street Journal*, March 18, 1938, 8.

76. Federal Reserve, *Twenty-Fifth Annual Report of the Board of Governors of the Federal Reserve System Covering Operations for the Year 1938* (Washington: GPO, 1939), 23.

77. J. H. Perkins to A. P. Giannini, June 15, 1938, National City Bank of New York – Bank of America Correspondence, 1929–1951, CITI, 1.

78. "Display Ad 10 – No Title," *Los Angeles Times*, January 21, 1936, 12.

79. American Bankers Association, *Survey Of Personal Loan Department Experience And Practice*, Bulletin 74, May 1938 (New York: American Bankers Association, 1938). A survey letter was sent to "518 banks known to be doing a personal loan business of appreciable volume," of which 258 banks answered. The responses came from all over the country.

80. Ibid., 10, 18.

81. Ibid., 15.

82. Bussing, *Report on Some Important Aspects,* 7.

83. United States Department of Labor, Bureau of Labor Statistics, United States Department of Agriculture, Bureau of Home Economics, et al., Study Of Consumer Purchases In The United States, 1935–1936 [Computer file]. 2nd ICPSR ed. Ann Arbor, MI: Inter-university Consortium for Political and Social Research [producer and distributor], 1999. This data set is skewed in its sampling, but oddly it is skewed to contain exactly the population to which bankers reported lending. Unlike data used in later chapters, it cannot be used to discuss the different uses of debt between populations, because of this basic sampling problem. This figure of 10 percent should be considered a provisional estimate, which nonetheless is as good as anything else available. The variables that were used, variables 1376 and 1377, were described as "Notes due to banks, insurance companies, or small loans companies" and did not include mortgages. It cannot be ascertained whether these funds came from personal loan departments, industrial banks, or other sources. But it is useful to see that such a high fraction of the urban population was using small loans from some kind of institution.

84. This recurrent theme is addressed thoroughly in chapter 1. The expansion of this entire system was an adaptation to a widespread wage system, away from the farming system of pledged future assets. It was the division of industrial production reshaping the credit system.

85. *United States Investor*, "Borrowers of Little Sums" (June 6, 1936), 1.

86. Paddi, "The Personal Loan Department," 140.

87. *United States Investor*, "Borrowers of Little Sums," 3.

88. John Paddi, Manufacturers Trust Company, "Investigation Process" 1937; "Operating Techniques," Box 92, RSF, 1.

89. The reliance on salaried employees was based on the social separation of labor from the means of production.

90. Without a universal identification number, like the social security number, keeping track of individuals across many addresses and name spellings was extraordinarily difficult. The concerns over the number's as universal ciphers have been borne out in the past century.

91. American Bankers Association, *Survey of Personal Loan Department*, 10.

92. Paddi, "The Personal Loan Department," 136.

93. Paddi, "Investigation Process"; "Operating Techniques," 2.

94. John Paddi, Manufacturers Trust Company, "Functions of the Local Interchange Bureau" (1937), "Operating Techniques."

95. Paddi, "Functions."

96. John Paddi, Manufacturers Trust Company, "Address File" (1937), "Operating Techniques."

97. Paddi, "Address File."

98. Paddi, "Functions."

99. *United States Investor*, "Borrowers of Little Sums," 3.

100. American Bankers Association, *Survey of Personal Loan Department*, 19.

101. Ibid., 19. Median net profit rate calculated by author.

102. "Inevitable That More Banks Will Recognize Possibilities of Personal Banking," *Wall Street Journal*, May 31, 1938, 9. This was not on unpaid balances, so the actual annual interest was approximately double.

103. "Personal Loan Profits Of Banks Found Higher Than on Other Assets," *Wall Street Journal*, June 12, 1940, 6.

104. "National City Shows Increased Profit for 1938," *Wall Street Journal*, January 11, 1939, 9.

105. *Wall Street Journal*, "Banks Beginning to Consider Personal Loans As Integral Part of Their Business," May 28, 1938, 3.

106. Nugent, *Banking*, 26; the main reason I have focused this history, after this point, on commercial banks rather than other lesser capitalized institutions is that commercial banks so quickly and decisively overwhelmed their lending volume, once they became interested in consumer lending.

107. William Trufant Foster, *Consumer Loans By Commercial Banks*, Pollak Pamphlet 40 (October 1940), 12–13.

108. M. R. Neifeld, *Law and Contemporary Problems* (Winter, 1941): 31. He estimated that personal loan department extended $592,000,000 during 1939. In 2004 dollars this would be $8,045,280,000.

109. D. J. Defoe, "Helps Them Get On Their Feet: Five Per Cent Personal Loans With An Optional Savings Plan That Converts the Borrower Into a Saver and Investor," *Burroughs Clearing House* (September 1927), "Operating Techniques," Box 92, RSF, 16.

110. Michigan and Virginia because of the state banking department; Arkansas, Missouri, Illinois, Nebraska, Ohio, Pennsylvania, Texas and Oklahoma because of usury laws.

111. *Survey of Personal Loan Department*, 19.

112. Ibid., "Borrowers of Little Sums," 2.

113. Mr. Alexander to Mr. Horbett, "Office Correspondence: National City Bank of New York," folder "430.1–17 – Personal Loan Department data Call Report," box 2006 "430.1–2 1925–1946 to 430.1–17 1937," RG 82 Records of the Federal Reserve System Board of Governors Central Subject file, 1919–1954, National Archives, College Park, MD, 2.

114. American Bankers Association, *Survey of Personal Loan Department*, 20.

115. Donald B. Thorburn, "Bank Credit Goes on a Retail Basis," *Burroughs Clearing House* (October, 1936), 9.

116. "Bank Group Gains Stir," *Los Angeles Times*, January 2, 1936, 17.

117. Thorburn, "Bank Credit," 11.

118. "Display Ad 7 – No Title," *Los Angeles Times*, March 11, 1938, 7.

119. "Display Ad 5 – No Title," *Los Angeles Times*, October 14, 1938, 6.

120. "Display Ad 10 – No Title," *Los Angeles Times*, January 21, 1936, 12.

121. "Bank of America Gains 38% in Year," *New York Times*, January 2, 1937, 20.

122. Ibid., 20.

123. "Bank of America Building Program Totals $1,000,000," *Los Angeles Times*, May 16, 1937, E6.

124. Ibid.

125. Donaldson Thorburn, "Bank Credit Goes On a Retail Basis," *The Burroughs Clearing House* (October 1936), 9.

126. P. I. Caplan, "Blind Spots in Consumer Credit," reprint from September/October 1939 *Credit Executive*, "1935–1940 General," Box 166, RSF.

127. *Los Angeles Times*, January 21, 1936; Thorburn, "Bank Credit," 9.

128. "Personal Credit Makes History in 10 Years," *Number Eight Magazine* 32 (May 1938), CITI, 1.

129. Steffan, "How Modernization Loans," 6.

130. Thorburn, "Bank Credit," 10.

131. Industrial banks continued to cater to working-class Americans unserved by personal loan departments at commercial banks. (William Foster, "Consumer Loans by Commercial Banks," Pollak Pamphlet, [October 1940], Historical Collections, Baker Library, Harvard University, 17.)

Chapter Four
War and Credit

1. Diner's Club International Website, "Diners Club history overview and timeline," http://www.dinersclubnewsroom.com/anniversary.cfm, accessed on August 15, 2006.

2. Lewis Mandell, *Credit* Card *Use in the United States* (Ann Arbor: University of Michigan Press, 1972) and Lewis Mandell, *The Credit Card Industry: A History* (Boston: Twayne Publishers, 1990). Mandell's narrative of the credit card's origin provides the basis for most other histories of consumer credit. Other, more recent critical or sociological books, like Bruce Manning's *Credit Card Nation*, rely on Mandell's findings for their arguments about contemporary indebtedness. A better, yet still incomplete, account of the early credit card is the more obscure article by Timothy Wolters, "'Carry Your Credit In Your Pocket': The Early History of the Credit Card at Bank of America and Chase Manhattan," *Enterprise & Society* 1 (June 2000): 315–54. Wolters acknowledges the existence of pre-existing credit systems, but still privileges individual entrepreneurs over structural changes and policies in explaining the emergence of credit cards. The greatest weakness of his argument, however, is the Whiggish privileging of bank credit cards over department store credit cards in the development of consumer credit practices. In chapter 5, moreover, I argue that while travel and entertainment cards, like Diner's Club, were successful with certain kinds of businessmen, the more important shifts in consumer practices of credit were in department stores, which had little to do with these more discussed forms of credit. Americans, I argue, learned to use charge cards with locally branded department stores, not national credit cards like Diner's Club. Though today's credit cards have an institutional lineage with these early bank plan cards, the ways in which consumers practiced credit does not.

3. The last major work to discuss Regulation W was written in the early 1950s while it was still in effect. Robert P. Shay, *Regulation W: Experiment in Credit Control* (Orono, ME: Maine University Press, 1953). Usury laws had been in force for generations, but they operated at the state-level and regulated only the

maximum interest that a borrower could be charged. In many states, installment credit relations were outside of these laws.

4. As initially written, the Trading with The Enemy Act (1917), though giving the president broad powers over the import and export of bullion as well as "credits in any form," specifically excluded control over "transactions to be executed wholly within the United States." In the heady days of the banking holiday, however, Congress extended the president's powers over the economy, legalizing Roosevelt's initially presumptuous economic regulations. The Emergency Banking Act (1933) extended the powers the president had over banks, partially by granting him those powers directly and also by revising the Trading With The Enemy Act through which he had initially justified, however illegally, the bank holiday. Though most of the amendments in 1933 and in subsequent years focused on the president's power to control and regulate the export of bullion and use of foreign-owned property, there was also an extension of his power over domestic debts. The Trading with the Enemy Act allowed the president, during war or national emergency, to "regulate or prohibit . . . transfers of credit between or payments by or to banking institutions as defined by the President." – Though Roosevelt defined "banking institutions" to include loan companies, finance companies, banks and anyone "engaged in the business of making or holding extensions of credit," clearly it was odd to classify a furniture store as a bank. It was through this revision that Roosevelt justified his executive order for Regulation W in 1941. See Trading with the Enemy Act, October 6, 1917, 40 Stat. 411, 415; "History Of Sec 5(B) of The Trading with The Enemy Act And Actions Taken By The President Thereafter," September 24, 1941, "Constitutionality of Regulation W (Jan 1940–1954)," box "502.01," RG 82, NARA, 2–7; William H. Maulsby, "Memorandum for Mr. McInerney, Chief, National Defense Section," December 1, 1941, folder "Constitutionality of Regulation W (Jan 1940–1954)," box "502.01," RG 82, NARA, 2.

5. As discussed in earlier chapters, installment credit allowed consumers to buy goods, usually durable goods, with a contract over a fixed length of time, with a fixed interest. Each purchase had an associated contract. On default, the seller had the right to repossess the goods. Charge accounts, by World War II, were so-called convenience accounts at stores that consumers would repay at the end of the month. Charge accounts had no limit and no contract. Arrangements would be made ahead of time with the credit manager of a store, who would approve the account to purchase any goods within a store. In practice, many consumers would not repay at the end of the month. These "slow pays" might take sixty or ninety days to repay their debts. In terms of social meaning, installment credit was associated with a lower-class standing while charge accounts were associated with a more affluent rank of customer.

6. Rolf Nugent and Leon Henderson, "Installment Selling and the Consumer: A Brief for Regulation," *Annals of the American Academy of Political and Social Science* 173 (May 1934): 93–103.

7. Ibid., 102.

8. Rolf Nugent, *Consumer Credit and Economic Stability* (New York: Russell Sage Foundation, 1939), 237.

9. John Hamm, *The English Hire-Purchase Act, 1938: A Measure to Regulate Instalment Selling* (New York: Russell Sage Foundation, 1940), 4. The British system of installment purchases was more akin to today's "rent-to-own" than to the American installment credit regime (Hamm, 10).

10. J. D. Kemper, "Results of the 1939 C.M.D. Installment Selling Study," *Credit Management Year Book 1940* (New York: National Retail Dry Goods Association, 1940), 41.

11. "Confidential: Consumer Debt Under Regulation W," December 9, 1942, folder "(Oct–Dec 1942)," box "502.3 – Installment Sales Credit," RG 82, National Archives of the United States, College Park, MD, 6. Hereafter I will refer to materials from the National Archives as NARA.

12. Marriner Eccles, "Conference of Representatives of the Board of Governors of the Federal Reserve System with Representatives of the Federal Reserve Banks, in Connection with the Regulation of Instalment [sic] Credit, Thursday, August 14, 1941" folder "July–August 14, 1941," box "252.W – Regulation W," RG 82, NARA,, 6–7.

13. Ibid., 6.

14. Nugent, *Consumer Credit,* 244.

15. Eccles, "Conference," 8/14/41, 2.

16. Ibid., 3.

17. Dietz, "Conference of Board of Governors of the Federal Reserve Banks, Representatives of Government Agencies, and Representatives of the Trade in Connection with the Regulation of Instalment [sic] Credit Friday, August 15, 1941," 15 August 1941, folder "Aug 15–16—1941 Regulations FR Board," box "252.W – Regulation W," RG 82, NARA, 188.

18. Eccles, "Conference," 8/14/41, 3.

19. Ibid., 12.

20. Ibid., 1.

21. Ransom, "Conference," 8/14/41, 78.

22. Cargile, "Conference," 8/15/41, 74; Ransom, "Conference," 8/15/41, 73–74.

23. Henderson, on a personal level, lost his job and his prominence in policy-making circles. Not until his appointment by Roosevelt to the OPA did Henderson regain his stature ("Up Again Henderson," *Time Magazine*, May 1, 1939).

24. Ransom, "Conference," 8/14/41, 46.

25. Ibid., 74.

26. Parry, "Conference," 8/15/41, 75.

27. Ibid.

28. Eccles, "Conference," 8/15/41, 5.

29. Carpenter, "Conference," 8/15/41, 17.

30. Ransom, "Conference," 8/15/41, 14.

31. See Jacobs, *Pocketbook Politics* for more on the OPA rationing program.

32. Ransom, "Conference," 8/14/41, 75.

33. Rolf Nugent to Carl Parry, 25 July 1941, folder "July–August 14, 1941," box "252.W – Regulation W," RG 82, NARA,, 2; Carpenter, "Conference," 8/15/41, 20.

34. Ransom, "Conference," 8/14/41, 46.

35. Ibid., 13.

36. Ibid., 34–36.

37. Dietz, "Conference," 8/15/41, 118; refrigerators had such long-term lengths because sellers sold them at the same per month price as ice deliveries. If the consumer was used to paying X dollars per month for ice, she could pay the same and get the use of a modern electric refrigerator, which after three years she would own and not have to pay anything more. Such pricing schemes made installments fit the conventions of peoples' prices and budgets for their daily expenses.

38. Nugent to Parry, 7/25/41, 1.

39. Ibid., 2.

40. David Craig to Federal Reserve Board, August 18, 1941, folder "(Aug 17–Oct 10, 1941) Regulations FR Board," box "252.W – Regulation W," RG 82, NARA, 1.

41. Ibid., 3.

42. Parry, "Conference," 8/15/41, 52.

43. Nugent, "Conference," 8/15/41, 142–43.

44. Edward Brown to Ronald Ransom, August 16, 1941, folder "Regulations FR Board," box "252.W – Regulation W Aug 15–16 — 1941," RG 82, NARA, 1–2; Edward Brown, "Conference of Representatives of the Board of Governors of the Federal Reserve System with Representatives of the Federal Reserve Banks, Government Agencies, and the Trade in Connection with proposed Amendments to Regulation W Friday, September 26, 1941," September 26, 1941, folder "(Aug 17– Oct 10, 1941) Regulations FR Board," box "252.W – Regulation W," RG 82, NARA, 13.

45. B. E. Henderson, "Conference of Representatives of the Board of Governors of the Federal Reserve System with Representatives of the Federal Reserve Banks, Government Agencies, and the Trade in Connection with Proposed Amendments to Regulation W Friday, September 26, 1941," September 26, 1941, folder "(Aug 17– Oct 10, 1941) Regulations FR Board," box "252.W – Regulation W," RG 82, NARA, 70.

46. Ibid., 71.

47. Roger Steffan to Chester Morrill, August 16, 1941, folder "(Comment's on 8/14/41 Draft Regulation W – FRBoard)," box "252.002–W," RG 82, NARA, 1.

48. Ibid.

49. Roger Steffan to Chester Morrill, August 16, 1941, folder "Regulations FR Board," box "252.W – Regulation W Aug 15–16, 1941," RG 82, NARA, 1.

50. Edgar Fowler to Chester Morrill, August 18, 1941, folder "(Aug 17–Oct 10, 1941) Regulations FR Board," box "252.W – Regulation W," RG 82, NARA, 5.

51. Steffan to Morrill, August 16, 1941, Regulations FR Board, 1.

52. Ransom, "Conference," 8/15/41, 13, 49; for an expanded discussion of open book credit, its practices and uses, please see chapter 1. In this time, open book credit was also called charge account credit. By the late 1940s, retailers began to distinguish between regular charge account credit, which was open book

credit, and revolving charge account credit, which was the new form of revolving credit that, in 1941, did not exist.

53. M. R. Neifeld, "Institutional Organization of Consumer Credit," 8 *Law and Contemporary Problems* 23 (1941): 30.

54. Haverty, "Conference," 8/15/41, 63.

55. Ibid., 54.

56. Some very large companies, like Sears, could extend a massive amount of open book credit—but only because they had such a good reputation for repayment and such a large amount of money that it could be considered wholesale financing. Sears eagerly complied with the regulation, however and did not attempt to evade its proscriptions ("Conference," 8/14/41, 119–20).

57. Fry, "Conference," 8/14/41, 118; Though some open book financing existed, it was costlier and rarer than installment financing, because instead of selling the debt to a third party the retailer borrowed the money from a third party.

58. Ibid., 114; by the end of the 1930s, suspicions had begun to arise about the reality of "convenience credit." Many consumers, instead of paying off their accounts at the end of the month, spread payments over many months. This practice was never officially sanctioned by the retailer (Arthur Hert, "Charge Accounts of Retail Merchants," Annals of the American Academy of Political and Social Science (March 1938), 111–20.)

59. Regional Fed banks compiled lists of newspapers to which to send announcements. Dallas, for instance, had a list of 432 newspapers. By November, the Kansa City Fed had arranged 61 talks for over 6,500 people, as was typical of all branches. Fed officials in Minnesota, for instance, met with concerned citizens at the Duluth Chamber of Commerce Ballroom, the Grand Rapids Village Hall, and in Winona's High School Auditorium. "Conference," November 17–19, 1941, 23–24; J. N. Peyton to Banks, Retailers, Finance Companies, and Others Extending Consumer Credit, May 14, 1942, folder "Federal Reserve Bank, Minneapolis credit control – economics conditions," box "502.-c(9) Circulars Federal Reserve Boards," RG 82, NARA, 1.

60. Carpenter, Section 9(h), "Conference," 8/15/41, 33.

61. Ransom, "Conference," 8/15/41, 42.

62. Dietz, "Conference," 8/15/41, 105; Peterson, "Conference," 106.

63. Roscoe, "Conference," 9/26/41, 103.

64. "Federal Reserve Conference on Regulation W," November 17–19, 1941, folder "(Oct 11–Dec 1941) Regulations FR Board," box "252.W – Regulation W," RG 82, NARA, 20.

65. Roscoe, "Conference," 9/26/41, 103.

66. Chester Morrill to Presidents of all Federal Reserve Banks, January 28, 1942, folder "(1941–Jan 1942) Credit Control," box "502.7 – Enforcement," RG 82, NARA, 1.

67. "Conference," November 17–19, 1941, 29.

68. Ibid., 10.

69. Ibid.

70. "Confidential: Consumer Debt Under Regulation W," December 9, 1942, folder "(Oct–Dec 1942)," box "502.3 – Installment Sales Credit," RG 82, NARA, 7.

71. "Furniture Sales On Time Cut 35%," *New York Times*, September 13, 1942, F7; The South was harder hit, on average, than the North. The Atlanta district reported drops as high as 50 percent, while Boston reported only 25 to 30 percent.

72. "Confidential: Consumer Debt," 12/9/42, 7.

73. "Consumer Credit in the First Quarter of 1943," May 13, 1943, folder "(Jan–May 1943)," box "502.3 – Installment Sales Credit," RG 82, NARA, chart 2.

74. "Confidential: Consumer Debt," 12/9/42, 7; for additional data on other lines see F. B. Hubachek to Ronald Ransom, November 16, 1942, folder "(Oct–Dec 1942)," box "502.3 – Installment Sales Credit," RG 82, NARA, which contains hand-drawn charts on percent change per month in various lines of installment credit goods.

75. Walter Gatzert, secretary-treasurer of Spiegel's to Federal Reserve Board, September 3, 1943, folder "(Aug 19–Oct 1943)," box "502.3 – Installment Sales Credit," RG 82, NARA, 8.

76. "Confidential: Consumer Debt," 12/9/42, 9.

77. Ibid.

78. Ibid.

79. Edward Condlon, "Non-defense Loans Facing Extinction," *New York Times*, March 8, 1942, F1.

80. George Coleman, "Investment Practices of Commercial Banks," *Law and Contemporary Problems* (1952): 109.

81. "Conference," November 17–19, 1941, 10–11.

82. Ibid., 14.

83. "Additional Suggestions Relating to The Proposed Regulations Governing Extension of Instalment [sic] Credit," C. A. Sienkiewicz to Chester Morrill, August 16, 1941, folder "Regulations FR Board," box "252.W – Regulation W Aug 15–16, 1941," RG 82, NARA, 2.

84. Ransom, "Conference," 8/14/41, 65.

85. Ibid., 74.

86. Zurlinden, "Conference," 8/14/41, 74.

87. Alfons Landa, Association of Retail Apparel Stores to Federal Reserve Board, June 5, 1942, folder "(Apr–Jun 10, 1942)," box "502.3 – Installment Sales Credit," RG 82, NARA, 1; Other installment credit store owners wrote to the Fed, like Pittsburgh's Harris Stores Company's H. H. Smit, but their arguments only echoed those of this group (H. H. Smit to J. A. Schmidt, November 11, 1942, folder "(Oct–Dec 1942)," box "502.3 – Installment Sales Credit," RG 82, NARA.)

88. "Notes," 6/2/42, 8–9.

89. Ibid., 8.

90. Ibid., 3. Calculated by author from figures in the letter. The group claimed total sales in 1939 of $155,443,000 compared with total installment sales of $3,947,000,000.

91. "Notes of Meeting with Association of Credit Apparel Stores," June 2, 1942, folder "(Apr–Jun 10, 1942)," box "502.3 – Installment Sales Credit," RG 82, NARA, 2.

92. Alfons Landa, Association of Retail Apparel Stores to Federal Reserve Board, 5 June 1942, folder "(Apr–Jun 10, 1942)," box "502.3 – Installment Sales

Credit," RG 82, NARA, 4; Other installment credit store owners wrote to the Fed, like Pittsburgh's Harris Stores Company's H.H. Smit, but their arguments only echoed those of this group (H. H. Smit to J. A. Schmidt, November 11, 1942, folder "(Oct–Dec 1942)," box "502.3 – Installment Sales Credit," RG 82, NARA.)

93. Parry, "Apparel stores – information from Mr. Althaus," May 28, 1942, folder "(Apr–Jun 10, 1942)," box "502.3 – Installment Sales Credit," RG 82, NARA, 1.

94. Nugent, "Conference," 8/15/41, 121.

95. Ransom, "Conference," 8/14/41, 54.

96. Dorothy Brady, "Expenditures and Savings of City Families in 1944," *Monthly Labor Review* (January 1946): 1.

97. Parry, "Conference," 8/14/41, 56.

98. Dietz, "Conference," 8/15/41, 119.

99. C. Harrell and Roger Clouse to Carl Parry, 27 July 1943, folder "(Jun–Aug 18 1943)," box "502.3 – Installment Sales Credit," RG 82, NARA, 3.

100. Bonnar Brown, "Partial Payments in so-called Charge Accounts and Short-term Instalment Contracts," July 12, 1943, folder "(Jun–Aug 18 1943)," box "502.3 – Installment Sales Credit," RG 82, NARA, 1.

101. "Partial Payments," 7/12/43, 1.

102. Ibid., 2.

103. Ibid.

104. Ibid.

105. E. A. Heath to J. H. Dillard, "Serial Liquidation of Charge Accounts Administrative and Investigative Policy," May 10, 1944, folder "Apr 1944–Aug 1950," box "502.32 Open Account Installment Credit Consumer Credit," RG 82, NARA, 1; see also Edwin Gahan, "Retailers Oppose New Credit Curbs," *New York Times*, June 6, 1943, S6; also, Edwin Gahan, "Evasion of Curbs on Credit Fought," *New York Times*, October 4, 1942, F1.

106. "Partial Payments," 7/12/43, 3.

107. Harrell to Parry, 7/27/43, 3.

108. C. A. Sienkiewicz to Carl Parry, August 5, 1943, folder "(Jun–Aug 18 1943)," box "502.3 – Installment Sales Credit," RG 82, NARA, 1.

109. Regulators' examined past business practices, intervals of payment, ratio of purchase price to buyer's salary, store advertising, equality of partial payments, and use of payment books. Curiously, whether or not the account had finance charges or interest was not used to determine the type of credit (ibid., 1–2).

110. C. Harrell and Roger Clouse to Carl Parry, July 27, 1943, folder "(Jun–Aug 18 1943)," box "502.3 – Installment Sales Credit," RG 82, NARA, 1.

111. Commercial Credit Company, "Summary of Comments of Trade Association," Feb. 6, 1942, 3.

112. Paul Hodge to Carl Parry, May 21, 1943, folder "(Jan–May 1943)," box "502.3 – Installment Sales Credit," RG 82, NARA, 2.

113. Lewis Dembitz to Parry, "Regulation W — down payments on articles sold for $6 or less," December 31, 1942, folder "(Oct–Dec 1942)," box "502.3 – Installment Sales Credit," RG 82, NARA, 3.

114. Paul Hodge to Carl Parry, May 21, 1943, folder "(Jan–May 1943)," box "502.3 – Installment Sales Credit," RG 82, NARA, 2.

115. "Notes," April 27, 1942, 3. Three months is actually an approximation for the curiously worded regulation. The actual restriction was forty days from the end of the month in which the purchase was made. So if a purchase was made on the first of the month, then payment would have to be completed by the tenth day of the second month after the purchase. The maximum number of days was about seventy and the minimum was about forty. Later exceptions were made in July 1942 in Amendment No. 5 for stores that used "cycle-billing." Cycle-billing—bills sent in groups over the course of the month to reduce accounting expenses—required specialized equipment just coming into vogue, but also did not permit all bills to be paid before the 10th of the month. For companies using cycle-billing, an exemption was made to permit them to have the accounts paid by the "40th day following the last day of the applicable monthly billing period." Technology that made accounting and billing easier also locked businesses into practices that made regulations more difficult to enforce. Since cycle-billing had just begun for most businesses, however, relatively few retailers used the cycle-billing exemption. Regulation W was equated with the 10th of the second month following in both the popular and professional memory of the experience of the regulation. ("Amendment No. 5 to Regulation W," July 2, 1942, folder "(Apr 28–Dec 1942)," box "252.W - Regulation W," RG 82, NARA, 1.)

116. Notes from conference, April 27, 1942, folder "(Feb 16–Apr 27) Regulations FR Board," box "252.W - Regulation W," RG 82, NARA, 1.

117. "Conference," 27.

118. "Regulation W Proposed Amendment No. 3 (Consolidated) Summary of Comments of Trade Association of Sales Finance Companies and Three Large Finance Companies," 6 February 1942, folder "(Jan–Feb 15, 1942)," box "252.W - Regulation W," RG 82, NARA, 3.

119. Board of Governors of the Federal Reserve System, "Statement for the Press," May 5, 1942, folder "(Apr 28–Dec 1942)," box "252.W - Regulation W," RG 82, NARA, 1, 3.

120. Thomas Conroy, "Stores Expecting Rise in Cash Sales," *New York Times*, July 12, 1942, F1.

121. "'Frozen' Accounts May Be Under 25%," *New York Times*, July 14, 1942, 32.

122. "Charge Account Relationships in the Sixth Federal Reserve District," November 18, 1943, folder "Nov 1943 - Mar 1944," box "502.32 Open Account," NARA, 5–6.

123. Ibid., 5, 8.

124. C.B. Ritz to Ronald Ransom, May 3, 1944, folder "Apr 1944–Aug 1950," box "502.32 Open Account Installment Credit Consumer Credit," RG 82, NARA, 1–2.

125. E. A. Heath, "Discussion of Regulation W Des Moines, Iowa Friday April 14, 1944, Hotel Kirkwood 6:30 p.m.," April 21, 1944, folder "Apr 1944–Aug 1950," box "502.32 Open Account Installment Credit Consumer Credit," RG 82, NARA, 1.

126. "Discussion of Regulation W Des Moines," 4/21/44, 1.

127. Ibid.

128. Norman Cassaday et al. to Board of Governors, May 25, 1944, folder "Apr 1944–Aug 1950," box "502.32 Open Account Installment Credit Consumer Credit," RG 82, NARA, 1.

129. C. B. Ritz to Ronald Ransom, May 3, 1944, folder "Apr 1944–Aug 1950," box "502.32 Open Account Installment Credit Consumer Credit," RG 82, NARA, 2.

130. Ritz to Ransom, 5/3/44, 2.

131. Bonnar Brown and Theodore Smith, "Visit to Philadelphia August 20 and 21, 1943," August 23, 1943, folder "(Aug 19–Oct 1943)," box "502.3 – Installment Sales Credit," RG 82, NARA, 3.

132. Theodore Smith, "Trip to Cleveland, October 25, 26 and 27, 1943," November 3, 1943, folder "Nov 1943–Mar 1944," box "502.32 Open Account," NARA, appendix. Various credit cards, which were small paper rectangles with the customer's name and an identification number, were at the end of the Cleveland report.

133. Strawbridge & Clothier, "Credit Control Refer List," August 31, 1943, folder "(Aug 19–Oct 1943)," box "502.3 – Installment Sales Credit," RG 82, NARA, 1.

134. J. N. Adam Credit Card, "Trip to Cleveland," November 3, 1943, appendix.

135. Ibid.

136. Part of the difficulty in historicizing economic practices is the problem of definitions, which economists love and historians loathe. Revolving credit might be defined as credit extended by a retailer or bank in which the borrower expects to repay only a portion of the debt every month and to be charged a service fee and/or interest on the outstanding debt. Revolving credit is basically what we are all familiar with in contemporary credit cards. On the ground, however, historical divergence from definition becomes clear. In this period, revolving credit had a strict, very low, limit. Interest charges were small. It was suspect. Some retailers charged interest only after a few months or on the unpaid balance, while others charged at the end of the month on the entire amount borrowed. The practice was in flux and rather than strictly define it and then show deviation from that definition, I would rather show the set of practices surrounding consumer borrowing and how these practices were understood at the time by businesses and consumers. Yes, definitions were offered and imposed, but these were secondary to the flux and experiment. In later chapters, the way in which revolving credit is practiced changes in important ways, even though retailers and consumers continue to call it "revolving credit."

137. U.S. Department of Commerce, *Business Statistics 1961 Edition: A Supplement to the Survey of Current Business* (Washington: GPO, 1961), 85.

138. "Statement for the Press," November 15, 1946, folder "(Jan 1943–Nov 1946)," box "252. – W," RG 82, NARA, 1.

139. Bonnar Brown, "Visit to New York January 4–6, 1944," January 13, 1944, folder "(Nov 1943 – May 1945)," box "502.3 – Installment Sales Credit," RG 82, NARA, 1.

140. "Visit to New York," 1/13/44, 2.

141. J. A. Kaufman to Chester Morrill, April 28, 1944, folder "(Nov 1943–May 1945)," box "502.3 – Installment Sales Credit," RG 82, NARA, 2.

142. "Demand Truman End Regulation W," *New York Times*, November 9, 1945, 28; The Retail Credit Institute would later merge with the National Foundation for Consumer Credit, an important postwar pro-credit lobbying group and trade association.

143. "Demand Truman," 11/9/45, 28; see Bruce Schulman's *From Cottonbelt to Sunbelt* (New York: Oxford University Press, 1991) for more on the wartime movement of industry to the South and West.

144. "Visit to New York," 1/13/44, 2.

145. Ibid., 5.

146. Ibid., 2.

147. "Post-War Credits Draw Mixed Views," *New York Times*, March 19, 1945, 27.

148. Ibid.; Thomas Conroy, "Credit Sales Ratio Shows Rising Trend," *New York Times*, January 27, 1946, F5.

149. "Statement for the Press," November 15, 1946, folder "(Jan 1943–Nov 1946)," box "252. – W," RG 82, NARA, 1.

150. Evans and Parry to Board, 14 June 1946, folder "(Jan 1943–Nov 1946)," box "252. – W," RG 82, NARA, 2.

151. "Urges Sound," *New York Times*, 1/16/47.

152. Ralph Young, "Role of Instalment Credit Regulation in the Current Financial Situation," December 7, 1948, Remarks before the Capitol Group of the Controllers' Congress of the National Retail Dry Goods Association, Washington, December 7, 1948, folder "(Oct 1948–Feb 1949)," box "502.3 – Installment Sales Credit," RG 82, NARA, 9.

153. William Brian, "Charga-Plate Service In Action," *Credit Management Year Book 1947* (New York: National Retail Dry Goods Association, 1947), 296.

154. "Consumer Credit Expanding Swiftly," *New York* Times, October 20, 1946, F6; Thomas Conroy, "Push Drive to Build Charge Accounts," *New York Times*, September 30, 1945, 66.

155. "Push Drive," 9/30/45, 66; Cash sale had risen faster, however, and accounted for 78 percent of 1944 sales compared to 65 percent of 1941 sales. Installment sales volume had plummeted from 12 percent in 1941 to 3 percent of retail sales in 1944. This was calculated by the author from published volumes of retail sales by sales type.

156. Thomas Conroy, "Credit Sales Ratio Shows Rising Trend," *New York Times*, January 27, 1946, F5.

157. "Urges Sound Basis for Retail Credit," *New York Times*, January 16, 1947, 38.

158. Ibid.

159. "Business Bulletin," *Wall Street Journal*, October 2, 1947, 1.

160. Frank MacMillen, "Bank Loans to Aid Business at New Peak and Still Rising," *New York Times*, August 18, 1946, 65.

161. "Consumer Credit Expanding Swiftly," *New York Times*, October 20, 1946, F6.

162. Ibid.

163. Ibid.

164. "Store Group Sets a 9-Year Record," *New York Times*, April 2, 1940, 37.

165. The editor of a postwar credit manager's yearbook noted that, "This type [revolving credit] of account was generally discontinued during the existence of Regulation W in its original form. However, after termination of Regulation W on November 2, 1947, they were revived and continue to operate under the revised regulation." ("Revolving Credit Analyzed," 118).

166. Proquest, the online full-text archive of the *New York Times*, contains only three advertisements for "permanent budget accounts" before 1946, after which they become more common for Bloomingdale's, and then other stores. Before 1946, the advertisements for permanent budget accounts were part of larger advertisements, while after 1946 they become the central point of the advertisements; "Display Ad 10 – No Title," *New York Times*, June 12, 1942, 7. See also "Credit Practices Revised by Stores," *New York Times*, May 7, 1942, 34. This ruling also affected the relatively common "ten-payment" plan for men's clothing, which was subsumed under the revolving credit programs in the postwar.

167. Ibid.

168. Ibid.

169. Robert O'Hagan, "Latest Developments in Revolving Credit," *Credit Management Year Book 1949* (New York: National Retail Dry Goods Association, 1949), 370.

170. John Kemper, "Credit Identification and Authorization Policies," *Credit Management Year Book 1947* (New York: National Retail Dry Goods Association, 1947), 272.

171. O'Hagan, "Latest Developments in Revolving Credit," 370.

172. Robert O'Hagan, "Bloomingdale's Permanent Budget Account," *Credit Management Year Book 1947* (New York: National Retail Dry Goods Association, 1947), 248.

173. Ibid.

174. R. H. Bulte, "Revolving Credit Analyzed," *Credit Management Year Book 1948* (New York: National Retail Dry Goods Association, 1948), 114.

175. Ibid., 243. Bloomingdale's had silver plates for the regular accounts and brown plates for the PBA accounts.

176. William Brian, "Charga-Plate Service In Action," *Credit Management Year Book 1947* (New York: National Retail Dry Goods Association, 1947), 296.

177. Ibid.

178. Ibid.

179. Farrington Manufacturing encouraged retailers to move to a centralized model. By the mid-1940s they were promoting a group Charga-Plate plan that combined Charga-Plate accounting and billing operations for many different stores, even of different companies. One Charga-Plate would work at different stores. (Ibid., 297).

180. Coupon books complicated the enforcement of department store credit during World War II. While the coupon book made life easier for the credit manager, it also made it harder on Fed officials. Such coupon books could be used for

any goods in the store and allowed an easy evasion of the down payment requirements for Regulation W, since they were equivalent to cash at checkout. Should all coupons have down payments, which would affect even non-listed articles, or should there be special Regulation W coupon books, which would increase the clerical headaches for department store credit departments? Eventually, stores created two coupon systems or excluded restricted goods from purchase with coupons. (Lewis Dembitz to Parry, "Regulation W – down payments on articles sold for $6 or less," December 31, 1942, folder "(Oct–Dec 1942)," box "502.3 – Installment Sales Credit," RG 82, NARA, 1–5.)

181. Kemper, "Results of the 1939 C.M.D. Installment Selling Study," 42.

182. Bulte, "Revolving Credit Analyzed," 113.

183. Ibid., 124, 131.

184. Bolen, "Revolving Credit Analyzed," *Credit Management Year Book 1948* (New York: National Retail Dry Goods Association, 1948), 115.

185. Ray Johnson, "Step-By-Step Planning and Installation of Revolving Credit," *Credit Management Year Book 1948* (New York: National Retail Dry Goods Association, 1948), 136.

186. S. C. Patterson, "Advantages of Revolving Credit and How to Capitalize on Them," *Credit Management Year Book 1951* (New York: National Retail Dry Goods Association, 1951), 221.

187. O'Hagan, "Bloomingdale's Permanent Budget Account," 246.

188. Watkins, "Revolving Credit Analyzed," *Credit Management Year Book 1948* (New York: National Retail Dry Goods Association, 1948), 116.

189. Norman Smith, "Revolving Credit Analyzed," *Credit Management Year Book 1948* (New York: National Retail Dry Goods Association, 1948), 114; Johnson, "Step-By-Step," 137.

190. O'Hagan, "Latest Developments," 370.

191. Bolen, "Revolving Credit Analyzed," 115.

192. O'Hagan, "Latest Developments," 370.

193. Ibid.

194. Patterson, "Advantages," 221.

195. Ibid., 225.

196. "Display Ad 45 – No Title," *New York Times*, December 16, 1946, 6.

197. Ibid.

198. "Display Ad 13 – No Title," *New York Times*, March 11, 1948, 14.

199. The gendering of consumption and male authority over credit, as expressed by the credit manager, continued in much the same way as it had in the 1920s. Please see chapter 1 for a detailed discussion of the ways in which gender structured credit relations for men and women.

200. "Display Ad 8 – No Title," *New York Times*, August 28, 1947, 8.

201. Ibid.

202. O'Hagan, "Bloomingdale's Permanent Budget Account," 247–48.

203. Van Lander, "Revolving Credit Analyzed," 117.

204. Charles Egan, "Installment Buying Is Curbed On Autos, Home Appliances," *New York Times*, September 9, 1950, 1.

205. Charles Egan, "Credit Buying is Tightened; More Down Except on Autos," *New York Times*, October 14, 1950, 7.

206. "Text of the President's Economic Message to Congress Setting Mobilization Program Goals," *New York Times*, January 13, 1951, 4.

207. "Text of Administration's Summary of Economic Mobilization Bill," *New York Times*, July 20, 1950, 13.

208. A. L. Trotta (Manager, Credit Management Division, National Retail Dry Goods Association) to Board of Governors, November 8, 1950, folder "Sep 1950–1953," box "502.32 Open Account Installment Sales Credit – Consumer Credit," NARA, 3.

209. Charles Sheldon to Alfred Williams, November 2, 1950, folder "Sep 1950–1953," box "502.32 Open Account Installment Sales Credit – Consumer Credit," NARA, 1–2.

210. Sherman to Leonard, "Excerpt from the minutes of the meeting of the Board on November 7, 1950," December 1, 1950, folder "Sep 1950–1953," box "502.32 Open Account Installment Sales Credit – Consumer Credit," NARA, 3.

211. Aaron Frank to Thomas McCabe, October 19, 1950, folder "Aug 1942 to 1950," box "502.322," NARA, 1–2.

212. Frank Neely to Thomas McCabe, July 17, 1950, folder "Apr 1944–Aug 1950," box "502.32 Open Account Installment Credit Consumer Credit," RG 82, NARA, 1.

213. Frank Neely to R. M. Beane, "Memorandum," September 15, 1950, folder "Sep 1950–1953," box "502.32 Open Account Installment Sales Credit – Consumer Credit," NARA, 1.

214. Sherman to Leonard, 12/1/50, 1.

215. Egan, "Credit Buying is Tightened," 1; "Installment Buying," 1.

216. "Credit Group Asks End of Controls," February 4, 1952, 24; Alfred Zipser, "Two-Day Meeting Here to Survey Effects of Credit Curbs on Trade," December 3, 1950, F1.

217. "Repeal Demanded for Credit Curbs," *New York Times*, June 8, 1951, 43.

218. "Credit Group," 2/4/52, 24.

219. "Text of the President's," 1/13/51, 4.

220. "Credit Controls Called A Failure," *New York Times*, March 13, 1951, 47.

221. "Reserve Board to 'Re-examine' Enforcement of Credit Curb Because of Bank Protests," *New York Times*, January 5, 1952, 18.

222. Philip Webster to Homer Jones, July 31, 1950, "Use of 'revolving' charge accounts with six months to pay, based on reports from Reserve Banks, July 21, 1950," folder "Apr 1944–Aug 1950," box "502.32 Open Account Installment Credit Consumer Credit," RG 82, NARA, 1.

223. Ibid.

224. Webster to Jones, 7/31/50, 1.

225. "Credit Trend Continues: Installment Buying Last Year Little Changed From 1952," *New York Times*, March 4, 1954, 40. Government statistics lumped revolving and installment credit statistics together (U.S. Department of Commerce, *Business Statistics 1961 Edition: A Supplement to the Survey of Current Business,* [Washington: GPO, 1961], 241.)

226. "Credit Trend Continues," 40.

227. Sachs advertisement, "Display Ad 98 – No Title," *New York Times*, February 10, 1952, 92.

228. Alfred Zipser, "Easing of Installment-Buying Curb Sets Off Battle Among Merchants," *New York Times*, May 11, 1952, F1.

229. Russell Porter, "Public Slow To Buy With Easier Credit," *New York Times*, May 9, 1952, 21.

230. "Dallas," *New York Times*, July 6, 1952, F6.

231. Porter, "Public Slow To Buy," 21.

232. "Display Ad 17 – No Title," *Los Angeles Times*, December 9, 1953, 21.

233. "New Credit Plan Put To Retailers," *New York Times*, May 27, 1955, 28.

Chapter Five
Postwar Consumer Credit

1. Wealth, as accumulated assets, can take many forms, from liquid assets like bonds and savings accounts to illiquid assets like houses.

2. This chapter, more than other chapters in *Debtor Nation*, relies heavily on statistical analysis of two data sets. The quantitative approach has important limitations. First, survey questions on future outlook can be used to see if they correlate with behavior, but the subtle chains of reasoning, so central to intellectual history, cannot be observed and the complicated ways in which consumers thought about borrowing in moral or religious terms is mostly absent from this data. Respondents' attitudes have important significance, I will argue, but "thick description" cannot be found. Second, ownership information is also limited. At no point, outside of autos and homes, does the survey ask consumers what goods they already owned, only what goods they planned to buy. The 1958 survey, concerned as it was with installment credit, does little to explain the changing usage of charge accounts, and the 1961 survey does not have the 1958 survey's detailed household financial information. The 1958 survey collected revolving credit account information but lumped it with other forms of installment credit, giving us little empirical sense of the rise of this important form of credit in the 1950s. Third, categories that today's surveyors would disaggregate, like race, are simplified into white, black, and "other," making analysis of Asian American or Latino uses of debt impossible to parse. Fourth, institutions that drive the analysis of many other chapters are also absent from the data. Beyond a simple question of whether borrowed money came from a person or an institution, there is little information about the institutional context of lending. The survey's collection methods tend to boil down the world to means, percentages, and probabilities that a historian's palate might find bland.

With those limitations in mind, however, survey data also allow access to populations underrepresented in the archives and for a range of questions that conventional archival sources cannot answer. The data enables the restoration of the African American experience to our understanding of the world of consumer finance. African American suburbanites, as Andrew Wiese in *Places of Their Own: African American Suburbanization in the 20th Century* (University of Chicago

Press: Chicago, 2004) has recently argued, have been excluded from most accounts of the suburbs. While still a minority, the suburban experience structured an important set of aspirations for African Americans everywhere in the postwar period. At the same time, when investigating suburban history, one immediately confronts its overlapping qualities of heterosexuality, education, whiteness, wealth, and space. How can we weigh the importance of these factors in how suburbanites borrowed and spent their money? Did suburbanites borrow more simply because they had more money? Statistical methods, unlike anecdotal weighing of factors, permit the disaggregation of these different qualities of borrowing. Controlling for income or location or race allows the salient demographic features of financial behavior to come to the fore. What is simple to accomplish mathematically would be impossible to do anecdotally. Only through such analysis can we know how much more frequently a black college graduate borrowed than a white college graduate—2.67 times. While quantitative methods have fallen into disfavor among historians, I think that when used as part of a historian's tool kit they can answer questions other methods cannot.

Though the published reports of Michigan's Economic Behavior Program do not directly answer the questions posed at the beginning of this chapter, the raw data it gathered does. While those reports showed how indebtedness broke down by income, they did at the same time not control for race, location, education, and the myriad other factors that historians wonder about. Contemporary statistical methods, additionally, allow for a richer and more statistically accurate analysis than could have been done in 1958. The 1958 Survey of Consumer Finance interviewed 3,117 households across the country, oversampling higher-income families. The analysis in this chapter has reweighed the data for both income oversampling and internally correlated sampling clusters, taking advantage of the survey set commands of Stata to adjust for primary sampling units. The second survey, the Survey of Consumer Attitudes and Behavior from Spring 1961, sampled 1,363 households across the country. The Harvard-MIT data center, drawing on the Inter-University Consortium for Political and Social Research (ICPSR), made both data sets available for download as raw ASCII files converted from the original punch cards with an accompanying scanned code book. Both data sets are widely available for download through ICPSR. All data cleaning, variable encoding, and dictionary creation was done by the author. The author's version of the data is available upon request. (Economic Behavior Program, Survey Research Center, University of Michigan, "Surveys of Consumer Attitudes and Behavior, Spring 1961," ICPSR Study 3629; Economic Behavior Program, Survey Research Center, University of Michigan, "Survey of Consumer Finances, 1958," ICPSR Study 3617.) All analysis was done using Intercooled Stata 9.2. The most important statistical advances made since the late 1950s, for the purposes of this analysis, are the ability to adjust for the internal correlation of primary sampling units, logistic regression, and censored normal regressions—all of which are used in this chapter, especially the first two mentioned. In terms of questions, this chapter pays far greater attention to the intersections of race, class, and location than the original published survey, which was mostly a collection of bar graphs and averages. For the less technically inclined reader, explanations of some of the statistical methods will be in the notes. For the more technically inclined reader, p-values of relevant tests and regressions have generally been put in the notes.

3. William H. Whyte, "Budgetism: Opiate of the Middle Class," *Fortune* (May 1956), 133, 136–37.

4. John Lebor, "Requirements for Profitable Credit Selling," *Credit Management Year Book 1959–1960* (New York: National Retail Dry Goods Association, 1959), 12.

5. Malcolm McNair, "Changing Retail Scene and What Lies Ahead," National Retail Merchants Association Convention Speech, January 8, 1962, Historical Collections, BAK, 12.

6. Calculating mean incomes over occupational categories in the survey, there were overlaps in the 95 percent confidence intervals. Office and factory workers earned roughly the same incomes.

7. Suburban mean of $7,983 compared to urban mean of $5,951, among those households with mortgages. The mean dollar amount for conventional mortgages was $7,046, while for federally insured mortgages it was $9,208.

8. Taking a subpopulation of suburban debtors, the regression found that the dummy for mortgage status ($P > 0.000$) and the income variable ($P > 0.013$) were significant, while race ($P > 0.248$) and liquid assets ($P > 0.241$) were not. Having a mortgage raised the indebtedness of a suburban household $571, after controlling for other factors.

9. Odds ratio 3.44 with ($P > 0.01$) [1.75, 6.79]. Logit regression of mortgage dummy variable on consumer debt dummy, controlling for race, home ownership, income, and liquid assets among suburban households. Income had no relationship ($P > 0.129$) on the odds of a suburban household borrowing.

10. Odds ratio 1.96 with ($P > 0.02$) [1.15, 3.34] controlling for race, income, and region.

11. Odds ratio 2.33 with ($P > 0.00$) [1.88, 2.89].

12. Logit regression of auto ownership dummy on debtor dummy, with odds ratio 2.60 with ($P > 0.0$) [1.78, 3.78] controlling for race, income, and location. Even after adjusting for suburb, race, and income, auto ownership was still a very strong predictor of indebtedness.

13. In these regressions, wealth refers to a household's liquid assets, bonds, and savings accounts, not the total value of all assets, which was not available in the data set. For the decision to borrow, however, liquid assets matter most. The liquid asset variable was significant in the logistic regression to see if a household borrowed ($P > 0.00$), but not significant in the linear regression to see how much a household borrowed ($P > 0.24$).

14. The mean liquid assets of working-class households with debt were $1,018 and $1,611 for households without debt. For households headed by a professional, manager, or business owner, the means were $3,994 and $6,426.

15. Regression of total personal debt among suburban indebted households with income, mortgage status, race, and liquid bonds. Income was significant ($P > 0.01$) with a coefficient of $b = 0.05$ [0.012, 0.09].

16. The odds ratio was 1.51 with a ($P > 0.023$) with [1.061, 2.154].

17. Means of total personal debt had overlapping confidence intervals. The confidence intervals of the liquid assets of the working and professional classes also overlapped.

18. James Foree, "League Gets Alarming Data On Credit Victims," *Daily Defender*, September 16, 1959, A7.

19. Ironically, after the 1968 riots, Urban League leaders would call on Congress to provide credit cards for ghetto residents as a way to prevent future unrest. See chapter 7 for a detailed discussion of the political economy of credit and ghetto riots in the 1960s. While this chapter focuses on middle-class African Americans, chapter 7 examines the plight of urban, working-class African Americans excluded from the credit systems discussed in this chapter.

20. "Negro Suburbia Is Fast Growing," *Chicago Defender*, September 17, 1959, 2.

21. While I do not discuss this explicitly in the chapter, I wonder if this is one the roots of the wealth inequality between today's white and black households. See Melvin Oliver's *Black Wealth, White Wealth: A New Perspective on Racial Inequality* (New York, Routledge, 1995), for more on the importance of wealth inequality compared to income inequality today. As discussed later in the chapter, at the same income levels, African Americans always borrowed more frequently than whites and had lower wealth levels.

22. This was determined by running a series of regressions on debt and liquid assets, while controlling for location, mortgage status, marital status, and income. P-values for liquid assets in all models ($P > 0.00$). For whites, the model had $R^2 = 0.12$ and for whites $R^2 = 0.41$.

23. Odds ratio 5.42 with ($P > 0.01$) [1.44, 20.41].

24. A linear regression with a suburban debtor subpopulation shows race ($P > 0.248$) and liquid assets ($P > 0.241$) to have no relationship to the amount borrowed unlike mortgage status ($P > 0.000$) and income ($P > 0.013$).

25. Suburban dummy variable for black households with ($P > 0.02$). Suburban dummy variable for white households with ($P > 0.15$). Clearly it seems that moving to the suburbs had more a statistically meaningful effect on debt use for black households than white households.

26. Logit regression with a suburban subpopulation of debtor dummy variable with income ($P > 0.118$), liquid assets ($P > 0.001$), mortgage status ($P > 0.003$), and race ($P > 0.004$).

27. See Thomas Sugrue, *The Origins of the Urban Crisis,* Princeton Studies in American Politics (Princeton, NJ: Princeton University Press, 1996).

28. Pearson test of ($P > 0.42$) for FHA and suburban dummy variables.

29. Odds ratio 3.69 with ($P > 0.02$) [1.23, 11.07].

30. See, for instance, Thurgood Marshall, special counsel to the NAACP to Franklin Richards, FHA Commission, December 22, 1949, folder "Racial Restrictive Covenants 1949," box 6, Commissioner's Correspondence and subject file, 1938–1958, RG 31 Records of the Federal Housing Administration, NARA.

31. *Shelley v. Kraemer*, 334 U.S. 1 (1948).

32. Franklin Richards to Field Directors, January 10, 1950, Commissioner's Clearance No. 1705, folder "Minority Group Housing – Field Letters"; The FHA required a form to filled out that explicitly showed that there was no such cove-

nant in place. At the same time, however, this policy only applied to loans made after February 15, 1950, not to existing FHA-insured mortgages.

33. DeHart Hubbard to George Bremer, March 25, 1949, folder "Minority Group Housing – Financial Institutions," box 3, Program Correspondence of the Assistant Commissioner for Operations, 1936–1956, RG 31 Records of the Federal Housing Administration, NARA; The five positions of racial relations officer was created in August 1947 to better connect the FHA and minority group associations and institutions.

34. See Catherine Willemin, "Concord Park: The Creation of an Interracial Postwar Suburb" (A.B. Thesis, Harvard University, 2007).

35. William G Weart, "U.S. Housing Drive to Aid Non-Whites," *New York Times*, September 6, 1953.

36. There was a boom in postwar guides to sell to African American consumers. See, for instance, William Bell, *Fifteen Million Negroes and Fifteen Billion Dollars* (New York: W.K. Bell Publications, 1956), as well as the republication of the 1930s advertising classic, Paul Edwards' *The Southern Urban Negro as a Consumer* (College Park, MD: McGrath Publishing Co., 1969).

37. "Negro Housing Projects: Originating and Secondary Mortgages," box 3, Program Correspondence of the Assistant Commissioner for Operations, 1936–1956, RG 31 Records of the Federal Housing Administration, National Archives, College Park, MD; FHA to Directors of all Field Offices, "Financing Minority Group Housing Projects," folder "Minority Group Housing – Financial Institutions," box 3, Program Correspondence of the Assistant Commissioner for Operations, 1936–1956, RG 31 Records of the Federal Housing Administration, National Archives, College Park, MD, 1; See also Mortgage Bankers Association, "A proposed analysis of problems and experiences in mortgage financing relating to housing production for minority groups in selected communities," folder "Minority Group Housing – Field Letters," box 3, Program Correspondence of the Assistant Commissioner for Operations, 1936–1956, RG 31 Records of the Federal Housing Administration, National Archives, College Park, MD.

38. See Franklin Richards, FHA Commissioner, "Address before the National Association of Real Estate Brokers and the National Builders Association, Detroit, Michigan," August 23, 1949, folder "Minority Group Housing – Field Letters," box 3, Program Correspondence of the Assistant Commissioner for Operations, 1936–1956, RG 31 Records of the Federal Housing Administration, NARA, 1–9; Redman, July 27, 1949, folder "Minority Group Housing – Financial Institutions," box 3, Program Correspondence of the Assistant Commissioner for Operations, 1936-56, RG 31 Records of the Federal Housing Administration, NARA; W. J. Lockwood to Directors of Field Offices, "Financing Minority Group Housing Projects," September 14, 1949, folder "Minority Group Housing – Field Letters," box 3, Program Correspondence of the Assistant Commissioner for Operations, 1936–1956, RG 31 Records of the Federal Housing Administration, NARA. The Lockwood letter details a long list of national and regional insurance companies bought the mortgages for such properties.

39. See for instance the discussion of North Carolina in J. P. McRae to Herbert Redman, July 25, 1949, folder "Minority Group Housing – Financial Institutions,"

box 3, Program Correspondence of the Assistant Commissioner for Operations, 1936–1956, RG 31 Records of the Federal Housing Administration, NARA, 1–2.

40. Warren Lockwood to B.T. McGraw, June 23, 1948, "FHA-Insured Loans Held by Members of the National Negro Insurance Association," folder "Minority Group Housing – Financial Institutions," box 3, Program Correspondence of the Assistant Commissioner for Operations, 1936–1956, RG 31 Records of the Federal Housing Administration, NARA, 1–2.

41. Guy T.O. Hollyday, FHA Commissioner to J. Leonard Lewis, President NNIA, November 6, 1953, folder "Minority Group Housing – Printed Material, Speeches, Field Letters, Etc., 1940–1950," box 4, Commissioner's Correspondence and subject file, 1938–1958, RG 31 Records of the Federal Housing Administration, NARA, 1–2.

42. Edith Lapish to Mr. Richards, "Leading Title VI Mortgages," September 6, 1946, "Portfolio Holdings – June 30, 1945, Insurance Companies," folder "Mortgages Leading Institutions Holding FHA Mortgages," box 9, Program Correspondence of the Assistant Commissioner for Operations, 1936–1956, RG 31 Records of the Federal Housing Administration, NARA. Total is for Section 203 loans for owner-occupied housing, the successor to the Title II mortgage loan program. Insurance companies accounted for 25 percent of all 203 mortgage loans.

43. B. T. McGraw to Warren Lockwood, Assistant Commissioner FHA, June 17, 1948, "FHA-Insured Loans Held by Members of the National Negro Insurance Association," Office Memorandum, folder "Minority Group Housing – Financial Institutions," box 3, Program Correspondence of the Assistant Commissioner for Operations, 1936–1956, RG 31 Records of the Federal Housing Administration, NARA; FHA officials saw African American insurance companies as the best opportunity to find capital for African American mortgages in the late 1940s and early 1950s. The FHA records are filled with long lists of names and companies.

44. Luigi Laurenti, "Effects of Nonwhite Purchases on Market Prices of Residences," *Appraisal Journal*, (July 1952): 314–29, folder "Minority Group Housing – Field Letters," box 3, Program Correspondence of the Assistant Commissioner for Operations, 1936–1956, RG 31 Records of the Federal Housing Administration, National Archives, College Park, MD.

45. Walter Greene, "Before National Urban League, Cleveland, Ohio," September 2, 1952, folder "Minority Group Housing – Printed Material, Speeches, Field Letters, Etc., 1940–1950," box 4, Commissioner's Correspondence and subject file, 1938–1958, RG 31 Records of the Federal Housing Administration, NARA, 6.

46. Kenneth Wells to Guy T.O. Holladay, June 24, 1953, folder "Minority Group Housing – Printed Material, Speeches, Field Letters, Etc., 1940–1950," box 4, Commissioner's Correspondence and subject file, 1938–1958, RG 31 Records of the Federal Housing Administration, NARA.

47. P-value = 0.0001.

48. Once again, race had a p-value of > 0.586. The racial co-efficient, moreover, dropped to only a little over $500.

49. Linear regression with mortgage-having subpopulation for mortgage amount, race (P > 0.586) was not significant, and location (P > 0.006) was.

50. Pearson test for suburban dummy variable was (P > 0.42).

51. Linear regression of mortgage controlling for race (P > 0.269), location (P > 0.019), federal loan status (P > 0.003), and income (P > 0.000). Even after controlling for other factors, households that used FHA and VA loans, with their lower costs, could afford to borrow an additional $2,052 over those who did not use a federally insured loan, which was more than the difference between suburban and urban mortgages of $1,861.

52. Linear regression of mortgage controlling for federal loan status (P > 0.000) and income (P > 0.000) among black households with mortgages with an R^2 of 0.42.

53. Logit regression with black subpopulation of FHA dummy variable on suburban dummy variable with odds ratio .485 with (P > 0.632) [–1.57, 2.54]. The model overall had an F-test of (P > 0.63). With such a high p-value the FHA dummy did not predict suburban or urban status for African American households.

54. Computed by author from multiple response variables in the 1961 survey.

55. Timothy Wolters, "'Carry Your Credit In Your Pocket': The Early History of the Credit Card at Bank of America and Chase Manhattan," *Enterprise & Society* 1 (June 2000): 315–54.

56. Ibid., 336–49.

57. National Cash Register Company, "A Bank's 'Charge-It' Plan," no. 4, April 8, 1953, *Bank Information Bulletin* (Dayton, OH), folder "Sep 1950–1953," box "502.32 Open Account Installment Sales Credit – Consumer Credit," NARA, 1.; "John C. Biggins Dies, Paterson Banker, 61," *New York Times*, September 19, 1971, 66.

58. Ibid., 1.

59. Ibid., 1.

60. Ibid., 2.

61. Ibid.

62. Ibid.

63. Ibid.

64. Eight percent is much higher than the 1 to 2 percent merchant discount fees that credit card companies charge today.

65. "Merchants' Charge Account Service is Unveiled by Franklin National," folder "Sep 1950–1953," box "502.32 Open Account Installment Sales Credit – Consumer Credit," NARA, 1–4.

66. Ibid., 1.

67. Ibid., 1; "Manufacturers Trust Acquires Flatbush National Bank," *Wall Street Journal*, May 11, 1946, 2; The relationship between father and son is shown in the granddaughter's engagement announcement. "Catherine Biggins Becomes Affianced," *New York Times* January 17, 1967, 38.

68. National Cash Register Company, "A Bank's," 2.

69. "John C. Biggins Dies."

70. Malcolm McNair, "The American Department Store, 1920–1960: A Performance Analysis Based on the Harvard Reports," Bureau of Business Research Bulletin no. 166 (Cambridge: Graduate School of Business Administration, Division of Research, 1963), BAK, 40. The gross margin remained fixed around 36 percent;

this gross margin was also stable across sizes of stores. There was no return to scale on margins by sales volume. (*Operating Results of Department and Specialty Stores in 1960*, Bureau of Business Research, Bulletin no. 161 [Cambridge: Graduate School of Business Administration, Harvard University, 1916], BAK, 6.)

71. Federated Department Stores (FDS), *Annual Report 1952*, 8. All the annual reports in this chapter come from the Historic Corporate Reports collection in Historical Collections at Baker Library (BAK).

72. FDS, *Annual Report 1955*, BAK, 9.

73. May Department Stores also had a similar experience of maintaining local identity while expanding across the country. By the 1960s, these two department store chains had consolidated the bulk of the industry.

74. FDS, *Annual Report 1951*, 7–8; FDS, *AR 1952*, 8; FDS, *AR 1956*, 4; FDS, *AR 1959*, 7; FDS, *AR 1964*, 18.

75. FDS, *AR 1951*, 7.

76. Howard Abrahams, "Promoting the New Branch," *Credit Management Year Book 1956–1957* (New York: National Retail Dry Goods Association, 1956), BAK, 303.

77. Ibid., 305.

78. Ibid.

79. The sample size (N = 23) of suburban African Americans for this particular test was too small to be meaningful.

80. Ibid., 303, 305.

81. Ibid., 305.

82. Ibid.

83. Question C12, Form C, Long Interview Form Questionnaire, Survey of Consumer Attitudes and Behavior, Spring 1961.

84. Dean Ashby, "Credit Sales Promotion Ideas Which Have Paid Off," *Credit Management Year Book 1954–1955* (New York: National Retail Dry Goods Association, 1954), BAK, 85.

85. Ray Johnson, "Yes – Credit Promotion Pays," *Credit Management Year Book 1954–1955* (New York: National Retail Dry Goods Association, 1954), BAK, 113.

86. Ibid.

87. Ibid.

88. Ibid.

89. Bessie Tearno, "How We Built Up Our Credit Volume," *Credit Management Year Book 1954–1955* (New York: National Retail Dry Goods Association, 1954), BAK, 217.

90. Ibid., 216.

91. Ibid., 220. Only 36 out of 16,000 accounts were higher than $120.

92. Norman Smith, "Credit Sales Promotion Ideas Which Have Paid Off," *Credit Management Year Book 1954–1955* (New York: National Retail Dry Goods Association, 1954), BAK, 78.

93. See any of the discussions from the mid-1950s in the *Credit Management Year Book*. Any time these issues were discussed, there were invariably audience members who denounced the expansion of credit or pointed to his store's able track record at restraining borrowing.

94. Robert Calvert, "Where Is the Charge Account Customer?" *Credit Management Year Book 1956–1957* (New York: National Retail Dry Goods Association, 1956), BAK, 247.

95. Ibid., 248.

96. George Watkins, "Planning and Installation of Martin's Extended Chart Account," *Credit Management Year Book 1956–1957* (New York: National Retail Dry Goods Association, 1956), BAK, 102.

97. "Bad Debt Loss Survey," *Credit Management Year Book 1954–1955* (New York: National Retail Dry Goods Association, 1955), BAK, 121.

98. Kenneth Oetzel, "Credit Sales Promotion Ideas Which Have Paid Off," *Credit Management Year Book 1954–1955* (New York: National Retail Dry Goods Association, 1954), BAK, 85.

99. FDS, *AR 1955, 5.*

100. Herbert Landsman, "The Flexible Credit Limit Plan," *Credit Management Year Book 1956–1957* (New York: National Retail Dry Goods Association, 1956), BAK, 88.

101. Ibid.

102. Ibid., 89.

103. Ibid.

104. Watkins, "Planning," 99.

105. Ibid., 101.

106. Ibid.

107. Landsman, "Flexible," 94.

108. Ibid., 90.

109. Watkins, "Planning," 103.

110. Landsman, "Flexible," 95.

111. Race had a χ^2 value of (P > 0.332).

112. χ^2 test with (P > 0.000).

113. χ^2 test with (P > 0.000).

114. All customers paid the same interest and repayment of the balance. Individual interest rates for department store shopping were not yet possible. Rather than create individual interest rates, stores simply denied credit to consumers who did not earn enough income.

115. C. L. Prowse, "Leading Detroit Stores Adopt the Option Plan," *Credit Management Year Book 1958–1959* (New York: National Retail Dry Goods Association, 1958), BAK, 138; "Analysis and Evaluation of New Trends in Credit Plans – All- Purpose Revolving Accounts," *Credit Management Year Book 1958–1959* (New York: National Retail Dry Goods Association, 1958), BAK, 155; "Survey of Credit Policies," *Credit Management Year Book 1958–1959* (New York: National Retail Dry Goods Association, 1958), BAK, 164.

116. This store credit manager also remarked that a third of his 30-day balances took as long as 90 or 120 days to pay off (Prowse, "Leading Detroit Stores," 129).

117. Charles Dicken, "Should the Credit Department Be Self-Supporting?" *Credit Management Year Book 1958–1959* (New York: National Retail Dry Goods Association, 1958), BAK, 92.

118. John Gribbon, "A New Approach To Credit," *Credit Management Year Book 1961–1962* (New York: National Retail Dry Goods Association, 1961), BAK, 10.

119. Josephine Hexdall, "Welcome – Mr and Mrs Charge Customer," *Credit Management Year Book 195–1957* (New York: National Retail Dry Goods Association, 1956), BAK, 59.

120. O. C. Faulkner, "Credit Sales Promotion Ideas Which Have Paid Off," *Credit Management Year Book 1956–1957* (New York: National Retail Dry Goods Association, 1956), BAK, 84.

121. Gribbon, "A New Approach to Credit," 10.

122. Prowse, "Leading Detroit Stores," 136.

123. Clare Prowse, "Results of Our Option Plan of Credit," *Credit Management Year Book 1959–1960* (New York: National Retail Dry Goods Association, 1959), BAK, 69.

124. Ibid., 69.

125. Dean Ashby, "Effect of Option Accounts on Consumer Buying Habits," *Credit Management Year Book 1959–1960* (New York: National Retail Dry Goods Association, 1959), BAK, 55.

126. Clare Prowse, "Results," 69.

127. Ashby, "Effect of Option Accounts," 55.

128. Ibid., 56.

129. Gribbon, "A New Approach to Credit," 7.

130. Robert Lynch, "Optional Terms for Smaller Stores," *Credit Management Year Book 1960–1961* (New York: National Retail Dry Goods Association, 1960), BAK, 253.

131. Ibid., 254.

132. Ibid., 255.

133. David Bollman, "Credit Sales Promotion – Opportunity Unlimited," *Credit Management Year Book 1956–1957* (New York: National Retail Dry Goods Association, 1956), BAK, 57.

134. Ibid., 57.

135. Gribbon, "A New Approach To Credit," 13.

136. Ibid.

137. Ibid.

138. Ibid. Surprising as it might be to the contemporary reader, Gribbon's ideas about profit and receivables were difficult for other credit professionals to understand. Following his talk, there was an audience discussion. The many questions reveal both that the audience did not understand the larger, general principles he espoused and that they were hostile to changing their everyday business practices, even if it meant more profit. Gribbon's paper was pronounced "provocative" by the session moderator. ("Open Forum Discussion report on Management Practices," *Credit Management Year Book 1961–1962* (New York: National Retail Dry Goods Association, 1961), BAK, 15).

139. The option plan completed reversed the habits and thinking of the revolving budget account. Compare Gribbon's reasoning to this quote from a Wanamaker's credit manager only five years earlier: "I would rather have a customer who is going to pay me $25 a month than a customer who is going to pay me $10

a month. Based on her ability to make those payments, the more I get the more she is open to buy" (Richard Westin, "New Techniques for Sound and Profitable Credit Selling," *Credit Management Year Book 1956–1957* (New York: National Retail Dry Goods Association, 1956), BAK, 78).

140. R. H. Bulte, "Credit Sales Promotion – The New Look," *Credit Management Year Book 1958–1959* (New York: National Retail Dry Goods Association, 1958), BAK, 95.

141. A. Leonidas Trotta, "Preface," *Credit Management Year Book 1959–1960* (New York: National Retail Dry Goods Association, 1959), BAK, v.

142. FDS, Form 10-K (1952), BAK, S–6.

143. FDS, Form 10-K (1958), BAK, S–7.

144. Ibid., S–4.

145. Lebor, "Requirements for Profitable Credit Selling," 14–15.

146. Gribbon, "A New Approach to Credit," 5.

147. Ibid, 6.

148. Ibid.

149. Ibid.

150. Lebor, "Requirements for Profitable Credit Selling," 20.

151. FDS, *AR 1960*, 4–5.

152. Sears Roebuck Acceptance Corporation, *Annual Report 1956*, 3.

153. Sears, Roebuck Company (SRAC), *Annual Report 1950*, 3.

154. SRAC, *Annual Report 1957*, BAK, 2–3.

155. SRAC, *Annual Report 1965,* BAK, 3.

156. SRAC, *Annual Report 1966,* BAK.

157. This comparison was evident in a picture from the 1967 *Annual Report*, which showed a picture of the board in Money Market Center that had a list of the interest rates and other financial information of all the major finance companies, including SRAC (SRAC, *Annual Report 1967*, BAK.)

158. Edward Sullivan, "How We Solved Our Money Needs For Expanding Credit Sales and Receivables," *Credit Management Year Book 1961–1962* (New York: National Retail Dry Goods Association, 1961), BAK, 225.

159. Ibid.

160. Ibid.

161. Commercial Credit Corporation and the emergence of other national finance companies are more fully discussed in chapter 1.

162. Sullivan, "How We Solved," 227. One reason that stores could borrow from finance companies was that finance companies did not require collateral, which typically accounted for 20 percent of the borrowed funds from banks. Though banks might charge a lower interest rate, they also tied up more capital in collateral that could not be loaned to consumers (James Newman, "A Simplified Method for Financing Retailers Accounts Receivable," *Credit Management Year Book 1961–1962* [New York: National Retail Dry Goods Association, 1961], BAK, 230).

163. Sullivan, "How We Solved," 227.

164. Ibid.

165. Newman, "A Simplified Method," 228.

166. Ibid., 229.

167. Ibid., 229.

168. GECC integrated the state-based finance companies setup by GE in the 1920s. See chapter 1 for more details.

169. GECC, *Annual Report 1952*, Historic Corporate Reports, Historical Collections, Baker Library, Harvard University, Allston, Massachusetts.

170. GECC, *Annual Report 1961, 5*.

171. GECC, *AR 1962*, 4.

172. GECC, *AR 1963*, 4.

173. GECC, *AR 1962*, 4.

174. H. A. Jaffe, "New Trends in Revolving Credit and Instalment Selling," *Credit Management Year Book 1956–1957* (New York: National Retail Dry Goods Association, 1957), BAK, 113.

175. E. O. Johnson, "New Trends in Revolving Credit and Instalment Selling," *Credit Management Year Book 1956–1957* (New York: National Retail Dry Goods Association, 1957), BAK, 113.

176. Davis, "New Trends in Revolving Credit and Instalment Selling," 113. Strangely, the installment contract, by the end of the 1950s, had become as legally fictitious as the actually fraudulent contracts of loan sharks in the 1910s. See chapter 1 for more on loan shark contracts and their psychological use in enforcement of debts.

177. GECC, *AR 1963*, 5.

178. Lebor, "Requirements for Profitable Credit Selling," 13.

179. Ibid.

180. Ibid.

181. GECC, *AR 1964*, 4.

182. Ibid., 6.

183. GECC, *AR 1966*, 3.

184. W. J. Noonan, "Customers, Credit, Computers – 'C's' The Opportunity," *Credit Management Year Book 1961–1962* (New York: National Retail Dry Goods Association, 1961), BAK, 80.

185. GECC, *AR 1966*, 16.

186. Other programs existed like "Unicard," which allowed consumers to use a card at multiple stores, but retailers were loath to pay the high fees to an outside firm and risk the loss of consumer loyalty. More than anything, department stores in the 1960s wanted to maintain their sales growth. Programs like Unicard threatened that and ultimately failed. Private labeling schemes, like GECC's however, grew. (On Unicard, see Victor Brown, "What the Credit Manager Should Know About Financing Receivables?" *Credit Management Year Book 1963–1964* (New York: National Retail Merchants Association, 1963), BAK, 151.

187. GECC, *AR 1968*, 8.

188. GECC, *AR 1969*, 7.

189. GECC, *AR 1972*, 6.

190. GECC, *AR 1972*, 9.

191. Lebor, "Requirements for Profitable Credit Selling," 20.

192. George Quist, "Survey of Authorization Procedures," *Credit Management Year Book 1961–1962* (New York: National Retail Dry Goods Association,

1961), BAK, 10. This survey was not entirely representative and I think, if anything, it overstates the ability of consumers to use bank cards in the early 1960s. Seven stores of twenty-nine respondents allowed the use of "national credit cards" in their stores.

193. Computed by author from ICPSR, "Surveys of Consumer Attitudes and Behavior, Spring 1961," ICPSR Study 3629, University of Michigan. See chapter 5 for a detailed discussion of the patterns of credit use.

194. Lebor, "Requirements for Profitable Credit Selling," 20.

195. Timothy Wolters, "'Carry Your Credit in Your Pocket': The Early History of the Credit Card at Bank of America and Chase Manhattan," *Enterprise & Society* 1 (June 2000): 317.

196. Overly careful readers will remember J. Andrew Painter from chapter 3, where he was involved in the formation of the first personal loan department at National City Bank and the planning of the FHA Title I loan program.

197. J. Andrew Painter, "Citibank Ready-Credit Plan," *Credit Management Year Book 1959–1960* (New York: National Retail Dry Goods Association, 1959), BAK, 83.

198. Ibid.

199. Ibid., 85.

200. Joseph Garcia, "American Express Credit Card," *Credit Management Year Book 1959–1960* (New York: National Retail Dry Goods Association, 1959), BAK, 86.

201. Robert Farrar, "Hilton's Carte Blanche," *Credit Management Year Book 1959–1960* (New York: National Retail Dry Goods Association, 1959), BAK, 87.

202. "Stop Stewing About Saving," *Changing Times* (August 1957), 16.

203. Joseph O'Mahoney, "Do Installments Peril the Economy?" *New York Times*, May 4, 1958, SM12.

Chapter Six
Legitimating the Credit Infrastructure

1. As a number of historians have explained, FHA policies led to the systematic disinvestment in black-owned housing in the middle of the twentieth century. The best remains Thomas Sugrue, *The Origins of the Urban Crisis,* Princeton Studies in American Politics (Princeton, NJ: Princeton University Press, 1996.)

2. Lizabeth Cohen and other historians have emphasized the importance of the welfare rights and consumer movements in transforming retailers' credit policies. While these protests no doubt affected specific retailers and consumers, I believe that overall the riots, legislative changes, and business competition played a more decisive role in changing access policies for groups denied credit. At the same time, the implied radicalism of these consumer movements should be questioned since they merely demanded access to credit and did not push for a larger critique of the credit, much less the capitalist, system. Lizabeth Cohen, *A Consumers' Republic* (New York: Random House, 2004), 381–85.)

3. Lizabeth Cohen has argued that rioters looted to satisfy unmet material ambitions that represented exclusion from the postwar consumer order. Instead

of focusing on the psychology of consumer demands, I would argue that many protesters had concrete grievances against local creditors, who rioters *experienced* as exploitative. Rather than protesting a lack of consumption, then, rioters protested the usurious credit with which they actually had used to shop. It was not an absence of consumption that spurred the rioting, then, but the conditions under which consumption had occurred (Cohen, *A Consumers' Republic*, 373–75.)

4. U.S. Kerner Commission, *Report of the National Advisory Commission on Civil Disorders*, New York Times reprint (Bantam Books: New York, 1968), 274.

5. Ibid., 274.

6. Ibid, 1.

7. While in the economy at large repossession had withered away to encompass only autos as discussed in earlier chapters, in the ghetto economy repossession, as will be discussed below, remained a vital part of the credit relation.

8. Sauter Van Gordon, "Flames Erase Long Stretch of Chicago's Madison Street," *The Washington Post*, April 7, 1968, A7.

9. Federal Trade Commission (FTC), *Economic Report on Installment Credit and Retail Sales Practices of District of Columbia Retailers* (Washington: GPO, 1968), Historical Collections, Baker Library, Harvard Business School, Harvard University, Cambridge, Massachusetts, ix; the study distinguished between "low-income market" retailers and "general-market" retailers. The low-income retailer sold to a limited market of low-income consumers with limited mobility and credit access, while the middle-class retailer sold to more affluent customers who could easily move between the city and the suburbs. Rather than the cumbersome "general-market," I have substituted "middle-class" for the FTC's original analytic category.

10. Ibid., x.

11. Ibid., 16.

12. David Caplovitz, *The Poor Pay More: Consumer Practices of Low-Income Families*, 1967 edition (New York: Free Press, 1967), 95, 97.

13. Credit references were personal communications between creditors while credit ratings were impersonal and filed with a credit bureau.

14. Congress, Senate, Committee on Banking and Currency, Subcommittee on Financial Institutions, "Consumer Credit and the Poor," 90th Cong., 2nd sess., April 19, 1968, 5–6.

15. Calculated by author from FTC, *Economic Report*, 43.

16. Benny Kass, Congress, Senate, Committee on Banking and Currency, Subcommittee on Financial Institutions, "Fair Credit Reporting Act," 91st Cong., 1st sess., May 19–23, 1969, 129–30.

17. FTC, *Economic Report*, ix.

18. This percentage is for unassigned installment contracts, which will be discussed in detail later in this chapter.

19. Congress, "Consumer Credit and the Poor," 7.

20. Ibid.

21. Ibid., 20. See chapter 5 for a discussion of the reasons why repossession, outside of autos and homes, became financially unjustifiable for durable good sales.

22. Ibid., 21.
23. Ibid.
24. Ibid.
25. The most important of these was Caplovitz's *The Poor Pay More: Consumer Practices of Low-Income Families* (New York: Free Press of Glencoe, 1963), which was widely discussed among policymakers and in the popular press as uncovering the hidden economy of low-income Americans.
26. FTC, *Economic Report*, ix.
27. Ibid., xii.
28. Ibid., 33.
29. Ibid., 34.
30. Ibid., xii.
31. Ibid. 19.
32. By this point, most installment paper was resold without recourse. The holder of the obligation could not force the original seller to take the merchandise back.
33. FTC, *Economic Report*, 18.
34. Ibid., 17.
35. Ibid., 20.
36. Ibid., 20.
37. Murray Seeger, "Washington Ghetto Smoldering Ruins Block After Block," *Los Angeles Times*, April 7, 1968, 18.
38. "Rampage & Restraint," *Time Magazine*, April 19, 1968.
39. Williard Clopton, "11,500 Troops Confront Rioters; Three-Day Arrest Total at 2686," *Washington Post*, April 7, 1968, A14.
40. "Avenging What's-His-Name," *Time Magazine*, April 19, 1968; "Generation Gap in the Ghetto," *Washington Post*, April 7, 1968, B6.
41. "Most Riot-Damaged Stores Have Credit Records Intact," *Washington Post*, April 11, 1968, A4.
42. FTC, *Economic Report*, xii.
43. Ibid., xv.
44. Paul H. Douglas, *In the Fullness of Time: The Memoirs of Paul H. Douglas* (New York: Harcourt, Brace, Jovanovich, Inc., 1972), 523–35.
45. Congress, "Consumer Credit and the Poor," 18.
46. Ibid., 12.
47. Ibid.
48. Ibid., 4.
49. Congress, Senate, Committee on Banking and Currency, Subcommittee on Financial Institutions, "Financial Institutions and the Urban Crisis," 90th Cong., 2nd sess., September 20 and October 1–4, 1969, 1.
50. Ibid., 183.
51. Congress, "Consumer Credit and the Poor," 8.
52. Ibid., 19.
53. Ibid., 1.
54. Ibid., 2.
55. Cross, "Financial Institutions," 389.
56. Ibid., 399.

57. Nick Ortiz, manager of Banco Popular bank in New York, "Financial Institutions," 400.

58. Senator Charles Percy (Illinois), "Financial Institutions," 24.

59. Ibid., 389.

60. Ibid., 397.

61. The federal bureaus began this program in 1965 across the country in Boston, New York, Chicago, Los Angeles, Washington, New Orleans, Miami, Houston, San Francisco, and Charleston (WV) ("Financial Institutions, 74).

62. Congress, "Consumer Credit and the Poor," 30–34.

63. Congress, "Financial Institutions," 74; of these credit unions, sixty were directly funded by the OEO. (ibid., 113.)

64. Congress, "Consumer Credit and the Poor," 35.

65. Congress, "Financial Institutions," 101. OEO officials, like Levine, believed that the "discontent and disorder in cities across the country is in no small part a consumer revolt against a system that has for years permitted exploitation of inner-city residents. OEO is convinced that the consumer problems of the poor must be solved if we are ever to eliminate poverty" (Written Statement of Robert Levine, Assistant Director for Research, Plans, Programs, and Evaluation Office of Economic Opportunity, "Financial Institutions," 106).

66. Congress, "Consumer Credit and the Poor," 34; Credit unions, additionally, were limited by law to investing 25 percent of their capital in other credit unions. Credit union advocates, like J. Orrin Shipe, the managing director of the credit union organization CUNA international, called for raising that limit to 50 percent (Congress, "Financial Institutions," 131).

67. Congress, "Consumer Credit and the Poor," 34.

68. Congress, "Financial Institutions," 82; Proxmire described the amount of money involved in these credit unions as "peanut" ("Financial Institutions," 120).

69. Congress, "Consumer Credit and the Poor," 106; OEO costs averaged $30,000, which included "a full time manager, bookkeeper, and tell counselor plus rent and other overhead" (Financial Institutions," 113).

70. Levine, "Financial Institutions," 114.

71. Walter Mondale citing a study of the Federal Reserve Board's Andrew Brimmer, "Financial Institutions," 3.

72. Congress, "Consumer Credit and the Poor," 35.

73. Congress, "Financial Institutions," 120.

74. Ibid.

75. The testimony of Stephen Miller, a black entrepreneur from Michigan, nicely illustrated this divide. Affirming the ideal of local control, he saw the community-focused leadership of economic development as important as the economic development itself. Turning development over white-run institutions would not be acceptable. While legislators were receptive to hearing that African Americans should own the businesses in black neighborhoods, envisioning greater stability, they were also concerned about the slow growth of these businesses and were willing to trade local control for greater stability. Miller rejected investment from white banks, but black–controlled banks, at the same time, had little money to invest. Small growth, from the perspective from the legislators, would not sta-

bilize the ghetto. Total self-determination was impractical for the goals of the committee, which was social stability, not autonomous black control. For most of the white businessmen who testified, investment in black businesses by white organizations was the only practical option. For self-determinationists like Miller, this option, however practical, was impossible. (Congress, "Financial Institutions," 114–26).

76. Ibid., 232.

77. Ibid., 233; this position reversed the Urban League's position on credit in the late 1950s. See chapter 5 for more on the Urban League's ideas of credit and prosperity.

78. Congress, "Consumer Credit and the Poor," 4.

79. Congress, "Financial Institutions," 235.

80. Ibid., 234.

81. Ibid.

82. Ibid.

83. Ibid.

84. Ibid.

85. Ibid.

86. Ibid., 238.

87. Ibid.

88. Congress, "Consumer Credit and the Poor," 20.

89. Ira Millstein, "Hearing on Availability of Credit to Women," May 22, 1972, unpublished, Folder "Hearings and Related Records Availability of Credit to Women," box 35, RG Records of the National Commission on Consumer Finance, 1970–1972, NARA, 3.

90. Howard, "Credit to Women," 5/22/72, 93.

91. Leonor Sullivan, "Credit to Women," 5/22/72, 6.

92. Ibid., 6.

93. Ibid., 59.

94. Friedman, "Credit to Women," 5/22/72, 50.

95. Ibid., 52.

96. McElhome, "Credit to Women," 5/22/72, 139.

97. Campbell, "Credit to Women," 5/22/72, 182.

98. Ibid.

99. Ibid., 184.

100. Howard, "Credit to Women," 5/22/72, 74.

101. Hagen, National Commission on Consumer Finance, "Hearing on Availability of Credit to Women," May 23, 1972, unpublished, Folder "Hearings and Related Records Availability of Credit to Women," box 35, RG Records of the National Commission on Consumer Finance, 1970–1972, NARA, 121.

102. Hagen, "Credit to Women," 5/23/73, 121.

103. Griffiths, "Credit to Women," 5/22/72, 11.

104. Litwiller, "Credit to Women," 5/22/72, 65.

105. "Credit to Women," 5/22/72, 60.

106. "Diners Club Application," Exhibit B, Folder "Testimony from hearings on availability of credit to women," box 35, RG Records of the National Commission on Consumer Finance, 1970–1972, NARA.

107. Abzug, "Credit to Women," 5/23/72, 46.
108. Ibid.
109. Ibid.
110. Stewart, "Credit to Women," 5/22/72, 153.
111. Ibid., 155.
112. Ibid., 154.
113. Griffiths, "Credit to Women," 5/22/72, 11; Representative Martha Griffiths (D-MI), 1955–1974.
114. Howard, "Credit to Women," 5/22/72, 74.
115. Divorces per 1,000 married women went from 9.6 to 18.2 from 1963 to 1973 (Table Ae507–513, "Marriage and Divorce Rates: 1920–1995," *Historical Statistics of the United States*, Millennial Edition On Line.)
116. Gallagher, 5/22/72, 194.
117. "Hearing," 5/23/72, 33.
118. "Credit to Women," 5/23/73, 122.
119. Hagen, "Credit to Women," 5/23/73, 133.
120. Ibid., 123–24.
121. Ibid., 125.
122. Ibid., 127.
123. Howard, "Credit to Women," 5/22/72, 78.
124. Ibid., 79.
125. Ibid., 80.
126. Hagen, "Credit to Women," 5/23/72, 134.
127. Barr, "Credit to Women," 5/23/72, 67.
128. This line of reasoning with regards to discrimination in markets was first advanced by Gary Becker in his landmark *Economics of Discrimination* (Chicago: University of Chicago, 1957).
129. Stewart, "Credit to Women," 5/23/72, 144.
130. Ibid., 146.
131. Ibid.
132. Ibid., 149.
133. Ibid., 150.
134. National Bank of North America advertisement, [1974], folder 59, box 30, National Organization for Women collection, Schlesinger Library, Radcliffe Institute, Harvard University, Cambridge, Massachusetts. National Bank of North America was, in 1970, 98 percent owned by the finance company C.I.T. and was the twenty-eighth largest bank in the United States (C.I.T. Annual Report, 1970, 4).
135. The advertisement, designed by Hicks & Griest, won a "positive image award" from NOW in 1974 (Leonard Sloane, "Advertising: Chock Full O' Beer," *New York Times,* August 26, 1974.)
136. Sharyn Campbell, "NOW TASK FORCE ON CREDIT," November, 1973, folder 59, box 30, NOW.
137. From Sharon Campbell to James Lowery, August 29, 1974, folder 59, box 30, NOW, 1.
138. Gene Boyer to Wisconsin Now Chapters, et al., August 6, 1973, folder 59, box 30, NOW, 1.

139. This critique of the middle-class women's liberation movement is most clearly articulated by bell hooks in her classic *Feminist Theory: From Margin to Center* (Boston: South End Press, 1984).

140. Such economic erasure extended beyond credit to other areas of upper-middle class life, such as stock ownership. One such story from the hearings concerned a woman who had owned stock before her marriage in 1970. After her marriage she was notified by her stockbroker, Merrill, Lynch, that she now had to have her husband sign a consent form for her to manage the stock because "women have squandered the grocery money on bad investments." Without his signature, the account would be frozen. Even after two years, the woman, "still trembling with rage from this dehumanizing experience," had not allowed her husband to sign the form. Merrill, Lynch did freeze the account. (Litwiller, "Credit to Women," 5/22/72, 64–65.)

141. Pressman Fuentes, "Credit to Women," 5/22/72, 188–89. Pressman Fuentes was, at that time, a lawyer with the Equal Employment Opportunity Commission, although in her testimony, she made clear that she was not testifying on behalf of that agency.

142. Seidenberg, "Credit to Women," 5/22/72, 115.

143. Ibid., 120.

144. Ibid., 122.

145. Ibid., 136.

146. Lynne Litwiller, "Report of National Task Force on Taxes and Credit," October 15, 1972, folder 59, box 30, 2; Bella Abzug's bills were HR 15546, HR 15547, and HR 15548.

147. Abzug, "Credit to Women," 5/23/72, 41.

148. Ibid.

149. Ibid., 54.

150. Ibid.

151. Abzug, "Credit to Women," 5/23/72, 57.

152. Untitled NOW press release on National Commission on Consumer Finance Hearings, folder 59, box 30, NOW.

153. John Spafford, Congress, Senate, Subcommittee on Consumer Credit, "Fair Credit Reporting Act–1973," 93rd Cong., 1st sess., October 1–5, 1973, 11a.

154. Ibid.

155. The so-called Gallagher hearings (U.S. House, "Commercial Credit Bureaus," March 12, 1968) had debated creating a state-run data bank with privacy protection to replace the private sector credit agencies. Though defeated, its threat caused the Associated Credit Bureaus to create privacy guidelines in November 1968. According to industry representative John Spafford, executive vice-president of Associated Credit Bureaus, these guidelines provided consumers the ability to correct errors in their credit reports. Spafford reminded the committee that some consumers wanted "pertinent" information erased from their records that reflect their spotty repayment records. Credit reports existed to, in Spafford's view, protect creditors. Credit was not a "basic right" but a privilege based on a consumer's "proven stewardship in meeting his obligations." ("Fair Credit Reporting Act," 142–43.)

156. "Fair Credit Reporting Act," 13.
157. Ibid., 31.
158. Ibid., 34.
159. Ibid., 52–53.
160. Ibid., 52.
161. J. S. Roberts, *The Spirit of the Retail Credit Company* (Atlanta: Retail Credit Company, 1965), 6–15. Open-book credit is discussed in detail in chapter 1.
162. Ibid., 39.
163. Ibid., 62.
164. "Fair Credit Reporting Act," 113.
165. Ibid., 119.
166. Jonathan Cottin, *Washington Daily News*, March 19, 1969, reprinted in "Fair Credit Reporting Act," 169.
167. "Fair Credit Reporting Act," 169.
168. Ibid., 172.
169. Ibid., 75.
170. Ibid., 81.
171. Westin, "Fair Credit Reporting Act," 88.
172. Angevine, "Fair Credit Reporting Act," 118.
173. "Fair Credit Reporting Act," 173.
174. Ibid., 179.
175. Ibid., 183.
176. Ibid., 183.
177. Ibid., 155.
178. Ibid., 92, 149.
179. Ibid., 223.
180. Ibid., 227.
181. Ibid., 231.
182. Ibid., 226, 231.
183. Ibid., 229.
184. Virginia Knauer, "Fair Credit Reporting Act," 12.
185. "Fair Credit Reporting Act," 17.
186. Through a series of acquisitions and sales, Credit Data Corporation formed the core of what eventually would become Experian, which, alongside Equifax and Transunion would form the three main consumer credit reporting agencies in the United States. Retail Credit Company bought up local credit bureaus around the country and computerized them. These events began as early as 1968, when TRW bought a minority share of Credit Data Corporation. (*New York Times*, December 9, 1968, 35.)
187. Donald Badders, director, legislative affairs, TRW Credit Data Division, TRW, Inc., "Fair Credit Reporting Act–1973," 149.
188. Sarah Newman, general secretary of the National Consumers' League, "Fair Credit Reporting Act," 127.
189. Curtis Martin, Congressional Research Service, Library of Congress, "Federal Consumer Credit Protection: A Summary and Overview," February 25, 1977, 10.

190. Martin, 46.

191. Ibid., 47; Indirect predictors of these statuses were also forbidden. Asking whether someone had a telephone registered in their name, for instance, was forbidden since it was usually registered in a husband's name and would discriminate against women. Asking whether a phone was in the house, however, was permitted (Martin, 48).

192. Gerald Ford, "Statement on Signing the Equal Credit Opportunity Act Amendments of 1976," March 23, 1976, in John Woolley and Gerhard Peters, *The American Presidency Project* [online]; Santa Barbara, CA: University of California (hosted), Gerhard Peters (data base), http://www.presidency.ucsb.edu/ws/?pid=5745; Gerald Ford, "Remarks Upon Signing the Equal Credit Opportunity Act Amendments of 1976 and the Consumer Leasing Act of 1976,"March 23, 1976, in ibid., ; http://www.presidency.ucsb.edu/ws/?pid=5743.

193. Sheldon Feldman, Assistant Director for Special Statutes, Federal Trade Commission, "To Amend the Equal Credit Opportunity Act of 1974," 52.

194. To create these models, creditors took a sample from their files that included reliable customers, defaulting customers, and rejected applicants. A computer performed a multivariate regression on the data to find out which factors best predicted the lending outcome. Then the rejected applicants were "augmented" to give them the outcomes that the model predicted to find out how well the previous selection criteria worked. The regression was then turned into an easy-to-use system to find out if a customer should be approved or denied. That model was then run against a second sample from the creditor's files to see how well it predicted the outcome of the loan. Over time, the model could be refined with newer information. (Congress, Senate, Committee on Banking, Housing, and Urban Affairs, Subcommittee on Consumer Affairs, "Credit Card Redlining," June 4–5, 1979, 247.)

195. Richard Cremer, Congress, House, Committee on Banking, Currency, and Housing, Subcommittee on Consumer Affairs, "To Amend the Equal Credit Opportunity Act of 1974," 94th Cong., 1st sess., April 22–23, 1975, 86.

196. Ibid., 91.

197. Numerous studies found zip codes to be statistically significant predictors of default. (Gail Rubino, National Retail Merchants Association representative, "Credit Card Redlining," 244.)

198. Dwight Golann, assistant attorney general, Massachusetts, "Credit Card Redlining," 262.

199. William Fair, "Credit Card Redlining," 220, 236. William Fair's company went on to create the well-known FICO score—Fair, Isaac Corporation—that is today synonymous with credit score.

200. Ibid., 222.

201. Author interview with John Reed, former CEO of Citigroup (June 5, 2009).

202. Of course, at the same time, credit reporting agencies with access to a predictive variable, like martial status or race, would be hard-pressed not use it. Again and again, credit bureau executives testified that they wanted to use whatever legal variables available to them to increase the predictive power of their models. If they had race or martial status, there would always be the temptation to use them.

203. Stewart, "Credit to Women," 5/23/72, 152.

204. Calculated by author from Board of Governors of the Federal Reserve System, *Supplement to Banking and Monetary Statistics* (Washington: GPO, 1963), 57 (in unadjusted dollars).

Chapter Seven
Securing Debt in an Insecure World

1. Robert Bennett, "Citibank's Credit Card Blitz," *New York Times*, July 23, 1978, 9.

2. Thomas Durkin, "Credit Cards: Use and Consumer Attitudes, 1970–2000," *Federal Reserve Bulletin* (September 2000), 624.

3. The Federal Reserve limited the return on deposits at commercial banks through Regulation Q. Savings and loan banks, in turn, were limited by the returns on their fixed rate mortgage portfolios.

4. Philip Brownstein, "The 1968 Housing Bill," Mortgage Banker (May 1968): 21.

5. I discuss the global dimensions of this crisis in greater detail in Louis Hyman, "The Policy Origins of Securitization," *The Shock of the Global* (Cambridge: Harvard University Press, 2010).

6. Congress, FHLBB, "A Study of Mortgage Credit," 90th Cong., 1st sess., May 22, 1967, 33.

7. Economic Report 1968, 22.

8. Congress, "A Study of Mortgage Credit," v.

9. Ibid.

10. Brownstein, "1968 Housing Bill," 23.

11. Congress, Senate, "Mortgage Credit," 90th Cong., 1st sess., 12, 26, 27, June 28, 1968, 274–75.

12. Congress, "A Study of Mortgage Credit," 18.

13. As will be described later, the mortgage-backed security is a financial instrument that channels both principal and interest payments of a group of mortgages to investors.

14. The Act had a number of other features as well, including riot insurance for the inner city, where these mortgage funds were intended to flow. Also, the Act freed the FNMA to borrow "flexibly" and exceed its historical 15:1 debt to capital borrowing limit (Congress, House, "Housing and Urban Development Act of 1968," 68).

15. The use of the term "subprime" in this essay is anachronistic but I believe to be accurate. While today subprime loans have a clear definition—as loans to individuals whose credit scores are too low to qualify for normal or "prime" mortgage loans—no such universal credit ratings existed in 1968. For ease of communication, I am using "subprime loan" in a nearly identical sense—meaning a loan that the borrower could not have acquired in the normal mortgage markets, but not because of a credit score (which was not used) but because of their low income. While there is a distinction to be drawn in the epistemological origins of the loan, I think those differences are trivial compared to the immediate clarity the word "subprime" provides the contemporary reader.

16. Spelman, "Federalization & Housing: At Point of No Return?" *Mortgage Banker* (June 1971), 54; Eugene Cowen, "The Nixon Program for Housing," *Mortgage Banker* (July 1971), 10.

17. Spelman, "Federalization & Housing,"56.

18. Philip Jackson, "The commitment is massive, but so is the problem," *Mortgage Banker* (June 1972), 6.

19. Ibid.

20. Department of Housing and Urban Development, *1970 HUD Statistical Yearbook* (Washington: GPO, 1970), 234.

21. Brownstein, "1968 Housing Bill," 20.

22. Spelman, "Federalization & Housing," 57; Robert Gray, "Good Counseling: The Answer In Successful 235 Housing," *Mortgage Banker* (August 1971), 14.

23. Congress, House, "Housing and Urban Development Act of 1968," 90th Cong., 2nd sess., 11.

24. Ibid., 2–3.

25. Ibid., 70.

26. FNMA and GNMA are hard to pronounce acronyms, so both have folksy artificial names: Fannie Mae (FNMA) and Ginnie Mae (GNMA). Later, FHLMC would be called Freddie Mac.

27. MBA Editorial, "Much Ado About Very Little," *Mortgage Banker* (May 1970), 4.

28. GNMA Annual Report, 1970, 5.

29. Ibid.

30. Woodward Kingman, "The Mortgage-Backed Security," *Mortgage Banker* (April 1970), 66.

31. Philip Greenawalt, "Title VIII — and 'Ginnie Mae,'" *Mortgage Banker* (September 1968), 14.

32. Philip Kidd, "One Year Old and Going Strong," *Mortgage Banker* (May 1971), 27.

33. The South and the West, for instance, funded 40 percent of their mortgages non-locally, compared to fewer than 4 percent in the Northeast (John Wetmore, "FHA Operation Now Vital to secondary mortgage market" *Mortgage Banker* [December 1973], 24, 27.)

34. The difficulty with conventional mortgages was the heterogeneity of the borrowers. While mortgages of a certain size and yield could be easily compared, there was no easy way in 1970 to compare the mortgagees. While credit histories were widespread, standardized credit scores did not exist yet. Fair, Isaac and Company were still developing their FICO score and credit rating agencies were making the difficult transition from experiential credit scores to statistical credit models.

35. Oliver Jones, "Pursuing the Elusive Conventional Mortgage," *Mortgage Banker* (November 1966), 38.

36. U.S. Congress, Senate, Committee on Banking, Housing and Urban Affairs, "Housing Goals and Mortgage Credit: 1975–80," 94th Cong., 1st sess., September 22, 23, and 25, 1975, 250.

37. Ibid., 244; Ronald Shafer, "Another Market?" *Wall Street* Journal,, March 27, 1974, 30.

38. "FNMA Explains Debt Financing Structure," *Mortgage Banker* (August 1973), 43.

39. FNMA's 5 percent cash dividend limit would be repealed and the HUD secretary would set a "fair rate of return." While FNMA paid federal taxes, it was exempted from state and local taxes. GNMA was exempted from all taxes (Congress, House, "Housing and Urban Development Act of 1968," 69, 125).

40. Congress, "Housing Goals and Mortgage Credit: 1975–80," 241.

41. Ibid., 242.

42. "FNMA Explains," 45.

43. Robert Pease, "The mortgage market: a crisis that seeks and demands a remedy," *Mortgage Banker* (April 1970), 51.

44. Ibid., 51.

45. Everett Spelman, "Federalization & Housing," 54; Eugene Cower, "The Nixon Program for Housing," *Mortgage Banker* (July 1971), 10.

46. Woodward Kingman, "We round out our first year with sales over $2 billion," *Mortgage Banker* (May 1971).

47. Untitled Advertisement, *Mortgage Banker* (May, 1969), 30.

48. Pease, "Mortgage Market," 64.

49. "The Washington Scene," *Los Angeles Times*, July 15, 1973, K23.

50. Russell Clifton, "FNMA Conventional Mortgage Program Shows Dramatic Growth," *Mortgage Banker* (July 1973), 52.

51. United States, GAO, "Government National Mortgage Association's Secondary Mortgage Market Activities," March 8, 1977, 46.

52. Congress, "Housing Goals and Mortgage Credit," 254.

53. Ibid., 233.

54. Ibid., 36.

55. David Seiders, "Junior Mortgage Financing and Other Borrowing Against Inflated Housing Equity," Working Paper No. 25, Credit Research Center, Krannert Graduate School of Management, Purdue University (c. 1980), 2.

56. Ibid., 11.

57. See chapter 2 for more on why the FHA forbade second mortgages.

58. "Refinancing can redouble profits for mortgage lenders" *ABA Banking Journal* (April 1983): 100.

59"Today's mortgage market has primary flexibility and secondary depth," *ABA Banking Journal* (April 1983): 118.

60. Rosemary Rinder, "How real is ARM 'payment shock'?" *ABA Banking Journal* (April 1984): 46.

61. Ibid., 47.

62. Mary Antoun-Fruscello, "Cash market hedging remains attractive" *ABA Banking Journal* (May 1984): 228.

63. Walter Shealy, "The Secondary Market Makes Mortgages Move" *ABA Banking Journal* (November 1983): 9.

64. Ibid., 10.

65. "Home Equity Lines of Credit," 363.

66. Recall the complications surrounding unamortized mortgages and the run-up to the Great Depression discussed in chapter 2.

67. "Who's Afraid of the Secondary Market?," *ABA Banking Journal* (August 1984): 50.

68. Glenn Canner et al, "Home Equity Lines of Credit," *Federal Reserve Bulletin* (June 1988): 362.

69. "Home Equity Lines of Credit," 364.

70. Household International, *Annual Report 1982*, 10.

71. Calculated by author. Return = pretax income/finance receivables. Household International, *Annual Report 1982*, 9.

72. "Instalment Lenders face Retail Banking Revolution," *ABA Banking Journal* (April 1983): 66.

73. "A Freddie Mac Offering Is Divided into 8 Parts," *New York Times*, November 22, 1985; Mark Clifford and Barbara Rudolph, "Who's Got the Risk?" *Forbes*, May 20, 1985, 194.

74. Leonard Sloane, "Your Money; Collateralized Mortgages," *New York Times* October 8, 1983.

75. Michael Quint, "Investing; A New Play in the Housing Securities," *New York Times*, March 25, 1984.

76. For more on "duration matching" and pension funds, see Zvi Bodie, "Pension Funds and Financial Innovation," *Financial Management* (Autumn 1990): 11–22.

77. "Freddie Mac's President to Leave Sept. 15," *Washington Post*, E14.

78. John Thackray, "Corporate Finance the golden age of innovation," *Forbes* April 29, 1985, 136.

79. "Brendsel Named Acting President of Freddie Mac," *PR Newswire*, September 4, 1985.

80. Ann Monroe, "Citicorp Unit Plans Mortgage Securities of $500 Million," *Wall Street Journal*, September 11, 1984.

81. Eric Berg, "Rise of a National Mortgage Market," *New York Times*, January 22, 1984.

82. Durkin, "Credit Cards," 624.

83. "Do State Rate Caps Make Sense?"; a 1973 Columbia University survey found that retail charge accounts were far more distributed across income groups than bank cards. In a survey of New York retail charge customers who already had a charge card, only households with incomes higher than $10,000 ($48,000 in 2009 dollars) more commonly had bank cards than did not have bank cards. Robert Shay and William Dunkelberg, *Retail Store Credit Use in New York*, Studies in Consumer Credit No 4. (New York: Columbia University Press, 1975), 18.

84. "Bank Cards Push For the Big Stores," *Business Week,* September 27, 1976, 107.

85. United States General Accounting Office, *U.S. Credit Card Industry: Competitive Developments Need to Be Closely Monitored* (GAO: April 1994), 19.

86. *U.S. Credit Card Industry*, 11. *Worthen Bank & Trust Co. v. National BankAmericard*, 345 F. Supp 1309 (E.D. Ark. 1972), rev'd, 486 F 2d 199 (8th Cir. 1973), cert. denied, 415 U.S. 918 (1974).

87. Robert Johnson, "Testimony on Senate Bills," *Credit World* (August 1981): 8.

88. Brennan, "Bank Cards Are Here To Stay," 79. The fee was subsequently struck down by a New York court in 1978.

89. Bennett, "Citibank's Credit Card Blitz," 9.

90. Ibid.

91. Advertisement, "GECC Credit Scoring," *ABA Banking Journal* (April 1983): 106

92. Robert Eisenbeis, "Problems in Applying Discriminant Analysis in Credit Scoring Models," Working Paper No. 18, Credit Research Center, Krannert Graduate School of Management, Purdue University (1978), 4.

93. Ibid., 7.

94. A. Charlene Sullivan and Robert Johnson, "Value Pricing of Bank Card Services," Working Paper No. 34, Credit Research Center, Krannert Graduate School of Management, Purdue University (c. 1980), 8.

95. "Conceptual Issues in Credit Scoring Models: Part II," *Credit World* (July 1983), 24.

96. Sullivan and Johnson, "Value Pricing."

97. Ibid., 9.

98. While the study used several different measures to rank the importance of the variables, the ranking of the Wilks' Lambda, which is considered today to be the best measurement, placed the self-reported ability to save first and race second.

99. Sullivan and Johnson, "Value Pricing," 9. While the study used several different measures to rank the importance of the variables, the ranking of the Wilks' Lambda, which is considered today to be the best measurement, placed the self-reported ability to save first and race second.

100. "Testimony on Senate Bills," 8.

101. Quoted in David Harvey, *The Condition of Postmodernity* (Oxford: Blackwell Publishers, 1990), 158.

102. *Marquette National Bank Of Minneapolis V. First Of Omaha Service Corp. et al , 439 U.S. 299*

103. "High Court Backs Bank Over Rate," *New York Times*, December 19, 1978, D3.

104. Brennan, "Bank Cards Are Here To Stay," 88.

105. "Looking At Credit Rates? Don't Be Myopic," *Credit World* (May 1983), 19.

106. "Instalment Lenders face Retail Banking Revolution," *ABA Banking Journal* (April 1983): 66.

107. Brennan, "Bank Cards Are Here To Stay,", 79.

108. "Variable rate loans rise," *ABA Banking Journal* (October 1984), 154.

109. "Tough future for small card plans," *ABA Banking Journal* (September 1984), 136.

110. "Retail Banking. It's terrible/it's wonderful," *ABA Banking Journal* (June 1980), 90.

111. Sullivan and Johnson, "Value Pricing," 4.

112. Michael Staten and Robert Johnson, "The Case for Deregulating Interest Rates on Consumer Credit," Monograph 31, Credit Research Center, Krannert Graduate School of Management, Purdue University (1995), 22.

113. Brennan, "Bank Cards Are Here To Stay," 80.

114. Staten, "Case for Deregulating Interest Rates," 30, 49.

115. Richard Peterson and A. Charlene Sullivan, "Consumer Use of Mortgage Credit," Working Paper No. 42, Credit Research Center, Krannert Graduate School of Management, Purdue University (1981), 1.

116. Bennett, "Citibank's Credit Card Blitz.".

117. Peter Yoo, "Charging Up a Mountain of Debt: Accounting for the Growth of Credit Card Debt," *Federal Reserve Bank of St. Louis Review* (March/April 1997), 4.

118. Donald Auriemma, "Help for tired card marketing" *CCM* (September 1984), 140.

119. "Cardholders' Reactions to Recent Price Increases," *Credit World* (October 1981), 7.

120. A. Charlene Sullivan, "Do State Rate Caps Make Sense," CCM (March 1992), 21.

121. "Looking At Credit Rates?," 18, 20.

122. "Tough future for small card plans," 136.

123. William Redig, "New 'golds' get off to a solid start," *ABA Banking Journal* (September 1983), 139.

124. Ibid.

125. Roughly $100 in 2008 dollars.

126. James Daly, "Marketer of the Year: Visa U.S.A. – Visa's AmEx Slayer," *CCM* (August 1992), 21.

127. Redig, "New 'Golds,'" 142.

128. Charles McCoy and Steve Swartz, "Plastic Battle: Big Credit-Card War May Be Breaking Out To Detriment of Banks—American Express 13.5% Rate Is Roiling the Industry; New Tax Law Plays Role—Do Consumers Really Care?," *Wall Street Journal*, March 19, 1987.

129. United States General Accounting Office, *U.S. Credit Card Industry*, 28.

130. Ibid., 34.

131. Auriemma, "Help for tired card marketing," 140.

132. MBNA prestige cards had balances of $1,500, $600 more than conventional credit cards.

133. Auriemma, "Help for tired card marketing," 146.

134. Ibid., 142.

135. Ibid., 146.

136. "After the Tax Triumph," *New York Times*, December 19, 1985, A30.

137. Michael Weinstein, "Home equity credit lines expected to boom; plan to end deduction for consumer-loan interest makes second-mortgage products more attractive," *American Banker*, August 5, 1986.

138. Ibid.

139. "U.S. Banking's dramatic loss of market share," *ABA Banking Journal* (November 1980), 66.

140. "Looking At Credit Rates?," 20.

141. For more on nonconsolidated finance company subsidiaries and the shady accounting ground they inhabited, see Martin Benis, "The Non-Consolidated Finance Company Subsidiary," *The Accounting Review* (October 1979), 808.

142. "Capital-strapped? Here's A Way Out," ABA Banking Journal (June 1980), 59.

143. "Capital-strapped?"; The special purpose subsidiary to move credit card debt off the balance sheet formed an important institutional bridge to the securitization of credit card debt, which did not happen until 1986.

144. Author Interview with Mark Stickle, April 9, 2009.

145. Lisabeth Weiner, "Hit the Market This Year," *American Banker*, January 7, 1987.

146. Ibid.

147. "Maryland National Bank and Morgan Guaranty Team Up to Securitize Credit Card Receivables," *American Banker*, January 9, 1987.

148. Sanford Rose, "The Capital-Cost Impact of Securitization," *American Banker*, January 17, 1988

149. George Yacik, "Citicorp to Pick Underwriters for Credit Card Sales," *American Banker*, May 31, 1988.

150. George Yacik, "Citicorp Selects Card Issue Underwriters," *American Banker*, June 14, 1988.

151. "First Chicago Net Aided By Non-Interest Income," Reuters, July 17, 1989.

152. "Maryland National Bank and Morgan."

153. Dennis O'Connell, "Banc One Sets Big Card Deal," *American Banker*, July 26, 1988.

154. For the best history of the origins of the Basel Accord, see David Andrew Singer, *Regulating Capital: Setting Standards for the International Financial System* (Ithaca: Cornell University Press, 2007).

155. Basel I had five risk weights of 0, 10, 20, 50 and 100, unlike the Basel II accord, which had more flexible computations of risk.

156. Capital to asset ratios at commercial had fallen from 10 percent in the 1950s to under 4 percent in the 1980s. Citicorp, for instance, which had a ratio of 4.73 percent in 1986 Japanese banks, had much lower ratios in the 2 to 3 percent range, which was why international agreements were necessary to collectively raise the ratio. (*Regulating Capital*, 46, 53, 62.)

157. Stickle Interview, 4/9/09.

158. United States General Accounting Office, *U.S. Credit Card Industry*, 19.

159. James Daly, "Ten Years of Covering Cards," CCM (May 1998), 14.

160. Kevin Higgins, "The comeback in card bonds" *CCM* (March 1995).

161. Ibid.

162. Linda Punch, "Legacy of card bonds," *CCM* (May 1998).

163. Linda Punch, "Jitters over the bond boom," *CCM* (September 1995), 40.

164. Higgins, "The comeback in card bonds."

165. Punch, "Jitters," 40.

166. Kevin Higgins "Crowded at the top," *CCM* (September 1996), 58.

167. John Stewart, "Is Wall Street Around the Corner," *CCM* (June 1992), 26.

168. Punch, "The Legacy of card bonds," 36.

169. "Ibid.

170. Michael Quint, "Favored Credit Card Holders Quietly Given Lower Rates," *New York Times*, November 13, 1991, D8; Lindsey Grusons, "On Credit Cards, D'Amato Finds Victory and Defeat," *New York Times*, November 19, 1991, B7.

171. A. Charlene Sullivan, "Do State Rate Caps Make Sense," *CCM* (March 1992), 21; Alison Rea, "Focus — Card Rate Cap Seen Bad for Economy, Banks," *Reuters* News, November 14, 1991; D'Amato's cap was variable and pegged to4 percent above the interest rate charged by the Internal Revenue Service, which in 1991 was 10 percent.

172. "Bill on Credit Card Rates Advances," *New York Times*, November 14, 1991, D22.

173. Kenneth Bacon, "Credit-card Cap Furor Will Have Big Effect, Economic and Political," *Wall Street Journal*, November 18, 1991, A1.

174. Irvin Molotsky, "Effort to Cap Credit Card Rates Is Attacked," *New York Times*, November 18, 1991, D7.

175. Bacon, "Credit-card Cap Furor."

176. GAO, *U.S. Credit Card Industry*, 27.

177. Molotsky, "Effort to Cap Credit Card," D7.

178. United States General Accounting Office, *U.S. Credit Card Industry*.

179. Ibid., 32.

180. Ibid., 4.

181. Ibid., 18.

182. John Stewart, "Goodbye, Fat City" *CCM* (March 1992), 70.

183. "Citi Devises Another New Twist in Card Securities," *Credit Card News*, June 1, 1992.

184. Kathie O'Donnell, "Citibank's $1.33 Billion Global Deal Seen as a First in Credit Card Market," *The Bond Buyer*, September 25, 1992.

185. "CEO Interview FIRST USA INC.," *Wall Street Transcript*, May 31, 1993.

186. Higgins, "The comeback in card bonds," 61; "FASB's High and Tight Fastball," *CCM* (March 1995), 63.

187. Anonylous, "Playing Games with debt," CCM (October 1996), 6.

188. GAO, *U.S. Credit Card Industry*, 19.

189. John Stewart, "The New Frugality," *CCM* (May 1992), 28.

190. Peter Lucas, "Say So Long to Booming Balances," *CCM* (April 1992), 60.

191. Stewart, "The New Frugality," 28.

192. GAO, *U.S. Credit Card Industry*, 3.

193. Stewart, "The New Frugality," 28.

194. Stewart, "Goodbye, Fat City"

195. Ibid.

196. Stewart, "The New Frugality."

197. Edward Bird, Paul Hagstrom, and Robert Wild, "Credit Cards and the Poor," Discussion Paper no. 1148-97 (October 1997), Institute for Research on Poverty, University of Wisconsin-Madison, 5

198. Bird, "Credit Cards and the Poor," 8.

199. Yoo, "Charging Up A Mountain," 6.
200. Ibid.
201. Bird, "Credit Cards and the Poor," 13.
202. Kevin Higgins, "Bottom Feeding," *CCM* (January 1994), 62.
203. Stewart, "Goodbye, Fat City"
204. Mark Borowsky, "BofA's battle to rebound," *CCM* (November 1993), 45.
205. Peter Lucas, "A card that breaks all the rules," *CCM* (July 1994), 12.
206. Peter Lucas, "GE lights up its card strategy," *CCM* (June 1993), 40.
207. Jeff Bailey and Scott Kilman, "Taking Credit: Here's What's Driving Some Lenders Crazy: Borrowers Who Think—Working Class Is Getting Hip To Lower Interest Rates; Card Surfing Is the Rage," *Wall Street Journal*, February 20, 1998, A1.
208. Ibid.
209. Kevin Higgins, "Calling all revolvers," *CCM* (March 1997), 60.
210. Ibid.
211. Ibid.
212. Ronald Fink, "God Is In the Details," *CCM* (November 1992), 54.
213. Linda Punch, "A Sobering Year for Collectors," *CCM* (June 1992).
214. Kathleen Pender, "Rating the Credit Customer" *San Francisco Chronicle* (February 17, 1992), B1.
215. Punch, "A Sobering Year for Collectors," 52.
216. Katherine Morrall, "The Rocky Advent of Profit Modeling," *CCM* (December 1992), 16.
217. Stewart, "Goodbye, Fat City"
218. Steve Gasner, "Forging A Link Between Retention and Profits," *CCM* (April 1992), 84.
219. Kevin Higgins, "Those naughty nonrevolvers," *CCM* (December 1996), 46.
220. Ibid.
221. Ibid.
222. "Citi's Net Soars 355%; Chemical Jumps 78% Banc One, Wells Also Post Gains," *American Banker*, October 20, 1993.
223. "The Downward Pressure Continues on Card Profits," *Credit Card News*, April 1, 1996.
224. Federal Reserve, "The Profitability of Credit Card Operations of Depository Institutions," (August 1997). http://www.federalreserve.gov/boarddocs/rptcongress/creditcard/1997/
225. John Stewart, "The Earnings Balloon," *CCM* (May 1994), 32.
226. Federal Reserve, "The Profitability of Credit Card Operations of Depository Institutions," (August 1998). http://www.federalreserve.gov/boarddocs/rptcongress/creditcard/1998/
227. "Moody's Sees Risks As Credit Card Issuer Competition Rises," *Dow Jones News Service*, March 30, 1994.
228. "Subprime marketing gets sophisticated," *CCM* (March 1998), 78.
229. "The Price of Growth: A Spike" *Credit Card News*, April 1, 1996.

230. Jeanne Hogarth and Kevin O'Donnell, "Banking Relationships of Lower-Income Families and the Governmental Trend toward Electronic Payment," *Federal Reserve Bulletin* (July 1999), 460.

231. Higgins, "Bottom Feeding."

232. Higgins, "Bottom Feeding."

233. Elayne Demby, "A new approach to credit reporting," *CCM* (September 1998), 56.

234. Mark Borowsky, "Who's Afraid of Big Bad Debt?" *CCM* (July 1995), 20.

235. Higgins, "Calling all revolvers."

236. Linda Punch, 'Subprime's dangerous waters," *CCM* (March 1998), 76.

237. Paul Demery, "Trying to out-score the competition," *CCM* (January 1998), 22.

238. Peter Brennan, "Card profits by the numbers," *CCM* (September 1993), 48.

239. "Shifting to a profit mode," *CCM* (np, 1998), S26.

240. Punch, "Subprime's dangerous waters."

241. "Competition and Expenses Put the Squeeze on Profits," *Credit Card News*, April 1, 1995.

242. Mark Borowsky, "The $10 Billion Question," CCM (March 1995), 34.

243. Ibid.

244. "A Desire to Shed Bad Debt Drives Portfolio Sales," *Credit Card News*, February 1, 1997.

245. Ibid.

246. Anonymous, "Risk-based repricing draws flak," *CCM* (January 1996), 13.

247. "A Desire to Shed."

248. "Fraying Credit Quality Leaves Investors Hanging," *Credit Card News*, July 1, 1996.

249. Ibid.

250. Linda Green, "Late Fees Upheld For Credit Cards," *New York Times*, June 4, 1996, A1.; *Barbara Smiley, Petitioner V. Citibank (South Dakota)*, N.A., 517 U.S. 735.

251. Paul Barrett, "Legal Beat: Justices' Ruling on credit cards favors banks," *Wall Street* Journal, June 4, 1996, B1; The *Smiley* decision followed on the heels of several state-level decisions like *Tikkanen v. Citibank*, *Greenwood Trust Co. v. Commonwealth of Massachusetts*, *Hill v. Chemical Bank*, and *Nelson v. Citibank*.

252. James Daly, "Ten Years of Covering Cards," CCM (May 1998), 14.

253. "Chargeoffs Take a Big Bite Out of Card Profits," *Credit Card News*, April 1, 1997.

254. "Card revenues and profits rebounded strongly in 1998," *Credit Card News*, April 15, 1999.

255. Ibid.

256. "Profits continued to build in 1999, paced by fees," *Credit Card News*, April 15, 2000.

257. "Subprime marketing could endanger profits, Fitch says," *Credit Card News*, May 1, 2000.

258. Ibid.

259. Leonard Groupe, "Home-equity plan frightens wife," *Chicago Sun-Times*, 11 January 1991.

260. Linda Punch, "Home-equity threat," *CCM* (September 1998).

261. Ibid., 112.

262. Ibid.

263. Anonymous, "Good News about bad debt," *CCM* (October 1998), 14.

264. Punch, "Home-equity threat."

265. Ibid.

266. Christopher Farrell, "Credit Card Wars: Profits are Taking a Direct Hit—Savage Competition and Hair-raising Default Rates are Zapping Issuers," *Business Week*, November 17, 1986, 166.

267. Steven Bergsman, "Mortgages on the MasterCard: Home Equity's Plastic," *Barron's*, February 16, 1987.

268. Mickey Meece, "Home Improvement: Equity Credit Card Doing Better the Second Time Around," *American Banker*, October 1, 1993.

269. Kenneth Harney, "Whip out your home-equity credit card and say: Charge it," *San Diego Union-Tribune*, May 7, 2000.

270. Ibid.

271. Christine Dugas, "Bills in full, using home equity," *USA Today*, June 27, 2000.

272. Lynn Adler, "Profit is in low credit sector—US Conference Panel," *Reuters News*, October 6, 1997.

273. "Home Equity Abs being Touted for Value," *Mortgage-Backed Securities Letter Investment Dealers' Digest*, May 17, 1993.

274. "Delinquencies Rise in Home Equity Securitizations," *National Mortgage News*, March 25, 1996.

275. See Anya Kamenetz, *Generation Debt* (New York: Riverhead Trade, 2006).

276. Charles Morris, *The Trillion Dollar Meltdown* (New York: Perseus Books, 2008), 142–47.

Epilogue
Debt as Choice, Debt as Structure

1. Gilbert Burck and Sanford Parker, "The Coming Turn in Consumer Credit," *Fortune* (March 1956), 99–100.

2. Ibid., 246.

3. Household Finance Corporation, Children's Spending (Chicago: Household Finance Corporation, 1971), 28.

4. Ibid., 28–29.

5. Ibid., 27.

6. The literature on the post-1970s return of inequality is vast. For a useful entry point into the literature see Katherine Newman's *Falling from Grace:*

Downward Mobility in the Age of Affluence (Berkeley: University of California Press, 1999).

7. At the center of the creation of the aerospace industry is the often-overlooked Defense Plant Corporation, whose methods were very similar to other New Deal financing schemes discussed in this book. See Gerald White, *Billions for Defense: Government Financing by the Defense Plant Corporation during World War II* (University: University of Alabama Press, 1980).

References

Archival and Manuscript Collections

Baker Library, Historical Collections, Harvard University, Allston, MA (BAK)

Historic Corporate Reports
Old Class Collection
Pamphlet Collection of the Sales Finance Association

Citigroup Archives, New York City, NY (CITI)

National City Bank

Harvard-M.I.T. Data Center, Harvard University, Cambridge, MA

Study of Consumer Purchases in the United States, 1935–1936
Survey of Consumer Finances, 1958
Surveys of Consumer Attitudes and Behavior, Spring 1961

Manuscript Division, Library of Congress, Washington, D.C. (RSF)

Russell Sage Foundation

National Archives, College Park, MD (NARA)

Federal Home Loan Bank Board
Federal Reserve Bank
Federal Housing Administration
National Commission on Consumer Finance
Federal National Mortgage Association

Schlesinger Library, Historical Collections, Harvard University, Cambridge, MA (NOW)

National Organization for Women

Selected Newspapers

Atlanta Constitution

Chicago Defender
Chicago Tribune
Chicago-Illinois Examiner
Chicago Journal

Los Angeles Times
Minneapolis News
New York Times
New York Amsterdam News
New York World
Toledo News-Bee
Pittsburgh Courier
Washington Post

Index

POLITICS AND SOCIETY IN TWENTIETH-CENTURY AMERICA

Civil Defense Begins at Home: Militarization Meets Everyday Life in the Fifties
by Laura McEnaney

The Politics of Whiteness: Race, Workers, and Culture in the Modern South
by Michelle Brattain

Cold War Civil Rights: Race and the Image of American Democracy
by Mary L. Dudziak

Divided We Stand: American Workers and the Struggle for Black Equality
by Bruce Nelson

Poverty Knowledge: Social Science, Social Policy, and the Poor in Twentieth-Century U.S. History
by Alice O'Connor

State of the Union: A Century of American Labor
by Nelson Lichtenstein

Suburban Warriors: The Origins of the New American Right
by Lisa McGirr

American Babylon Race and the Struggle for Postwar Oakland
by Robert O. Self

Changing the World: American Progressives in War and Revolution
by Alan Dawley

Dead on Arrival: The Politics of Health Care in Twentieth-Century America
by Colin Gordon

For All These Rights: Business, Labor, and the Shaping of America's Public-Private Welfare State
by Jennifer Klein

Impossible Subjects: Illegal Aliens and the Making of Modern America
by Mae M. Ngai

The Other Women's Movement: Workplace Justice and Social Rights in Modern America
by Dorothy Sue Cobble

The Radical Middle Class: Populist Democracy and the Question of Capitalism in Progressive Era Portland, Oregon
by Robert D. Johnston

Cities of Knowledge: Cold War Science and the Search for the Next Silicon Valley
by Margaret Pugh O'Mara

Labor Rights Are Civil Rights: Mexican American Workers in Twentieth-Century America
by Zaragosa Vargas

More Equal Than Others: America from Nixon to the New Century
by Godfrey Hodgson

Pocketbook Politics: Economic Citizenship in Twentieth-Century America
by Meg Jacobs

Taken Hostage: The Iran Hostage Crisis and America's First Encounter with Radical Islam
by David Farber

Defending America Military Culture and the Cold War Court-Martial
by Elizabeth Lutes Hillman

Morning in America: How Ronald Reagan Invented the 1980s
by Gil Troy

Phyllis Schlafly and Grassroots Conservatism: A Woman's Crusade
by Donald T. Critchlow

The Silent Majority: Suburban Politics in the Sunbelt South
by Matthew D. Lassiter

White Flight: Atlanta and the Making of Modern Conservatism
by Kevin M. Kruse

Troubling the Waters: Black-Jewish Relations in the American Century
by Cheryl Lynn Greenberg

In Search of Another Country: Mississippi and the Conservative Counterrevolution
by Joseph Crespino

The Shifting Grounds of Race: Black and Japanese Americans in the Making of Multiethnic Los Angeles
by Scott Kurashige

Americans at the Gate: The United States and Refugees during the Cold War
by Carl J. Bon Tempo

School Lunch Politics: The Surprising History of America's Favorite Welfare Program
by Susan Levine

Trucking Country: The Road to America's Wal-Mart Economy
by Shane Hamilton

The Straight State: Sexuality and Citizenship in Twentieth-Century America
by Margot Canaday

Little Rock: Race and Resistance at Central High School
by Karen Anderson

Debtor Nation: The History of America in Red Ink
by Louis Hyman

No Man's Land: Jamaican Guestworkers in America and the Global History of Deportable Labor
by Cindy Hahamovitch

Philanthropy in America: A History
by Olivier Zunz

Between Citizens and the State: The Politics of American Higher Education in the 20th Century
by Christopher P. Loss

Mothers of Conservatism: Women and the Postwar Right
by Michelle M. Nickerson

The Second Red Scare and the Unmaking of the New Deal Left
by Landon Storrs